T0330203

Marx: Key Concepts

NEW DIRECTIONS IN MODERN ECONOMICS

Series Editor: Malcolm C. Sawyer, *Professor of Economics, University of Leeds, UK*

New Directions in Modern Economics presents a challenge to orthodox economic thinking. It focuses on new ideas emanating from radical traditions including post-Keynesian, Kaleckian, neo-Ricardian and Marxian. The books in the series do not adhere rigidly to any single school of thought but attempt to present a positive alternative to the conventional wisdom.

For a full list of Edward Elgar published titles, including the titles in this series, visit our website at www.e-elgar.com.

Marx: Key Concepts

Edited by

Riccardo Bellofiore

Formerly Professor of Political Economy, University of Bergamo, Italy

Tommaso Redolfi Riva

Liceo Enrico Fermi, Cecina, Italy

NEW DIRECTIONS IN MODERN ECONOMICS

Edward Elgar
PUBLISHING

Cheltenham, UK • Northampton, MA, USA

Cover image by Alessandro Dinetti

Published by
Edward Elgar Publishing Limited
The Lypiatts
15 Lansdown Road
Cheltenham
Glos GL50 2JA
UK

Edward Elgar Publishing, Inc.
William Pratt House
9 Dewey Court
Northampton
Massachusetts 01060
USA

A catalogue record for this book
is available from the British Library

Library of Congress Control Number: 2023948563

This book is available electronically in the **Elgar**online
Economics subject collection
http://dx.doi.org/10.4337/9781800880764

ISBN 978 1 80088 075 7 (cased)
ISBN 978 1 80088 076 4 (eBook)

Printed and bound in Great Britain by
TJ Books Limited, Padstow, Cornwall

Contents

Contributors

Riccardo Bellofiore was Professor of Political Economy at the University of Bergamo, Italy. His interests are Marxian theory, the development and crisis of capitalism, the macro-monetary approach (Circuitism and Minsky), history of economic thought, and economic philosophy. He has recently published, with Giovanna Vertova, *The Great Recession and the Contradictions of Contemporary Capitalism* (Edward Elgar Publishing, 2014) and 'The Adventures of *Vergesellschaftung*' (in *Consecutio Rerum*, 2018). With Tommaso Redolfi Riva he has edited in Italian the writings of Hans-Georg Backhaus on the *Dialectics of the Form of Value*, and with Stefano Breda the Italian translation of Michael Heinrich's *Science of Value*.

Stefano Breda studied philosophy in Venice and obtained his PhD at the Freie Universität Berlin. His research interests focus on Marx's critique of political economy, the structural role of the credit system in the capitalist mode of production, and the epistemological status of a materialistic dialectic. On these topics he has published several articles and the book *Kredit und Kapital – Kreditsystem und Reproduktion der kapitalistischen Vergesellschaftungsweise in der dialektischen Darstellung des Marxschen 'Kapital'* [Credit and Capital – Credit System and Reproduction of the Capitalist Mode of Socialization in the Dialectical Exposition of Marx's 'Capital']. He works as a high school teacher. In parallel, he translates texts by and about Marx from German into Italian. He has recently translated Michael Heinrich's *Die Wissenschaft vom Wert* [The Science of Value], co-edited with Riccardo Bellofiore.

Emanuela Conversano has a PhD in History of Ideas, Philosophy and Science from the Scuola Normale Superiore, Italy, and is a Visiting Research and Editorial Assistant at the Berlin-Brandenburg Academy of Sciences and Humanities, Germany, for the project of *The Complete Works of Marx and Engels (MEGA)*. Her research interests include Marxian theory of history and philosophy of praxis within the broader context of his dialectical thought. In particular, she is currently working on Marx's notebooks on ancient, global history and ethnology.

Frank Engster, Berlin, wrote his PhD thesis *Das Geld als Maß, Mittel und Methode. Das Rechnen mit der Identität der Zeit* (2014) on the subject of time, money and measure. He is interested in the different – (post-)operaist, (post-)

structuralist, form-analytic, (queer) feminist, and so on – readings of Marx's critique, especially money as a technique and its connection with measurement, quantification, time and (natural) science. Some of his publications are published on academia.edu.

Roberto Fineschi is Professor in Political Philosophy at the Siena School for Liberal Arts, Italy. His research interests include Marx's and Hegel's thought, theory of history and society, political economy, and Italian political thought. He has engaged in academic research, and has extensively published articles and books in several languages.

Bob Jessop is Emeritus Professor of Sociology at Lancaster University, UK. He taught in Lancaster from 1990 to 2021 and was previously in the Department of Government, University of Essex, UK. He is a specialist in Marxist political economy, critical state theory, critical governance studies, welfare state restructuring, and cultural political economy. His recent publications include *Putting Civil Society in its Place* (2020), *The State: Past, Present, Future* (2016), and *Towards a Cultural Political Economy: Putting Culture in its Place in Political Economy* (co-authored with Ngai-Ling Sum, 2013). His work is widely accessible on the Internet.

Luca Micaloni is a Postdoctoral Researcher at Università 'Sapienza' di Roma (Rome, Italy). His work has focused on the philosophical aspects of Marx's critique of political economy and on the systematic role of psychoanalysis in the development of Frankfurt School Critical Theory.

Vittorio Morfino is Professor in History of Philosophy at the University of Milan-Bicocca, Italy, and Director of the Masters in Critical Theory of the Society. He has been a Visiting Professor at the Universidade de São Paulo, Brazil; the Université Paris 1 Panthéon-Sorbonne and the Université Bordeaux-Montaigne, France; and the Universidad Nacional de Cordoba, Argentina; and has been Directeur de Programme at the Collège international de philosohie. He is the author of *Il tempo e l'occasione. L'incontro Spinoza Machiavelli* (Milano, 2002; Paris, 2012), *Incursioni spinoziste* (Milano, 2002), *Il tempo della moltitudine* (Roma, 2005; Paris, 2010; Madrid, 2013; Santiago, 2015), *Plural Temporality. Transindividuality and the Aleatory between Spinoza and Althusser* (Leiden, 2014), *Genealogia di un pregiudizio. L'immagine di Spinoza in Germania da Leibniz a Marx* (Hildesheim, 2016), and *Intersoggettività e transindividualità. Materiali per un'alternativa* (Roma, 2002). He is an editor of *Quaderni materialisti* and *Décalages. An Althusserian Journal*.

Kirstin Munro is Assistant Professor in Economics at the New School for Social Research in New York, USA. Her research concerns the relationship between the reproduction of capitalist society and work outside the wage-relation, a topic which she investigates in a number of articles and her book *The Production of Everyday Life in Eco-Conscious Households: Compromise, Conflict and Complicity.* She serves on the editorial board of the *Review of Radical Political Economics.*

Chris O'Kane is Adjunct Associate Professor in the Department of Economics and Finance at St John's University, Queens NY, USA. He works on theories of social domination and social emancipation in critical social and political theory and political economy. Along with Werner Bonefeld, he is the co-editor of *Adorno and Marx: Negative Dialectics and the Critique of Political Economy.*

Gianluca Pozzoni is a Postdoctoral Researcher at the University of Milan, Italy.

Tommaso Redolfi Riva teaches Philosophy and History at Liceo Statale Enrico Fermi in Cecina, Italy. He is an independent researcher. He graduated in Philosophy at the University of Pisa, Italy, and has a PhD in History of Economic Thought from the University of Florence, Italy. He has published several articles on Marx, Marxisms and the *Neue Marx-Lektüre*. He is co-editor with Riccardo Bellofiore of *Ricerche sulla critica marxiana dell'economia* (2016), an Italian collection of the most important articles by Hans-Georg Backhaus.

Sebastiano Taccola has a PhD in Cultures and Societies of the Contemporary Europe from the Normale School of Pisa, Italy. His research interests include philosophy of history, critical theory, critique of political economy, history of Marxism. His recent book (*Categorie marxiste e storiografia del mondo antico. Critica e storia in un dibattito italiano degli anni Settanta*) investigates the relation between historical materialism and critique of political economy in a historiographical debate concerning ancient societies, that took place in Italy during the 1970s. He teaches history and philosophy in high schools.

Frieder Otto Wolf. Born 1 February 1943, he studied philosophy and political science at Kiel University, Germany, and at the Sorbonne University, École pratique des Hautes Études and École Libre Protestante in Paris (France). Since 1966 he has held various posts in research and teaching in Saarbrücken and Berlin (Germany), and Coimbra (Portugal); Since 1973 he was a Lecturer in Philosophy at the Freie Universität Berlin, until becoming Honorary Professor in 2006. From 1979 onwards he engaged in active political work in Germany and in Europe, especially in initiatives for an alternative Left: from 1984 to 1999 in the Green Group in the European Parliament, the last five years as an MEP. Main publications: *Die neue Wissenschaft des Thomas Hobbes*

(1969, 2nd edn 2024); *Umwege* (1983); *Radikale Philosophie* (2002, 2nd edn 2009); *Arbeitsglück* (2005); *Rückkehr in die Zukunft* (2012); *Humanistische Interventionen* (2019). Editor of the *Collected Works* of Althusser in German; co-editor of the book series Luxemburg International Studies in Political Economy.

Introduction to *Marx: Key Concepts*

Riccardo Bellofiore and Tommaso Redolfi Riva

In the last 30 years we have witnessed an overall renaissance of interest in Marxian work. This renaissance can be attributed to the following factors.

First, the systemic crisis of the neo-liberal accumulation regime of capitalism has profoundly intensified social and geographical inequalities, calling into question the chances of survival of human beings on the planet. Social movements need to equip themselves with a conceptual apparatus capable of understanding the dynamics of the crisis and, at the same time, to acquire the tools capable of facing it practically.

Second, the fall of the regimes of 'actually existing' socialism. The danger of establishing a too easy correspondence between Marx's thought and the political trajectory of Eastern Europe after the Second World War can be now definitely dispensed with.

Third, the renewal of Marxian studies originated from *MEGA²*, the new historical-critical edition of the collected works of Marx and Engels. The conclusion of the publication of the second section (containing *Capital* and the preparatory works) has allowed us to read many new unpublished manuscripts and *Capital* itself in a way that is much more articulated and stratified than that which had emerged following the Engelsian edition of Volume 2 and Volume 3. The (still ongoing) publication of the fourth section (containing excerpts, notes and marginalia) has allowed scholars to shed light on lesser-known aspects of Marxian interests, in particular in relation to forms and modes of production other than capitalism.

In the last few years, we note the release of a series of books that attempt to take stock of the theoretical and political ferment we have mentioned above, showing the new acquisitions and the new research directions that have emerged. Our book fits into this publishing climate. Although organized according to thematic headings, it is not intended to give an account of a process that has taken place and is historically situated 'behind' us as authors. The individual chapters collected here aim to show the research in its making, the theoretical possibilities not yet undertaken, the liveliness of the debate, the inexhaustible dialectic between our questioning from the present, and the answers that could come from a Marxian approach and its latest developments.

The cover of the first 2023 issue of the German magazine *Der Spiegel* featured a buoyant Marx with a question at the bottom: '*Hatte Marx doch recht?*' Was Marx right, after all? It is an interrogation recurrently proposed whenever a systemic structural crisis appears in this day and age, and it looks as though there is no way out. Even more so, when multiple crises are on the horizon.

Paradoxically, too often Marx is mentioned in support of perspectives willing to save capitalism from itself. Instead of a deepening of the radicality of his inquiry, the name 'Marx' becomes an empty signifier, which can be again and again refilled with petitions in favour of state interventions in the economy, of less social inequalities, of the conservation of the natural environment, and against the perverse effects of capitalist production and consumption, and so on. Marx is resurrected as a 'classic' thinker, just as valid as Smith, Hegel or Keynes, in an anaesthetizing modality.

What appears undigestible and out of tune with our modernity is what we think is instead more alive in his legacy: the insistence on, and the fight against, the increasing exploitation of labour, the many forms of capitalist domination, the widening class structure of society, and finally, the spectre of communism as a possible superior form of social organization of production. The expulsion of these themes from what it is deemed sensible to discuss makes any reference to Marx useless.

Carlo Ginzburg reminds us in the field of historical research that asking anachronistic questions, and thus looking at the past from the practical and theoretical problems posed by the present, is an excellent heuristic method, once we become aware that anachronism in answers is a mortal sin. It is because they are convinced of the necessity to advocate a Marxian categorical framework for understanding our present, at the same time pursuing radical answers, that the authors have contributed to this book.

This book aims to provide a wide-ranging journey through some of the central ideas of Marx, with a focus on a few key concepts that have defined his thought. The book consists of 14 chapters that aim to cover the full range of his critique of political economy: the method, the theory of value, the theory of capital, confronting the classical and contemporary receptions of Marx in the economic, sociological and philosophical debates.

The aim of Chapter 1 by Tommaso Redolfi Riva is to explain the concept of critique of political economy in Marx's mature work. Starting from the different meanings that critique of political economy assumes (as the analysis of the conditions of possibility of an autonomous science of political economy;

as the presentation of the exploitation of labour-power; as the inquiry into and naturalization of capital relationships based on the exchange of things on the market), Redolfi Riva aims to explain the peculiarities of such a critical project. In particular, he focuses attention on the critique of political economy as a critique of capital as an objective–subjective totality: on the one hand, as a system of social production whose aim is the valorization of capital, based on the appropriation of unpaid labour, and generating a system of socialization of production increasingly becoming autonomous from the social agents which establish it; on the other hand, as the place of constitution of the categories of political economy, whose defects cannot only be brought back to the methodological lack of the economists because such categories, as a part of the capitalistic reality itself, are products of capitalistic social relationships. What emerges from this perspective is that the critique of political economy, as the presentation of the system of capitalistic relationships, is the critique of a specific science put forth by means of the critique of its own specific object.

Chapter 2 by Stefano Breda provides a comprehensive analysis of materialism and dialectics in Marx's critique of political economy. A materialist understanding of the method followed by Marx in his critique of political economy requires going beyond both the traditional logical-historical interpretation of dialectics and the logical-systematic interpretation developed within the *Neue Marx-Lektüre*, since both interpretations ultimately lead to an idealistic reading of *Capital*, albeit in different ways. The dialectical exposition of the capitalist mode of production should be conceived neither as a conceptual reconstruction of historical development, nor as an independent logical movement of economic categories. Rather, it must be conceived as an immanent critique of what is empirically given. All economic categories that follow one another in the dialectical development are taken *a posteriori* by Marx. None of them can be logically deduced from the previous one, but each category expresses some necessary conditions for the existence of the phenomena expressed in the previous category. The forward movement of the categories thus discloses the structural connections between phenomena that are all taken as empirically given, but necessarily manifest themselves as if they were independent from each another.

The purpose of Frieder Otto Wolf's Chapter 3 is to reject a Hegelian interpretation of Marx's dialectical method, and from this perspective, to lay the basis for a development of Marxism as a 'finite' theory. Materialist dialectics is neither an *a priori* method nor something that Marx had to abandon to reach the purpose of the analysis of modern bourgeois society. Marx's dialectical method is coherent with the finite character of its object of investigation, as can be seen following the very practice of Marx's theoretical presentation in which money, labour-power as commodity and landed property are assumed as historical contingent givens. *Capital* is not built upon the circular kind of argument underlying Hegel's logic; on the contrary, Marx's dialectical development is interrupted in certain points where historic-empirical elements are introduced. Such interruptions and integrations must be understood in accordance with the limits of a dialectical presentation. In Marx we can find theoretical objects that cannot be fully constructed by the dialectical order of presentation, and that must be introduced in a different way. If in Hegel the development of the concept can be seen as an *a priori* process, this is no longer possible in Marx, where the dialectical presentation needs to be preceded by the process of research. Such a 'finite' character opens a space for a renewal of materialist dialectics that has to be developed through gradual integrations coming from different fields of research and political struggles.

In Chapter 4, Bob Jessop explores the neglected role of cell biology in the constitution of Marx's method in *Capital*. The point of departure is the 1857 Introduction and the two opposite methods of political economy that Marx presents. Even if in this Introduction Marx seems to opt for a synthetic method, *The Wealth of Nations* being a paradigmatic example, this is not consequently followed in *Capital*. Instead of starting with exchange-value, money, capital, as concretely occurs in *Grundrisse*, from 1859 Marx adopts the commodity – the simplest, most elementary, most abstract element of capitalist mode of production – as the starting point of the presentation. Commodity is the elementary existence of the capitalist form of wealth and, as the 1867 Preface explicitly states, it is the economic cell form. Marx's choice of the commodity as the point of departure for the presentation can be better understood if we consider Marx's (and Engels's) interest in the development of cell biology. From this perspective, what has always been read as a simple metaphor taken from the natural sciences acquires a different argumentative importance. Six key foundational principles of cell theory – taken from the texts with which Marx was acquainted, directly or indirectly – could have inspired Marx's profound shift in the choice of the starting point for his critique of political economy between the 1857 Introduction and the 1867 first edition of *Capital*.

For Riccardo Bellofiore (Chapter 5) a (if not the) key concept in Karl Marx's critique of political economy is 'absolute value'. This category has been lost in the English secondary literature. Its specific meaning can be understood by re-reading Marx's confrontation with Samuel Bailey and David Ricardo. Unfortunately, the available English translation of the *Theories of Surplus Value* is seriously deficient. The chapter reconstructs this theoretical path, whilst also considering his previous writings (*Grundrisse, A Contribution, Urtext*), and provides a first survey of the relevant secondary literature (in German, Italian, French and English). The adjective 'absolute' refers to the two following, and entwined, circumstances. First, that the commodity, beyond being use value, is value as long as it materializes as exchange-value in another commodity. Value within the commodity is separated (or 'abstracted') from the use value of that commodity itself and enters a relation where money becomes the 'body of value': 'value embodied'. Second, the 'unsocial sociability' between the isolated producers is separated (or 'abstracted') from them, and controls them. 'Absolute' also stands for the development of value into an 'automatic subject' as an overgrasping and self-reproducing totality. Unfortunately, the foundation upon which Marx's reasoning is erected is fragile. The category of labour as the substance of absolute value is not properly grounded, and it maintains an internal necessary reference to 'money as a commodity' which should be rejected. The answer to Marx's question – what is it that grounds the reference of value to labour? – lies in the 'consumption' by capital of the living bearers of labour-power: that is, in the use of their labour-power, and hence in the (antagonistic) extraction of their living labour, turning into the new value added. This outcome cannot be taken for granted in capitalism's historically socially specific situation, and that is why capitalist production is nothing but labour. This is the ultimate foundation of Marx's (monetary) value theory of labour. The monetary imprinting must be given by an *ex ante* validation of the living labour expended, by finance to production (the buying and selling of labour-power).

In Chapter 6, Frank Engster focuses his attention on money and on the specific role it assumes in capitalism. In this specific form of production, money becomes a measure that has to quantify pure social relations. Furthermore, money itself in its measuring and quantifying function presents itself as essential to the constitution of the same social objectivity and totality that it mediates. To clarify this question, Engster borrows from quantum physics the concept of entanglement. Engster concentrates his analysis on the development of the different functions of money. Marx's analysis of the form of value shows in a logical way how a measure is given by the exclusion of one arbitrary commodity; which, by its exclusion, fixes an ideal value-unit, while all other commodities in turn are set in a quantitative relation as pure values. All commodities share an ideal value-unit as their common measure, but this sharing falls into the practical realization of their relation in the exchange process. Hence, what seems to be an exchange of commodities and money is the realization of the capital, and what seem to be exchange-values are the magnitudes determined by the productive power of the valorization of labour-power and capital. Money in its capitalist form measures a valorization process in which money itself constantly enters. It is as if this form of self-measurement functions for the capitalist society as the practical self-reflection of an 'automatic subject'.

Luca Micaloni (Chapter 7) examines the concept of 'automatic subject' used by Marx to describe capital's process. First, Micaloni traces this Marxian expression back to Hegel's philosophy: 'subject' is self-reference, negation of alterity, circular movement; 'automatic' entails the subjective prerogative of being principle, cause, beginning and end of one's own movement. In the following paragraphs Micaloni shows how Marx's characterization of large-scale industry and of interest-bearing capital proves to be coherent with the circular self-movement illustrated in the general formula. If manufacture still rests on labourers' artisan abilities, in large-scale industry it is capital itself that elaborates and organizes the labour process, considering the worker only as an element of the process. Technology, as an element of capital, is what organizes the productive process according to valorization demand, and the instruments of labour, instead of labour-power, are now the starting point of the analysis of the process of production. The automation of the labour process in large-scale industry represents for Marx an implementation of the general formula of capital as 'automatic subject'. In interest-bearing capital (D-D'), where the process of production is hidden and capital presents itself as a thing producing value, the automatic subject acquires its complete form. Finally, Micaloni discusses the 'homology thesis' between Marx's concept of capital and Hegel's logic.

Roberto Fineschi (Chapter 8) focuses on the notion of 'reproduction'. Reproduction has two fundamental meanings in Marx's work. On the one hand, it is accumulation, that is, the specific form in which capital produces and reproduces itself. On the other, it is a general concept, pertaining to the general trans-historical human reproduction. As accumulation, reproduction has a key role in Marx's *Capital*, and on it rests the logical validity of the whole presentation. A dialectical theory must reproduce as its own results the elements that at the beginning were assumed as presuppositions, not posited by the theory itself. Only 'posing its own presuppositions capital' can properly become a process. The moment of reproduction represents in *Capital* the position of the presuppositions. Fineschi recalls the changes in the order of presentation of 'reproduction/accumulation' that Marx thought would have been necessary in the different drafts of the theory on the basis of the level of abstraction (generality, particularity, singularity). He then outlines the fundamental alteration concerning 'accumulation' in the different editions of *Capital* Volume 1. Fineschi also deals with reproduction in a broader sense, as a trans-historical category characterizing human beings living together in their relation with nature: the object of the discourse is here the relationship between general and historical-specific categories in Marx's theory of historical process.

Sebastiano Taccola (Chapter 9) proposes a re-examination of Marxian 'primitive accumulation'. First, primitive accumulation is presented as a diachronic process, capable of explaining the historical genesis of the capitalist mode of production, especially as it took place in England (through the Enclosures Acts, the clearing of the estates, and so on). Then, attention is focused on the permanence of this kind of accumulation. Primitive accumulation cannot just be seen as a process existing 'behind the back' of the production of capital, as a mere historical presupposition. It also has to be understood as the constantly expanding class separation reproduced in the accumulation of capital. It is a lever that drives this on a global scale, the synchronic process playing a crucial role in the reproduction of capital. Systemically and structurally, primitive accumulation represents a pivotal articulation in the explanation of economic, social and political phenomena typical of capitalism such as 'accumulation by dispossession' (Harvey), 'uneven development' (Amin), and so on. Finally, Taccola looks at the critical role that the category assumes in Marx's systematic presentation. This interpretation of primitive accumulation is grounded on that inner genesis of categories which is immanent to the Marxian critique of political economy and its method of presentation.

Chris O'Kane's attention in Chapter 10 is on the concept of 'domination'. He pursues the standpoint proposed by Alfred Schmidt of a backwards reading of Marx's early critique of bourgeois society from the perspective opened by the critique of political economy. After showing that Marx's early critiques of Smith, Hegel, Proudhon and bourgeois society are based on the anthropological standpoint of estrangement and alienation, O'Kane moves to Marx's later critique of the historically specific constitution and reproduction of bourgeois society. Where in precapitalist society personal domination was the basis of power relations, in bourgeois society all personal relations of dependence are dissolved in production. What arises is an objective and impersonal bond that rests on (the accumulation of surplus) value. Value presupposes the separation between subjective and objective conditions of production – the historical process of constitution of classes built on conquest, enslavement, robbery, murder; in short, force – that is constantly reproduced on a larger scale through the production process of capital. We have here an objective and abstract form of 'domination' (value) that expands the class division between the owners of means of production and workers. In this social condition, state laws protecting private property are not neutral, but an essential moment of the preservation of capitalistic class relations. On the one hand, Marx's theory presents a critique of bourgeois society self-understanding: market freedom, division of labour and the state are not institutions promoting social freedom, but forms of constitution and perpetuation of capital domination. On the other hand, showing that the condition of exploitation and misery to which the working class is forced by an objective impersonal form of compulsion, Marx's theory is a critical social theory of domination.

Chapter 11 by Gianluca Pozzoni concentrates on the concept of 'real abstraction'. Abstraction plays a crucial role in Marx's theory. In early works, in
particular in his critique of Proudhon, the category has a methodological role
against the universalization and naturalization of historical social relationships
put forth by political economy. It is only when Marx's methodological critique
evolves into a comprehensive scientific approach to political economy that
abstraction reveals its conceptual potential. In Marx's critique of political
economy, abstraction is located in the social process of production: the abstraction of labour is not a mental generalization, but a practical process going on
within private commodity exchanges under a production system dominated
by an accumulation of capital resulting from workers' exploitation. Pozzoni
emphasizes the fundamental role played in the critical theory of society by
real abstraction, especially in the reflections of Sohn-Rethel and Adorno, as
well as in contemporary critical social analysis. As Pozzoni shows, this notion
can serve to recast Marx's critique of political economy as an 'open' research
programme rather than as a closed system.

In her Chapter 12, Kirstin Munro proposes a critical account of the concept of
'social reproduction' developed by Marx and used by Marxist-feminists as the
core of what is known as social reproduction theory. First, she distinguishes
the Marxian concept of social reproduction from its use in Bourdieusian sociology. Marx's concept is inextricably linked to the accumulation and reproduction of capital as a whole. Bourdieusian sociology refers to social reproduction
as the intergenerational transmission of culture put forward by the education
institutions. The conflation between the Marxian category and biological
reproduction is contested. If social reproduction presupposes biological reproduction, the former refers to the reproduction of capital relation, that is, the
reproduction of the separation between subjective and objective conditions
of production. Munro insists on the point of departure of the current social
reproduction theorists: the unwaged activities necessary for the reproduction
of labour-power. In such an approach there is a progressive shift of the analysis
from the reproduction of labour-power as a moment of the reproduction of
capitalist society as a whole, to the reproduction of labour-power as a separate
section in which are amassed all the 'life-making activities'. Such activities are
presented by social reproduction theorists as not capitalistic. For this reason
they are often depicted as virtuous, and alternative to capital's subsumption of
labour-power in production. What the appealing expression 'life-making activities' conceals is what emerges if the view is broadened to society's reproduction as a whole. Such activities must reproduce a commodity (labour-power)
that has to be sold on the labour market, to be used by capital for the production
of surplus value. Building on Simone Clarke, Moishe Postone and Michael
Heinrich, Kirstin Munro emphasizes the necessity to understand class and

power relations from the point of view of the all-encompassing law of capital accumulation. From this perspective she presents a simple model of capitalist society in which is highlighted the structural relationship going on between the reproduction of labour-power and the reproduction of capital.

Vittorio Morfino (Chapter 13) develops a penetrating interpretation of the notes of *Capital* Volume 1 in which Lucretius and Darwin are quoted. The point is not to provide an additional reconstruction of the relation between Marx and Lucretius or between Marx and Darwin. The purpose is rather to discover the function of these authors in Marx's presentation. After presenting and commenting on the references, Morfino explains what is hidden behind Lucretius and Darwin. Three different levels of analysis are suggested, going from the more certain to the more conjectural. At the first level, Lucretius and Darwin represent only 'anti-finalism' and a stance for reason and science. At the second level, recognizing Spinoza behind Lucretius, the point is the denial of anthropocentrism, and the positive affirmation of a kind of 'materialism' where complexity and historicity are interconnected and irreducible. At the third and final level, building on Althusser and the problem of structural causality, Morfino argues that Lucretius/Spinoza and Darwin stand for a form of 'mechanism' in which totality still has a role, and an 'organicism' escaping teleology.

Emanuela Conversano (Chapter 14) analyses the method and content of the late Marx's *Ethnological Notebooks*. An alternative interpretation from that of Engels in his Preface to *The Origin of the Family, Private Property and the State* is suggested. Marx's inquiries are neither a mere further development of the 1840s historical materialism, nor a sudden anthropological turn in the name of Morgan. It is necessary to go beyond these interpretations in order to understand what is the actual legacy of these late Marx studies, and their role in the contemporary world. The societies under examination – which are different from the Western bourgeois society in time and space – act as a 'litmus test' for the understanding of capitalism as a historically (and geographically) developed social form. By helping to recognize the 'transient nature' of the capitalist mode of production, the topics of the excerpts are not to be conceived as material for historiography or philosophy of history. They instead call into question – even if not directly and explicitly – the conditions of possibility for the revolution at the global level.

1. Critique

Tommaso Redolfi Riva

> The path of dialectic, which attempts to move beyond the specialist and highly circumscribed perspective of logic and epistemology, would be one which did not content itself with simply identifying the point which requires criticism and then declaring: 'Look! There is a mistake in the reasoning here, you have got yourself entangled in contradiction – the whole thing is therefore worthless.' Rather, the next step would be to show why, within the constellation of such thinking, the relevant mistakes and contradictions inevitably arise, what has motivated them within the movement of such thought, and thus how far they reveal themselves, in the total context of thought, to be significant in their own falsehood and contradictoriness.
>
> (Adorno [1958] 2017, p. 157)

1.1 INTRODUCTION

The categories of political economy represent for Marx a privileged access to the reality of the mode of capitalist production, not only because they are moments of a theory whose aim is to penetrate 'the inner connection, the physiology, so to speak, of the bourgeois system', but also because they are a 'nomenclature' of *economic* phenomena, reproduced 'for the first time in the language and [in the] thought process' (Marx [1861–63] 2010a, pp. 390–391). If it is true that the object of Marx's theory is the mode of capitalist production, the access to this object is possible only through the mediation of concepts (see Schmidt 1968; Fineschi 2006, particularly pp. 168–169). Political economy represents for Marx the conceptual mediation to economic phenomena, and that is the reason why the discussion with economists acquires a fundamental role in Marx's works. Nevertheless, Marx's relation with the categories of political economy is mainly critical. At a first glance Marx's critique seems to trace economic categories back to the historical conditions of capitalist accumulation, showing the development of ideas in its inner connection with the real development of the mode of production. In this way theoretical reflections are led back to the 'earthly kernel' from which they arose. But even if this movement *from conditioned to condition* is necessary and unavoidable, it is only generic. Given that 'the only materialist method' consists in developing 'from the actual relations of life the corresponding celestialised forms [*verhim-*

melten Formen] of those relations' (Marx [1867] 1906, p. 406, trans. mod.), the critique of political economy, as the 'critique of economic categories' (Marx [1858] 2010, p. 270), has to be able to understand categories as 'forms of being, the characteristics of existence' of 'modern bourgeois society' (Marx [1857–58] 1993, p. 106). According to this perspective, Marx's critique has to begin with the presentation of the object of the science of political economy, and from it to deduce the categories as moments of capitalist totality. In this way the theoretical inadequacy of political economy is no longer generic, it is rather a specific result of the very object to which political economy applies.

1.2   THE CONDITIONS OF POSSIBILITY OF POLITICAL ECONOMY AS AN AUTONOMOUS SCIENCE

In order to understand analytically the method of Marx's critique, first it is necessary to address the *object* of the critique, and from there to understand why for Marx it is essential to turn attention to political economy in order to understand the form of motion [*Bewegungsform*] of modern society. This issue has to do with an appropriate understanding of Marx's famous claim in the Preface to *A Contribution to the Critique of Political Economy*, according to which 'the anatomy of civil society has to be sought in political economy' (Marx [1859] 2010, p. 262).

A first approximation to the concept of 'critique of political economy' can be reached by starting from the understanding of the conditions of possibility of political economy as an autonomous science. From this point of view, the analysis of the constitution of political economy as a separate field of social science has not simply to do with the history of social science, from which it is easy to conclude that since ancient times there is a part of human knowledge that has to do with production and reproduction of human beings in society, and that such knowledge reaches its *classical* form in political economy. For Marx, the understanding of the constitution of political economy as an autonomous science means – materialistically – to reflect on how it can appear as an isolable segment of the reality that we designate as the sphere of economic relations. The historicity of the science of political economy – its appearing as an autonomous science (as *the* science of modern society) – has to be brought back to the appearance of the 'material relations of existence' [*den materiellen Lebensverhältnissen*] (Marx [1859] 2010, p. 262) as an autonomous sphere of society. The science that inquires into the *origins and the causes of wealth* can arise only when the production of wealth, the sphere of the 'material relations of existence', separates itself from political and ethical bonds characterizing pre-capitalist economic formations. Political economy can arise as a separate science only where its object acquires a distinction and a specific autonomy.[1]

If we now turn our attention to Marx's aforementioned statement that 'the anatomy of civil society has to be sought in political economy', we can see that, from this perspective, it acquires a clearer meaning that cannot simply be referred to as a generic and transhistorical 'materialist conception of history' [*die materialistiche Anschauung der Geschichte*] (Engels [1878] 2010, p. 254), where the word '*Anschauung*' seems to refer to a methodology in which the subject (the social scientist) perceives, distinguishes and selects from a mishmash of social facts. Nor can it be referred to as the construction of a historiographic canon, as in Croce's ([1900] 1914) interpretation. Marx's statement alludes to the autonomous constitution of a section of the reality – the material relations of existence – of which political economy is the science.

The autonomization of the economic sphere does not imply that material relations of existence can be understood beyond the state or beyond the political or juridical dimension, but that in the mode of production characterizing modern society, the determination of property and distribution relations, as well as the allocation of social labour, occurs outside the sphere of political deliberation, and within a system of private autonomous and independent processes of production without any coordination except that arising from a system of exchange of private produced commodities.[2]

In this perspective the part of the 1857–58 manuscript on the 'pre-capitalist economic formations' is a privileged access point. Here Marx wants to sketch the presuppositions on which capitalist social relation is based and to understand its *differentia specifica* compared with previous economic forms.[3]

In pre-capitalist epochs, production is not an autonomous segment divided from the other moments characterizing human relations. Production is finalized to the reproduction of the community that precedes and determines the

---

[1] On the issue of the 'materialistic deduction' of political economy, see the fundamental reflection of Lorenzo Calabi (1976).

[2] As Ellen Meiksins Wood states:
The point, then, is to explain how and in what sense capitalism has driven a wedge between the economic and the political – how and in what sense essentially political issues like the disposition of power to control production and appropriation, or the allocation of social labour and resources, have been cut off from the political arena and displaced to a separate sphere. (Meiksins Wood [1981] 2016, p. 20)

[3] It is in this sense, and not as a first attempt at a historiographic account of ancient economy, that these pages continue to be important. On this issue, with different emphases and perspectives, see Cazzaniga (1981), Meiksins Wood (2008), Basso (2008).

production itself. The community, outside and before the production, defines property relations, the distribution of resources and the allocation of labour.

Regardless how the relations between production, material relations of existence and social totality are presented, case by case, in the pre-capitalist economic formations the aim of production according to Marx lies outside of (and before) the production itself. Production is always oriented by a social aim that precedes it: it is only a means to an end that lies behind it. In pre-capitalist forms of production 'the economic aim is hence the production of use values, i.e. *the reproduction of the individual* within the specific relation to commune in which he is the basis' (Marx [1857–58] 1993, p. 485).

Since production is a means to an end that precedes and determines it, Marx shows that an analysis of the economic sphere as separated from the other moments of society has no documented existence. Political economy as a separated social science does not exist and cannot exist in antiquity:

> we never find in antiquity an inquiry into which form of landed property etc. is the most productive, creates the greatest wealth ... The question is always which mode of property creates the best citizens. Wealth appears as an end in itself only among the few commercial peoples ... who live in the poroes of the ancient world. (Marx [1857–58] 1993, p. 487)

Only where capital self-valorization becomes the 'directing motive, the end and aim' (Marx [1867] 1906, p. 363) of capitalist production, does political economy first emerge as an autonomous science. As Marx states:

> Political economy, which as an independent science, first sprang into being during the period of manufacture, views the *social* division of labour only from the standpoint of *manufacture*, and sees in it only the means of producing more commodities with a given quantity of labour, and, consequently of cheapening commodities and hurrying on the accumulation of capital. In most striking contrast with this accentuation of *quantity* and *exchange-value*, is the attitude of the writers of classical antiquity, which hold exclusively by *quality* and *use-value*. (Marx [1867] 1906, pp. 400–401)

The aim of capitalist production does not lie outside material production, in the reproduction of society or in a social configuration that precedes production. The driving motive of the process is the production of abstract wealth, money: the greatest possible production of surplus value: M-C-M'. As Marx shows, political economy can reach the status of a separate science only where material relations of existence become autonomous, where the 'directing motive, the end and aim' of production, is production itself; that is, where the production process assumes the form of valorization. Only because capitalist production is the production of surplus value, and as such has no other driving purpose and determining scope except valorization, is it *ab-solute* and hence autonomous.

1.3   THE CRITIQUE OF THE CAPITALIST MODE OF PRODUCTION *JUXTA PROPRIA PRINCIPIA*

Starting from capitalist production as the production of surplus value, it is possible to understand a second determination that the concept of the critique of political economy assumes. For Marx, what characterizes capitalist production is the form labour acquires as wage labour. The separation between subjective and objective conditions of production is the result of the historical genesis of capital:

> the encounter with the objective conditions of labour as separate from him, as *capital* from the worker's side, and the encounter with the *worker* as propertyless, as an abstract worker from the capitalist side ... presupposes a *historic process* ... which ... forms the history of the origins of capital and wage labour. (Marx [1857–58] 1993, p. 489)

For Marx, the historical genesis of capital relation is at the same time 'the *historic origin* of the bourgeois economy, of the forms of production which are theoretically or ideally expressed by the categories of political economy' (Marx [1857–58] 1993, p. 489). The historical genesis of political economy, as a separate science that can address material relations of existence in their purity and autonomy, presupposes the historical genesis of the capitalist mode of production, that is, the scission between subjective and objective conditions of production: 'the capitalist epoch is therefore characterized by this, that labour-power takes in the eyes of the labourer himself the form of a commodity which is his property; his labour consequently becomes wage-labour' (Marx [1867] 1906, p. 189).

Starting from capitalist production as a specific stage of human social production, and wage labour as a specific historical form of existence of subjective conditions, Marx is able to understand the production process as a process of valorization, and to solve the problem upon which political economy was beached: that is, the creation of profit starting from the exchange of equivalents on the market. Leaving behind the preclassical theory of 'profit upon alienation', according to which profit came from commodities being sold above their value, classical political economy linked profit with the mass of advanced capital (Ricardo), but it was not able to relate this proportionality to the law of value. This lack became the limit of Ricardo's system and of his law of value.

Since objective (means of production) and subjective (workers) conditions of production are structurally separated, production – presupposing the unity of the separate conditions – can occur only by means of an exchange between the owner of capital and the worker. The exchange relation does not occur between capital and labour, as conceived by political economy, since labour exists only potentially in the worker (given that they cannot exercise labour on any means of production before the exchange). The exchange occurs between capital and labour-power; that is, between capital and labouring capacity [*Arbeitsvermögen, Arbeitsfähigkeit*]. This is an exchange of equivalents, since the wage received by the worker is equivalent to the quantity of labour necessary to the reproduction of the worker. Nevertheless, the formation of surplus value depends on the use by capital of the commodity labour-power: capital buys the commodity labour-power at its value, but it uses this commodity – that is, it makes the worker work – for a greater number of hours than are necessary for the reproduction of the wage.

Only entering the 'hidden abode of production' allows Marx to understand the production of surplus value and, at the same time, to develop an immanent critique of the laws of the circulation of commodities. From this standpoint, the critique of political economy is a critique of the capitalist system and of its own self-representation as the '*Eden of innate rights*' where '*Freedom, Equality, Property*' are effective. The equivalence characterizing the exchange of commodities on the market is based on surplus value production, on capital's appropriation of surplus labour, carried out by labour-power beyond the labour necessary to the reproduction of the worker:

> property turns out to be the *right*, on the part of the capitalist, to appropriate the *unpaid labour of others* or its product and to be the impossibility, on the part of the labourer, of appropriating his own product. The *separation of property from labour* has become the necessary consequence of a law that apparently originated in their *identity*. (Marx [1867] 1906, p. 640)

The mode of capitalistic production becomes the object of critique exactly on the same basis upon which exchange rests: the circulation of commodities presents the owner of the means of production and the worker as free and equal persons. Their exchange has the form of an equivalent exchange, but from the point of view of production it is appropriation of surplus labour, carried out by labour-power beyond the labour necessary for its own reproduction.[4] The

---

[4]   On this question, the reflection developed by Ellen Meiksins Wood is very interesting. Meiksins Wood shows that in pre-capitalist modes of production the appropriation of the product of other people's labour is based on the practice of an extra-economic power (military, political, and so on); while in the capitalist mode of production what guarantees the appropriation is the relation between labour and capital itself, which only from a formal perspective is a contract between free and equal persons. Reproducing on the one hand the free worker (free both as a person and as

equivalence is only a façade and the critique of political economy becomes a *self-critique*: a critique of the mode of capitalist production *juxta propria principia*.[5]

1.4 CRITIQUE OF THE ABSOLUTIZATION OF CAPITALIST SOCIAL RELATIONS

As we have seen, capitalist modernity is the terrain in which political economy arises as an autonomous and separate science. Political economy presents itself as the *science of civil society*, in the double sense of subjective and objective genitive: on the one hand, as the science studying the capitalist mode of production; on the other, as the science which is the result of the capitalist mode of production and, in itself, is incapable of overcoming the capitalist standpoint.[6] From this perspective we can understand the critique of political economy as

---

lacking the means of production on which execute their labour), and on the other hand the owner of the means of production, the labour contract reproduces the capital relation. In the capitalist mode of production, it is not possible to understand the production process as a mere technical moment: from the beginning, it is a social relation of production, in the actuation of which political and juridical elements occur. The political aspect of the relation of production cannot be considered an ancillary or superstructural moment, since: 'The "sphere" of production is dominant not in the sense that it stands apart from or precedes these juridical-political forms, but rather in the sense that these forms are precisely forms of production, the *attributes* of a particular productive system' (Meiksins Wood [1981] 2016, p. 27).

5   Adorno refers to this immanent critique when he states that the aim of the critique is to measure 'that which "is the case" [*der Fall ist*] in society, as Wittgenstein would have put it, by what society purports to be, in order to detect in this contradiction the potential, the possibilities for changing society's whole constitution' (Adorno [1968] 2000, p. 31), 'to ask if society conforms to its own rules, if society functions according to laws which it claims as its own' (Adorno [1962] 2018, p. 158). For Adorno, the model for the critique of society is Marx's critique of political economy which:

> attempts to derive the whole that is to be criticized in terms of its right to existence from exchange, commodity form and its immanent 'logical' contradictory nature. The assertion of the equivalence of what is exchanged, the basis of all exchange, is repudiated by its consequences. As the principle of exchange, by virtue of its immanent dynamics, extends to the living labours of human beings it changes compulsively into objective inequality, namely that of social classes. Forcibly stated, the contradiction is that exchange takes place justly and unjustly. (Adorno [1969] 1977, p. 25)

6   This duplicity of political economy can also be recognized in Hegel's *Outlines of the Philosophy of Right*:

> This [political economy] is one of the sciences which have arisen out of the conditions of the modern world. Its development affords the interesting spectacle (as in Smith, Say, and Ricardo) of thought working upon the endless mass of details which confront it at the outset and extracting therefrom the simple principles of

the critique of the absolutization and naturalization of capitalist social relations put forth by political economy.

Marx's analysis does not lie *a parte subiecti*, just like the understanding of the autonomous constitution of political economy does not find an exhaustive answer in the historiographical examination of social science in its diachronic development: the lack of historicity of political economy is not a subjective mistake. According to Marx, the unsatisfactory conceptual elaboration of political economy is rather the result of the object it addresses, and can be explained only by means of the presentation of the object itself.

The autonomization of material relations of existence, of the economic sphere, is easily understandable if we reflect on the fact that the objects around us can be predicated of a supersensuous property – value – according to which they are exchanged, bought and sold. Value is the constitutive dimension of economic science.[7] Just as classical physics addresses objects having mass, so political economy addresses objects having value: political economy conceives value as a natural and constitutive dimension of the relation between human beings and objects. And this is true both for classical political economy and for marginalism.

Classical political economy focuses attention on the moment of production: the value of an object is determined by the quantity of labour expended in its production. In Smith's and Ricardo's 'Robinsonades' we can find original hunters and fishers exchanging their products according to labour expended in the production of their objects. For political economy, products are value since they are concretions of labour, regardless of the social form of labour, that is, the specific social form in which they are produced. Marginalism focuses attention on the moment of consumption, and determines the value of the object according to marginal utility. Value appears as a structural constituent of the relation between human beings and things, and modern economics represents itself as the science studying human conduct as 'the relationship between ends and scarce means which have alternative uses' (Robbins 1932, p. 15). Independently of the alternative theories of value, what completely

---

the thing, the understanding *effective* in the thing and directing it. (Hegel [1821] 2008, p. 187)

What political economy is able to grasp, bringing the multiplicity of single facts back to the unity of the law, is only the 'understanding in the thing', that is, the fixed determinations of what is presupposed to the analysis, of what is given. It is exactly the absolutization of the given, the inability to reconstruct its genesis starting from the specific form of social relations, that compels political economy to the role of the understanding of the system of needs.

7   On this question the whole work of Hans-Georg Backhaus is fundamental, particularly the essay *Zur Marxschen 'Revolutionierung' und 'Kritik' der Ökonomie: die Bestimmung ihres Gegenstandes als Ganzes 'verrückter Formen'*, in Backhaus (1997).

transcends the point of view of the economic science is the form of value: value as dimension, and not as quantity.

When economic science has to explain the exchange of two objects, it tries to bring back the proportion in which they are exchanged to an external and independent variable (see Dobb 1937, pp. 6–8): for classical political economy, objectified labour; for marginalism, utility at the margin. What economic science does not take into consideration is the fact that, first and foremost, the objects have to be predicated of a peculiar property, not characterizing their material objectuality: a supersensuous property. What remains outside the theoretical standpoint of political economy is the form of value.

Only when the issue of the *form* of value is at the centre of the discourse does the question of the conditions of possibility of the supersensuous property of the economic objects – value – become *the* problem of the science. From this perspective the commodity form – that is, the form the wealth obtains in societies in which the capitalist mode of production prevails – represents the result of a specific form of the organization of the social production.

For Marx, the commodity form can become the universal form of the wealth only where labour-power is a commodity, and labour is wage labour. Capitalist production is the production of commodities insofar as it presupposes a specific form of organization of the expenditure and socialization of labour. When Marx talks about commodities, he is not talking about objects, products of labour; he is talking about products as the result of a specific form of the organization of labour in the society:

> objects of utility become commodities, only because they are products of the labour of private individuals or groups of individuals who carry on their work independently of each other. The sum total of the labour of all these private individuals forms the aggregate labour of society. Since the producers do not come into social contact with each other until they exchange their products, the specific social character of each producer's labour does not show itself except in the act of exchange. In other words, the labour of the individual asserts itself as a part of the labour of society, only by means of the relations which the act of exchange establishes directly between the products, and indirectly, through them, between the producers. (Marx [1867] 1906, pp. 83–84)

The commodity form presupposes separate and autonomous units of production, producing for the exchange. The relationship among the different units of production, among the different expenditures of private labour, among the individual processes of valorization, is determined by the mutual exchange of commodities. There is no previous organization of social production. The labour expended in the production of commodities is private labour that becomes social, and hence part of total social labour, only by means of the exchange of the objects on the market. This organization of production and of the socialization of labour is historically specific: it belongs to the capitalist mode of production; but other forms of socialization of labour are possible.[8]

Marx sketches different forms of socialization of labour in which the product of labour does not acquire the commodity form (see Marx [1867] 1906, pp. 88–92). The fundamental difference lies in the fact that products have a social character before the exchange, in the production, while expended labour, although moments of the social division of labour, has a previous coordination that makes the products immediately social.

In the capitalist mode of production, since it is the production of commodities, the social relationship among productive units that determines the socialization of private labour occurs by means of a system of individual and separate commodity–money exchanges. There is no organization of the allocation of labour before the production: labour becomes social labour – that is, labour that society evaluates as necessary for its own reproduction – only when produced commodities are exchanged with money, when concrete labour expended in the production becomes abstract. Contra to classical political economy, the substance of value is not concrete labour expended in production, but abstract labour, that is, labour which by means of the exchange with money confirms itself as part of total social labour.

The value form of the products of labour is the result of a specific form of the organization of social production, in which every production unit is dependent from the others, but where each production unit behaves independently: a social division of labour without coordination before production. The sale of the product is the manner in which labour expended in the production becomes socially necessary labour: it is the manner in which the labours expended by an individual unit of production relates with the others. The economic science, understanding value as a constitutive element of the (productive or consuming) relation between human beings and things, cannot conceive the genesis of value, that is, the origin of that specific organization of production whose end is valorization.

---

[8]   On the specificity of the socialization of labour in the capitalist mode of production, see Fineschi (2001), Heinrich (1999, 2017). It is interesting to read the effort put forth by Riccardo Bellofiore (2018a, 2018b) to establish a link between the socialization that occurs in circulation, and the immediate socialized or collective labour [*unmittelbar vergesellschafteter oder gemeinsamer Arbeit*] (presented in the chapter on 'Machinery and Large-Scale Industry' of Marx's *Capital*), showing the different meanings that the 'social labour' category assumes in Marx's work.

1.5 THE CATEGORIES OF POLITICAL ECONOMY AS MOMENTS OF SOCIAL REALITY

Marx's reflection is not confined to the recognition of the absolutization of capital relationship put forth by economic science. The next step of his critique is the inquiry into the reasons and causes of this absolutization: Why does political economy naturalize the specific forms of capital production? Why does political economy remain trapped in the fetish character of the commodity? Where does the absolutization arise from? For Marx, naturalization, absolutization and fetishism of political economy depend directly on the form of thing assumed by the social relation: political economy fetishism is not a methodological mistake of the science. The exchange of things on the market – the form of capital socialization of labour – shows the specific characters of capitalist production as objectual properties of the products of labour, 'socio-natural properties of these things':

> the commodity reflects the social character of man's own labour as objectual [*gegenständliche*] character of the products of labour themselves, as socio-natural properties [*gesellschaftliche Natureigenschaften*] of these things, hence it also reflects the social relation of the producers to the sum of total labour as a social relation between things [*Dinge*], a relation which exists apart from and outside the producers (Marx [1867] 1906, p. 83, trans. mod.)

The social relation connecting productive units is realized by means of exchanges of things; it obtains an objective form and it faces social agents. This objectual form is the source of the eternization of the mode of capitalist production put forth by political economy.

The displacement of the social relation among units of production in a social relation among things shows the social relations among people as properties of things exchanged: it is 'an inversion and causes relations between people to appear [*erscheinen*] as attributes of things and as relations of people to the social attributes of these things' (Marx [1861–63] 2010b, p. 507). The fetish character of capitalist socialization is the source of political economy's fetishism: the naturalization of capital and of the form of value products of labour obtain.[9]

From this point of view, the critique of political economy is, on the one hand, the critique of the fetishism; on the other, the deduction of the fetishism from the presentation of the object of political economy: the fetish character of

---

9   The distinction between 'fetishism' and the 'fetish character' has been stressed by Riccardo Bellofiore (2013, 2014).

capitalist socialization, that is its objectual character, is the source of political economy's fetishism.

1.6   CRITIQUE OF POLITICAL ECONOMY AND CRITIQUE OF VALUE

Reflecting again on the theory of value, and leaving behind the fetishism of political economy, it is possible to distinguish a further sense of Marx's critique. Once value is understood as a social relation, it is possible to develop a critique of political economy as a critique of value, that is, as the critique of that social relation of production established by means of social agents' actions but imposed as a law of nature to which they are subjected.[10]

The law of value, as the fundamental relation regulating the form of motion of capitalist society, is not consciously executed by the exchangers – as it occurs in Smith's idea of labour as 'toil and trouble' – it is a superindividual process acting objectively and to which every social agent is subjected: as Marx states: 'we are not aware of this, nevertheless we do it' (Marx [1867] 1906, p. 85). Every capitalist, having as their aim the maximum valorization of their own capital, organizes the process of production with the technology (and the information about social demand) they have at their disposal. In this way, they can determine the quantity of concrete labour their commodities have to contain. Nonetheless, how much of that labour confirms itself as abstract labour – socially necessary labour, value – cannot be known before the selling of the commodities on the market: if concrete labour is present in the conscious thought of the producer, abstract labour is the result of a superindividual process realizing in circulation and objectively imposing itself on economic agents 'as an average' acting after and independently from individual expenditure of labour.

Marxian theory aims 'to show *how* the law of value asserts itself' (Marx [1868] 2010, p. 68), and to understand the objective process that necessarily realizes itself behind any possible control of social agents. In this sense, the critique of political economy is the 'anamnesis of the genesis' of the autonomization of social relations and strives for a human re-appropriation of the form of motion of society.[11]

---

[10]   The expression 'critique of value' is used here in the sense of a critique of the capitalist mode of production and of its specific form of socialization, and not with reference to theoretical work developed around the journal *Krisis* and Robert Kurz.

[11]   'Anamnesis of the genesis' is the expression by which Adorno ([1965] 1989) defines historical materialism in a dialogue with Sohn-Rethel. See Reichelt (2008), Redolfi Riva (2013), Bellofiore and Redolfi Riva (2015), Taccola (2019).

1.7   CONCLUSION

The concept of 'critique of political economy' expounded in this chapter makes it possible to develop some considerations on the method of the critique. It is important to stress the double nature of the Marxian method of the critique. It is the critique of the categories and of the form of knowledge of political economy, hence the critique of the conceptual elaboration of capitalist mode of production developed by the science; and at the same time it is the critique of a specific *science* insofar as it is the science of a specific *object*. The critique of the science turns out to be the critique of the object of the science, and the understanding of social objective conditions that originate that specific form of science. We could say that the critique of political economy is the critique of capital as objective–subjective totality: on the one hand, as a system of production whose end is self-valorization based on the appropriation of unpaid labour and realizing an autonomous (from social agents) system of socialization; on the other hand, as the place of constitution of the categories of political economy, whose inadequacy cannot be simply brought back to a subjective lack of knowledge, precisely because the categories are the reflection, manifestation and product of capitalist social relations – they are a moment of social reality. Since categories are a 'form of thought which are socially valid, and therefore objective, for the relations of production belonging to *this historically determined* mode of social production' (Marx [1867] 1906, p. 87, trans. mod.), Marx can describe his work both as a 'critique of economic categories' and 'a critical exposé [*Darstellung*] of the system of the bourgeois economy', that is, an 'exposé and, by the same token, a critique of the system' (Marx [1858] 2010, p. 270).

REFERENCES

Abbreviation:
    MECW = *Marx–Engels Collected Works*, London: Lawrence & Wishart.

Adorno, T.W., [1958] (2017). *An Introduction to Dialectics*. Cambridge: Polity Press.
Adorno, T.W., [1962] (2018). Theodor W. Adorno on 'Marx and the Basic Concepts of Sociological Theory'. *Historical Materialism*, 26(1), pp. 154–164.
Adorno, T.W., [1965] (1989). Notizien von einem Gespräch zwischen Th. W. Adorno und A. Sohn Rethel am 16.04.1965. In A. Sohn-Rethel, *Geistige und körperliche Arbeit. Zur Epistemologie der abendländichen Geschichte*. Weinhem: VHC, pp. 221–226.
Adorno, T.W., [1968] (2000). *Introduction to Sociology*. Stanford, CA: Stanford University Press.
Adorno, T.W., [1969] (1977). Introduction. In T. W. Adorno et al., *The Positivist Dispute in German Sociology*. London: Heinemann, pp. 1–67.

Backhaus, H.G., (1997). *Dialektik der Wertform. Untersuchungen zur marxschen Ökonomiekritik.* Freiburg: ça ira.

Basso, L., (2008). Tra forme precapitalistiche e capitalismo: il problema della società nei 'Grundrisse'. In D. Sacchetto and M. Tomba (eds), *La lunga accumulazione originaria. Politica e lavoro nel mercato mondiale.* Verona: Ombre Corte, pp. 58–73.

Bellofiore, R., (2013). Il Capitale come Feticcio Automatico e come Soggetto, e la sua costituzione: sulla (dis)continuità Marx–Hegel. *Consecutio Temporum*, 3(5). http://www.consecutio.org/2013/10/il-capitale-come-feticcio-automatico-e-come -soggetto-e-la-sua-costituzione-sulla-discontinuita-marx-hegel/.

Bellofiore, R., (2014). Lost in Translation: Once Again on the Marx-Hegel Connection. In F. Moseley and T. Smith (eds), *Marx's 'Capital' and Hegel's 'Logic': A Reexamination.* Leiden and Boston: Brill, pp. 164–188.

Bellofiore, R., (2018a). *Le avventure della socializzazione. Dalla teoria monetaria del valore alla teoria macro-monetaria della produzione capitalistica.* Milano: Mimesis.

Bellofiore, R., (2018b). 'The Adventures of *Vergesellschaftung*'. *Consecutio rerum*, 5, pp. 503–541.

Bellofiore, R. and Redolfi Riva, T., (2015). The Neue Marx-Lektüre. Putting the Critique of Political Economy back into the Critique of Society. *Radical Philosophy*, 189, pp. 24–36.

Calabi, L., (1976). Adam Smith e la costituzione dell'economia politica. *Critica marxista*, 3–4, pp. 213–253.

Cazzaniga, G., (1981). *Funzione e conflitto. Forme e classi nella teoria marxiana dello sviluppo.* Genova: Liguori.

Croce, B., [1900] (1914). *Historical Materialism and the Economics of Karl Marx.* New York: Macmillan.

Dobb, M., (1937). *Political Economy and Capitalism: Some Essays in Economic Tradition.* London: Routledge & Sons.

Engels, F., [1878] (2010). Antidühring. In: *MECW*, vol. 25. Digital edition. London: Lawrence & Wishart, pp. 1–312.

Fineschi, R., (2001). *Ripartire da Marx. Processo storico ed economia politica nella teoria del 'capitale'.* Naples: La Città del Sole.

Fineschi, R., (2006). *Marx e Hegel. Contributi a una rilettura.* Roma: Carocci.

Hegel, G.W.F., [1821] (2008). *Outlines of the Philosophy of Right.* Oxford: Oxford University Press.

Heinrich, M., (1999). *Die Wissenschaft vom Wert. Die Marxsche Kritik der politischen Ökonomie zwischen Wissenschaftlicher Revolution und klassischer Tradition*, 4th edn. Münster: Westfälisches Dampfboot.

Heinrich, M., (2017). Socializzazione ex post e carattere monetario del valore. In P. Garofalo and M. Quante (eds), *Lo spettro è tornato! Attualità della filosofia di Marx.* Milano: Mimesis, pp. 133–146.

Marx, K., [1857–58] (1993). *Grundrisse. Foundations of the Critique of Political Economy*, 2nd edn. Harmondsworth: Penguin.

Marx, K., [1858] (2010). Letter to Ferdinand Lassalle, 22 February 1858. In: *MECW*, vol. 40. Digital edition. London: Lawrence & Wishart, pp. 268–271.

Marx, K., [1859] (2010). *A Contribution to the Critique of Political Economy*, Part One. In: *MECW*, vol. 29. Digital edition. London: Lawrence & Wishart, pp. 257–417.

Marx, K., [1861–63] (2010a). Economic Manuscript of 1861–63. In: *MECW*, vol. 31. Digital edition. London: Lawrence & Wishart.

Marx, K., [1861–63] (2010b). Economic Manuscript of 1861–63. In: *MECW*, vol. 32. Digital edition. London: Lawrence & Wishart.

Marx, K., [1867] (1906). *Capital. A Critique of Political Economy. Volume One*. New York: The Modern Library.

Marx, K., [1868] (2010). Letter to Ludwig Kugelmann, 11 July 1868. In: *MECW*, vol. 43. Digital edition. London: Lawrence & Wishart, pp. 67–70.

Meiksins Wood, E., [1981] (2016). The Separation of the 'Economic' and the 'Political' in Capitalism. In E. Meiksins Wood, *Democracy against Capitalism: Renewing Historical Materialism*. London and New York: Verso, pp. 19–48.

Meiksins Wood, E., (2008). Historical Materialism in 'Forms which Precede Capitalist Production'. In M. Musto (ed), *Karl Marx's Grundrisse: Foundations of the Critique of Political Economy 150 Years Later*. London and New York: Palgrave, pp. 79–92.

Redolfi Riva, T., (2013). Teoria critica della società? Critica dell'economia politica. Adorno, Backhaus, Marx. *Consecutio Temporum*, 3(5). http://www.consecutio .org/2013/10/teoria-critica-della-societa-critica-delleconomia-politica-in-adorno -backhaus-marx/.

Reichelt, H., (2008). *Neue Marx Lektuere. Zur Kritik sozialwissenschaftlicher Logik*. Hamburg: VSA Verlag.

Robbins, L., (1932). *An Essay on the Nature and Significance of Economic Science*. London: Macmillan.

Schmidt, A., (1968). On the Concept of Knowledge in the Criticism of Political Economy. In VV. AA., *Karl Marx 1818–1968*. Bad Godesberg: Inter Nationes, pp. 92–102.

Taccola, S., (2019). Anamnesi della genesi e critica della politica. Note per una politica critica. In M. Di Pierro and F. Marchesi (eds), *Crisi dell'immanenza. Potere, conflitto, istituzione*. Macerata: Quodlibet, pp. 123–134.

2. Materialism and dialectics

Stefano Breda

2.1   A THEORETICAL TENSION FIELD

If one had to choose two unavoidable keywords to characterize Karl Marx's philosophy, these would probably be 'materialism' and 'dialectics'. The two terms even came to be merged together in the official philosophical doctrine of Marxism–Leninism, the DIAMAT, which stands for 'dialectical materialism'.

In 1974, however, Cesare Luporini pointed out that the terms 'dialectics' and 'materialism' are not immediately in harmony with each other. The significance of their connection cannot be taken for granted, since, as such, it defines just a 'theoretical tension field' (Luporini 1974, VII) in which a more precise meaning of this connection still has to be sought. A large part of philosophical Marxism can be seen as work within this tension field, work that produced an incredible multiplicity of methodological and epistemological positions, each with different theoretical and even political consequences.

Since the 1960s, with the development of heterodox currents in Marxism, scholars belonging to different schools have highlighted the limits of dialectical materialism, which, as a philosophical doctrine with a claim to universality, tends to translate into an all-encompassing and supra-historical Marxist worldview. Although such a doctrine can find support in the philosophical reflection of Friedrich Engels, it is hardly compatible with Marx's insight into philosophy, its limits and its relation to the empirical world. Having rejected the orthodoxy of dialectical materialism, heterodox Marxist scholars have more often focused on the notion of 'materialist dialectics' as a philosophical method used by Marx in his critique of political economy. At the time of writing in 2021, however, we are still a long way from giving the term 'materialist dialectics' a reasonably agreed and unambiguous meaning.

The question of the specificity of the dialectical method followed by Marx in his critique of political economy with respect to an idealist dialectics has been at the centre of heated debates since the first publication of *Capital* vol. 1. The inconsistency of the famous metaphor of inversion through which Marx defined the relationship between his dialectical method and that of Hegel was convincingly highlighted by Louis Althusser ([1965] 2005, 87ff.), who, however, did not provide any real comprehensive alternative. More concrete indications can be found in some fundamental intuitions of Theodor W. Adorno, and in their elaboration by the *Neue Marx-Lektüre*, the new reading of Marx developed in Germany since the 1960s. If we follow these indications, Marx's revolution of dialectics does not consist in an inversion of subject and predicate with respect to its Hegelian form, but rather in the recognition that dialectics *tout court* is merely the philosophical expression of those specific social relations in which subject and predicate are objectively inverted: capitalist relations (see Reichelt [1970] 1972, 81; Colletti 1969, 113f., 433f.). If, then, dialectics in its Hegelian form presents an upside-down world, we do not bring it down to earth by overturning it as a system of thought, but by revealing its objective roots in capitalist relations and criticizing an inversion operating in these relations. At most, then, it is the material relations that are to be overturned, not the dialectics: rather, dialectics is to be denaturalized, demystified by identifying its historically determined presuppositions. Much more appropriate than any image of inversion is therefore an image of delimitation: 'the dialectical form of exposition is only correct if it knows its limits' (Marx [1858/61] 1980, 91), that is, the points at which the dialectics, from *explanans*, becomes itself part of the *explanandum*, as a historical product in need of an equally historical explanation.

All this, however, remains only an abstract general conception of dialectics until a satisfactory answer has been given to the fundamental problem raised by Althusser: to demystify dialectics means not only to think of it in different terms, but also, at the same time, to transform its operative principles. Now, if the demystification of dialectics corresponds to its limitation, the problem arises in these terms: what does it mean, operationally, to use the dialectical form of exposition, knowing its limits?

Here I want to argue that in order to answer this question it is necessary to overcome some basic limitations of the meta-theoretical proposals of the *Neue Marx-Lektüre*, whose conception of dialectics remains too much in line with the Hegelian project of absolute knowledge.

Since it is a question of working within what Luporini called the 'theoretical tension field' generated by the juxtaposition of the two poles 'dialectics' and 'materialism', it is necessary to find the coordinates of this tension field first. In order to do so, it is useful to ask what, according to Marx's methodological self-understanding, characterizes his procedure as dialectical, and what marks its distance from an idealistic procedure. Starting from the second point, the oppositional lines shown in Table 2.1 can be extrapolated from Marx's statements.

Table 2.1   *Differences between materialistic and idealistic dialectics in Marx's self-understanding*

The unfolding of the 'peculiar logic of the peculiar object' (Marx [1843] 1982, 101)	instead of	the application of a ready-made logic to a specific object (see Marx and Engels [1856/59] 1963, 275)
An *a posteriori* reconstruction of this logic		an 'a priori construction' (Marx [1872] 1987, 709)
An appropriation of the concrete 'as a concrete in thought [*als ein geistig Konkretes*]' (Marx [1859] 1961, 632)		a reconstruction of the 'process of formation of the concrete itself' (Marx [1859] 1961, 632)

Instead, the main features that make Marx's method dialectical are the following:

1. 'The concrete is concrete because it is the synthesis [*Zusammenfassung*] of many determinations, hence unity of the diverse' (Marx [1859] 1961, 632). The appropriation of the concrete 'as a concrete in thought' has therefore to 'grasp the multiplicity of determinations in their unity' (this is the synthetic method according to Hegel [1812–16b] 2003, 511).
2. This process leads from the 'immediate manifestation of the relations' to their 'inner connection' (Marx and Engels [1864/67] 1965, 313).
3. The existing concrete has to be appropriated in such a way that 'in the positive comprehension of what exists' lies 'at the same time the comprehension of its negation' (Marx [1872] 1987, 709).

These Marxian indications just localize a theoretical tension field which has to be worked in to interpret Marx's exposition (*Darstellung*) of the capitalist mode of production, which is structured as a dialectical development of the concept of capital (see Marx and Engels [1864/67] 1965, 313).

On the one hand, according to these indications, the dialectical nature of this development lies in the fact that it starts from a historical result which appears as something immediate, and arrives at the same result as mediated, thereby denaturalizing the capitalist mode of production and bringing its peculiar structure to light. This development from immediacy to mediateness takes place through an 'immanent critique' of the categories of political economy (see e.g. Backhaus 1997, 505), that is, a critique that does not originate from their absolute negation, but from their 'determinate negation' (see Hegel [1812–16a] 1969, 49), which is included in the positive comprehension of these categories.

On the other hand, the materialistic character of this development comes from the following features:

• Thesis 1: The dialectical development fully takes place on a logical level (corresponding to the third line of the oppositions chart).
• Thesis 2: The dialectical development is not closed in on the logical level (corresponding to the second line of the oppositions chart).
• 1 + 2: As a result of the combination of these two features the dialectical development is not closed in on itself.

The first thesis, if expressed in this generic form, can be seen as the common feature of the *Neue Marx-Lektüre* (see Elbe 2010, 88ff.). This thesis implies rejecting the 'historicizing reading' of *Capital*, which reads the critique of political economy as a dialectical or – more generally – conceptual presentation of historical development (see e.g. Iljenkow 1971; Haug 2003, 384) and dates back to Engels's theorization of Marx's method as a logical-historical method (Marx [1859] 1961, 475).

The second thesis, though, leads also beyond the logical-systematic method developed by the *Neue Marx-Lektüre*, and implies a rejection of the so-called germ-cell dialectics (*Keimzellendialektik*), that is, of such interpretations that read the *Darstellung* as a process of logical deduction of categories from one another. According to such interpretations, Marx identified an initial category from which the whole capitalist mode of production could be deduced, thanks to the driving force of the contradictions inherent to this category.

2.2   ON THESIS 1: LOGIC AND HISTORY

As to the first thesis, it descends from the nature of Marx's object of inquiry. According to the first line of the oppositions chart, the dialectical development must be the development of the peculiar logic of a peculiar object, and this object is the 'specifically capitalist mode of production' (Marx [1890] 1974, 533, 652, 653, 657). Hence, the dialectical development of the concept of capital has to grasp the peculiarity of the capitalist mode of production. The object of inquiry is neither a capitalist society in its geographical and historical definiteness (see Fineschi 2003, 10), nor capitalism as 'a comprehensive socio-historical formation' (Wolf 2009, 4) in which the capitalist mode of production dominates, but rather the economic structure of capitalist societies, that is, their peculiar mode of provision and socialization of labour. The concept of capital as the object of the dialectical development is therefore a logical object which cannot exist as such in the historical temporality. The object of a historical investigation can only be the different ways in which the capitalist mode of production has established itself and developed in different societies;

that is, a history of 'capitalisms'. Moreover, in order for dialectical development not to be resolved into a *petitio principii*, the delimitation of its object (its historicization) cannot take place *a priori*, through a historical comparison with other modes of production. If this were the case, it would arbitrarily set as a premise what has, instead, to be identified, namely the specificity of the capitalist mode of production. The delimitation of the object of development must therefore be a result of development itself. Dialectical development and historical investigation thus have different objects, and correctly positing the object of the latter is only possible after the former (see Marx [1857/58] 1976, 369, also 42).

However, a development implies in any case some kind of temporality. In the *Grundrisse*, Marx also refers to the object of his exposition with the expression 'contemporary history [*kontemporäre Geschichte*]' (Marx [1857/58] 1976, 368) of capital, opposing the latter to the history of the constitution of capital and identifying it instead with the 'actual system of the mode of production dominated [by capital]'. It is clear from the context of the passage, which is devoted to the distinction between the historical and logical presuppositions of capital, that Marx by 'contemporary history' does not refer to the recent history of capital, an interpretation that would lead one to read the critique of political economy as a phase study.[1] A simple reflection on the etymology of the adjective *kontemporär* – from the Latin *cum-tempus*, which literally corresponds to the Greek *syn-chrònos* – suggests the meaning to be given to the expression: it does not refer to a 'mode of historicity', as Wolfgang Fritz Haug (2003, 386) claims, but to a mode of temporality, namely synchronicity. The word 'history' expresses here a peculiar way of dealing with this mode of temporality. To write the history of a synchrony means to unfold this synchrony as a development, to unfold the internal temporality of a logical object. This is exactly the meaning of the expression 'dialectical development'.

The dialectical development of the concept of capital is thus the unfolding of its logical temporality (see Fineschi 2008, 148). This unfolding takes the form of a succession of categorial transitions. These do not correspond to events that have occurred or may occur in the course of the historical development of capitalist relations, but to logical connections constantly presupposed by the very existence of those relations. The only history that is the object of dialectical development is the one that 'goes on stage every day before our very eyes' (Marx [1867] 1983, 102), not a history made up of successive unique events,

---

[1]   The German term for 'contemporary history' as a branch of the historical disciplines would be *Zeitgeschichte*, or *zeitgenössische Geschichte*, but the concept itself was not yet firmly established in Marx's time.

then, but a set of elements that always reproduces itself according to the same structured order.

To read the development of economic categories in *Capital* as if it corresponded to a development in historical temporality is, Marx explicitly states, not only wrong, but 'unfeasible' (Marx [1857/58] 1976, 42), because 'the simplest economic category ... can never exist other than as an abstract, one-sided perspective on an already given, concrete, living whole' (Marx [1857/58] 1976, 38f.).

The categories that follow one another in *Capital* thus express abstract moments of a whole, assumed as given. Their abstract character derives from the fact that they are indeed forms of expression of that whole, but they can only ever express it in a unilateral way. The whole, on the other hand, is to be regarded as concrete insofar as it expresses these moments that belong together in their unity. In the course of development, the concept of capital must express precisely those specific connections between the different phenomenal forms of capitalist relations without which none of these phenomenal forms could arise; in short, it must express the structure of capitalist relations. It is a dialectical concept insofar as it possesses an internal temporality in the course of which different economic categories gradually reveal themselves to be its abstract moments.

A first limitation of the dialectical method thus consists in the fact that the validity of dialectics must be limited to the logical level. Dialectical development can only be defined as materialist if, as dialectical, it is intended to discover the inner structure, and therefore the specificity, of an object of research taken as having become, and not to explain the historical becoming of this object. Transferring the logically necessary character of categorial development to the level of historical development inevitably leads to determinist philosophies of history. A dialectical method that wants to distinguish itself from an idealization of history can provide a key to understanding historical becoming only insofar as it allows us to identify the logical presuppositions for the existence of the becoming, and thus allows us, in a second step that already lies beyond the dialectical method itself, to identify also which passages of historical development were the decisive ones for it to result in what it actually resulted in. But explaining how and why those historical passages occurred remains an open task, to be solved not with the tools of dialectics, but with those of historiography (see Marx [1857/58] 1976, 369).

2.3   FROM THESIS 1 TO THESIS 2: LOGIC AND DIALECTICS

If the task of the dialectical exposition (*Darstellung*) is defined as above, it is clear that it cannot be a mere presentation of the results of the inquiry

(*Forschung*). Rather, the exposition is to be understood as a new work on the material from the inquiry, from which new information about this material, not accessible before the exposition, is to emerge. In other words, the aim of the exposition is not simply to express the 'peculiar logic of the peculiar object', but also to discover this logic. The argument about the logical character of the object of exposition, however, has often led to a misunderstanding: calling the method followed by Marx a 'logical method' or a 'logical-systematic method' (see e.g. Reichelt [1970] 1972, 126; Schmidt [1971] 1977, 74; Elbe 2010, 67; Wolf 2008, 10ff.). However, the fact that the object of the exposition is a logical object does not mean that the method should be defined in the same way. The only reason why it seems natural to define the method of exposition as logical is that logical – rather than historical – is the order in which the categories are exposed. But defining the method of exposition on the basis of the order in which the categories are exposed is tantamount to asserting that the peculiar logic of the peculiar object is already determined before the exposition, and that it is only a matter of following the criterion provided by this logic, without losing the thread that links the various categories together from the outset. The definition of the method should in fact refer to how this 'logic of the thing itself' is to be discovered. In this sense, the most appropriate adjective remains 'dialectical'. This is not merely a matter of definition, because not distinguishing between the dialecticality of the method and the logicality of the object easily leads to interpreting the dialectical development of the concept of capital as a 'circle screwed on itself' (Hegel [1812–16b] 2003, 571), in the manner of Hegelian absolute knowledge. This is precisely what has often been the case in the *Neue Marx-Lektüre*, whose logical-systematic conception of method implies a 'germ-cell dialectics' whereby the internal logic of the concept of capital is to be determined by following this logic in its own development. The concrete, that is, the multiplicity of determinations in their unity, would then already be contained *in nuce* in the initial category as an abstract determination, and would have to be revealed by following precisely the logical development of this category. Dialectical development would then become the self-development of the logic of the concept of capital. But such a self-development presupposes the identity of subject, object and method of development, as realized in the Hegelian concept. Identifying the (logical) object and (dialectical) method of Marx's exposition therefore means asserting the identity of subject and object for it too, and thus interpreting it in terms of Hegelian absolute knowledge, self-knowledge of the object of knowledge, knowledge without presuppositions insofar as it is able to transcend its own posited character and become knowledge *a priori*. Such an interpretation contradicts the second thesis advanced here, on the materialistic character of Marx's exposition.

2.4   ON THESIS 2: DIALECTICS AND EMPIRICS

As to the second thesis, it could be read as a restrictive clause to the first one. Although the dialectical development of the concept of capital takes place entirely on the logical level, it is not closed in on logicality; hence, it is not closed in on itself.

It is well known that Marx's exposition does not begin with a concept, but with a certain result of historical development presented 'in the form in which it manifests itself' (Marx [1880/83] 1962, 369), that is, the commodity as the form in which 'the wealth of the societies in which the capitalist mode of production dominates manifests itself' (Marx [1872] 1987, 69). Marx's initial category thus has the character of an empirical, *a posteriori* category. This is not to be understood, however, in a positivistic sense, for this category is not posited either as a concept or as a positive description of a phenomenon. Rather, it corresponds to the way in which a social phenomenon is perceived by the subjects who experience it. The empirics with which Marx begins his work are thus the economic relations as they manifest themselves in the eyes of the subjects involved and the theorists of these relations. The categories of political economy thus represent, for Marx, the self-understanding of bourgeois societies. The key that sets the Marxian dialectical development in motion is the problematization of the empirical experience expressed by the economic categories (see Establet and Macherey [1965] 1977, 65), that is, the questions: How is this experience possible? Under what conditions can the economic phenomenon manifest itself as it does?

The point is that, once a given experiential datum has been posited as an initial category, the entire chain of categorical transitions cannot be generated from its problematization as an absolute logical development, that is, independent of further historical-empirical presuppositions, so that it would be able to transcend its *a posteriori* character by coming at the end of the process to pose as the result of its autonomous movement the same empirical datum from which it started. Such a transformation of an *a posteriori* cognitive process into an *a priori* categorical development would again presuppose the identity of subject and object of the development[2] (see Colletti 1969, 32f.). On the contrary, the materialistic character of Marxian dialectical development resides in the fact that not only the beginning of the dialectical movement, but each of its fundamental steps is characterized by an assimilation and transformation of historical-empirical data, without which the dialectical development of the categories could not advance. For instance, the transition from the

---

[2]   In Hegel, only insofar as 'the pure concept ... has itself as its object' is it able to 'overcome its own position as content and object' (Hegel [1812–16b] 2003, 572).

sphere of simple circulation to that of capital could not take place without introducing into the exposition, from the outside, wage labour, the purchasability of labour-power as a commodity (see Wolf 2006). The cognitive process therefore never transcends its *a posteriori* character; on the contrary, as the dialectical development proceeds, the exposition is charged with ever new empirical presuppositions. The fact that the exposition develops entirely at the level of the logical temporality of its object does not therefore mean that the historical dimension is expelled from Marx's method. It is only the historical temporality that is expelled. Instead, the historical dimension constantly enters the exposition in the form of empirics, that is, in the form of the results of historical development taken in their phenomenal forms. Only in this way can Marxian exposition achieve its scientific aims. In fact, the need to go beyond the empiricist point of view, and the impossibility of a categorial development independent of empirics, both originate in the new kind of problem that Marx finds himself facing and that informs the specific epistemological terrain of the critique of political economy. This problem is that it is not enough, in order to grasp capitalist relations in their inner structure, to emancipate oneself from ideology, subjectively understood, and observe the empirical world 'as it offers itself to anyone who approaches it without preconceived idealistic reverie' (Engels [1886] 1962, 292),[3] because the ideological content of the categories of political economy itself originates from the social objectivity of capitalist relations. Marx refers to this with the expression 'real mystification' (Marx [1858/61] 1980, 128). In their phenomenal forms, the relations defined by the categories of value, money, commodity, labour and capital do not manifest themselves in their reciprocal connections; on the contrary, as they objectively appear in the empirical experience they do not even present themselves as relations, but rather as 'things'.[4] What is false in the categories of political economy is thus itself part of the truth of capitalist relations. Marx, therefore, cannot simply set aside the errors of political economy and turn directly to pure 'facts', because the truth of capitalist relations can only be understood by understanding the falsity of the categories of political economy. This is why the exposition of the capitalist mode of production and the critique of political economy are inseparably linked in Marx. If this is the problem that Marx has to face, the rejection of empiricism and the adoption of a dialectical procedure is an obligatory choice. On the other hand, however, through dialectical exposition Marx must trace the categories of political economy taken as 'socially valid,

---

[3]   This positivist conception of materialism in Engels clearly played a fundamental role in his interpretation of Marx's exposition as a conceptual reflection of historical becoming.

[4]   Regarding this objective appearance, it is essential to embrace Bellofiore's distinction between fetish character and fetishism. See Bellofiore (2014).

hence objective forms of thought' back to those specific 'forms of human life' (Marx [1872] 1987, 106) on the basis of which the *post festum* development of those objective forms of thought was possible; that is, he must identify the concrete and historically determined presuppositions of those objective forms of thought that bear no trace of those historically determined presuppositions, but instead present themselves as universal. It is only in this way that Marx can historicize the categories of political economy in an immanent way. The fundamental question that must guide Marx's exposition is therefore: What results of historical development does the empirical existence of the objective forms of thought corresponding to the categories of political economy presuppose? This question could not be answered by a self-contained logical development whose course is independent of experiential data. Because, on the one hand, the categories that are to be gradually posited as determinations of the concept of capital must be objective forms of thought that can be detected as results of historical development; on the other hand, these categories must be developed by relating each of them to its own historically determined presuppositions, which are themselves empirical data resulting from historical development. If the entire categorial development were already contained in the initial category, this would mean that the capitalist relations in their inner structure would already be reflected in this first form of thought; only, they would be reflected there in an unconscious and unexpressed way, and would have to be brought to expression by developing the contradictions inherent in this category. But this 'germ-cell dialectics' denies exactly the problem that makes a dialectical procedure necessary: the fact that capitalist relations, as they objectively manifest themselves, and thus primarily as they manifest themselves in the categories of political economy, are not relations in their inner structure. In order to grasp their inner structure, it is necessary to go beyond the categories that express these relations and to identify their historically determined presuppositions. The achievement of the aims of the critique of political economy thus implies the effective recourse to empirical inquiry, which in itself has nothing to do with dialectical development. Inquiry and exposition are therefore to be considered as two epistemologically and methodologically distinct moments, but not chronologically opposed to each other, since the results of inquiry must constantly enter the exposition as extraneous elements that it could not produce on its own, in order to become an integral part of it. Here, then, is a second limitation of the dialectical method in Marx: the dialectical character of the method must be limited to the mode of exposition.

2.5   AN IMMANENT CRITIQUE OF THE EMPIRICAL

After having theoretically defined how a materialistic dialectical method should look, the problem is to understand how dialectical development can practically assimilate the contents of experience, that is, to identify a principle of reading that responds to both aforementioned claims. Such a principle can consist in reading the dialectical development as an *a posteriori* reconstruction of the conditions of existence for what is given. An analysis of the Marxian method at work shows that such a formulation can be applied both to the relation of the whole development to the entire research object and to the single conceptual steps of the development.

On the one hand, the dialectical development of the concept of capital, as a whole, reconstructs the totality of the conditions of existence of specifically capitalist relations. On the other hand, this development consists in a chain of categorial transitions in which each category expresses the conditions of existence of the relations expressed by the preceding categories. In fact, as argued above, the dialectical exposition of the capitalist mode of production has the task of reconstructing that specific mode of labour provision and socialization that must underlie bourgeois societies in order for capitalist social relations to manifest themselves as they *de facto* do. This means not only that the mode of manifestation of capitalist relations is assumed as given in the exposition, and, therefore, that the development as a whole takes place *a posteriori*, but also that this *a posteriori* character is not transcended at any stage of the dialectical development, since every category that arises in the course of development is assumed as the objective given phenomenal form of capitalist relations. In other words, each category corresponds to an experiential content found by Marx 'at the surface of the bourgeois world' (Marx [1857/58] 1976, 174) and expressed in the economists' theories.

The task that the categorial development has to fulfil is therefore not to deduce one category from the other, but rather to establish implication relations between them and, consequently, between the contents of experience that they express. Hence, in the transition from one category to the other, the content of the latter has not to be deduced from the content of the former; just as the former, it rather expresses a content of experience, found at the 'surface of the bourgeois world'; it must, however, turn out to be that particular content of experience without which the content of the former category could not manifest itself in the way it does in that category. In the transition, the empirical immediateness of the one category vanishes, because this category turns out to be necessarily mediated through the other. What comes to light in this way is the specific mediateness of the manifold manifestations of capitalist relations; that is, the specific connections between the phenomena without which each phenomenon could not be given, in short, the structure of the capitalist relations.

If the term 'empirical' is understood to mean not only the immediate empirical data, but also the objective forms of thought crystallized in the categories of political economy, then the dialectical development of the concept of capital could be appropriately called an immanent critique of the empirical. A critique of the empirical, because it denies the immediacy of the various relations expressed by the categories of political economy (universal commodity exchange, value, monetary circulation, labour, capital, credit, and so on), that is, it denies the way in which these relations objectively manifest themselves in empirics. Immanent critique of the empirical, because the way in which bourgeois relations manifest themselves empirically is critiqued through the establishment of logically necessary connections between different experiential contents, which thus turn out to be phenomenal forms of a whole; the immediacy of a given empirically posited content is thus always denied by showing another empirically posited content as its condition of existence.

This interpretation framework provides a solution to the long-standing question about the criteria for selecting the empirical material to be included in the exposition of the capitalistic mode of production (see e.g. Luporini 1974, 166ff.). Indeed, in order to expose the specifically capitalistic mode of production, Marx has to outline exclusively the invariant structure of this mode of production, logically implicated by the way in which the capitalist relations manifest themselves in any bourgeois society. For this reason, the dialectical exposition has to be restricted to the necessary conditions of existence of these relations. Defining the conditions of possibility for specifically capitalistic socialization means at the same time defining its whole range of possibilities. In fact, according to the proposed reading principle, a specific empirical occurrence, such as the availability of a labour force as a commodity, or the existence of a monetary circulation, turns out to be a part of the structure of the capitalist mode of production and to play a specific role within it, because it happens to be that specific circumstance that fulfils a specific claim of the exposition and therefore it turns out to be a necessary condition for the existence of the research object. The integration of an empirical fact – such as the availability of labour-power as a commodity – into the dialectical development produces information that could not have been found through empirical analysis alone; for instance, the impossibility of abolishing the wage–labour relationship without undermining universal commodity exchange.[5] Other cir-

---

[5]   This kind of information has a crucial political importance and allows the critique of political economy to be a fundamental instrument for the revolutionary change of social relations, even though the characterization of its object made at the beginning makes it clear that it cannot be directly used as if it were a political work. Various intermediate steps are required, but it is on the basis of such knowledge of structural connections that Marx can, for example, reject Proudhon's political proposals, and brand them as utopian. In fact, the critique of political economy cannot provide a scientific political theory, yet it can give political thought the possibility of a grounding in scientific knowledge; that is, knowledge of social objectivity.

cumstances that can be empirically found alongside it, such as the dominance of factory work or the existence of a gold standard, shall be interpreted either as historical figures of the structural forms (see Fineschi 2008, 154), or simply as strictly contingent occurrences, as long as they do not play a specific role in the dialectical development.

Hence, which results of empirical inquiry are to be integrated in the dialectical exposition, and which role they have to play within it, can be only found out in the course of the exposition itself. It is therefore through the dialectical exposition that the object of the exposition itself is outlined. This does not mean that the exposition follows a logical path of its own, independent from the inquiry: first, because the logical connection between two categories could not be established if the connection between the actual social relations expressed in these categories were not already a factual result of historical development; and second, because the dialectical movement from one category to the other could not take place without effective recourse to factual data that could in no way be deduced from the first category. The immanent development of the first category, in itself, leads only to the recognition of its logical non-self-sufficiency, but the elements necessary to overcome this category are not contained in it and cannot, therefore, be logically developed from it.

2.6   CONCLUSIONS

The above interpretative principle represents a solution to the problem of the theoretical tension field 'dialectics/materialism'. The coordinates of this tension field were found at the beginning by referring to Marx's meta-theoretical self-understanding. However, it can be definitely excluded that Marx had sufficient awareness of the epistemological status of his dialectical exposition. This is proven not only by the ambiguity of several methodological statements, such as the aforementioned metaphor of inversion, but also by the fact that in some passages of his critique of political economy Marx commits theoretical errors evidently due to inadequate meta-theoretical awareness. In this respect, it is significant that the aspects of the theory of capital that have proved weakest – such as the transformation of values into prices, the status assigned to the law of the tendential fall of the profit rate, or the failure to overcome metallism in the theory of money – are also those in which Marx's procedure does not allow itself to be read according to the principle of the immanent critique of the empirical.

Particularly eloquent is also the fact that in Marx persists, at times, a theory of truth as unveiling, such that to identify capitalist relations in their own interconnection (*in ihrem eigenen Zusammenhang*) would be equivalent to finding the essence (*Wesen*) behind the phenomena (*Erscheinung*). To understand that this theory of truth is not compatible with a materialist dialectics interpreted as proposed here it is sufficient to ask what the materialistic character of this dialectical procedure consists of. 'Materialism' obviously does not refer to a materialistic reductionism in the mechanistic sense, since, on the contrary, in the course of the dialectical exposition Marx goes so far as to show how factors such as money, commodity and capital, which in political economy and in the common consciousness are considered as material things, are in fact the reification of social relations (see e.g. Marx [1861/63] 1978, 1404f.; Marx [1851] 1986, 365). Nor does 'materialism' refer to the materiality of economic interests as opposed to ideal motivations, as one might think by applying to the critique of political economy a cliché that is at most valid in other areas of Marxist theory. In fact, in the critique of the reification of social relations, subjective economic interests are as irrelevant as ideal motivations; what matters is rather the social objectivity of the mechanisms of reproduction of capitalist relations, that is, their ability to impose themselves on the backs of the subjects involved, even in spite of their subjective interests.

The materialist character of the dialectical procedure, rather, is to be found in its ability to go beyond the immediacy of phenomena without, however, going beyond the phenomena themselves, but rather rising above them to grasp them in their mutual mediation.

The materialism/idealism opposition, which – particularly by the proponents of so-called Hegelomarxism – has often been seen as an obsolete and empty formula, not without some reason, finds here a precise meaning again. Although a materialist dialectics and an idealist dialectics necessarily have in common the rejection of empiricism, an idealist dialectics is one that rejects the empirical world as well, considering it as a concealment of an essence that lies behind it, and claiming therefore to reach an absolute knowledge, literally meaning a knowledge that is independent from the experience (for which it could properly be called metaphysics); a materialist dialectics is one that remains tied to the empirical world and carries out an immanent critique of it.

REFERENCES

Abbreviations:
   MECW = *Marx–Engels Collected Works*. London: Lawrence & Wishart.
   MEW = *Marx–Engels Werke*. Berlin: Dietz.
   MEGA = *Marx–Engels–Gesamtausgabe.* Berlin: Dietz.

Althusser, L., (1965). *Pour Marx*, ed. 2005, Paris: La Découverte/Poche. (Eng: Althusser, L. *For Marx*, ed. 2005, London: Verso Books.)
Backhaus, H.G., (1997). *Dialektik der Wertform. Untersuchungen zur Marxschen Ökonomiekritik*, Freiburg: Ça ira Verlag.

Bellofiore, R., (2014). Lost in Translation? Once Again on the Marx–Hegel Connection. In: Moseley, F. and Smith, T. (eds), *Marx's Capital and Hegel's Logic*, Leiden, Boston: Brill. pp. 164–188.

Colletti, L., (1969). *Il marxismo e Hegel*, Bari: Laterza.

Elbe, I., (2010). *Marx im Westen. Die neue Marx-Lektüre in der Bundesrepublik seit 1965*, Berlin: Akademie Verlag.

Engels, F., [1886] (1962). *Ludwig Feuerbach und der Ausgang der klassischen deutschen Philosophie*. In: *MEW* Band 21. Berlin: Dietz Verlag. Transl. by A. Lewis (2010). *Ludwig Feuerbach and the End of Classical German Philosophy*. In *MECW*, vol. 26. Digital edition. London: Lawrence & Wishart, pp. 353–398.

Establet, R. and Macherey, P., (1965). *Lire le Capital IV*, ed. 1973, Paris: Maspero. (Eng: Althusser, L. et al. *Reading Capital: The Complete Edition*, ed. 2016, London: Verso Books.)

Fineschi, R., (2003). Il *capitale* dopo la nuova edizione storico-critica (MEGA²). Pubblicazione e teoria. https://www.scribd.com/document/36926784/Roberto -Fineschi-Il-capitale-dopo-la-nuova-edizione-critica-Pubblicazione-e-teoria (accessed 30 January 2021).

Fineschi, R., (2008). *Un nuovo Marx. Filologia e interpretazione dopo la nuova edizione storico-critica* (MEGA²), Roma: Carocci.

Haug, W.F., (2003). Historisches/Logisches. *Das Argument*, 251, pp. 378–396.

Hegel, G.W.F., (1812–16a). *Wissenschaft der Logik I*, in *Werke*, vol. 5, ed. 1969, Frankfurt/M: Suhrkamp. (Eng: Hegel, G.W.F. *The Science of Logic*, ed. 2010, Cambridge: Cambridge University Press.)

Hegel, G.W.F., (1812–16b). *Wissenschaft der Logik II*, in *Werke*, vol. 6, ed. 2003, Frankfurt/M: Suhrkamp. (Eng: Hegel, G.W.F. *The Science of Logic*, ed. 2010, Cambridge: Cambridge University Press.)

Iljenkow, E.W., (1971). Die Dialektik des Abstrakten und Konkreten im 'Kapital' von Marx. In: Schmidt, A. (ed), *Beiträge zur marxistischen Erkenntnistheorie*, Frankfurt/M: Suhrkamp.

Luporini, C., (1974). *Dialettica e materialismo*, Roma: Editori Riuniti.

Marx, K., [1843] (1982). *Zur Kritik der Hegelschen Rechtsphilosophie*. In *Werke, Artikel, Entwürfe. März 1843 bis August 1844*. In: *MEGA* Abteilung I. Band 2. Berlin: Dietz Verlag, pp. 3–137. Transl. by M. Millerman and B. Ruhemann (2010). *Contribution to the Critique of Hegel's Philosophy of Law*. In *MECW*, vol. 3. Digital edition. London: Lawrence & Wishart, pp. 3–129.

Marx, K., [1851] (1986). *Exzerpte und Notizen März bis Juni 1851*. In: *MEGA* Abteilung IV, Band 8. Berlin: Dietz Verlag.

Marx, K., [1857/58] (1976). *Ökonomische Manuskripte. 1857/58. Teil 1*. In: *MEGA* Abteilung II, Band 1. Berlin: Dietz Verlag. Transl. By Martin Nicolaus (1973). *Grundrisse. Foundations of the Critique of Political Economy (Rough Draft)*. London: Penguin Books.

Marx, K., [1858/61] (1980). *Ökonomische Manuskripte und Schriften 1858–1861*. In: *MEGA* Abteilung II, Band 2. Berlin: Dietz Verlag.

Marx, K., [1859] (1961). *Zur Kritik der politischen Ökonomie*. In: *MEW*, Band 13. Berlin: Dietz Verlag. Transl. by S.W. Ryazanskaya (1970). *A Contribution to the Critique of Political Economy*. Moscow: Progress Publishers.

Marx, K., [1861/63] (1978). *Zur Kritik der politischen Ökonomie (Manuskript 1861–1863). Teil 3*. In: *MEGA* Abteilung II, Band 3.4. Berlin: Dietz Verlag.

Marx, K., [1867] (1983). *Das Kapital. Kritik der politischen Ökonomie. Erster Band. Hamburg 1867*. In: *MEGA* Abteilung II, Band 5. Berlin: Dietz Verlag.

Marx, K., [1872] (1987). *Das Kapital. Kritik der Politischen Ökonomie. Erster Band, Hamburg 1872*. In: *MEGA* II Abteilung, Band 6. Berlin: Dietz Verlag. Transl. by B. Fowkes (1976). *Capital. A Critique of Political Economy. Volume One.* Harmondsworth: Penguin Books.

Marx, K., [1880/83] (1962). *Randglossen zu Adolph Wagners Lehrbuch der politischen Ökonomie*. In: *MEW* Band 19. Berlin: Dietz Verlag. pp. 335–383. Transl. by T. Carrell (2012). *Notes on Adolph Wagner*. In Marx, K. *Later Political Writings*. Cambridge: Cambridge University Press.

Marx, K., [1890] (1974). *Das Kapital. Kritik der politischen Ökonomie. Erster Band*. In: *MEW* Band 23. Berlin: Dietz Verlag. Transl. by S. Moore and E. Aveling (2010). *Capital. A Critique of Political Economy. Volume 1*. In *MECW*, vol. 35. Digital edition. London: Lawrence & Wishart.

Marx, K. and Engels, F., [1856/59] (1963). *Briefe. Januar 1856 – Dezember 1859*. In: *MEW* Band 29. Berlin: Dietz Verlag. Transl. by P. and B. Ross (2010). *Letters 1856–1859*. In *MECW*, vol. 40. Digital edition. London: Lawrence & Wishart.

Marx, K. and Engels, F., [1864/67] (1965). *Briefe. Oktober 1864 – Dezember 1867*. In: *MEW* Band 31. Berlin: Dietz Verlag. Transl. by C. Upward and J. Peet (1987). *Letters 1864–1868*. In *MECW*, vol. 42. London: Lawrence & Wishart.

Reichelt, H., (1970). *Zur logischen Struktur des Kapitalbegriffs bei Karl Marx*, ed. 1972, Frankfurt/m, Wien: Europäische Verlagsanstalt/Europa Verlag.

Schmidt, A., (1971). *Geschichte und Struktur. Fragen einer marxistischen Historik*, ed. 1977, München: Carl Hanser Verlag. Transl. by Jeffrey Herf (1981). *History and Structure. An Essay on Hegelian-Marxist and Structuralist Theories of History*, Cambridge, MA: MIT Press.

Wolf, D., (2008). Zur Methode in Marx' 'Kapital' unter besonderer Berücksichtigung ihres logisch-systematischen Charakters. Zum Methodenstreit zwischen Wolfgang Fritz Haug und Michael Heinrich. In: Elbe, I., Reichardt, T. and Wolf, D. (eds), *Gesellschaftliche Praxis und ihre wissenschaftliche Darstellung. Beiträge zur Kapital-Diskussion*, Wissenschaftliche Mitteilungen Heft 6, Hamburg: Argument Verlag.

Wolf, F.O., (2006). Marx' Konzept der 'Grenzen der dialektischen Darstellung'. In: Hoff, J., Petrioli, A., Stützle, I. and Wolf, F.O. (eds), *Das Kapital neu Lesen. Beiträge zur radikalen Philosophie*, Münster: Westfälisches Dampfboot.

Wolf, F.O., (2009). What 'capitalism' is, what it means to be against it, and what it takes to end it: Some remarks to prevent a renewal of blind alleys. Paper for the conference 'Kapitalismustheorien', Wien, 24 and 25 April 2009. https://ifg.rosalux .de/files/2014/06/Frieder-Otto-Wolf-Capitalism-Farris-2012-2.pdf (accessed 5 February 2021).

3. Finite Marxism

Frieder Otto Wolf

In order to advance a double goal of improving Marxist contributions to critical science and Marxist contributions to emancipatory politics, in this chapter I refer back to Althusser's little-known 1978 essay 'Marxism as a Finite Theory' ('Le marxisme comme théorie finie', in Althusser 1998, pp. 281–294), especially linking his problematics of a finite theory to the Marxian topic of the 'limits of dialectical presentation'. On this basis I propose the notions of a finite project and a finite initiative as a starting point for rethinking 'Marxist politics', and for establishing the groundwork for a Marxian philosophy which is capable of articulating an idea of 'finite plurality' as an attractive alternative to the notion of a 'monist infinity', as well as to that of an 'anything-goes infinity'.

3.1 A PROBLEMATIC ALTERNATIVE IN THE DEBATE OF THE LIMITS OF DIALECTICAL PRESENTATION IN *CAPITAL*[1]

Althusser's hints about Marxism as a finite theory[2] have directed attention to the task of clearly defining our perspectives on the notion of 'materialist dialectics' which has been central for traditional conceptions of Marxism: Can we consider it as a kind of a theoretical *a priori* or do we have to understand it

---

[1]   Cf. Wolf (2004).

[2]   Where the French playful ambiguity should not be overheard, as '*Marxisme fini*' designates simultaneously a 'finished' and a 'finite' Marxism. Also in English, at least 'infinite' may be understood as 'unending', so that talking about 'finite Marxism' seems to conjure up some sinister or promising 'ending' of Marxism. I am convinced that the contrary is true: 'finite Marxism' – in addressing specific problematics such as the domination of the capitalist mode of production in modern bourgeois societies, and the way modern politics have been reclaimed so far by the modern state – is, indeed, breaking the limits in which the postulated 'infinite' character of 'DiaMat' *cum* 'Histomat' (or its Hegelianizing alternatives) had, in effect, enclosed historical Marxisms since the 1920s. Looking into the mathematical debates about 'infinites' (cf. esp. Lorenzen 1957) will certainly be helpful to overcome the red herring of the traditional idea of an 'absolute infinite' supposed to be beyond the grasp of human reason.

as an abandoned project, that is, which Marx has found compelled to drop with his advances in the investigation of 'modern bourgeois societies'?

I defend the thesis that this alternative is a false one and has to be rejected, and that the 'contradicting answer' to this 'false question' can be largely clarified by reading Marx's *Capital*. There Marx – in the very practice of his theoretical presentation[3] – has fully attended to the finite character of his 'critique of political economy', that is, his critical theory of the domination of the capitalist mode of production as it is realized in 'modern bourgeois societies' by, in fact, strictly observing the 'limits of dialectical presentation' as they are determined by this finite character (although only partly making them explicit). This can be concretized and verified by looking closely at the main examples occurring already in *Capital I*: the money-commodity, labour power as a commodity, landed property, which all have to be taken up as a contingent 'given' which – as such – cannot be 'derived' from the preceding determinations, as any idealist version of dialectics would have to do.

To sum up a long-winded and complicated debate, the following thesis may be formulated. As a materialist dialectics, Marx's method of presentation in *Capital* operates on the basis of the historical givenness of the conditions and presuppositions under which it operates, without submitting to the idealistic temptation of a totalizing closure of the cycle of reproduction of the domination of the capitalist mode of production. This acceptance of the 'finitude' of its objects of scientific enquiry does not imply a closure concerning the specific infinities of human cultural practice or human self-reflection; which, however, are not to be confused with processes of scientific discovery.

3.2   A RADICALLY MATERIALIST NOTION OF METHOD: MATERIALIST DIALECTICS AS AN EMERGING PROJECT

On this basis a radically materialist notion of dialectics may be developed as a 'method of presentation',[4] which may not be unduly applied to the procedures and practices of research, as these are contingent on the really existing structures of the objects under enquiry, as well as on occasions and capabilities of enquiry or on given prejudices and preconceptions, or on accepted

---

[3]   I propose to read Marx's distinction between the 'process of inquiry' and the 'process of presentation' not as a literary device, but as an important methodological distiinction between the process of scientific discovery and the process of scientific theory building (cf. Kuruma 1969).

[4]   Which I take to have been Marx's way of referring to the construction of an appropriate sequence of scientific theories, not just using a good literary device for the presentation of his findings.

presuppositions,[5] on the part of the part of the subjects of enquiry,[6] that is, on the state of the development of the respective fields of science, as well as on the prejudices existing in the community of such subjects. Such a materialist notion of 'dialectics' will indicate and reflect the need for supplementing and 'underpinning' the scientific work of theoretical construction by properly taking account of historical and empirical facts as an unavoidable given. And it will, likewise, make it possible adequately to construct central concepts for deliberating in debates on strategy and tactics,[7] such as the notions of 'finite projects' and 'finite initiatives'.

In such a perspective of materialist dialectics all claims to a universalizing of transcendental positions, or to articulating the point of view of an effectively all-embracing totality, have to be critically rejected.[8] Or, in other words, in this methodological perspective, the specific objects, stakes and perspectives of, for example, wage struggles, gender struggles, environmental struggles, in terms of struggles within ongoing reproduction processes or – which is hard to distinguish, but highly important – of struggles opening up into transformation processes of the existing structures of domination, will have to be specifically reconstructed, in order to develop adequate criteria for orienting the practices of social movements, civil society organizations, trade unions, political organizations or political parties towards a strategically adequate[9] radicalization of their struggles.[10]

---

[5]   Marx could serve as a prime example of these problematics: in contradistinction to his French or British colleagues he could not relate immediately to the established structures of modernity, but he had to 'work himself out' of the attempts by Hegel and Feuerbach to develop a modern perspective in and out of the retrograde 'German situation'.

[6]   Which should be distinguished from the 'psychological subjects' which, of course, do provide the unavoidable basis of their scientific activities of research and theory construction.

[7]   The strong distinction between these two dimensions of planning one's activities has been especially elaborated by Clausewitz (cf. Herberg-Rothe 2001).

[8]   This presupposes that it is possible, following Althusser, to establish a tenable distiction between the Hegelian 'totality' and the Marxian 'whole'; which is certainly more complicated than Althusser's first indications seem to assume. I take it to be possible, even keeping in mind Hegel's often non-deductivist practice of his dialectics, by insisting on the un-exhaustible material 'givenness' of the fields of enquiry in Marx's practice of research, which can be neatly marked off from Hegel's dialectics of the 'forms of consciousness'.

[9]   That this is really difficult to distinguish, in actual practice, provides an explanation for the widespread resistance against Lenin's insistence on this distinction; which, however, remains central to any kind of real efficacy of political action.

[10]   The adequacy of such criteria cannot be judged on the basis of scientific findings alone. Due to the structural incapacity of scientific analysis ever to analyse the very 'present moment' or the 'actual situation' (which always opens to a specific future) in

This should not be misunderstood to imply that subjective motives, triggered by the 'contradictions' we have to live in – that is, the real antagonisms which determine our lives and which make us resist or rebel – such as suffering, indignation or solidarity, would not and should not have an important role in the building of common motivations for action. It rather serves to indicate the requirements for developing rationally justified courses of action, tactics or strategies.

This kind of radically materialist notion of dialectics can help us to fully understand the contradictory – that is, antagonistically determined – character of all of these organizations and institutions. On the one hand, they are – without any possibility to avoid this, and without any exception – spaces of struggle, where domination meets resistance, and where moments of liberation are conquered. On the other hand, they always – with the exception of successful 'processes of revolution' – tend to reproduce the domination of the dominating forces, even if with some unavoidable transformations of the very structures and processes of their domination.

By stressing the underlying structural dynamics and 'laws of development' of these real struggles, finite Marxism, as I defend it, takes its critical distance from all kinds of empiricism limiting scientific inquiry to a description of empirical findings, and clearly articulates the efficacy of these structures and laws within specific historical processes as they can, indeed, be described on the basis of lived experience; without falling into the idealist mistake of reducing the complexity of the overdetermined and contingently materialized real processes to their generalizable structures. Accordingly, finite Marxism cannot fall back upon a general theory of society[11] which has been made use of to function as a short-cut, avoiding the specific analysis of historically given

---

which any action has to take place (in order to bring such a future about), there is an unavoidable intuitive element (presumably based upon actual practical 'experience' in a very broad sense), as well as an element of choice in real judgements about 'what is to be done'. If this is properly reflected, it brings us to a position which overcomes the exaggerated rationalism of Lenin implicit in his combination of a totally justified insistence upon the 'concrete analysis of the concrete situation' as the imprescindible condition of rational political action, with the naive assumptions that: (a) scientific research could ever reach it, as its 'highest point'; and (b) also the subjects of practice could 'digest' the results of scientific research 'just in time', without giving in to the open irrationalism professed by 'decisionism', as propagated by Carl Schmitt ([1927] 2015; cf. critically Löwith 1927), which glories itself on the very unfoundedness of the resolutions to action which it propagates.

[11] As classically elaborated by the founding fathers of sociology, Durkheim, Weber and Parsons.

societies.[12] And, therefore, for finite Marxism, there is no way of avoiding the effort of either properly taking up relevant empirical findings, or of critically establishing the theoretically determined structures capable of explaining the situations and trends found by empirical or historical research.[13] And it becomes clearly visible, that taking stock of the actual situation in which action (or inaction) is called for is a radically different procedure from summing up the 'state of the debate' of the relevant sciences.

3.3   THE DIFFERENCE FROM POSTMODERN MARXISM

In order to avoid a number of misunderstandings about the approach of finite Marxism, as I defend it, which otherwise, quite patently, are likely to arise, I now critically discuss the project of 'postmodern materialism', briefly discussing some epistemological/methodological key points as articulated in its programmatic publications (Callari and Ruccio 1996; Resnick and Wolff

---

[12]   A lot of general talk about capitalism in general falls into that category (cf. Wolf 2009).
[13]   In so doing, it can and should be measured by the achievements of critical action research, as exemplified in recent German history by Willi Pöhler's conception of 'the social conflict as the main aspect of sociological research on industrial relation' (cf. Pöhler 1979), which went beyond contemporary liberal 'theories of conflict' (as in Dahrendorf 1957; Coser 1956; cf., critically, Krysmanski 1971) and competed rather successfully with the (then) contemporary research on industrial relations carried out in the 'Frankfurt School' which had been developing in a Marxian horizon. His under-lying theses – which can be traced back to Simmel (cf. 1992 [1908]; cf. Stark 2002; Schmitt [1908] 2012) – especially that social conflicts are not always already decided in advance and tend to build societal structures anew while reproducing them, constitute an important challenge to a finite Marxism working to make visible the materialist dialec-tics of the processes of class struggle inherent in the very reproduction of the structures of modern bourgeois societies, and to the Marxist claim to produce a kind of knowledge that may be used by the very subjects of class struggle to analyse the specific historical conditions under which they are operating. This intimate relation to Marxism emerges very clearly in an unfinished and unpublished study by Pöhler, where he has attempted to show in which way the 'grand sociologies' of Weber, Simmel and Parsons have all failed to fully take up the challenge of Marx's theorizing the domination of the capital-ist mode of production in modern bourgeois societies, going so far as attempting to take up central reflections of Mao Dze Dong on the conditions of social enquiry (very prob-ably *Oppose Book Worship*, from 1930, as well as *On the Relation between Knowledge and Practice, between Knowing and Doing*, from 1937), as well as of a group of con-temporary Czech Marxists (very probably Klofáč and Tlutsy 1963). [I have to thank Helmut Martens (http://www.drhelmutmartens.de), cf. especially Martens (1994), his contribution to the Pöhler-Festschrift, for this information about a manuscript which apparently has got lost in the library of the Sozialforschungsstelle Dortmund (sfs) at Dortmund; which I do hope will be found again somewhere.]

2006). I have taken the liberty of summing up the key positions of this post-modern materialism in the following theses, which I shall comment upon, one by one.

1: The concept of 'contradiction' is used to designate the diversity, differences and conflicts which characterize the constitution of each aspect of the social totality.

This is also true to some degree, of course, for the project of 'finite Marxism'. However, the totalizing and in some way 'ontological' assumption that these conflicts characterize the constitution of each aspect of the social totality is not taken up, for two reasons. One, that the very concept of the social totality should be problematized. Two, it is an unfounded ontological assumption that this applies to the constitution of each aspect of the social totality; some aspects may not be characterized by such diversity, differences and conflicts. It does, of course, make sense to talk about a given 'societal formation' (*Gesellschaftsformation*) 'as a whole', but this does not justify applying the Hegelian concept of 'totality', as the social totality may very well remain heterogeneous and impossible to reconcile in all its constitutive parts and dynamics.

2: The concept of 'overdetermination' is used to designate the complex consti-tution of each aspect/process by all the others.

This is, again, criticized by 'finite Marxism' as overly totalizing. Practical experience and scientific research are needed in order to be able to distinguish between those aspects and processes of societal reality which are constituted mutually (although possibly with very different impacts upon each other), and those which are not, that is, those which are not totally 'overdetermined' in this sense, as they are part of the external conditions and presuppositions of the existing complex structure of processes.

3: Thinking/theory is understood as a part of the social totality as a larger whole.

This is, of course, fully shared by 'finite Marxism'; with the precautionary caveats, however, that: (1) as just remarked, the whole of a given 'societal for-mation' is not a 'totality'; and (2) at least scientific thinking or theory is a very specific part of the respectively given social whole, for example, distinguished from ideology by the epistemological breakthroughs it realizes, as well as by the kind of ascertained and reliable, though 'relative', truths it produces.

4: Each overdetermined theory has its own notions of proof and truth, hence the rejection of notions of 'absolute truths'.[14]

For 'finite Marxism' overdetermination is not predicated on theories, but on real structures, as they are articulated or 'captured' by theories. Therefore, the notions of proof and truth – insofar as they are, indeed, specifically used within given theoretical fields in order to address the respective fields of reality – are not only determined by or within these respective theories: they always relate back to a layer of more general notions concerning the constitutive differences of scientific enquiry and of scientific findings. The rejection of 'absolute truths' does not, therefore, necessarily lead to the hyper-relativism articulated in this thesis.

5: Contradictions constituted in the thinking process appear as opposed theories and as inconsistencies within theories.

This is, indeed, a key issue, and a really difficult one. We are convinced, however, that the problem of the foundations in reality (*fundamentum in re*, as the scholastics have expressed it) cannot be eliminated by just looking at theories. Even there, the issue of their relation to reality seems unavoidable; at the very latest, when theory has to be applied to practice. And we tend to assume that the ways in which contradictions appear within theories are rather more variegated, also including, for example, blockades of thinking, imaginary 'experiences' never had, or 'evidence' never put into question.

6: The centrality of overdetermination rules out any notion that any social aspect, such as the economic, can be ultimately determinant of other social aspects.

This is certainly also true in the perspective of 'finite Marxism'. And yet, although 'the lonely hour of the last instance never tolls' (Althusser; in Elliot n.d.), there are relevant distinctions to be made between, for example, the material process of reproduction of a given society, and the way it is reflected and justified within the dominant ideologies. This has been expressed by Engels using the metaphor of the difference of weight existing between the diverse 'factors' of societal reality: none of them is excluded from impacting upon the overall result of historical social processess, but the impact of some

---

[14]   This is a common argument in the German tradition of critical theory since Horkheimer's comprehensive discussion of the notion of truth (Horkheimer 1935); cf. more recently e.g. Alfred Schmidt (1977).

does take place more often, and has a stronger weight in determining the specific outcomes of such 'encounters'.

Likewise, it must be underlined that there is no total autonomy of these various 'social aspects'. While, indeed, each of them works according to its own rules within its given field of action, they are all, in parallel, 'overdetermined' by some other fields working at the same time, although not all by all.

7: Marxist theory deploys its specific concepts of overdetermination, contradiction and class as its distinctive basis for making sense of the social totality, for constructing its particular version of the concrete totality.

The specific concepts named are taken up from the Althusserian (re-)construction of Marxist philosophy;, which of course is not an objection, as Marx has not articulated a full-fledged version of his philosophy, accompanying his 'science' – that is, the unfinished project of the critique of political economy (cf. Rojas 1988), and a still more unfinished, merely inchohative critique of politics (as it has been plausibly argued by Balibar et al. 1979) – which of course, does not constitute any objection from my part, as the 'finite Marxism' I am advocating takes its bearings largely from the same source. It should only be underlined that this is a specific approach within Marxism which has had 'competitors' that should not be overlooked, such as the early critical lines within Soviet Marxism (such as Bucharin, Deborin, Rjazanov, Rubinstein, Varga and Paschukanis), the 'critical theory' of Horkheimer, Adorno and the Frankfurt School, or the Italian currents of Marxism looking back to Antonio Gramsci.[15]

The main problem, however, with this formulation lies, in my eyes, in the lack of clarity concerning 'social totality' and 'concrete totality'. Even the capitalist mode of production in its 'ideal average' is certainly no 'closed totality', and the social formations dominated by it cannot be understood as 'concrete totalities', if we really take into account their overdetermined, and therefore also fragmented character. And, maybe, it should be underlined that Marx's theoretical reconstruction of the domination of the capitalist mode of production in modern bourgeois societies does more than just 'make sense' of them: it explains its (contradictory) 'general tendencies' and it grasps their underlying structures by constructing a conceptual framework, while at the same time marking the limitations of this theoretical reconstruction.

---

[15] These currents are certainly not yet critically worked upon, nor 'sublated' by Althusser's important philosophical initiatives in the late 1950s and in the 1960s.

8: Marxian theory does not need, nor can it sustain, any claim that its particular theories grasp the essence or the truth of the social totality of reality.

Again, this is – in one sense – fully shared by 'finite Marxism': science, politics and philosophy do not produce 'absolute truths'. The traditional practice of 'essentalism' in this sense – as has also been widespread and current within the Marxist tradition – certainly has to be overcome. However, this does not imply dropping the category of truth from the practices of science, politics or philosophy. On the contrary, the verification and falsification processes within scientific practice have to be consciously cultivated, the 'truth politics' characteristic of philosophy (cf. Wolf 2002, pp. 128ff.), and the truth claims raised within politics – as in the claim to make a 'true life' possible – have to be properly met, instead of dropped. And, as already indicated, 'the social totality of reality' seems to be a rather underdetermined, unclear and even misleading category, which helps to maintain the illusion that knowing about all the scientific findings available for a given situation is sufficient to grasp what is at stake and what is really possible in a given situation of action. Practised in this way, Marxist analysis of a given situation of action will be no less misleading than the dogmatic assertions of theoretical Stalinism.[16]

3.4   AN ALTERNATIVE TO POSTMODERN, AS WELL AS TO TRADITIONAL MARXISM

I shall now sketch my own position in two moves: first by referring back to the implicit method of Marx's *Capital*, and then by elaborating a distiction between the finitude of the sciences and the rational infinity even of Marxist philosophy.

The 'Analytic' Beginning of *Capital* and the 'Limits of Dialectical Presentation' in its 'Synthetic' Line of Argument

In contrast to the procedure proposed by 'postmodern' Marxism, I propose to re-read *Capital*, where Marx has presented his method of presentation in its most elaborate and most developed form.[17] It is often overlooked, in spite of a rather explicit remark by Marx, that *Capital* is not at all built upon the kind of circular argument underlying Hegel's *Logic*. Not only does the first

---

[16]   Which were 'held together' by the conviction that 'the leader' was always right. In 'postmodern' Marxism this is, indeed, overcome; at the price, however, of lapsing into open subjective arbitrariness.

[17]   Cf. the most recent reconstruction by Stefano Breda (2018).

chapter present an 'analytic' argument which in the end produces the concept of value, as the starting point of the 'synthetic' development of the concept of 'capital' which occupies the rest of the book; but furthermore, the 'dialectical development' that Marx gives of his theoretical concepts by exposing them systematically[18] is consciously interrupted at a number of points, where Marx consciously and carefully respects what he has called 'the limits of dialectical presentation',[19] by introducing historico-empirical reconstructions, for example of the rise of gold (and silver) to the role of the 'money-commodity', of the availability of labour power for wage labour, or of land use (as an example of 'ecological exploitation').

An explicit comprehension of both movements in Marx's argument – that is, the analytic and the synthetic, taken together – allows us to fully understand and reconstruct the way in which Marx's systematic science of the reproduction of the domination of the capitalist mode of production in modern bourgeois societies in its 'ideal average' – a process of reproduction which in this very process tends to produce 'occasions' for its revolutionary overcoming – is capable of reconstructing the forms and the 'laws of motion' of this process, as it underlies modern history until today.

In so doing, Marx has taken the everyday notion of the 'wealth' of modern bourgeois societies (as it had served as the title notion of Adam Smith's classical work) for his analytical argument in 'finding' the key concept for his further theoretical, 'synthetical' reconstruction of the capitalist mode of production, that is, the concept of value; and I take this to give the key to Marx's fully developed understanding of the relation of his new science of the critique of political economy to experience. In contradistinction to Hegel, who attempts to reconstruct the 'experience of consciousness', Marx refers back to the practical experience of living in the modern world – in which, indeed, 'the wealth of societies' appears in the form of a collection of commodities, on offer in the market – and this starting point is evident from lived experience to each and everyone. Marx's 'construction of the concept' does not start with this 'wealth' or with the single 'commodities' by which it is constituted, but with the concept of 'value' which results from his analysis of the form of the commodity (as a 'use value' bearing an 'exchange value'). And this is, then, the starting point of Marx's synthetic 'development of the concept', which is Marx's Hegelianizing way of referring to the exposition of his theory.

This reliance upon historical everyday experience, as it underlies Marx's presentation of his analytical move in the first chapter of *Capital*, has nothing

---

[18]   In which every new step of 'conceptual development' sheds new light, retrospectively, on the preceding stages of this exposition of Marx's theory.
[19]   I have discussed this in detail in Wolf (2006, 2007).

to do with any reliance upon individual subjectivity. It is based upon collective, shared experiences which cannot be reduced to 'sense experience', but have to be understood in their given complexity. Or as, for example, Josiah Royce has put it in a prespective of pragmatism: 'Truth and falsity are indeed relative to insight, to experience, to life, to action, to the constructions which pragmatism emphasizes. But unless these constructions are what they ought to be, they are not true.'[20] In the comparable perspective, to be constructed to articulate Marx's 'method of presentation', which is the way of proving the truth of his theory, relying on experience has nothing to do with 'methodological individualism' or with empiricism.

Accordingly, the Marxian distinction between 'presentation' and 'research' lays the ground for Marx's most significant self-reflective category: for that of the 'limits of dialectical presentation'. These limits stabilize the mediating process, making it impossible for it to vanish entirely, and thereby very clearly demarcate Marx's from Hegel's dialectics. In Marx, we find theoretical objects which cannot be fully constructed by the dialectical 'order of presentation' of his own systematic theory, and which therefore have to be introduced into it in a different way. I contend that this also means that they cannot be fully reproduced in practice by the capitalist mode of production without the concurrent complicity of something else, of some 'other' of the capitalist mode of production.

Such objects include money as the specific value commodity, the wage labourer as a key object of Marx's theory, and the social relation of landowners to pieces of the planet Earth. Their very existence has at least one important implication: whereas in Hegel it is at least possible to mistake the 'development of the concept' (*Entwicklung des Begriffs*) for an *a priori* process – due to its coinciding with the very process of articulating reality – this is no longer possible in Marx, where the 'dialectical presentation' can only begin in time, after the process of research has been basically completed. And by bearing the marks of the double requirement of finding an analytical path to the elementary category of the capitalist mode of production, the category of value, and of respecting the materially defined 'limits of dialectical presentation' within its very 'presentation', as scientific theory which at certain points ceases to be 'dialectical', in order to become merely historical about contingent facts, Marx's dialectics present themselves as being situated, finite and irreversible, like real human practice, in space and time.

This insight opens a specific space for a controlled and conscious renewal of materialist dialectics – which definitely puts an end to make use of the excuse

---

[20]   Royce (1903) https://brocku.ca/MeadProject/Royce/Royce_1904.html.

of 'dialectics' for covering up authoritarian manipulation or woolly thinking – and should and can effectively proceed on the following main lines:

- Full recognition of post-Fregean formal 'mathematical' logics.
- Making use of structural dynamics of theorizing, as allowed by formal logic, without attempting to substitute it: addressing fields of reality to be theoretically articulated in scientific enquiry, especially 'structures with dominance', singularities and 'concrete situations'.
- Addressing the reality of historical antagonisms, their possible mediations and their solutions without any guarantee.
- Theoretically reconstructing historical relations of domination within given fields which form articulated wholes: accumulation of capital, gender relations, international relations of dependency and ecologies of humankind on all of its levels;
- Weighting constellations of overdetermination in given 'concrete' situations, as in the writing of history (concerning the past) or in the anticipation of possible futures (politics, consultative forecasting).
- Interventions by a radical way of philosophizing understood as an argumentative struggle within a politics of truth: following and applying the principle of admitting and talking to each and everyone, the principle of inquiry prior to judgement, the principle of making use of arguments open to challenging their pertinence and validity, the principle of not denying one's own lived experience, and the principle of articulating and applying an explicit method.

All this, of course, would not produce any kind of an infallible method, but it would certainly help to improve the quality of critical scientific practice, especially in those fields where scientific reflection is needed in order to overcome the effects of ideology, by making explicit what is specifically at stake in a debate to be unfolded.

The Specific Finitude of the 'Labour of the Concept' in the Marxian Sciences and the Rational Infinity of Radical Philosophical Reflection

Once scientific research – in the fields concerning the domination of the capitalist mode of production in modern bourgeois societies (that is, the 'critique of political economy') which Marx has left to posterity as an 'unfinished project',[21] as well as his 'critique of politics' which he had only begun to sketch[22] – has begun really to grasp its real object by constructing an adequate theoretical object of its further inquiry, it is capable of reconstructing the specific objects of its research in terms of scientific theory. Although this is restricted, according to Marx's developed theory, to the rather 'abstract' level of the 'ideal average' – with the implication that any re-application of this theory to real historical developments requires an additional effort of reseach – the examples illustrating the theory in its actual presentation are just the examples, and should not be confused with such a reconstruction of concrete historical realities, their underlying antagonisms and their dynamics.

And even this, once achieved – for example, as could be argued, with good arguments, in Lenin's class analysis of Russia – does not provide a sufficient basis for taking 'realistic' political initiatives: these have to operate not only on the level of the specific history of a country as a historical and geographical singularity, but also, what is even more important, on the level of a given situation, of a concrete conjuncture, in which a way of taking initiatives and realizing actions has to be found in deliberation.

This does not, as such, put brakes on the imagination and the hopes of people active within this reality, nor does it limit the free play of philosophical projections and anticipations; while it certainly distinguishes them from the kinds of specifically grasping socio-historical reality in terms of occasions for action or of possibilities for research, as they are constitutive for political deliberation or for scientific enquiries. Yet this relative liberation from the 'principle of reality' comes at a high cost: that is, at the cost of immediate irrelevancy. Such a liberation may, in principle, serve as a necessary precondition for building the will to transformative action, but it implies the real danger of 'getting lost in transition', that is, of losing the capacity of ever touching the present realities again, in which historical action must be pertient to be successful.

Philosophy, today, is not just the Hegelian synthesis of the European philosophical tradition, nor just a return to the unexhausted philosophical alternatives of Baruch Spinoza or David Hume: it has constituted itself as a polyphony of reflection opened up by European pioneers such as Kierkegaard, the young Marx, Nietzsche and Mach, while at the same time becoming aware of the plurality and complexity of human self-reflection existing in non-European traditions. The materialist philosopher has to go beyond the realm of the materialist scientist (or politician) in taking up the unending labour of answering these

---

[21]   Cf. Rojas (1988), and in a more specifically constructive perspective, Breda (2018).
[22]   Cf. the sketches of an important work of reconstruction urgently to be taken up again provided by Balibar et al. (1979).

strands of reflection. In so doing, they cannot claim to grasp an object outside of this world of practices of human argumentative orientation-building, and yet they must be aware of doing a work with real practical impacts. The materialist philosopher will ever and again make visible how the free flight of 'idealist' philosophizing is referring back to (and intervening in) specific historical situations and problems, and is thereby subservient to attempts of looking for an imaginary way out, and yet they cannot expect ever to finish this critical work.[23]

This turn to radical philosophy is neither just another fashion in the rapid sequence of philosophical fashions that has marked the real history of philosophy since the end of its European tradition line, nor can it pretend to be the last fully rational philosophy. The full liberation of human societies will also liberate the human capacity for creative self-reflection and creative self-invention which can certainly be expected to go beyond it, with all the marks it still bears from the history of human submission to domination.

3.5   THE DISILLUSIONING EFFECT OF 'FINITE MARXISM' AS A LIBERATION

Finite Marxism overcomes the illusion of traditional 'historical materialism'[24] as a formulated general theory of human history, by clearly bringing out the singularity and specificity of the object of Marxist critical science, that is, modern bourgeois societies as (and insofar as) dominated by the capitalist mode of production (and, eventually, the modern form of politics). Instead, it clarifies how this example of a scientific breakthrough realized by Marx may serve as an inspiration – although not as a model simply to be copied – for further research on human history, its societies and its politics.

Finite Marxism recognizes the historical contingency of Marxist philosophy which has to function as a practice of intellectual orientation in confrontation with different and divergent specific constellations of economic struggles, ideological orientations and political directions which still today are far from historically uniform, in a global perspective; and therefore can never take an autonomous, 'systematic' shape, forced, as it is, to 'take the trains, as they go'.[25]

---

[23]   In so doing, they will fill with life, as Louis Althusser has predicated about 'Marxist philosophy': 'there can exist no Marxist philosophy in the classic sense of the word philosophy, and … the revolution that Marx brought to philosophy consisted in practising it in a new way' (Althusser 2017, p. 139).

[24]   Which – by the critical publication of the German ideology manuscripts (cf. Vileisis and Wolf 2018) – in the meantime has lost its traditionally assumed philological basis.

[25]   Cf. Althusser (2017, p. 139; cf. Sotiris 2020, pp. 302–311).

Finite Marxism recognizes the 'unfinished character' of Marx's scientific theories as an unavoidable effect of their opening the way for further scientific research capable of continuing and deepening its epistemological and scientific breakthroughs. And, more specifically, it is attentive to their constitutive characteristic of addressing an 'ideal average' amenable to scientific theoretical reconstruction.[26]

At the same time, finite Marxism recognizes the existence of structures and processes of domination outside class struggle, such as gender domination or international dependency. Its proponents, therefore, are working on developing a culture of dialogue and alliance-building between the subjects involved in these substantially different liberation struggles; not in the sense of mutual isolation, but in a perspective of more fully understanding the specificities and the existing or emerging interactions of the struggles against capitalist domination, modern patriarchal subalternization and imperial exploitation.

As an unavoidable consequence of these considerations, finite Marxism therefore addresses the resulting polyphony of Marxist and other voices in the politics of today as a factor of success, and of opening up further possibilities, instead of attempting to impose a necessarily violent unification of all of them, while at the same time working upon how to develop productive effects of non-antagonistic, although unavoidable contradictions, in order to make a concerted polyphony of Marxist and other radical voices in politics an effective and sustainable reality.

ACKNOWLEDGEMENT

I have to thank Darren Roso for his helpful comments and suggestions; the responsibility for the outcome is, of course, exclusively mine.

REFERENCES

Althusser, L., (1998). Le Marxisme comme théorie finie (1978). In: Althusser, L., *La solitude de Machiavel et autres textes*, ed. Y. Sintomer. Paris: Presses Universitäires de France, pp. 281–296.
Althusser, L., (2017). *How to be a Marxist in Philosophy*, transl. by G.M. Goshgarian. London: Bloomsbury.

---

[26]   Marx himself still makes use here of a slightly misleading Hegelian terminology. By speaking about the '*Entwicklung des Begriffs*', the unfolding of the concept, his wording may mislead into a properly Hegelian reading of his theoretical work; which is, however, incapable of doing full justice to Marx's epistemological breakthroughs to a fully scientific treatment of the fields of modern political economy, as well as to that of modern politics.

Balibar, É., Luporini, C. and Tosel, A., (1979). *Marx et sa critique de la politique.* Paris: Maspéro.

Breda, S., (2018). *Kredit und Kapital. Kreditsystem und Reproduktion der kapitalistiscen Vergesellschaftungsweise in der dialektischen Darstellung des 'Kapital'.* FUB Diss., Berlin (published by Königshausen & Neumann, Würzburg, in 2019).

Callari, A. and Ruccio, D.F., (eds) (1996). *Postmodern Materialism and the Future of Marxist Theory. Essays in the Althusserian Tradition.* Hanover and London: Wesleyan University Press.

Coser, Lewis A., (1956). *The Functions of Social Conflict.* Glencoe, IL: Free Press / London: Routledge & Kegan Paul.

Dahrendorf, Ralf (1957). *Soziale Klassen und Klassenkonflikt in der industriellen Gesellschaft.* Stuttgart: Enke.

Elliot, Gregory (n.d.). The Lonely Hour of the Last Instance Louis Pierre Althusser, 1918–1990. rp57_obituary_althusser.pdf (radicalphilosophyarchive.com).

Herberg-Rothe, Andreas (2001). *Das Rätsel Clausewitz. Politische Theorie des Krieges im Widerstreit.* München: Fink Verlag.

Horkheimer, Max (1935). On the Problem of Truth. In: *Between Philosophy and Social Science: Selected Early Writings.* Cambridge, MA: MIT Press, pp. 177–215.

Klofáč, J., and Tlustý, V. (1964). *Empirische Soziologie: kurzer Abriss der modernen bürgerlichen empirischen Soziologie.* Berlin: VEB Deutsche Verlag der Wissenschaften.

Krysmanski, Hans Jürgen (1971). *Soziologie des Konflikts. Materialien und Modelle.* Reinbek: Rowohlt.

Kuruma, Samezō (1969). Discussion of Marx's Method. Translated from: *Marx-Lexikon Zur Politischen Ökonomie* vol. 2, March 1969, part 1. https://www.Marxists.org/archive/kuruma/method-discussion1.htm, part 2 https://www.Marxists.org/archive/kuruma/method-discussion2.htm.

Lorenzen, P., (1957). Das Aktual-Unendliche in der Mathematik. *Philosophia naturalis*, vol. 4, pp. 3–11.

Löwith, K., (1927). Politischer Dezisionismus (C. Schmitt). Archiv für Sozialwissenschaft und Sozialpolitik.

Mao Dze Dong (1930). *Oppose Book Worship.* https://www.Marxists.org/reference/archive/mao/selected-works/date-index.htm#1930.

Mao Dze Dong (1937). *On Practice. On the Relation between Knowledge and Practice, between Knowing and Doing.* https://www.Marxists.org/reference/archive/mao/selected-works/volume-1/mswv1_16.htm.

Martens, H., (1994). Gesellschaftlicher Umbruch und gewerkschaftliche Reform. *Gewerkschaftliche Monatshefte*, no. 3, pp. 78–92.

Pöhler, W., (ed) (1979). *Damit die Arbeit menschlihcer wird – Fünf Jahre Aktionsprogramm Humanisierung des Arbeitslebens.* Bonn: Verlag Neue Gesellschaft.

Resnick, S.A. and Wolff, R.D. (2006). *New Departures in Marxian Theory.* New York and London: Routledge.

Rojas, R., (1988). *Das unvollendete Projekt. Zur Entstehungsgeschichte von Marx' 'Kapital'.* Hamburg: Argument.

Schmidt, A., (1977). *Drei Studien über Materialismus: Schopenhauer, Horkheimer, Glücksproblem.* München: Hanser.

Schmitt, C., ([1927] 2015). *Der Begriff des Politischen* (9th corr. edn). Berlin: Duncker & Humblot.

Schmitt, Lars ([1908] 2012). Georg Simmel: Der Streit. Konflikt als Form sozialer Wechselwirkungen. *Konfliktdynamik*, vol. 1, no. 1, pp. 82–83.

Simmel, Georg (1992). Der Streit [1908]. In: Simmel, G., *Soziologie. Untersuchungen über die Form der Vergesellschaftung*, Frankfurt a. M.: Suhrkamp, pp. 284–382.

Sotiris, P., (2020). *A philosophy for communism: Rethinking Althusser*. Leiden: Brill.

Stark, C., (2002). Die Konflikttheorie von Georg Simmel. In: Bonacker T. (ed) *Sozialwissenschaftliche Konflikttheorien*. (Friedens- und Konfliktforschung, vol 5.). Wiesbaden: VS Verlag für Sozialwissenschaften.

Vileisis, D. and Wolf, F.O., (2018). Marx und Engels im Umbruch: Zur kritischen Neuedition der Texte zur Deutschen Ideologie. *Deutsche Zeitschrift für Philosophie*, vol. 66, no. 1, pp. 134–141. https://doi.org/10.1515/dzph-2018-0012.

Wolf, F.O., (2002). *Radikale Philosophie. Aufklärung und Befreiung in der neuen Zeit*. Münster: Westfälisches Dampfboot.

Wolf, F.O., (2004). The 'Limits of Dialectical Presentation' as a Key Category of Marx's Theoretical Self-Reflection. *Capitalism, Nature, Socialism*, 3 (Sept.), pp. 79–85 (revised and enlarged German version in J. Hoff (ed), *Das Kapital neu lesen*. Münster: Westfälisches Dampfboot, 2006, pp. 159–188). (German version at: http://www.rote-ruhr-uni.com/cms/IMG/pdf/FOW_Grenzen.pdf.)

Wolf, F.O., (2006). 'Marx Konzept der, Grenzen der dialektischen Darstellung'. In: Jan Hoff, Alexis Petrioli, Ingo Stützle, and Wolf, F. O. (eds), *Das Kapital neu lesen. Beiträge zur radikalen Philosophie*, Münster: Westfälisches Dampfboot, pp. 159-188.

Wolf, F.O., (2007). 'The Missed Rendezvous of Critical Marxism and Ecological Feminism'. In: *Capitalism, Nature, Socialism*, vol. 18, issue 2, pp.109–125. https://doi.org/10.1080/10455750701368358.

Wolf, F.O., (2009). 'What Capitalism Is', electronic publication. Revised print edition in: S.R. Farris (ed) (2016). *Returns of Marxism. Marxist Theory in Times of Crisis*, Amsterdam: IIRE, pp. 101–127.

4.   The economic cell form

Bob Jessop

4.1   INTRODUCTION

Writing on 19th-century scientific developments, Engels noted that Feuerbach (*1804–†1872) 'had lived to see all three of the decisive discoveries – that of the cell, the transformation of energy, and the theory of evolution named after Darwin' (Engels [1886] 1990, p. 372). The same holds, of course, for Karl Marx (*1818–†1883), who was interested in contemporary science and tried to keep up to date with advances in many fields. Engels had already corresponded to Marx about the first two discoveries on 14 July 1858, when he referred to cell theory and thermodynamics (Engels [1858] 1983, p. 326; and on Darwin's book, Engels [1859] 1983, p. 551; Marx [1860] 1986, p. 232). All three decisive discoveries are taken up in Marx's analysis of the capitalist mode of production in the first volume of *Capital*.

The most discussed of these three discoveries in commentaries on Marx's work is Darwin's theory of evolution. *Origin of Species* was published in the same year as Marx's *Zur Kritik der politischen Ökonomie* (*Contribution to the Critique of Political Economy*) and had a far bigger impact, including in Germany, than Marx's work of that year (Marsden 1999, pp. 102–104). Marx considered Darwin to have achieved in natural history what he and Engels had realized for the domain of human history.[1] In the Preface to the first German edition of *Capital I*, Marx described how 'the evolution of the economic formation of society is viewed as a process of natural history' (Marx [1887] 1996, p. 10; cf. Afterword to the second German edition, Marx [1887] 1996, p. 18). He proceeded to identify analogies between natural selection and the evolution of tools and technology in the division of labour (Marx [1887] 1996, p. 346; cf. pp. 489–491). He interpreted competition as a crucial mechanism of natural selection in relations among those 'hostile brothers', individual capitalists,

---

[1]   Marx read *The Origin of Species* three times, from mid-November to mid-December 1860, in early to mid-June 1862, and in French sometime before mid-February 1869 (Sheasby 2004, p. 68).

in whose competition, 'one capitalist always kills many' (Marx [1894] 1998, p. 252; [1887] 1996, p. 750). He commented, probably semi-seriously, on 'natural selection' in the labour force (Marx [1887] 1996, pp. 274–275); and he almost certainly drew his contrast between a bee's hive-building capacities and the achievements of the worst architect from Darwin's discussion of hive-bees' 'inimitable architectural powers' (Darwin 1859, pp. 227–228; Marx [1887] 1996, p. 188).

Thermodynamics and energetics became an important influence in Marx's critique of political economy. This has been recognized more recently. This occurred through examination of Marx's *Exzerpthefte* (excerpt notebooks) from the 1850s and his published and unpublished drafts of *Capital* rather than because of Marx's public pronouncements or correspondence. Its significance emerged through his analysis of the transformative power of the steam engine in industrial production and his reading of texts on labour-power (Wendling 2009). The growing unification of theories about energy embraced animal and human physiology, another topic on which Marx made extensive notes. An important result of this discovery for Marx is his discussion of *Arbeitskraft*, translated as 'labour-power', the capacity or potential to perform living labour; a concept that was absent from classical political economy. According to Anson Rabinbach (1990), Marx appropriated the concept of *Arbeitskraft* from the physicist Hermann von Helmholtz (e.g., 1847). This was a key innovation in Marx's analysis of labour-power as well as machinery, especially of human labour and machines as alternative forms of motive power (Marx [1887] 1996, pp. 378ff.). Marx regarded his concept of labour-power as one of two 'best points' about *Capital*, because it allowed him to describe the twofold character of labour once it is divided into concrete and abstract labour (Wendling 2009, p. 52; citing Marx [1867] 1987, p. 407). The abstract character of labour-power is continually rebased through innovation and competition, and becomes socially necessary labour time in specific spatio-temporal contexts (Postone 1993). Temporality and (ir)reversibility were also key emerging themes in thermodynamics at the time (expressed in the notion of entropy), and crucial to Marx's exploration of the political economy of time. Moreover, as John Bellamy Foster and Paul Burkett (2008, p. 3) note, thermodynamics also provided the foundations for an ecological economics.

The significance of cell biology is the least remarked of the three scientific discoveries in relation to Marx's work. This could be because commentators are less familiar with its background, especially as, apart from one explicit reference in his magnum opus to the commodity as the economic cell form of the capitalist mode of production, clues are scattered in published correspondence and dispersed among other metaphors and analogies in relevant preparatory and published texts. Cell biology also tends to be subsumed into Marx's more general interest in physiology and its relevance to anthropology and land economy,[2] and as far as metabolism (*Stoffwechsel*) is concerned, could be conflated with the influence of thermodynamics, which took the term over from cell biology (Pawelzig 1997; Angus 2018; Otani et al. 2019, pp. 855–857). Moreover, his interest in cell theory belongs more to the discovery phases (the role of analogies and metaphors as heuristic devices) than to the more systematic research and presentation phases[3] of his developing critique of political economy; and, in this regard, two of the relevant excerpt notebooks have not yet been published in the *Marx–Engels Gesamtausgabe* (*MEGA²* *IV-10* and *IV-23*). The volume of excerpts and marginalia is also smaller than for mechanics, chemistry, agriculture, and so on (Griese and Sandkühler 1997, pp. 129–150). Another reason for neglect of the influence of cell biology may be that Marx more often refers to the commodity as the 'elementary form' of the capitalist mode of production (CMP). While this evokes the idea of the cell form as the elementary unit of organic life, it is less explicit and more easily overlooked. Further, given that Marx also employs many other analogies, similes and metaphors drawn from the natural sciences, humanities and literature, the role of cell theory as a heuristic device and extended metaphor can disappear among a plethora of other references. For example, metabolism figures in agronomy and is vital to Marx's account of metabolic rift (Foster 2013); but Marx also applied it to industrial production and the circuits of capital. This dual use obscures its important links to cell biology.

4.2   METHOD IN POLITICAL ECONOMY

In the Preface to the first German edition of *Capital Volume I*, Marx wrote: 'every beginning is difficult, holds in all sciences' (Marx [1887] 1996, p. 7). This could be an indirect reference to Hegel's concern in the *Science of Logic* with 'the difficulty of finding a beginning in philosophy', especially as for Hegel this was also a science, indeed, a pure science (*reines Wissen*) (Hegel [1831] 1998, p. 67; cf. [1816] 2010, p. 28). For Marx, however, regarding *Capital*, it refers in the first instance to the difficulties that he anticipated that his readers might have with the opening chapters (Marx [1887] 1996), which he reworked several times and across different editions. It could also refer indirectly to the difficulties that the Physiocrats and their opponents found in

---

[2]   For example, Schleiden and Schmid (1850), annotated by Marx, considered, *inter alia*, the relevance of plant and animal physiology to land economy.

[3]   These phases are not sequential and linear, but overlap and interact.

establishing the starting point of political economy. For, as Marx observed in
the *Grundrisse*:

> the crucial issue was not what kind of labour creates *value* but what kind of labour
> creates *surplus value.* They were thus discussing the problem in a complex form
> before having solved it in its elementary form; just as the historical progress of all
> sciences leads only through a multitude of contradictory moves to the real point of
> departure. (Marx [1859] 1987, p. 297)

Marx's quest for an entry point likewise involved many contradictory moves.
Thus, his comment could also refer to his own difficulties in finding the right
starting point for his critique of the categories, practices and dynamic of political economy.

These challenges pervaded not only the method of research but also the
method of presentation that was appropriate for reproducing the real-concrete
as a concrete-in-thought. *A fortiori*, this concerned the interweaving of phases
of research, drafting and final editing. Marx discussed method in political
economy in the 1857 Introduction, which juxtaposes two approaches that ultimately do not seem to figure in his choice of starting point in *Capital*.

The first approach starts with a real and concrete precondition of production
that remains an empty phrase, amounting to a chaotic conception of the whole,
until it has been decomposed into its simplest determinations and then recom-
posed, this time as 'a rich totality of many determinations and relations' (Marx
[1857] 1986, p. 37). This approach corresponds to the 'descending' method of
political economy in the 17th century (Marx [1857] 1986, p. 37). Early political economy took population as its 'comprehensive' starting point in the real
world; a category that was the most visible form in which the object of national
economics appears. It then aimed to reproduce this 'real starting point' in
thought 'as a synthesis of many determinations' (Marx [1857] 1986, p. 38).
While focusing on political economy, Marx also criticized Hegel's phenomenology. Specifically, he attacked its idealist premises that take the real starting
point as the product of the thinking mind, rather than as having an existence
'outside the mind and independent of it' (Marx [1857] 1986, pp. 38–39).

The second approach takes the simplest (or most abstract) element of
a specific mode of production as its point of departure. It then explores the
historical presuppositions of this element (its 'concrete substratum'), the historical development of this elementary form into its most abstract expression;
and its articulation with other elements to form more complex moments of
production. It may also seek to show how more complex moments can be
derived logically, with due recognition of historical contingencies, from the
simple, elementary form that is chosen as the starting point. This 'ascending'
approach is characteristic of classical political economy, as exemplified in

Adam Smith's synthetic method in *The Wealth of Nations*. While praising Smith's theoretical breakthroughs, Marx also criticized his treatment of bourgeois categories as universal or transhistorical and, relatedly, his emphasis on the formal rather than material aspects of capitalist production. He nonetheless proposed to adopt the ascending approach in his critique of political economy. He aimed to identify the historical *differentia specifica* of the CMP vis-à-vis the elements common to production in general. He illustrated this approach from Hegel's analysis of possession as the simplest legal relation, as the starting point for Hegel's philosophy of law. Referencing Smith, he then considers labour (not, be it noted, labour-power) as the simplest element identified in classical political economy, and comments on the historical conditions in which 'labour as such' (rather than specific kinds of labour) can become an abstract starting point for the analysis of modern political economy, as labour becomes 'a means to create wealth in general' (Marx [1857] 1986, pp. 39–42). Thus, after presenting the general abstract determinations that characterize all forms of society, attention must turn to 'the categories which constitute the internal structure of bourgeois society and on which the principal classes are based' (Marx [1857] 1986, p. 45). Next comes a progressive movement from more abstract-simple to more concrete-complex categories, culminating in the world market.

While Marx indicated his preference in the Introduction for the second method of inquiry, he did not fully follow this method in subsequent texts on capital. Instead he chose the commodity as the simple, elementary or most abstract starting point for his analysis, rather than labour or other core categories mentioned in the Introduction. Commodities are mentioned only once in the 1857 Introduction, and in relation to commodity prices rather than the commodity form. In contrast, money is referenced 11 times, capital in different forms appears 28 times, and labour and wage-labour together figure around 50 times (Marx [1857] 1986, pp. 17–44). The *Grundrisse* (1857–58) manuscripts begin effectively with Chapter 2, on money, which ends rather than begins with some remarks on the commodity, which rehearse the arguments in the *Poverty of Philosophy*, and then move to Chapter 3, on capital, which is ten times longer than that on money. In contrast, the commodity as the 'elementary existence' of the capitalist form of wealth is the first topic of Chapter 1 in *Contribution to the Critique of Political Economy* (1859), followed by a chapter on money, with the expected chapter on capital being absent from the published version.

Table 4.1 suggests that Marx adopts a third method in *Capital* compared with his various preparatory manuscripts. This method is indebted to the example of cell biology, which led Marx to take the simplest element of the CMP as his starting point. This does not mean that Marx employed the cell metaphor slavishly to transfer its concepts and mechanisms to the capital relation. But

Table 4.1   *From the 1857 Introduction to* Das Kapital, *Vol. 1 (1867)*

	1857 Introduction		Kapital I (1867)
	Method 1	Method 2	Marx's method
Example	Early political economy	Classical political economy	Critique of political economy
Starting point	A chaotic conception of the whole as it appears at first sight to a naïve observer	Decomposition of the whole by an informed theorist into analytically distinct but connected parts	Identify the ultimate morphological element that is also the nucleus of all further development
Initial object	The real-concrete	Several abstract-simple elements	The simplest element
Method	Descending analysis into constituent elements to better grasp the whole	Ascending synthesis to create a rich totality that reproduces the real-concrete as a concrete-in-thought	Logical-historical analysis of dialectical relations between the simplest element as both a presupposition and the posit of the whole

Source: Adapted with permission from Jessop (2018a).

his reading of cell biology does seem to have affected the substance of his argument as well as its starting point. The substance is, of course, an unfolding of the value form of the commodity as the presupposition and posit of the unfolding dynamic, contradictory character, and inherent crisis-tendencies of the capital relation.

As Roberto Fineschi notes, the commodity provides the ideal starting point because it is not abstract content but a unity of form and content. Specifically:

> 1) ... the economic cell must at the same time express *the universal character of the content and the formal determinacy it assumes in the capitalist mode of production.* The commodity seems to respond to this need: this is the criterion for choosing it [as the starting point]. 2) Its ability to represent at the most abstract level possible the unity of material content and social form is not, however, enough to characterize [the commodity as] the economic cell: *it must contain, potentially, in itself, the exposition of the whole theory of capital.* (Fineschi 2001, p. 44, my translation)

This excludes both the one-sided descending and one-sided ascending methods of early and classical political economy. It requires a unique combination of: (1) logical analysis based on 'the force of abstraction' (Marx [1887] 1996, p. 8) to identify the simplest social relation of the CMP that can be linked *in potentia*, by virtue of its inherent contradictions, to other bourgeois social relations; (2) historical analysis of the genesis of specific economic and social forms and their changing significance in different contexts; and (3) attention to the empirical details of relevant contemporary examples of the CMP to identify emergent tendencies and/or demonstrate the plausibility of logical arguments. This can be labelled a 'logical-historical-empirical method'.

4.3   THE COMMODITY AS STARTING POINT

So, what happened between 1857 and 1867 to prompt Marx to begin *Capital* with the commodity form rather than one or more of the economic categories that received far more attention in the 1857 Introduction: wage-labour, value, money, price, capital, and so forth? In addition to occasional remarks in correspondence and hints in the excerpt notebooks, we have four main sources for explaining this choice: Marx's Preface to the first German edition (1867); different editions of Volume I (1867–83); the initially unpublished Chapter 6, 'Results of the Direct Process of Production' (Marx 1861–64 [1989]), which was the intended bridge at the end of Volume I to Volume II; and Marx's 1881 'Marginal Notes on Adolph Wagner's *Lehrbuch der politischen Oekonomie*' (Marx 1881 [1975]).

I begin with clues in the Marx–Engels correspondence. Specifically, on 14 July 1858, Engels wrote to Marx:

> One has no idea, by the way, of the progress made in the natural sciences during the past, 30 years. Two things have been crucial where physiology is concerned: 1. the tremendous development of organic chemistry, 2. the microscope, which has been properly used only during the past 20 years. This last has produced even more important results than chemistry; what has been chiefly responsible for revolutionising the whole of physiology and has alone made comparative physiology possible is the discovery of the cell – in plants by Schleiden and in animals by Schwann (about 1836). Everything consists of cells. The cell is Hegelian 'being in itself' and its development follows the Hegelian process step by step right up to the final emergence of the 'idea' – i.e. each completed organism. (Engels [1858] 1983, p. 326)

This observation could have been a trigger, especially as Marx acknowledges in a letter written on 4 July 1864 that, in the natural sciences, Engels is always ahead of him and 'I always follow in your footsteps' (Marx [1864] 1986, p. 546).

Engels's letter to Marx was written in the year following the penning of the 1857 Introduction. It may explain why, in contrast to the latter's focus on method in political economy, the 1867 Preface highlights method in the natural sciences. This analogy concerns their capacity to drill down to the micro-foundations of macro-level phenomena. Specifically, in an allusion to the newly burgeoning field of histology and its accompanying cell theory or cell doctrine, Marx mentions the role of microscopy and chemical reagents (staining agents for making tissue structures more visible):

> The value-form, whose fully developed shape is the money-form, is very elementary and simple. The human mind has for more than 2,000 years sought in vain to get to the bottom of it all, whilst on the other hand, to the successful analysis of much more composite and complex forms, there has been at least an approximation. Why? Because the body, as an organic whole, is more easy of study than are the cells of that body.[4] (Marx [1887] 1996, p. 8)

Marx then presents '*mikrologische Anatomie*' (where 'micrological' refers to the analysis of phenomena at a microscopic scale) as the model for his point of departure, with a view to moving from the commodity as the economic cell form of the CMP through the process of cell formation, differentiation, repetition (simple reproduction) and growth (expanded reproduction or accumulation), to provide a complete account of the whole organism formed by a social formation dominated by the CMP. Since microscopy cannot be applied in the analysis of social forms, it must be replaced by 'the force of abstraction' (Marx [1887] 1996, p. 8). Abstraction is not a purely logical procedure. It is guided by the English case as the closest parallel to physicists' observation of natural processes where they exist in their most typical (*prägnateste*) form with the least external disturbance, and/or to their conduct of experiments in conditions that isolate the normal case (in German, *rein* or 'pure') (Marx [1887] 1996, p. 8). Later, Marx will show growing interest in the United States as a site of even more advanced forms of the capital relation regarding the enterprise form and finance (see, e.g., Marx [1878] 1991, p. 344; Griese et al. 2011, p. 725).

I now present six key propositions in cell theory that could have inspired Marx. These propositions draw on texts in cell biology, physiology, histology, and so on, that Marx and Engels were likely to have known directly or indirectly:

1. All living organisms – plants and animals alike – are composed of one or more cells (Schwann 1847). Or, as Virchow put it: 'the cell is really the ultimate morphological element in which there is any manifestation of life, and … we must not transfer the seat of real action to any point beyond the cell' (Virchow 1858, p. 3; 1860, p. 3).

---

[4]   Kölliker's *Gewebelehre* (*Histology*) opens with two remarks: microscopic anatomy (*mikroskopische Anatomie*) is now just as much one of the foundations of medicine as the anatomy of the organs and systems; and a basic study of physiology and pathological anatomy is impossible without exact knowledge of the most minute form relations (Kölliker 1852, p. iii, my translation). His book surveys the elementary parts (*Elementartheile*) of the body and the finer construction (*Bau*) of organs (ibid.).

2. Following from this, the cell is the most basic unit (*Elementarteil*) of life (Schwann 1847).
3. Cells lead independent lives that, at least in animals, are shaped by the life of a larger organism of which they are part (ibid.).
4. *Omnis cellula e cellula*, that is, 'all cell arises from other cells'[5] (Virchow 1855, p. 23; 1860, p. 27).[6]
5. Cellular reproduction depends on metabolic exchanges with the environment (including other cells) that convert food/fuel into energy to run cellular processes, create the building blocks for cell formation, and eliminate waste.
6. Embryonic cells can – but need not – differentiate into other kinds of cell, generating higher-order forms (specialized tissues, organs) that comprise a functioning organism.[7]

These points find parallels, conscious or unconscious, in Marx's analysis of the commodity, the circuits of capital, and the differentiation of different moments of the value form and other categories of the capital relation. Here I draw on the preparatory works to *Capital*, different editions of *Capital*, and the comments on Wagner. Thus:

1. The living organism or *Gesellschaftskörper* (social body) of the CMP depends on the dynamic arrangement of the value form and its cognate forms into concrete-complex relations (Marx [1857] 1986, p. 24; [1859] 1987; [1887] 1996).
2. The elementary unit (*Elementarteil*) of the value form is the commodity (Marx [1887] 1996, p. 45), which is also the economic cell form (*Zellenform*) of the CMP (Marx [1887] 1996, p. 8).
3. Commodities lead independent lives that are shaped by the life of the CMP of which they are a part; they are both presupposition and posit of both simple and expanded reproduction.
4. *Omnis merx e mercibus*, that is, every commodity from commodities.[8] This can take the form of simple commodity circulation, that is, C-M-C,

---

[5]   Raspail (1825, pp. 224, 384) was the first to state that *omnis cellula e cellula* (Harris 1999, p. 33).

[6]   This phrase, introduced in Virchow's 1855 article, is not in the first German edition of his book, although the idea is present (Virchow 1858, p. 25); it appears as an interpolation in the second edition, from which the English translation cited here was made (Virchow 1860, p. 27).

[7]   Schwann (1847), for example, identified five types of human tissue that could emerge from an embryonic cell.

[8]   Cf. Sraffa's (1960) analysis of production of commodities by means of commodities.

or of the circuit of capital, with the power of expanded reproduction, that is, M-C-M'. As Marx wrote, '[i]n capitalist production of products as commodities, on the one hand, and the form of labour as *wage-labour*, on the other, becomes absolute' (Marx [1861–64] 1989, p. 445; cf. Marx [1861–64] 1989, p. 375).

5.   Production, distribution and exchange are analysed as metabolic processes, examining how different elements are converted into each other and how a 'metabolic rift' can produce pathological effects in the overall production process as it unfolds in time–space (see esp. Foster 2000; Saito 2017).

6.   Embryonic contradictions in the commodity as cell form (or germ form) of the value relation generate further developments in the capital relation. These include the initial two special commodities (labour-power and money as universal equivalent), the price form, money as capital, and so on. For example, the commodity form of value 'is a mere germ [*Keimform*], which must undergo a series of metamorphoses before it can ripen into the price form' (Marx [1887] 1996, p. 72).[9] More generally, contradictions drive the metamorphosis of the value form and of capitalist societalization.

While the first two points need no elaboration here, the other four points do merit discussion. In point 3, the simple commodity is the presupposition of distinctive capitalist forms. Marx therefore proceeded from 'the simplest social form in which the product of labour presents itself in contemporary society, and this is the "*commodity*"' (Marx [1881] 1975, p. 544). On this basis, Marx could then explore the 'double life' of the commodity: as a commodity (which nonetheless presupposes that other commodities exist), and as an integral part of the CMP's overall logic. As he wrote in the *Grundrisse*:

> If in the fully developed bourgeois system each economic relationship presupposes the other in a bourgeois-economic form, and everything posited is thus also a premiss, that is the case with every organic system. This organic system itself has its premises as a totality, and its development into a totality consists precisely in subordinating all elements of society to itself, or in creating out of it the organs it still lacks. This is historically how it becomes a totality. Its becoming this totality constitutes a moment of its process, of its development. (Marx [1857–58] 1986, p. 208)

---

[9]   Cf. McCarthy (1988, pp. 115–116) on the commodity as the 'simplest category', the '*Keimform*' (or germ form), that 'contains within itself the totality of all forms of capitalist social structure and their contradictions of the capital relation'.

Similar arguments are presented in the original draft of the chapter on money for *Contribution to the Critique of Political Economy* (Marx [1858] 1987, pp. 497–498). In addition, in the 1861–63 *Manuscript*, Marx writes:

> It is as such a prerequisite that we treat the commodity, since we proceed from it as the simplest element in capitalist production. On the other hand, the product, the result of capitalist production, is the commodity. What appears [*erscheint*] as its element is later revealed to be its own product. Only on the basis of capitalist production does the commodity become the general form of the product and the more this production develops, the more do the products in the form of commodities enter into the process as ingredients. (Marx [1861–63] 1989, pp. 300–301; cf. Marx [1887] 1996, p. 376)

In point 4, regarding the proposition that every commodity stems from commodities, Marx argued in the unpublished Chapter 6 (written in 1864) that:

> *Commodities,* i.e. use-value and exchange-value directly united, emerge from the [labour] process as *result*, as product; similarly, they enter into it as constituent elements. But nothing at all can ever emerge from a production process without first entering into it in the form of the conditions of production. (Marx [1861–64] 1989, pp. 387–388)

The idea that every cell develops from other cells and that the simple cell can generate different kinds of tissue anticipates the idea of the stem cell. Today, it is recognized that stem cells reproduce themselves through simple repetition, but are also pluripotent, having the capacity to form very different kinds of cell with different properties and functions. The value form of the commodity can be seen from these perspectives too. The first perspective concerns either simple commodity production, which takes the form of C-M-C, or the metamorphosis (metabolism) in the circuit of capital in the form of M-C-M'. The second perspective – the pluripotency of the commodity form – indicates how the elementary contradiction in the value form of the commodity between use value and exchange value leads to differentiation. In addition to wage-labour and money, Marx discusses other forms of the capital relation. These also have their own specific properties, contradictions and impact on the expanded reproduction of capital and the character of capitalist social formations. While the stem cell metaphor enables these arguments to be stated more clearly, they are already implicit in cell theory as it existed between 1857 and 1867, when Marx was drafting *Capital*. Thus, the heuristic power of adopting the stem cell analogy hinges on its capacity to generate further insights.

In point 5, highlighting metabolic conversion in the unpublished Chapter 6, Marx wrote:

> The conversion of money, which is itself only a converted form of the commodity, into capital only takes place once labour-power [*Arbeitsvermögen*] has been converted into a commodity for the worker himself ... Only then are all products converted into commodities, and only then do the objective conditions of each individual sphere of production enter into production as commodities themselves. (Marx [1861–64] 1989, p. 359, translation modified)

There are many similar comments in the preparatory and actual texts of *Capital*.

In point 6, the commodity form is the common principle of development for other social forms and therefore provides its most elementary form. In this sense, the commodity contains the embryonic contradiction that becomes the germ form (*Keimform*) of other contradictions. All forms of the capital relation can be unfolded dialectically from the value form of the commodity, considered as the unity of exchange-value and use-value, as a unity of (historical) form and (universal) content. So, Marx soon moves from the commodity to two of its special forms: first, labour-power (which also has a dual character as use-value and exchange-value and, in his later analyses, is further explored through its dual character as concrete labour and abstract labour) (cf. Marx [1881] 1975, p. 546); and, second, money as the universal commodity, which is later analysed in terms of its metamorphosis into capital. Subsequently, Marx will explore another special commodity: land as private property and forms of rent (Marx [1894] 1998). In these and other cases, the commodity is the simple *concretum* from which all other forms can be derived through a combination of logical reflection and historical analysis in order, eventually, to reproduce the real-concrete as a concrete-in-thought, as 'a rich totality of many determinations and relations' (Marx [1857] 1986, p. 37).

4.4   THE LIMITS OF ANALOGY

Ludwig Kugelmann tried to use the publication of Marx's *Capital* in 1867 to convert the cell pathologist Rudolf Virchow, who was a vocal and influential German liberal, to scientific socialism. He informed Marx that he had sent Virchow a copy of the book:

> In making him aware of your work, I told him how you regard commodities as cells, [how you] analyse bourgeois society, etc., that you follow the same method in political economy as he does in medicine: that your *Capital* could therefore be dubbed the social pathology of bourgeois society, etc. (cited in de Rosa 1964, p. 595)

Marx replied to Kugelmann on 17 April 1868:

> You have done me a great service with your lines to Virchow, though I doubt whether he will have the patience and time to immerse himself in a subject out of his line. I know it cost me a great effort to read his Cellularpathologie [1858] in Manchester, particularly because of the way it was written. (Marx [1868] 1988, p. 13)

More generally, *pace* Kugelmann, Marx and Engels opposed categorical political arguments based on analogies with biology and other natural sciences (Darwinism, society as a federation of cells, or the body politic). Such arguments were already criticized in the first German edition of *Das Kapital I*, when Marx noted:

> The weak points in the abstract materialism of natural science [*abstrakt naturwissenschaftlichen Materialismus*], a materialism that excludes history and its process, are at once evident from the abstract and ideological conceptions of its spokesmen, whenever they venture beyond the bounds of their own speciality. (Marx [1887] 1996, pp. 375–376n)

The principal limits to the analogy are presented in Table 4.2. In essence, whereas cells are the universal basis of organic life and operate through known universal chemical, physiological and metabolic processes, the value form of the commodity as the economic cell form of the capital relation is historically specific, and its laws and tendencies are doubly tendential, in the sense that, they exist only to the extent that the contradiction-rife and crisis-prone capital relation is reproduced in and through social practices that are historically contingent and contested. Further, while the failure of cell replication and differentiation can lead to harmful or morbid developments in the organism, the mechanisms of cellular pathology have nothing in common with capital's crisis-tendencies, which must be grounded in the immanent logic of the capital relation, and its instantiation in social formations dominated by the capital relation.

4.5   CONCLUSIONS

This chapter has explored the neglected role of cell biology as a paradigm-shifting natural scientific discovery in Marx's critique of political economy. There are several good reasons why this influence has been neglected, but it should be taken seriously now. I suggest that there are six key foundational principles of cell theory that could have inspired Marx's profound shift in the choice of starting point for his critique of political economy between the 1857 Introduction and the 1867 first edition of *Das Kapital*. My argument is based

Table 4.2   The limits of the analogy

Cell theory	Economic cell theory	Limits of analogy
All living organisms are composed of cells	Social body of the CMP is composed of value forms	Not a universal truth but historically specific
The cell is the most basic element of life (single cells can exist)	The commodity is the elementary unit of CMP	A single commodity without other commodities is irrational; commodities are always plural
Cells lead independent lives but are shaped by the larger organism	Commodities circulate as commodities but are shaped by the overall logic of the CMP	Cell theory's ontological claim versus Marx's methodological use of presupposition and posit
Omnis cellula e cellula	*Omnis merx e mercibus*	Not automatic for CMP: it requires generalization of the commodity or price form to all inputs into M-C-M'
Cellular reproduction involves fallible metabolism (hence cellular pathology)	Production, distribution, exchange involve fallible metabolism (hence crises)	Metabolism of CMP is internally contradictory, conflictual, crisis-prone
Embryonic cells may differentiate into other kinds of cell	Contradictions in basic cell form generate more developed social forms	Ontological statement versus logical-historical-empirical analysis of successive forms

Source: Adapted with permission from Jessop (2018a).

only on the texts in cell theory with which Marx was acquainted, directly or indirectly, and on clues in Marx's relevant methodological texts, the economic manuscripts and correspondence. Crucial here is the identification of the nucleus (cytoplast) in cell formation, differentiation and reproduction.[10] The analogy in the commodity is the nucleus (*Keimform*) of the contradiction between use-value and exchange-value as two necessary moments of the value form of the commodity.

In addition, the idea that the commodity is the 'economic cell form' of the CMP provides an essential mediating link between the scientific presentation of Marx's critique of the CMP and the use of Hegel's *Logic* as a rhetorical device in unfolding this argument. Marx was aware of the limitations of taking arguments from the natural sciences beyond their appropriate field of application, and criticized German 'scientific materialists' for doing so, especially

---

[10]   Huxley (1853, pp. 302–307) critiques Schleiden and Schwan for adopting an inertial, structural account of the cell's development potential, in favour of an epigenetic concept of the germ cell that also reflects its interaction with the cell's environment. It is unlikely that Marx knew this text, but he attended Huxley's lectures on evolution in London in 1862 and knew some of his colleagues.

where they invoked natural science to critique the scientific socialism that he and Engels were developing in the 1870s and 1880s. This is why I present cell biology as having positive heuristic value in the process of discovery: being a source of inspiration and self-clarification along with other metaphors and analogies. In contrast, say, to thermodynamics, chemistry or agronomy, it is not a crucial part of the substantive research process in political economy, which focuses on the historically specific features of the CMP. Nor, given the limits of the analogy, could or should cell biology have played a major role in the presentation of Marx's scientific results in *Capital*. The influence of cell biology is more subterranean, but no less important for that. For, during the discovery process, it seems to have suggested ways to link the commodity as its simplest morphological element to the logic of the CMP as an organic totality. Recognizing the limits of taking the logic of the natural sciences as a model for the social world (whilst noting the unity of the natural and social worlds), it would make little sense to derive and develop the analysis of the CMP through strict analogical unfolding with cell biology, thermodynamics or the evolution of natural species. Here the method of presentation relies on a dialectical method that owes more to Hegel than to the pioneers of cell biology. Yet it also goes beyond Hegel, because of its emphasis on the contingently necessary development and dynamic of the capital relation and their mediation in and through social action. After all, human beings make their own history, but not in circumstances of their own choosing.

ACKNOWLEDGEMENTS

This chapter draws on Jessop (2018a, 2018b, 2019). Pradip Baksi sent me relevant historical material as I was preparing this chapter; it was also stimulated by reading Han (1995). Moishe Postone and Riccardo Bellofiore encouraged me to clarify some points. Remaining errors are mine.

REFERENCES

Abbreviation:
    MECW = Marx–Engels Collected Works. London: Lawrence & Wishart.

Angus, I., (2018). *Marx and Metabolism: Lost in Translation? Climate and Capitalism – Online*, 1 May. climateandcapitalism.com/2018/05/01/marx-and-metabolism-lost-in-translation, accessed 2 February 2021.
Darwin, C., (1859). *On the Origin of Species by Means of Natural Selection.* London: John Murray.
de Rosa, R., (1964). Rudolf Virchow und Karl Marx: zu einem unveröffentlichten Brief von Kugelmann an Marx über Virchow (1868), *Virchows Archiv* 337. Pp. 593–595.

Engels, F., [1858] (1983). Engels to Marx, 14 July 1858. In: *MECW* vol. 40. pp. 325–327.

Engels, F., [1859] (1983). Engels to Marx, 11 or 12 December 1859. In: *MECW* vol. 40. pp. 550–551.

Engels, F., [1886] (1990). Ludwig Feuerbach and the end of classical German philosophy. In: *MECW* vol. 26. pp. 353–398.

Fineschi, R., (2001). *Ripartire da Marx: Processo storico ed economia politica nella teoria del 'capitale'*. Rome: La Città del Sole.

Foster, J.B., (2000). *Marx's Ecology*. New York: Monthly Review Press.

Foster, J.B., (2013). Marx and the rift in the universal metabolism of nature. *Monthly Review* 65(7). pp. 1–19.

Foster, J.B. and Burkett, P., (2008). Classical Marxism and the second law of thermodynamics: Marx/Engels, the heat death of the universe hypothesis, and the origins of ecological economics. *Organization and Environment* 21(1). pp. 3–37.

Griese, A., Krüger, P., and Sperl, R., (2011). Einführung. In: idem, eds, *MEGA² IV/26, Karl Marx Exzerpte und Notizen zur Geologie, Mineralogie, und Agrikulturchemie, März bis September 1878*. Berlin: Akademie Verlag. pp. 691–741.

Griese, A. and Sandkühler, H.J., eds, (1997). *Karl Marx – Zwischen Philosophie und Naturwissenschaften*. Berlin: Peter Lang.

Han, S., (1995). *Marx in epistemischen Kontexten: Eine Dialektik der Philosophie und der 'positiven Wissenschaften'*. Berlin: Peter Lang.

Harris, H., (1999). *The Birth of the Cell*. New Haven, CT: Yale University Press.

Hegel, G.W.F., [1816] (2010). *Encyclopedia of the Philosophical Sciences in Basic Outline. Part I: Science of Logic*, trans. K. Brinkmann and D.O. Dahlstrom. Cambridge: Cambridge University Press.

Hegel, G.W.F., [1831] (1998). *Hegel's Science of Logic*, trans. A.V. Miller. Amherst, NY: Humanity Press.

Helmholtz, H. von, (1847). *Uber die Erhaltung der Kraft, eine physikalische Abhandlung vorgetragen in der Sitzung der physikalischen Gesellschaft zu Berlin am 1847*. Berlin: G. Reimer.

Huxley, T.H., (1853). Cell-theory. *The British and Foreign Medico-Chirurgical Review* 12(2). pp. 285–314.

Jessop, B., (2018a). 'Every beginning is difficult, holds in all sciences': Marx on the economic cell form of the capitalist mode of production. *Consecutio Rerum* 3(5). pp. 173–197.

Jessop, B., (2018b). From the 1857 Introduction to the 1867 Preface: reflections on Marx's method in the *Critique of Political Economy*. *Politeia* 8(2). pp. 15–36.

Jessop, B., (2019). 'Every beginning is difficult, holds in all sciences': Marx on the economic cell form of capital and the analysis of capitalist social formations. In: M. Musto, ed., *Marx's Capital after 150 Years: Critique and Alternative to Capitalism*, Abingdon: Routledge. pp. 54–82.

Kölliker, A., (1852). *Gewebelehre des Menschen für Aerzte und Studierende*. Leipzig: Wilhelm Engelmann.

Marsden, R., (1999). *The Nature of Capital: Marx after Foucault*. London: Routledge.

Marx, K., [1857] (1986). Introduction. In: *MECW* vol. 28. pp. 17–48.

Marx, K., [1857–58] (1986). *Outlines of the Critique of Political Economy* (Rough draft of 1857–58) [First Instalment]. In: *MECW* vol. 28. pp. 49–537.

Marx, K., [1857–58] (1987). *Outlines of the Critique of Political Economy* (Rough draft of 1857–58) [Second Instalment]. In: *MECW* vol. 29. pp. 1–255.

Marx, K., [1858] (1987). From the preparatory materials. In: *MECW* vol. 29. pp. 420–532.

Marx, K., [1859] (1987). *A Contribution to the Critique of Political Economy*. In: *MECW* vol. 29. pp. 257–417.

Marx, K., [1860] (1986). Letter to Engels, 19 December 1860. In: *MECW* vol. 41. pp. 231–233.

Marx, K., [1861–63] (1989). *Economic Manuscript of 1861–63* (Continuation). A contribution to the critique of political economy. In: *MECW* vol. 32. pp. 3–541.

Marx, K., [1861–64] (1989). Chapter 6. Results of the direct production process. In: *MECW* vol. 34. pp. 354–466.

Marx, K. [1864] (1986). Letter to Engels, 14 July 1864. In: *MECW* vol. 41. pp. 545–547.

Marx, K., [1867] (1987). Letter to Engels, 24 August 1867. In: *MECW* vol. 42. pp. 407–408.

Marx, K., [1868] (1988). Letter to Kugelmann, 17 April 1868. In: *MECW* vol. 43. pp. 12–13.

Marx, K., [1878] (1991). Letter to Nikolai Danielson, 15 November 1878. In: *MECW* vol. 45. pp. 343–344.

Marx, K., [1881] (1975). Marginal notes on Adolf Wagner's *Lehrbuch der politischen Oekonomie*. In: *MECW* vol. 24. pp. 531–559.

Marx, K., [1887] (1996). *Capital, volume 1. MECW* vol. 35.

Marx, K., [1894] (1998). *Capital, volume 3. MECW* vol. 37.

McCarthy, G.E., (1988). *Marx's Critique of Science and Positivism: The Methodological Foundations of Political Economy*. Dordrecht: Kluwer Academic.

Otani, T., Saito, K., and Graßmann, T., (2019). Einführung. In: Idem, eds, *MEGA²* *IV-18, Karl Marx Friedrich Engels. Exzerpte und Notizen. Februar 1964 bis Oktober 1868, November 1869, März, April, Juni 1970, Dezember 1872*. Berlin: Akademie Verlag. pp. 834–886.

Pawelzig, G., (1997). Zur Stellung des Stoffwechselsbegriffs im Denken von Karl Marx. In A. Griese and H.J. Sandkühler, eds, *Karl Marx – Zwischen Philosophie Und Naturwissenschaften*. Berlin: Peter Lang. pp. 129–150.

Postone, M., (1993). *Time, Labor and Social Domination: A Reinterpretation of Marx's Critical Theory*. Cambridge: Cambridge University Press.

Rabinbach, A.G., (1990). *The Human Motor: Energy, Fatigue, and the Rise of Modernity*. New York: Basic Books.

Raspail, F.V., (1825). *L'analyse microscopique et le développement de la fécule dans les céréales*. Paris: Imprimerie de Fain.

Saito, J., (2017). *Marx's Ecosocialism: Capitalism, Nature and the Unfinished Critique of Political Economy*. New York: Monthly Review Press.

Schleiden, M.J., and Schmid, E.E., (1850). *Encyclopädie der gesammten theoretischen Naturwissenschaften in ihrer Anwendung auf die Landwirthschaft*. Bd. 1–3. Braunschweig: Vieweg.

Schwann, T., (1847). *Microscopical Researches into the Accordance in the Structure and Growth of Animals and Plants*. London: Sydenham Society.

Sheasby, W.C., (2004). Karl Marx and the Victorians' nature: the evolution of a deeper view: Part two: The age of aquaria. *Capitalism, Nature, Socialism* 15(3). pp. 59–77.

Sraffa, P., (1960). *Production of Commodities by Means of Commodities*. Cambridge: Cambridge University Press.

Virchow, R., (1855). Cellular Pathologie. *Archiv für pathologische Anatomie und Physiologie und für klinische Medicin* 1. pp. 1–39.

Virchow, R., (1858). *Die Cellularpathologie in ihrer Begründung auf physiologische und pathologische Gewebenlehre*. Berlin: Georg Reimer.

Virchow, R., (1860). *Cellular Pathology as Based upon Physiological and Pathological Histology* (English trans. of 2nd German edition). New York: Robert M. De Witt.

Wendling, A.E., (2009). *Karl Marx on Technology and Alienation*. Basingstoke: Palgrave Macmillan.

5.   Absolute value

Riccardo Bellofiore

Marx's abstraction is not an invention but a discovery. It does not exist in Marx's head but in the commodity economy. It has not an imaginary existence, but a real social existence: so real that it can be cut, hammered, weighed, and coined. The abstract human labour discovered by Marx is, in its developed form, none other than money. (Luxemburg [1900] 2004, p. 150)

5.1   INTRODUCTION

Looking for the meaning of 'essay' in a dictionary, one finds as a suggestion something like 'initial and tentative effort on a particular topic, dealt from a personal point of view'.[1] This is what this chapter is. Though the subject – the relationship between value, money, and labour in Marx – has been discussed countless times, and though I have extensively written about it, I deal with it only from a limited (and even idiosyncratic) angle here. I investigate how Marx connected the notion of 'absolute value' with the question: *What is it?* What is it that makes labour the *unity* which is exhibited in money, through 'value' as the *universal power of exchangeability*? The main text that I am considering is Marx's critique of Bailey in the *Economic Manuscript of 1861–63*, in the part initially published as *Theories of Surplus Value (TSV)*.[2]

Mine is a chapter written in English and hence mainly devoted to those who read Marx in this language without at the same time having access to the original. This is a severe disadvantage to the understanding of the argument, and a liability in the debate. As I have argued at length elsewhere, I am convinced that almost all the translations of Marx in English need to be revised. This

---

[1]   This chapter is part of a much larger manuscript (*'What Is It?' Intrinsic Value, Absolute Value, and Exploitation*) where I consider Marx's trajectory in his investigation of absolute value. In that manuscript there is not only a more detailed interpretation of the texts on absolute value in the entire Marx's *oeuvre*, that here had to be brutally abridged, but also a more substantial review of the secondary literature.

[2]   Even though I quote from MEGA[2], where the manuscripts are in six volumes, I refer in the text to *TSV2* or *TSV3* according to the pages I am quoting in the English translation, to help readers to locate the argument.

problem, however, is more intensely acute in the only translation of *TSV* that we have (or at least that I know of). The same cannot be said about translations in other languages.

My perspective in what follows is that *Marx's* – note: neither Ricardo's nor Bailey's – notion of absolute value is the crucial theoretical intermediate link leading from *intrinsic* value to capital as value *in process*. Mine is partially also a self-criticism since, in the past, I wrongly identified 'intrinsic' with 'absolute' value, as most literature (both supportive or critical) does. I now think this identification is wrong and dangerous (my work on Sraffa and Marx alerted me to this). But, in fact, the elements to reach my conclusions in this chapter on the distinction between intrinsic and absolute value were already there in my past work. Moreover, my perpetual journey of reading, interpreting and reconstructing Marx – three very different endeavours, by the way – has been instrumental in allowing me to come to decipher these pages of *TSV*. Marx's pages on Bailey (on the background of what he argued in the *Grundrisse* and *Contribution*) are the preamble to understand the dialectical derivation of the form of value that *Capital*, in its various drafts, tried to pursue from 1867 onwards, never reaching a definitive formulation that satisfied him.

Another way to characterize this chapter is as an exercise in 'plagiarism'. In exposing Marx's statements, I stick to a close English rendition of his (mostly) German *TSV* text, alternative to the one available in English. 'Mostly' German, because Marx also partially writes directly in English; interestingly enough, even in this case, the English translation 'corrects' his English without notice. It is not plagiarism narrowly defined, for three reasons. First, I depart system-atically from the available English translation, and it would be impossible to specify my alterations continuously (though I will do that parsimoniously). Second, I freely interpolate changes where I think different formulations can sensibly portray more mature positions by Marx which are, however, already implicit in *TSV* (for example, I make explicit the distinction between 'value' and 'exchange value', sometimes evidencing it in brackets, even crossing out '(~~exchange~~) value', when I think value is at issue). Third, I elaborate on Marx's argument for clarification. Finally, when I believe that the indication of the German term behind my English translation could help the reader get a more profound comprehension, I do not refrain from adding the relevant word in brackets.

The structure of the chapter is as follows. In section 5.2, I summarize Marx's argument about absolute value in his critique of Bailey in *TSV*. In section 5.3, I provide some hints at how Marx's argument looks before and after *TSV*. In section 5.4, I maintain that 'exploitation' (in my understanding of the notion) is the proper answer to what is the *unity* allowing us to speak of a value theory of labour, thus suggesting an alternative way to ground the value theory *of labour*. A short Conclusion follows. In Appendix I, I give the conventions that I use to translate some of the more relevant and controversial expressions in Marx's text (though some key terms are discussed as the chapter unfolds). Finally, in Appendix II, I give a short survey of the secondary literature.

The 'interpretation' of Marx which I present here unveils the richness but also the blind alleys of his various attempts to answer the critical question he posed (*what is it?*). At the same time, it provides many elements useful to the 'reconstruction' of Marx's critique of the political economy, along the lines I have undertaken elsewhere, which is essential for the reader to understand my conclusions fully.

5.2   'WHAT IS IT?' MARX ON BAILEY IN THE 1861–63 *ECONOMIC MANUSCRIPT*

Marx deals with Bailey first in *TSV2*, discussing how Ricardo grasped 'absolute' and 'relative' value without a proper understanding of the 'form of value'.[3] Bailey's criticism of Ricardo's confusion about the determination (*Bestimmung*) of 'value' is also essential for our understanding. Ricardo begins from *relative values* (or 'exchangeable values'): behind the equivalence among commodities, there must be equality in 'substance' (*Substanz*), labour. *Because of that*, they are 'values' which are only different in 'magnitude' according to the amount they 'contain'.

This is the Ricardo with whom Marx establishes a (critical) relation of continuity. Ricardo, however, does not analyse the character of this 'labour': he does not look at the 'shape' (*Gestalt*) taken by labour, that is, the *particular* determination of it as it creates value and as it is exhibited (*darstellt*) in 'exchange value'. Misunderstanding the 'character' of this labour, he cannot figure out the internal connection between labour and money: that is, on the one hand, the *determination* of value through labour time; and on the other hand, how commodities necessarily *progress* into the 'formation' of money. These two limits account for his erroneous theory of money. The immediate exclusive interest in the magnitude of value induces Ricardo to disregard all the mediations.

For Ricardo, 'value in exchange' is first specified as the relative power of purchasing other *goods*, as in Bailey. It corresponds to how value is manifested phenomenally (*erscheint*) in circulation. However, this definition is soon overcome by 'comparative value': 'exchangeable value' of commodities depends on the *labour* time *relatively* bestowed in producing them. Relative value may remain the same if the 'absolute' *difficulty of producing* commod-

---

[3]   The reference is here to Marx [1861–63] (1978) – MEGA[2] II/3.3, especially at pp. 815–825. See MECW 31, pp. 394–399.

ities (assessed in their separate productive processes) changes proportionally. Marx also attributes to Ricardo a definition of 'absolute value' according to which this is a specific kind of comparative or relative value. The relative or comparative value, thus conceived, as the real exhibition (*realen Darstellung*) of the exchange value of one commodity in the use value of another *or* in money, as if unmasking the comparative determination by labour, is labelled by Ricardo as *absolute value*. Note that Ricardo's absolute value, as long as it offers to our view the comparative changes in labour time, is nevertheless a *relative* concept, which is also named by him as 'real value' or value 'as such' (*schlechthin*).

In this discourse, Bailey only finds 'contradictions' and raises objections because Ricardo regards value *not* as a relation between *objects*, but as a 'positive' result produced by a definite quantity of labour: in this sense, Ricardo would see value as something both intrinsic *and* absolute.[4] In other words, Bailey ascribes to Ricardo the same *identification* of intrinsic value with absolute value too often attributed to Marx as a characteristic pertaining to the *single* commodity, independently *from* commodity exchange, and arising from production *in isolation*. This complaint is not without reason because of Ricardo's faulty exposition, due to his neglect of the investigation into the determinate *form* taken by labour as abstract-universal (*abstrakt-allgemeinen*) and social, and the fact that he only gives attention to the magnitude of value. However, what Bailey does not see is precisely that the *relativity* of the concept of value is in no way eliminated because all commodities, as values, are looked at by Ricardo as proportional 'expressions' (*Ausdrucke*) of social labour time.

Indeed, the relativity in question is not merely about the ratio of the exchange of *each* commodity with *one* another. Instead, it refers to the relation between *all of them* and the *social labour* as their substance (*Substanz*). In fact, Marx attributes Ricardo aspects of his position and, of course, comments that this is correct. Ricardo must be criticized for quite the opposite reason: because he almost always conceives only 'relative' or 'comparative' values (even though as ratios of distinct labour amounts) and forgets 'absolute value'.[5]

In *TSV3*, with very few exceptions, Marx uses the term 'unity' (*Einheit*) instead of 'substance', and he goes deeper in his understanding of 'absolute value' as opposed to Ricardo's. Before illustrating this, I have to refer to the *TSV2* pages where Marx advances a first opinion on Ricardo's search for an *invariable standard of value*. His first take on this issue is quite dismissive.[6] He writes that Section VI, *On an invariable measure of value*, deals with the

---

4   Marx [1861–63] (1976) – MEGA² II/3.1, p. 90. See MECW 30, pp. 101–102.
5   Marx [1861–63] (1978) – MEGA² II/3.3, p. 825. See MECW 31, p. 399.
6   Marx [1861–63] (1978) – MEGA² II/3.3, p. 850. See MECW 31, p. 426.

measure of value without giving any significant contribution. The connection between value, its 'immanent' measure through (*durch*)[7] labour time, and the necessity of an 'external' measure of commodity values, is not understood, nor is it even raised as a question. A *perfect* measure of value – that is, a standard assessing the *absolute* (unchanging in time) difficulty of production of commodities in terms of labour time – could be a 'divining rod' to assess in which commodity a change in relative price originates. Unfortunately, due to the unequal time structure of production, that is not enough to construct an invariable measure of value: assuming a uniform rate of profit and unchanged labour content, wage variations determine modifications of the relative prices of commodities. Ricardo recognizes that a measure of value of this kind is 'perfect' only for the commodities produced with precisely the same production conditions. For Marx, Ricardo's is not an adequate discussion, and in no way does it allow the construction of an invariable money medium.

Let us move then to Marx's discussion of Bailey on Ricardo in *TSV3*. Here Marx evaluates the limits and merits of Bailey's main point of attack against Ricardo's whole system. The indictment is of having transformed value, which is always relative, into something 'absolute'. In Marx's view, the problem stems from the failure to distinguish the different and successive *moments* of 'value'. The value must be grasped as a *processual* concept *in movement* which cannot be frozen in any of its determinations. Marx sets apart the inquiry about the *quantitative* relation between commodities in circulation from the 'display' (*Darstellung*) of value itself. The existence of the (intrinsic) value of commodities cannot be shown by their *particular* use value: it must appear in their expression in *other* use values; that is, in the relation in which these *other* use values exchange for those commodities. This is clarified by Marx himself in English (I have reinstated here his original, discarding the 'corrections' by the translator, which are recorded in square brackets):

> If we speak of the *value in exchange* for a thing, we *mean* the *relative quantities* of every [all] other commodity that can be exchanged with the first commodity. But, on further consideration, we shall find that for the proportion, in which one thing exchanges with an infinitive [infinite] mass of other things, which have nothing at all in common with it ... all those various heterogeneous things must be considered as proportionate representations, expressions of the *same* common *unity*, [of] an element quite different from their natural existence or appearances. We shall then furthermore find that if our meaning has any sense, the value of a commodity is something by which it not only differs from or is related to other commodities but is a *quality* by which it differs from its own existence as a thing, a value in use.[8]

---

[7] In the English translation the 'through' is omitted, and becomes 'i.e.'.
[8] Marx [1861–63] (1979) – MEGA² II/3.4, p. 1316. See MECW 32, pp. 315–316.

Marx's argument against Bailey here is that what is 'absolute' – that is, *independent* – is use value. Value is instead *posited* (by living labour) in a certain relation to socially necessary equal labour time. Value, therefore, is eminently *relative*: so much so that its magnitude varies if the labour time to reproduce that commodity is altered compared to what was required for its own production. Marx then defines Bailey as a *fetishist* since he attributes the social 'power of exchangeability' to things as *natural* objects, even though he does that referring not to the *individual* commodity but to all of them *in concert*, so to speak:

> I mentioned that it is characteristic of labour based on the private exchange that the social character of labour is exhibited [*darstellt*] in an upside-down way [*verkehrt*] – as the property of things [*Dinge*]; that a social relation is manifested phenomenally [*erscheint*] as a relation between things (between *products, values in use, commodities*). This form of manifestation (*Erscheinung*) is accepted as something effective [*etwas wirkliches*] by our fetish-worshipper, and he, in fact, believes that their properties determine the exchange value of things *as things* and is altogether *a natural property* of things.[9]

Marx too stresses the relation: not between things, like Bailey; not of the commodities exchanged against a supposedly invariable standard, like Ricardo; rather, *as exhibitions of portions of social labour in commodity circulation.* In this relation, things are *not* independent (*selbständiges*) and hence 'autonomous' entities: they are instead outer *expressions* of the way social production is internally organized. This requires investigating the movement of value *from the inner to the outer* in concert with the one about the exhibition of value in the *co-determination* of commodity production and commodity circulation. In fact, for Marx, the two perspectives, though distinct, refer to the same conceptual determination of what value is.

The claim that value, being relative, *is not* to be devised as an *entity* does *not* dispense altogether with a concept of 'absolute value'. *Quite the opposite*: it opens the way to the proper construction of this notion in Marx, in a formulation coherent with his articulation of the couple fetish character/fetishism. This latter distinction is crucial for Marx's strategy of showing that the *Darstellung* (exhibition) of value is, at the same time, an *Offenbarung* (revelation)[10] of the human practice embedded in value itself.

Marx makes the case that in exchange, commodities must impart to their value a separate or autonomous (*selbstständigen*) 'being-there', which is different from and independent of (*verschiednen und unabhängig*) the body of

---

9   Marx [1861–63] (1979) – MEGA² II/3.4, p. 1317. See MECW 32, p. 317.
10   The term, with theological overtones, is about an identity revealing at the end of exposition an identity between form and content, and between external and internal.

their own use values. Commodity circulation must evolve into the formation (*Bildung*) of money. How does money 'grow out of' commodities? First of all, through the 'imagined' anticipation in price: this is properly speaking a *Vorstellung*, a 'representation'. Commodities to be exchanged are *ex ante notionally* 'materialized' in the body of money against which they are sold.[11] They are now all *one* in the *same* identical 'form' of labour: as such, they are discrete amounts of a unitary substance. Marx emphasizes that the *Einheit*, the unity, is *anterior* to the actual commodity exchange on the market.

Marx's claim that commodities are *already* presupposed to be equal in a 'third' (even *before* final circulation) – so that they are just different amounts of an identical unity – does *not* refer to some objectified value either a produced commodity or an invariable measure of value. His perspective is detailed in this dense quote:

> [T]he labour which constitutes the unity [*Einheit*][12] of value is not only homogeneous, simple, average labour; it is the labour of a private individual exhibited in a determinate product. But, as value, the product must be the embodiment of *social* labour [*Verkörperung der gesellschaftlichen Arbeit*] and, as such, be immediately convertible from one use value into any other. (The determinate use value in which labour is immediately exhibited so that it can be converted from one form into another is irrelevant.) Thus, the *private labour* has to be immediately exhibited as its opposite, *social* labour; the labour thus transformed as its immediate opposite is *abstract universal labour*, which is therefore exhibited in a universal equivalent. Only through this alienation/externalisation [*Veräusserung*] individual labour is exhibited as its opposite. The commodity, however, must have this universal expression before it is alienated/externalised [*bevor sie veräussert ist*]. This necessity to exhibit individual labour as universal labour is equivalent to the necessity of exhibiting a commodity as money.[13] The commodity receives this exhibition in so far as money serves as a measure of value, and it is an expression of the value of the commodity, in its *price*. It is only through sale (i.e., its actual metamorphosis into money), that the commodity acquires its adequate expression as exchange value.[14] The first transformation is just a theoretical process, the second is an actual one.[15]

---

[11] It anticipates in thought a *Materiatur* (see Appendix I).

[12] In the English translation *Einheit*, 'unity', becomes 'substance'.

[13] The reader is alerted that when I refer to this notion by Marx I use the expression 'money as a commodity', to express that in Marx money is an excluded commodity *unlike* any other, distinguishing it from the Ricardian and neoclassical theories, where money is a commodity *like* any other.

[14] According to the argument of this chapter, the point Marx is making is that the (intrinsic) value of the commodity is eventually expressed in 'absolute value' as exchange value. If this fails, the product is not a commodity but just a use value.

[15] Marx [1861–63] (1979) – MEGA² II/3.4, p. 1322. See MECW 32, p. 323.

In the context I am discussing, Marx is playing on an alternative meaning of *Veräusserung*, which is 'divestment' and 'undressing', an *externalization*.[16] More specifically, it refers to a kind of *disembodiment* of the ghostly objectivity of value from the individual *internal* objectification of labour within the commodity. Value as the 'soul' of that commodity is released, and it seizes the use value of money as its own external 'body'. It is precisely a 'possession' like in a gothic novel: the *coming into being* of the ghost of value in the body of money as a commodity. That is why 'money as money' is defined by Marx as *value embodied*. It is a *fetish* (or, better, *the* Fetish), *truly* socially endowed with social powers. However, these social powers are *mistakenly* assumed to belong to things *as if* by nature, which is a *fetishist* illusion. The labour of individuals is exhibited in the universal equivalent as its opposite: it is a social, abstract, and universal labour displayed through a process involving reification *and* thingification.[17]

Even though it is only through a sale that the commodity eventually becomes 'exchange value', the commodity develops an universal expression of value being sold. This occurs through money as *a measure of value* in its price. It is a *Verwandlung*: a metamorphosis, a change of shape, as if by supernatural means. The commodity as (intrinsic) value must be converted into money,[18] which is the *immediately social* 'embodiment' (in the universal equivalent) of abstractly universal social labour. As such, all commodities have an identical form, possess the same shape, and manifest themselves phenomenally as the immediate incarnation (*Inkarnation*) of social labour. As soon as it is sold, the commodity is transfigured into money. Then, value – thanks precisely to this *dual* movement of *externalization* (from the commodity) and *possession* (its embodiment, *Verkörperung*, in gold as money) – now holds an autonomous existence, separate from its use value. It now is *absolute* value.

In money as *absolute value*, the 'being-there' of value as a given amount of social labour time is achieved. Marx insists that in this 'absolute' *echangeabilité* that the commodity possesses as money, in its 'absolute' efficiency as *valeur d'echange* (which, he stresses, has nothing to do with the magnitude of value), no quantitative determination is shown: only qualitative identity. The processual development of the commodity makes its value self-sufficient and really exhibits it in 'free shape' (*freier Gestalt*)[19], as an *outer* 'exchange value' alongside the 'use value' in which it is embedded, and this is already ideally

---

[16]   Arthur (1986, pp. 147–148), is useful about the translation of *Veräusserung*.
[17]   For the difference between 'reification' and 'thingification', related to the difference between *Sache* and *Ding* (see Appendix I), see Tairako (2017).
[18]   It is a *Verwandlung*: a change of form.
[19]   The English translation as 'separate aspect' (MECW 32, p. 324) does not convey the idea of what Marx is claiming here.

anticipated in its price (tag). This conclusion is valid *only* because money is a commodity, though an excluded commodity: as such, it can be exchanged immediately against any other commodity.

While Bailey chastises 'absolute value' as a *scholastic* invention of Ricardo, which denies the relationality of value, and thinks that it has to be categorically rejected, Marx goes in the opposite direction and radicalizes the notion in ways forbidden to Ricardo. 'Absolute value', for Marx, is the effective separation of the intrinsic values, which (to begin with) are *cut away* from the commodities bearing them, and (afterwards) are *embodied* in the exterior use value of money as a commodity. *Absolute* 'value' is then nothing but the independent exhibition of intrinsic value through money as a *real abstraction*.[20]

In Ricardo, it is very different: absolute value refers to the 'comparative value' between each and every commodity and the standard, while the latter is conceived as the *invariable* measure of value. Marx insists instead on the claim that the *variability* of the standard *cannot* be avoided. Though it may be thought of as an 'imperfection' of the standard, its variability *necessarily* arises from the fact that (the *intrinsic* value of) the commodity needs to be expressed *relatively* in an exhibition which *posits* the commodity to be sold as 'equal' to money as *another* commodity: it is as commodities that they share the same *unity*, and are thus qualitatively *identical*. Being a commodity (though a very special, 'excluded' one), money *must* by definition be of a *changeable* value. This *qualitative* aspect is crucial and fundamental. Hence, Marx's version of the labour theory of value does not have room for an invariable standard of value.

In his *TSV3* comments on Bailey and Ricardo it is already clear that Marx's conceptualization of 'autonomous value' becomes even sharper when it progresses from the notion of *money* to that of *value-in-process*, namely, *capital*. 'Capital', as the relation between value as the *presupposition* (*vorausgesezten Werth*) of the process of production, and value as resulting (*resultirenden Werth*) or *posited*, is the overgrasping/dominating Subject determining the entire capitalist production process (*Übergreifende und Bestimmende des ganzen capitalistischen Productionsproceß*).[21] The condition for value-as-capital to reproduce itself and increase in a spiral as value-in-process (*processirender*

---

[20] The point was clear to Luxemburg ([1900] 2004), as the epigraph to this chapter confirms.

[21] Marx [1861–63] (1979) – MEGA² II/3.4, p. 1318. See MECW 32, p. 318. Maybe this is one of the occasions in which the English translation (p. 318) can be commended – even though *Darstellung* is translated as 'expression' and *processirenden* as 'dynamic', both questionable choices. On the contrary, 'all-embracing and decisive' is close enough to the idea of what Marx means for *Capital* as *the* Subject. All this reappears conspicuously at the beginning of Chapter 4 of *Capital I*.

Werth) is to measure its own growth in *a common monetary standard*, notwith-standing the changes in the multifarious physical components which serve as the bodies (*die ihm als Leiber dienen*). And that – Marx argues against Bailey – *exactly requires that relative value is converted into value as an absolute*.

Suppose my interpretation is not too far off the mark. In that case, it follows that it would be spectacularly wrong to argue that Marx withheld altogether from a concept of absolute value because value is relative, although this may seem counterintuitive. As a matter of fact, Marx writes: 'If commodities exchange themselves in the relation in which they exhibit the same amount of labour-time, then their being-there [*Dasein*] as objectified labour-time, their being-there [*Dasein*] as embodied labour-time, is their *unity*, their *identical* element.'[22] The indication about the *embodiment* through labour time means that the identity of commodities as bearers of value is exposed when the (abstract) labour time *objectified* in the commodities is already mirrored in the (concrete) labour time *embodied* in money as *absolute value*.[23] They exhibit an identical quality; but this, Marx insists, gives no immediate quantitative determination.

The *relativity* of value may be understood in opposite alternative ways. Like in Bailey, it can be conceived as the ratio of exchange *between the use values* of the commodities traded. Marx instead portrays it as the quantitative proportion among their *absolute values* as relative *shares* of a common 'third' something. In this case, Marx argues directly in English that it is not the rate at which two commodities exchange that determines their value, as Bailey thinks, but rather the other way around: their value determines the rate at which they exchange.[24] For value, he means here the 'absolute' value: that is, their 'intrin-sic' value, *if* and *when* expressed and exhibited in money as *exchange value*. The 'immanent measure' of commodities is what *expresses* in circulation (as an inner–outer movement from production) the *unity* between commodity and money since they are *both* objectifications of living labour in production.

Marx writes (once again, in English): 'the *absolute* expression of its *rel-ative* value would be its expression *in time of labour*, and by this absolute expression it would be expressed as something relative, but in the absolute relation, by which it *is* value'.[25] It is a crucial passage. The internal connection of an individual commodity with the others in terms of labour time must be

---

[22]   Marx [1861–63] (1979) – MEGA[2] II/3.4, p. 1315. See MECW 32, p. 315.

[23]   As I have shown elsewhere (e.g. Bellofiore 2014), *abstract* labour is 'contained' (from *enthalten*), while *concrete* labour is 'embodied' (from *verkörpern*). Also see Appendix I. This is particularly relevant to understand the dialectical derivation of the form of value.

[24]   Marx [1861–63] (1979) – MEGA[2] II/3.4, p. 1319. See MECW 32, p. 319.

[25]   Marx [1861–63] (1979) – MEGA[2] II/3.4, p. 1320. See MECW 32, p. 320.

determined as an *absolute* expression of *relative* value, since in this way the relativity between the commodities does reveal them as *portions* of the *social* totality of *dissociated* labour. On the one hand, one is here reminded of Saint Bonaventure: *omne respectivum fundatur super aliquo absoluto*: that is, everything relative (*respectivus* and *relativus* are equivalent) is founded on something absolute.[26] On the other hand, the reference is to Kant. In a bourgeois society as *ungesellige Geselligkeit* ('unsocial sociability'), the social relationships among human beings are detached from themselves, reified in a thing and turned into a fetish.[27]

It is exactly in this 'absolute' relation that the commodity *is* value, not just a product or use value. Absolute does not mean 'non-relative' but 'made separate from' (*ab*) and 'detached' (*solvere*). As André Doz observes, 'the word *absolutus* itself says a relation'.[28] For Marx, the adjective 'absolute' refers to the two following entwined circumstances. First, the commodity, beyond being use value, *is* 'value'; but it is value only as long as it *materializes* as 'exchange value' in *another* commodity. In this way, the value within the commodity is *separated* (or 'abstracted') from the use value of that commodity itself and enters into a relation where money becomes an *embodied value*, the 'body of value' (*als verkörperter Werth, als Werthkörper*), as Marx writes in *Capital I*.[29] Second, and in the same movement, this same peculiar kind of sociality between the isolated producers is *separated* (or abstracted) from them and controls them. 'Absolute' refers not only to this 'detachment' but also to the *consequent* 'despotic command'. The abstracted moment (here, the 'form' of money as absolute value) is considered in the relativity with the correlativity from which the process of isolation and separation begins (here, the form of the *commodity*, inseparable from its own use value). 'Absolute' refers to developing value into *an overgrasping and self-reproducing totality*.

Marx, who in *TSV2* was so critical about the search by Ricardo of an 'invariable standard of value', has now something favourable to say about it. He writes that Ricardo often sounds, and sometimes actually speaks, as if 'the quantity of labour' were a solution to the false or misplaced problem of an 'unvariable

---

[26] As quoted in Doz (1996, p. 8). Bonaventure from Bagnoregio was a Franciscan, living from 1217 to 1274.

[27] The Kantian concept of *ungesellige Geselligkeit*, 'unsocial sociability', that characterizes bourgeois society and capital, is crucial in Lucio Colletti. See Colletti ([1969] 1972, pp. 159–160), for a long quote from the fourth and fifth theses of the *Idea of a Universal History from a Cosmopolitan Point of View* (1784).

[28] See the article quoted before: Doz (1996, p. 8).

[29] Marx [1872] (1987) – MEGA II/6, p. 84. See also MECW 35, p. 62; Penguin edition, p. 143.

measure of values'. This 'false semblance' (*false Schein*)[30] stems from the fact that, as Marx already suggested, Ricardo did not grasp that the *single* labour must exhibit itself as abstract *universal* labour and, in this form, as (a specific kind of) social labour. To understand how this *Darstellung* becomes possible, Ricardo should have figured out how the *formation* of money is connected with the *essence* of value and with its *determination* through labour time: and this, in my interpretation, is *exactly* what is implied by absolute value as *embodied value*. Bailey's objection has the merit of dispelling the confusion between money as the outer 'measure' exhibiting value (with money being a commodity mirroring other commodities), and the immanent measure of the substance of value.[31] Nevertheless, he fails to recognize in money the conversion or transfiguration (*Verwandlung*) of value. Marx will rephrase the same concept in *Capital I*, arguing that this transformation is *transubstantiation*: the *sensible* body of gold (as money) is changed over into the embodiment of the *supra-sensible* soul of the commodity, externalized and incarnated in the excluded commodity. The conclusion in *TSV3* is that Bailey stops at the mere superficial consideration of the measure of value: this latter, being an external (*äusseren*) one, *already presupposes value*.

Marx's point is that Ricardo never asks the proper question. The fact of being posited as equal means that there should be something in common between the commodities exchanged:

> The *unity* of the two commodities A and B is, at the first view, their exchangeability. They are 'exchangeable' objects. As 'exchangeable' objects they are magnitudes *of the same denomination*. But *this 'their' existence* as an 'exchangeable' object *must be different from their existence as values in use*. ***What is it?***[32]

Value is *the* 'power of purchasing', yet purchasing presupposes not only value but money itself; therefore, presenting the issue in this way implies that the externalization of value into money is aborted or inverted. Yes, value is a *relation*. Nevertheless, Marx thinks that in the commodity unquestionably, something *intrinsic* and *positive* is acting as a 'power' in exchange. 'Value'

---

[30]   Note how the adjective, 'false', reinforces the noun, 'semblance', resulting in something like a 'deceiving pretence'. Marx's intent is to proclaim that the quantitative determination of labour has *nothing to do* with 'measuring' value against an unchanging benchmark.

[31]   Marx [1861–63] (1979) – MEGA² II/3.4, p. 1324. See MECW 32, pp. 324–325.

[32]   Marx [1861–63] (1979) – MEGA² II/3.4, p. 1345. See MECW 32, pp. 346–347. Marx is here writing directly in English. I put the interrogation 'what is it?' in italic for emphasis. It is the key question of this chapter, and in fact the primary and ultimate subject-matter involved in Marx's (monetary) value theory of labour, distinguishing it from any other value theory.

must be found *before* expressing it. This power is not to be found *in the use value dimension*, in its particularity. Marx compares commodities *in the value dimension* to points in the space dimension. Supposing that both commodities which are exchanged are contained in this value dimension:

> If we speak of the distance as a relation between two things, we suppose something 'intrinsic', some 'property' of the things themselves, which enables them to be distant from each other ... we speak of their difference in space. Thus we suppose both of them to be contained in the space, to be points of the space. Thus we equalize them as being both existences of the space, and only *after* having them equalized *sub specie spatii* we distinguish them as different points of space. To belong to space is their unity.[33]

The unity which Marx is speaking about cannot be traced back to 'utility'; neither to some relation that commodities entertain with each other as *natural* things, nor as some relation which they have as natural things to *human needs*. It is not the *degree* of their utility that determines the quantities in which they exchange.[34] I interpret Marx as arguing that, like distance, value is a relation, but at the same time, it is something distinct from that relation and the 'absolute' ground of that relation. If exchange value as the *expression* of a commodity's value requires *another* commodity, both must be part of that *common* space. Then, once more, the question: *what is this 'unity', their 'identity', that something by which they become exchangeable, in a certain amount?*

Marx thinks that *within* the commodity a value 'in itself' can be discovered only in relation to 'social labour' considered as 'another thing'. As long as commodities are produced not as objects of direct consumption but as bearers of value, they are a kind of 'cheque' on a given quantity of *all* the exhibitions of social labour, and they are all *forced* to give themselves, *as values*, a form of existence *distinct* from their existence as use values. The formation of money

---

[33] Marx [1861–63] (1979) – MEGA² II/3.4, pp. 1328–1329. See MECW 32, p. 330. Marx is again writing directly in English.

[34] Here Marx is too quick in rejecting a subjective utility theory of value. I agree with Napoleoni (1976, p. 55), my translation from the Italian original:

> In the first chapter of *Capital*, Volume I, Marx arrives at determining value as objectified labour through a process that can give the impression of successive elimination of various characteristics of commodities, so that, in the end, there remains, as a residue, the fact, precisely, that they are products of labour. If this were indeed the case, it would certainly be right the traditional objection according to which one cannot see why one should choose labour, rather than, for example, utility: if they are all products of labour, commodities are also all useful. Marx's problem is not one of identifying a note that all commodities have in common, and then abstracting it from all the others ... It is instead of identifying what the commodity is in a historically determined social function.

is brought about as the development of the labour contained in commodities as tentatively social labour: the inner–outer movement, the movement of 'expression'. Marx is transparent that for him it is the development of *their* value which necessarily brings with it the formation of money: the *independent* form of 'being-there' of (value as) exchange value (*selbstständige Daseinsformen des Tauschwerth*).[35]

Bailey is right that money, as an extrinsic measure of value, is perfectly adequate to the task: the problem of the 'invariable measure of value' *disappears*, since money, as the exclusive third, *must* be of variable value. But he erroneously infers from this that the inquiry about the *concept* of value and the problem of its *determination* are meaningless. For him, value is the same as (any arbitrary) relative price, and there is no difference between the price of a commodity expressed in money or in whatever other commodity. But all these myriads of relative prices are just *particular* expressions of the same value, while money price is the *universal* expression of it. In other words, Bailey is right in saying that money need not be a commodity of *invariable* value; but he wrongly concludes that no independent determination of value, *distinct from the commodity itself*, is necessary. Ricardo's vain quest for the 'invariable measure of values' concealed the search for the concept of value itself, and Bailey's attack against Ricardo is based on an untenable identification between *determination* and *measure* of value. The value of commodities is a *result*, and it is inherently 'changeable': (abstract) labour is the activity *constituting* value and is not a commodity; it is instead a *fluid* which is objectified in variable amounts.

The closing stage of Marx's arguments, wrapping up his perspective vis-à-vis Bailey (and Ricardo), can be once again paraphrased following his own statement in English very closely.[36] First, the inquiry must:

> [find] the value, *before* expressing it; finding in what way the values in use, so different from each other, fall under the common category and denomination of *values*, so that the value of the one may be expressed in the other. Moreover, [i]f the values of different commodities are expressed in the same third commodity, however variable its value may be, it is of course very easy to compare these *expressions*, already possessed of a common denomination.

---

[35]   Marx [1861–63] (1979) – MEGA² II/3.4, p. 1329. See MECW 32, p. 331.
[36]   Marx [1861–63] (1979) – MEGA² II/3.4, p. 1343. See MECW 32, p. 345.

The difficulty consists in equalizing a commodity with any portion of another, and:

> this is only possible if a common unity exists for them because they are different representations[37] of the same unity. If all commodities are to be expressed in gold, [as] money, the difficulty remains the same. There must be a common unity between gold and each of the other commodities ... They are equivalents: they are both *equal* expressions of values ... only different or equal in quantity, but always quantities of the same quality. The difficulty is to find this quality.

After this quality is unearthed, and the value of commodities is given as their common unity,[38] measuring or expressing their relative value becomes the same thing, as Bailey maintains. But, contrary to Bailey's views, *estimating* value is *not* expressing it, and one does not arrive at 'expression' until one arrives at a unit *distinct* from the *immediate* being-there of commodities.

The theoretical perspective is unambiguous. The reference to 'quantity of labour' is sensible in the *genetical* inquiry about the nature of value, while the reference to 'value' concerns values sought as an external measure of value. In the latter case, the issue concerns the monetary expression of value as *part* of its 'exhibition'. In the former case, the issue concerns the *cause* of value, which is *independent of* and *presupposed to* the 'exhibition'. Labour as the immanent measure of value *transforms* use values into value; money as the extrinsic measure *presupposes* the existence of value, as distinct from that commodity's use value. Gold, for example, can only measure the value of cotton if gold and cotton, as values, possess a unity that is distinct from both as use values. Once money, as a measure of value, develops into the standard of price, money *presupposes* the *theoretical* transformation from the commodity to money: if the values of all commodities are exhibited as money prices, they can be compared; in fact, they are *already* compared through 'representation'.

This is followed in *TSV3* by a clear description of the exchange process as based on a *real* and *practically 'objective'* (that is, not a conceptual and psychologically 'subjective') *abstraction* acting behind the back of the producers. The same circumstances (independent of the mind, although acting on it) that compel producers to sell their products as commodities give them an *exchange value* that also, for their minds, is independent of their use value. This is, I think, an allusion to money as *embodied* and *absolute* value. At this point, thanks to this separation and autonomization of value, the producers'

---

[37] Marx uses 'to represent' for his own *darstellen*. This gives pause for thought for those who (like me) are very insistent on the need to find the proper English rendition of Marx's German terminology.

[38] The English translation for *gemeinschaiftliche Einheit* has been 'common entity' (MECW 32, p. 345). Entity is not a synonym of unity.

consciousness may well ignore the existence of what determines value; the fundamental thing is that they find themselves placed within relationships that determine their mind without them having to know, just like everyone can use money as money, without knowing what money is.

5.3   'WHERE TO HAVE IT?' IMMATERIAL SUBSTANCES AND TANGIBLE THINGS

I have no space here to go into Marx's confrontation with Bailey before and after the *1861–63 Economic Manuscript*, hence I will limit myself to a quick sketch. Bailey is not there in the *1844 Economic and Philosophical Paris Manuscripts*. He is mostly mentioned in the *Grundrisse* (Marx [1857–58] 1973) about specific monetary issues. Discussing Ricardo, Marx asserts that the notion of 'absolute value' is *nonsense*.[39] However, he quotes from Sismondi[40] that trade has separated the 'shadow' from the 'body' and has introduced the possibility of *possessing them separately*. In the last pages of the *Grundrisse*, dealing with 'money as money',[41] Marx writes that during international crises, gold and silver in their metallic form are the '*absolute* means of payment' and the '*absolute* equivalent': they are value *für sich seiender* (which is 'being-for-itself').[42] This reference to absolute value when discussing money as money will return in all later writings (and I will not follow this recurrence).

In *A Contribution to the Critique of Political Economy* (1859) the argument about 'absolute value' is expanded and deepened. At this theoretical juncture, there is an apparently contradictory vicious circle, as Marx himself admits. The (exchange) value of the commodity has been first introduced as *our* abstraction, or in the consciousness of exchanging producers. Still, it can *actually* exist *only* in circulation, where commodities relate *to one another*. To display itself as exchange value, as *objectified* universal labour time, the commodity must pass through *disembodiment* of its use value. *However*, this 'externalization' *already* presupposes its *being-there* as an exchange value. While it *latently* exists in commodities, *nevertheless* social labour time reveals

---

[39]   Marx [1857–58] (1981) – MEGA² II/1.2, p. 455. See MECW 29, p. 480. Penguin, p. 560.
[40]   Marx [1857–58] (1976) – MEGA² II/1.1, p. 144. See MECW 28, p. 144. Penguin, p. 217.
[41]   Marx [1857–58] (1981) – MEGA² II/1.2, pp. 733–734. This is from a Miscellaneous section (*Vermischtes*).
[42]   Hegel [1831] (2010), pp. 126–127: 'something is for itself inasmuch as it sublates otherness, sublates its connection and community with other, has rejected them by abstracting from them'.

itself only in their exchange process.[43] Commodities must enter the process of exchange as objectified universal labour time; yet, the objectification of the private labour time of individual producers as universal is itself only the result of the exchange process.

Many traits of the 'absolute value', as I spotted it in *TSV*, are anticipated, but in *A Contribution* money as a commodity looks like a way to solve 'practically' a theoretical difficulty, which in any case continued to trouble Marx afterwards. Marx writes that in prices all commodities strive for gold as money as the *universal commodity*,[44] the latter being exactly a term he borrows from Bailey, as his *Index* confirms.[45] As the *absolute* form of value in exchange and as the universal means of payment money is 'the absolute commodity of contracts', as Bailey again writes in *Money and its Vicissitudes*.[46]

In August–November 1858, before finalizing *A Contribution*, Marx wrote the Notebooks later known as the *Urtext* (*Fragment des Urtextes von Zur Kritik der politischen Ökonomie*). Notebook 'B' has on its cover the phrase: 'As means of payment, money – money for itself – should stand for value as such; in fact, however, it is only an identical quantum of variable value'. MECW editorial comment rightly identifies this as Marx's 'free personal summary' of some of Bailey's points in *Money and Its Vicissitudes*.[47] Marx's (versus Ricardo's) notion of absolute value is unmistakably delineated. In the *Urtext*, there are important integrations to *A Contribution*'s argument: on the phenomenal manifestation of the law of appropriation in simple circulation; and on the transition from money (as money) to capital. The absolutization of value is depicted as the condition where society must exist vis-à-vis separated individuals in the form of money as an equally independent, external, accidental, reified relation. It is a relation expressed as the *palpably subjectivized* universal commodity, hence as a *tangible thing*.[48] When money (as absolute

---

[43]   Marx [1857–61] (1980) – MEGA² II/2, for example at p. 120. See MECW 29, pp. 282–283.

[44]   Marx [1857–61] (1980) – MEGA² II/2, p. 212. See MECW 29, p. 289. See also Marx [1857–58] (1981) – MEGA² II/1.2, p. 162 (MECW 29, p. 328): 'It is the "beyond" of the commodities because in their *alienation as externalization* the *bodies* of their use-values *leap over* to the side of money, while their soul, which is [~~exchange~~] value, *jump within gold* as money itself.'

[45]   Marx [1857–61] (1980) – MEGA² II/2, p. 3; See MECW 29, p. 421. But see the entire *Index to the 7 Notebooks*.

[46]   Marx [1857–61] (1980) – MEGA² II/2, p. 206: 'Money is the general commodity of contract, or that in which the majority of bargains about property, to be completed at a future time, are made. [Samuel Bailey, *Money and its Vicissitudes*, London, 1837, p. 3]' See, MECW 29, both at p. 189 and p. 376.

[47]   Fn 105 at p. 549, which is about the quote in MECW 29, p. 508.

[48]   Marx [1857–61] (1980) – MEGA² II/2, pp. 53–54. See MECW 29, p. 468.

value) stands opposite commodities, it is a 'purely fantastic' *and* 'material' existence.[49] The emphasis is increasingly on the process behind value 'in becoming': a sort of dynamic version of the 'absolutization' of value, *detached from any fixed shape.*

Capital value must remain qualitatively identical in the different phases of the circuit so that a quantitative comparison can be made, which is what Bailey does not understand in his criticism of Ricardo. At this point, 'absolute' takes on another connotation deriving from its etymological origin in the Latin verb *absolvere*, turned into the German *absolvieren*: something differentiated, accomplishing its end, reaching perfection, and becoming One.

Both money and commodities are nothing but *objectified* labour; thereby, the 'third' must be *not-objectified* labour: labour *as subjectivity*. This is the second crucial theme of the last section of the *Urtext*. On this major integration to the argument in *A Contribution*, I will return near the Conclusion of this chapter. For now, I want to stress that to understand Marx's discourse about 'intrinsic value' and 'absolute value' as distinct though related notions, it is mandatory to go through the logical structure of the first section of Volume I of *Capital*. Mostly I will refer to the 1872 second German edition since I cannot elaborate on other versions for space reasons.

At the beginning, we find the commodity, as a *singularity*, articulated in an 'inner duality', where the body of the product to be sold on the market (its use value) is declared to be the bearer of an exchange value. Exchange values, at first, are phenomenally manifested (*erscheint*) as the quantitative ratios in which 'physical' use values are traded, according to proportions which seem (*scheint*) somewhat arbitrary, depending on the perpetual fluctuations of supply and demand. This is exactly the view of Bailey as a 'vulgar' political economist: an 'intrinsic value', a *valeur intrinsèque* (that is, an inner 'exchange value', immanent *within* the commodity), would be a *contradictio in adiecto*, because the adjective predicates something contradictory with the noun. Marx clearly disagrees and qualifies this opinion as a 'semblance' (*Schein*). This unfolds a problem-setting leading to a second, more appropriate, definition of 'exchange value': the *exteriorization* of a communal identity positing commodities as homogeneous and immanent to them, which is phenomenally manifested in exchange value.[50]

---

[49]   Marx [1857–61] (1980) – MEGA² II/2, p. 64; See MECW 29, p. 479.
[50]   Marx [1872] (1987) – MEGA² II/6, pp. 70–71. See MECW 35, p. 46; Penguin, p. 126. In the Penguin translation 'to appear' translates both *erscheinen* and *scheinen*, which is confusing; in MECW *erscheinen* is translated as 'to present itself' and *scheinen* as 'to appear', which could be accepted, but I remind my reader that I use 'to appear' for *erscheinen* and 'to seem' for *scheinen*. See Appendix I.

Marx acknowledges that one may twist and turn a commodity as one pleases; it remains 'immaterial' *as a thing of value*. The point is clarified through his quote from Shakespeare. The natural (*crude and tangible*) objectivity of the *single* commodity as a use value is immediately accessible. On the contrary, its peculiar 'value-objectivity' (*Werthgegenständlichkeit*) is unlike Dame Quickly in *Henry IV*: 'One does not know where to have it'.[51] At this moment of the exposition, value is nothing but a *ghost*: an 'ethereal' presence which does not yet exist. Etymological research is once again enlightening. 'Ghost' derives from a proto-West Germanic word meaning 'super-natural being', and can be associated to the Latin *spiritus* (meaning a *disembodied* soul) and to the Greek *φάντασμα* (an apparition or phantom which has only *seeming* reality). In 'ghost', there is thus an intriguing ambiguity between two meanings, which quite well lays bare what is going on. On the one hand, it is an illusory, non-existent image. On the other, it is a shadow, a spectre, or a frightening vision of some dead person haunting the living. In both cases, the 'objectivity' of this uniquely social reality is not obvious.

The ghosts that the commodities contain *take possession of a body* through their 'embodiment' (*Verkörperung*) in money as a commodity: gold (or silver) as a product of labour. Money is defined as 'embodied value' (*verkörperter Werth*),[52] the isolated 'absolute value' as a *fetish*. Marx is going to dissolve the *fetishism* that spontaneously arises from this *fetish character*; showing, first, how this 'thing-of-value' springs necessarily from the social relation that *commodities* entertain with each other; and second, how that reified social relation conceals a specific social relation going on among *human beings* in their practical form of life under capital as universalized production of commodities.

To accomplish this task, and hence *reveal*[53] the mystery of money, Marx turns to the 'form of value' as a *polar relation* (opposing and uniting) the commodities. It is something which was not there at the time of his comments about Bailey; it was, in fact, his confrontation with Bailey that oriented him in this direction.

I cannot explore the issue adequately in this section, so I content myself with a reminder that: (1) in the *simple form of value*, the commodity in the *relative form of value* is playing an 'active' role and thereby outwardly *expresses* the inner ghostly objectivity of *its* value, while the body of its own use value is playing no function at all; (2) the commodity in the *equivalent form of value*, which is playing the 'passive' role, displays in its own use value that ghostly objectivity, now *incarnated* in a *thing*, in an adequate material form

---

51 Marx [1872] (1987) – MEGA² II/6, p. 80. See MECW 35, p. 57; Penguin, p. 138.
52 Marx [1872] (1987) – MEGA² II/6, p. 84. See MECW 33, p. 62; Penguin, p. 143.
53 According to the meaning of *offenbaren* clarified in Appendix II.

(a *Materiatur*). The theoretical wording alluding to incarnation lets us see what is happening here. The use value of gold as money (displayed in circulation as 'absolute value'; that is, as 'embodied value') acts as the phenomenal form of the commodity's value 'as such'.[54] At the same time, the concrete (and private) labour producing 'money as a commodity' acts as the phenomenal form of the commodity's abstract (and social) labour. In a certain sense, money is *the* commodity.

This (*a-Ricardian*) commodity nature of money cannot be too easily thrown out, as the post-1970s literature has done. It has nothing to do with a ground-less theoretical assumption derived from peculiar historical circumstances. It performs a *cogent* and *central* logical role in the 'internal connection'. Within this train of thought, the reference to *absolute value* is plainly there for those who are alert enough to see it. Relevant here is a quote from Chapter 3. I report Hans Ehrbar's translation, which has the merit of fully making explicit Marx's nuances:

> Money is the absolutely alienable commodity [*die absolut veräußerliche Ware*] because it is the *disembodied* shape [*entäußerte Gestalt*] of all other com-modities, the product of their universal *externalization*, alienation [*allgemeinen Veräußerung*].[55]

In his 1871–72 *Ergänzungen und Veränderungen zum ersten Band des Kapital* (*Additions and Changes to the First Volume of Capital*), Marx writes that the nature of the value of the commodity is that of being a 'thingly' expression (*dinglicher Ausdruck*) and 'reified' shell (*sachliche Hülle*) of the human labour power spent in its production, that is, gelatine (*Gallerte*) of human labour, abstract human labour pure and simple (*schlechtin*). The other commodity can be posited as equal (*gleichgesetzt werden*) only as long as it is regarded just as a 'mere thing of value' (*blosses Werthding*). That is: *as long as its material consists of objectified human labour, its body exhibits nothing but human labour.* Money can thus be a *value-thing* because it is itself a commodity, that is produced by labour.[56] In the value relation between commodities, the equiv-alent, hence gold as money, is at once the 'common *body* of commodities'

---

[54]   A sensible, more transparent, translation for *schlechthin* is 'pure and simple', as below.

[55]   Ehrbar (2010), p. 774. See Marx [1872] (1987) – MEGA² II/6, p. 134. See MECW 35, p. 120; Penguin, p. 205.

[56]   Marx [1872] (1987) – MEGA² II/6, p. 9. There is no English translation that I know of.

(*gemeiner Waarenkörper*), and the '*ghost* made flesh' (*Gespensterleib*): and as this latter it is also the 'chrysalis' (*Verpuppung*) of abstract human labour.[57]

Once the duality within the commodity (between 'useful-thing' and 'value-thing') is consolidated in universal exchange – which is, in fact, assumed by Marx from the beginning of *Capital*: there is no place in his theory for Engels's simple commodity production as a historical stage underpinning universal simple exchange – the character of value is *already* taken into consideration in production itself. *From this moment on*, the private labours of producers take on a double social character *before* commodity circulation:

> The value of a commodity *exists* only in its own body. Iron, linen, and corn are values because human labour has been expended in their production. But their value *does not come into sight* in their actuality, in their bodies. The *relative form* in which it sensuously *comes* to light is, therefore, only *a merely ideal, represented form* because it is distinct from *the actual being-there of its value*. What is true of the relative form of value, in general, is also true of *price*. In their prices, iron, linen, grain, etc., possess a figure of value in so far as they *represent* gold quanta. Gold is a sensuously [*sinnlich*] distinct *thing* from them, and in their prices, they refer to gold as *another thing*, which is, however, their *equivalent in value*. They are therefore displayed as values in that they are represented as *gold-equal*.[58]

In these pages, Marx is tracing the path from the ethereal ghost to the existence within the *single* commodity (through price 'representing' gold), and then its conversion into *the* Subject; Marx will add the adjective 'automatic' only in 1871–72.[59]

---

[57] Marx [1872] (1987) – MEGA² II/6, p. 13. In *Capital I*, second edition, Marx writes that the universal relative form of value of the commodity world assigns to the 'excluded' equivalent commodity the character of the universal equivalent. The natural form of this latter is their common shape of value (*Werthgestalt*), directly exchangeable with all other commodities. The bodily form (*Körperform*) counts as the visible incarnation, the universal social chrysalis of every human labour. The *TSV* 'absolute value' is translated into the 'polarities' of the form of value (Marx [1872] (1987) – MEGA² II/6, p. 98). On chrysalis and butterfly, ghosts and vampires, I have written extensively for the last 20 years at least: one example is Bellofiore (2016), whose title has been defined as 'exotic' by a reviewer (though it is certainly unusual, it is quite close to Marx's texts).

[58] Marx [1872] (1987) – MEGA² II/6, p. 47.

[59] In *Capital I*, second edition, what is lost from the first chapter of the first edition is the explicit homology that Marx there pointed out between the *absolutization* of value and Hegel's *absolute* Idea. I think that this is unfortunate. Even though Marx's reading of *Hegel* as absolute idealist was problematic, it is *that* Hegel who allowed Marx to grasp the peculiar ontology of capitalism.

5.4   WHAT HAS EXPLOITATION GOT TO DO WITH IT?

Marx's critique of Bailey revolves around one big theme, which is at once also a critique of Ricardo: the inability to understand the 'externalization' and 'absolutization' of value. It is the process by which the inter-temporal condensation of value is embodied in money (as absolute value), and by which money is transformed in capital as value-in-process (absolute value as the Subject). 'Absolute value' is the expression, in the form of a *thing*, of something inherently 'relative': the *social relation* between human beings, on the one hand, and their mutual productive activity as a *separate* entity governing them, on the other. This *incarnation* of intrinsic value (value as a 'ghost') in money as *value embodied* (value as 'chrysalis') exhibits what *unites* the world of commodities: all of them are portions of a specifically social labour, bearing a peculiar 'form determination'.

I build on the point Marx is advancing in Part I of *Capital I*. Behind the *quantitative* ratios of exchange in commodity circulation, there must be a previously grounded *qualitative* unity (*Einheit*). He finds this foundation in production. It is *labour*, and the (immanent) 'measure' being in (socially necessary) time. This identity (*Identität*) is *not immediate*, however. It has to pass through money as the (external) measure. This 'measurement' leads to a monetary expression of that labour time.[60] The exhibition of values 'as such' in circulation is also an expression *from the inner to the outer*.[61] The argument is that commodities can be compared quantitatively because they are identically equal because of this qualitative 'unity'.

Suppose gold is money as a commodity produced by labour, and that it is exchanged with the other commodities produced by labour. In that case, prices are performing *in advance* a quantitative homogenization (*Gleichung*), as 'value-as-form', of commodities' 'value-as-content'. In other words, the commodity enters the market *with an already given value* in terms of gold as money, and is conceptually made equal with the other commodities *beforehand*. Producers' expectations may be disappointed.[62] When commodities

---

[60]   See Fineschi (2001, pp. 79–84), for the distinction between: (a) *measure* (according to which the 'immanent' or inner measure is the socially necessary labour time); (b) *measuring device* (the 'external' or outer measure, money); and (c) *measurement* (which happens only *ex post* within commodity circulation).

[61]   After Part I the exhibition will be explicitly of the (class) relation of production: a term encompassing the 'buying and selling of labour power' and 'immediate production'.

[62]   In Napoleoni (1976, p. 58), it is clarified that Marx's law of value is *at the same time* a theory of equilibrium *and* disequilibrium, of order *and* disorder.

are produced to be sold on the market, the measured commodities and the measuring commodity must be identical in a *tertium*, this *tertium* being labour as *living* activity (the 'cause') once it is 'congealed' as *dead* labour in the commodity product. This identity of values in social labour justifying labour as the (immanent) measure arises (logically) *earlier*; the (external) measuring through the expression of those values in money prices follows *later*.

The determination (that is, *generation*) of value refers to labour as the activity in-becoming, which *posits* value; value measurement refers instead to commodities and money as already *presupposed* objectified entities. It is true that the extrinsic measure in the display of value has to do with the *Darstellung* in the unitary 'co-determination' of production and circulation, but the inner ground and cause of value has to do with the *Ausdruck*, the movement 'from' production (where the constitution or formation of value emerges) 'to' circulation (where the exhibition of value is displayed). Napoleoni was right in observing that 'abstract labour and value are in fact the same thing, seen, on the one hand, as an activity and, on the other hand, as a result',[63] if this is translated, *à la* Rubin, in a *processual* reconstruction of abstract labour, value and money as only capitalistic notions.

Labour-in-becoming, the activity objectified in value-as-content, is, as Backhaus claimed, the *ens realissimum*, the motor of the movement of capital. In my reconstruction, however, value 'in general' is no longer pre-monetary, like in Backhaus, since it is *ante*-validated by money as finance to production (like in monetary circuit theory), it is also validated *before* circulation by 'value-as-form' (or ideal money), thus avoiding any risk of a 'two-worlds view'.[64] Marx's argument is based on the doubtful assumption that looking for a 'unity' behind the values of commodities (as *objectified* labour) is equivalent to tracing back the latter to labour. Here, the *Urtext* is fundamental in allowing to convincingly ground new value in the objectification of (*living*) labour. To show this, let me go back and complete Marx's argument on the transition from money (as money) to capital in this 1859 'Fragment'.

The absolutization of value presupposes circulation as a developed moment and presents itself as a continuous process, which posits circulation and always returns from it to pose it again. Active value is the only value that posits surplus value. Money that has become autonomous as exchange value in circulation, multiplied in it and through it, is *capital*. As capital, money has lost its rigidity: from a *tangible thing*, it has become a *process*. The becoming autonomous of capital stands in a relationship with a 'third', but this cannot be

---

[63]   Napoleoni (1972), p. 21n.
[64]   Like in Heinrich, at least according to the interpretation by Backhaus and Reichelt: see Appendix II on interpretations.

commodities, nor money, because both are *objectified* labour. The only antithesis to objectified labour is *not-objectified* labour. Therefore, Marx concludes, it is *subjectified* labour. The antithesis to spatially existing labour, *past in time*, is living labour, *present in time*.[65] The latter is the living subject's capacity for work or the capacity of labour that exists as a subject.

The only exchange through which money can become capital is that which the possessor of money concludes with the possessors of the living labour capacity, that is, with workers. The only commodity they have to offer is precisely *their* living labour capacity, present in *their* living corporeity; its use value is labour as an activity when that capacity is put in motion, making *them* work. The real non-capital is 'labour' itself. For money as capital there is no other use value. Labour capacity itself is the use value whose consumption immediately coincides with the objectification of labour, thus with positing value and exchange value. This is where the *Urtext*'s argument leads, and the logical step forward is in *Capital I*, Chapter 7, second paragraph. *Verwertungsprozeß*: the valorization *process*.

Bailey is right in criticizing Ricardo's circular determination of value by the value of labour. Labour power must be recognized as a commodity and distinguished by labour as such. The proper answer to the question 'What is it?' is recognizing that the 'third thing' – which cannot be either a value or a commodity – is not circular but linear, going back to what transforms products into commodities and *constitutes* them as values. This obliges us to investigate the problematic internal connection of 'labour power' and 'labour as activity' *within* 'living labour power' (that is, workers themselves). 'Labour capacity' is *attached to them*, and 'labour in motion' *springs from them*. If it is so, the 'third thing' ultimately must be identified with *the whole* of living labour as a 'fluid': that is, with the *total* social labour, which is objectified as direct labour.

I think that this constellation reveals an Aristotelian moment in Marx's value theory. In Aristotle, we can distinguish the moments of abstract 'potentiality' (as *the generic possibility of becoming something*: ἐνδέχεσθαι), and the concrete 'possibility' (as the 'potency', or *the power of producing reality*: δύναμις). The latter is relevant for Marx, the reference being exactly to a processual reading of the real abstraction of labour as *a movement or process capable of making explicit an implicit form*. Aristotle gave primacy to actuality over potentiality. In the Scholastic reprise of this same theme, the hierarchy

---

[65]   This is what actually is wrongly labelled as 'living labour' in most secondary literature. That is why for some years I have distinguished it, as in the following phrases, from direct labour (the labour which *has been* spent within the period) as the objectification of *living* labour (labour-in-motion: a fluid, not-yet-determined until the end of immediate production). Steedman is right that 'after the harvest', to borrow Sraffa's phrase, Marx's value is redundant.

was sometimes reversed, which appears to be what happened with Marx. This Aristotelian moment was, I think, particularly evident in the *Grundrisse* and in the *Urtext*, and should be regained in the more mature Marx of *Capital I*, where it is less visible.

The reference to Aristotle is also decisive in appreciating the meaning of 'substance' in Marx. As David Andrews argues:[66]

> The choice of *substance* to express Aristotle's οὐσία is particularly egregious. In modern English and German, these terms have lost any connection whatsoever with Aristotle's (and therefore Hegel's and Marx's) meaning. This was not a problem for Hegel and Marx because they were deeply engaged with Aristotle in the original Greek. They could use Latin terms without misunderstanding when writing in German. For us the situation is completely different: their use is complete fantasy.

The point can be made clearer by referring to Joe Sachs's introduction to a translation of Aristotle's *Physics*:[67]

> In the central books of the *Metaphysics*, Aristotle captures the heart of the meaning of being in a cluster of words and phrases that are the most powerful expressions of his thinking. The usual translations of them not only fall flat but miss the central point: that the thinghood (οὐσία) of a thing is what it keeps on being in order to be at all (τὸ τί ἦν εἶναι), and must be a being-at-work (ἐνέργεια) so that it may achieve and sustain its being-at-work-staying-itself (ἐντελέχεια). In the standard translations of those words and phrases, that rich and powerful thought turns into the following mush: the substance of a thing is its essence, and it must be an actuality, so that it may achieve and sustain its actuality.

I think Andrews and Sachs are absolutely right, and I think my reference to Guido Calogero[68] is attempting to go in the same direction.

I would add a third Aristotelian moment, in my interpretation and reconstruction at least: intrinsic value within the *single* commodity must be regarded

---

[66] What follows is indebted to email conversations with David Andrews, who I have already referred to in Bellofiore (2018b, fn 57 at p. 536). This article was published after Bellofiore (2018a), which was a book-length expansion of the same argument, and includes some theoretical developments, especially on this point.

[67] Sachs (2004, pp. 14–15).

[68] See Calogero's entries in *Enciclopedia Treccani*:
'Possibilità' (1935): https://www.treccani.it/enciclopedia/possibilita_%28Enciclopedia -Italiana%29/;
'Potenza' (1935): https://www.treccani.it/enciclopedia/potenza_res-d8942172-8bb5 -11dc-8e9d-0016357eee51_%28Enciclopedia-Italiana%29/;
'Soggetto' (1936): https://www.treccani.it/enciclopedia/soggetto_%28Enciclopedia -Italiana%29/;
'Sostanza' (1936): https://www.treccani.it/enciclopedia/sostanza_%28Enciclopedia -Italiana%29/.

as the '*synolon*', σύνολον (that is, as the *compound*) of value-*as-content* (that is, latent *abstract labour*) and value-*as-form* (that is, ideal money).

5.5   CONCLUSION

Marx's is a journey *from Ghost to Fetish*,[69] where intrinsic value turns into money as absolute value, which becomes capital. Value is portrayed as a self-determining integral whole (*Gestalt*),[70] which has (so to speak) conquered an autonomous, independent reality: *only then* is 'intrinsic value', grasped at the beginning just as an *ethereal* ghost, transformed into a *material* (though *only social*) 'substance' of the value *internal* to the single commodity. As the etymology suggests, this *sub*-stance is literally 'coming *from under*', though admittedly, Marx is far from transparent here (at least for the modern reader). From this perspective, as I have just concluded, substance is to be understood as the 'compound' (σύνολον) of value-*as-content*, which is a labour amount, and value-*as-form*, which is its ideal money representation (*Vorstellung*) in the price tag. It cannot be reduced to a non-monetary or pre-monetary dimension.

Marxian theory of value was directly concerned with explaining *how* valorization is possible, to account for the source of the value added and thus to understand the generation of surplus value. The *Urtext* and Chapter 7 of *Capital I* suggest that the answer lies in the 'consumption' of the living bearers of labour-power: that is, in the (antagonistic) extraction from them of living labour by capital *as a vampire*. This outcome cannot be taken for granted in capitalism as a historically social specific situation. As the whole of Volume I shows, it depends on what Étienne Balibar has called 'class struggle in pro-

---

[69]   See Bellofiore (2019) for a comprehensive presentation of Marx's argument.

[70]   See, on this, Blunden (2022). He also argues that in Marx *Gestalt* can be brought back to Goethe's meaning as 'the overall dynamic configuration of a living thing'. See https://ethicalpolitics.org/ablunden/works/gestalt.htm. See also Blunden's translation from Goethe:

> The Germans have a word for the complex of existence presented by a physical organism: *Gestalt*. With this expression they exclude what is changeable and assume that an interrelated whole is identified, defined, and fixed in character. But if we look at all these *Gestalten*, especially the organic ones, we will discover that nothing in them is permanent, nothing is at rest or defined – everything is in a flux of continual motion. This is why German frequently and fittingly makes use of the word *Bildung* to describe the end product and what is in process of production as well. Thus in setting forth a morphology we should not speak of *Gestalt*, or if we use the term we should at least do so only in reference to the idea, the concept, or to an empirical element held fast for a mere moment of time.

See *Gestalt* in the Glossary of Terms in the Marxist Internet Archive: https://www.marxists.org/glossary/terms/g/e.htm.

duction'. That is why capitalist production is *nothing but labour*, and *this* is the ultimate foundation of Marx's value theory of labour.

The living labour objectified is displayed in the money value added. This monetary exhibition is true to be looked at as the *exchange value*. It is the labour contained in the commodities comprised in the net product and bought by money in circulation: *absolute value*, abstracted (separated) and autonomized. The 'value added' in the period is conflictually shared between the capitalist class and the working class. This macro-social division of the total labour pumped out from capital is accurately portrayed in the social accounting in terms of labour contained.[71]

If Marxian theory is reconstructed as a monetary analysis in the sense of Schumpeter and Keynes, and if it is prolonged to become a truly macro-monetary theory of capitalist production and distribution,[72] the notion of absolute value does not disappear. The *qualitative* 'unity' (*Einheit*) that Marx identifies is redefined as a *quantitative* total magnitude: the labour contained in the new value which has been added during the period, which is the macro-foundation having priority over individual pricing. The 'exchange value' for the current commodity output (the 'world of commodities') is the monetary exhibition of the objectification of total living labour. The same notion of individual 'exchange value' – that is, the simple or direct price as the ratio between the labour required to produce the commodities exchanged – is maintained as the necessary intermediate category between value and price of production. Circulation at exchange values (simple or direct prices)[73] follows that price rule which gives a 'perspicuous presentation' (*übersichtliche Darstellung*)[74] of the confrontation between capital and labour in the

---

[71] The capitalist price-setting of individual commodities determines a divergence between the amount of labour *required to produce the commodities* and the amount of labour *commanded in circulation by the price of those commodities*. It is a necessary distortion in the phenomenal manifestation of surplus value (as gross monetary profits) and the value of labour-power (as the monetary wage bill): an example of what, in Backhaus terminology, are the *Verrückte Formen*, that is, 'deranged', 'crazy' and 'displaced' forms. This point was not realized by Marx himself. See Bellofiore and Coveri (2021).

[72] As I have clarified many times, the meaning of the expression 'macro-monetary' is quite distant from the use of the term in contemporary Marxists such as Fred Moseley (2016). The label 'macro-monetary' in my case directly descends from the use of the term in Italian monetary circuit theory, in authors such as Graziani, Messori and myself, since the early 1980s.

[73] The expression 'direct price' comes from Anwar Shaikh; the expression 'simple price' comes from Michel De Vroey, in writings of the late 1970s and early 1980s.

[74] I am borrowing the expression from Wittgenstein, according to which a 'perspicuous presentation produces precisely that kind of understanding which consists in "seeing the connections". Hence the importance of finding and inventing *intermedi-*

labour process as contested terrain: 'absolute value' (that is, the condensation of living labour as total new value in commodity circulation) and 'exchange values' (the price ratios proportional to the labour contained in commodities) make transparent the class allocation of the objectification of living labour, and supply the mediation from the macro dimension to the micro determination.

Marx's macro-monetary value theory of labour is here grounded in *exploitation*: deciphered both as the consumption of workers as the human bearers of labour power (resulting in total living labour), and as the prolongation of living labour over and above necessary labour (resulting in surplus labour). This argument does not require 'money as a commodity' and can retrospectively justify the assumption at the beginning of *Capital* which relates value back to labour.

Within a view where the valorization process is ante-validated by the banking system financing the production of the firm sector, Graziani wrote at the end of the article, 'Let's rehabilitate the theory of value':[75]

> the problem of valorization comes upon the class of capitalists in its relations with workers; the exchange of commodities as a phenomenon within the capitalist class is a quite different problem. Surplus value and profit can only derive from a relation between the two classes, but the exchange of commodities is quite a different thing inasmuch as it is a phenomenon within the class of capitalists ... This area is governed by the rules of competitive equilibrium (analyzed a thousand and one times from the general equilibrium of Walras to Sraffa's theory of prices). These rules indeed explain the determination of relative prices in the exchange of commodities. Such exchanges do not shape relations between classes and have nothing to do with the phenomenon of valorization ... analysis of the relations between the classes, or social macroeconomic analysis on the one hand, and analysis of relations within a class or competitive microeconomic analysis on the other, are disparate phenomena that for that reason are governed by their own logic.

In this reconstruction of Marx's reasoning, it remains valid that the exhibition of values 'as such' in circulation is also an 'expression' from the inner to the outer, but in a different formulation (crucial from the point of view of the constitution of capital as a social relation): the 'inner' does not refer anymore just to 'immediate production', but encompasses the 'buying and selling of labour power' before it.

---

ate links' (§ 122 of *Philosophical Investigations* in the modified translation of Martin 2016, p. 104). The term is translated very often as 'surveyable' or 'perspicuous representation', in French as *tableau synoptique*, in Italian *rappresentazione perspicua*. I prefer 'perspicuous presentation' (see also the note on *Darstellung* in Appendix I on translation).

[75]   Graziani ([1983] 1997), p. 25.

Maybe Marx's is a discourse not too far from what Sraffa had in mind when in the 1920s he wrote a note entitled 'Cause and measure of value',[76] arguing that the 'classics, when they speak of "invariable measure" mean really *cause*', quoting Marx's *TSV* (in a French translation), and Bailey's *Dissertation*. Maybe this view does not sit too well with the investigation about the Standard Commodity, it is nevertheless in continuity with his 1940 note about the *Use of the Notion of Surplus Value*, and the consequent possible interpretation of the normalizations in his 1960 book (the net product as *numéraire*, and direct labour as unit) as compatible with Marx's value theory of labour.

REFERENCES

First, I list the references to Marx (in the original German, followed by translations in English), then the references to the secondary literature.

Marx

Abbreviations:
MEGA² II = *Marx–Engels GesamtAusgabe, Zweite Abteilung: 'Das Kapital' und Vorarbeiten*
MECW = *Marx–Engels Collected Works*

Marx, K., [1857–58] (1973). *Grundrisse*. London: Penguin.
Marx, K., [1857–58] (1976). *Ökonomische Manuskripte 1857/58. Teil 1*. MEGA² II/1.1. Berlin: Dietz Verlag.
Marx, K., [1857–58] (1981). *Ökonomische Manuskripte 1857/58. Teil 2*. MEGA² II/1.2. Berlin: Dietz Verlag.
Marx, K., [1857–61] MECW 28. *Economic Works 1857–1861*. London: Lawrence & Wishart.
Marx, K., [1857–61] MECW 29. *Economic Works 1857–1861*. London: Lawrence & Wishart.
Marx, K., [1857–61] (1980). *Ökonomische Manuskripte und Schriften 1858–1861. (Zur Kritik der politischen Ökonomie u. a.)*. MEGA² II/2. Berlin: Dietz Verlag.
Marx, K., [1861–63] (1976). *Zur Kritik der Politischen Ökonomie (Manuskript 1861–1863). Teil 1*. MEGA² II/3.1. Berlin: Dietz Verlag.
Marx, K., [1861–63] (1978). *Zur Kritik der Politischen Ökonomie (Manuskript 1861–1863). Teil 3*. MEGA² II/3.3. Berlin: Dietz Verlag.
Marx, K., [1861–63] (1979). *Zur Kritik der Politischen Ökonomie (Manuskript 1861–1863). Teil 4*. MEGA² II/3.4. Berlin: Dietz Verlag.
Marx, K., [1861–63] MECW 30. *Economic Manuscript of 1861–63*. London: Lawrence & Wishart.
Marx, K., [1861–63] MECW 31. *Economic Manuscript of 1861–63*. London: Lawrence & Wishart.

---

[76] SP D1/22.14.

Marx, K., [1861–63] MECW 32. *Economic Manuscript of 1861–63*. London: Lawrence & Wishart.

Marx, K., [1872] (1987). *Ergänzungen und Veränderungen zum ersten Band des Kapital*. MEGA II/6, Berlin: Dietz Verlag.

Marx, K., [1872] (1987). *Das Kapital. Kritik der Politischen Ökonomie. Erster Band. Hamburg 1872*. MEGA² II/6. Berlin: Dietz Verlag.

Marx, K. [1887] (1976). *Capital. Volume I*. Translated from the third German edition by Ben Fowkes. London: Penguin Books.

Marx, K. [1887] (1996). MECW 35. *Capital. Volume I*. Translated from the 3rd German edition by Samuel Moore and Edward Aveling. London: Lawrence & Wishart.

Others

Albinus, L., (2016). Wittgenstein, Frazer, and the Apples of Sodom. In L. Albinus, J.G.F. Rothhaupt and A. Seery (eds), *Wittgenstein's Remarks on Frazer. The Text and the Matter*. Berlin: De Gruyter, pp. 339–365.

Arthur, C.J., (1986). *Dialectics of Labour. Marx and his Relation to Hegel*. Oxford: Blackwell.

Arthur, C.J., (2022). *The Spectre of Capital: Idea and Reality*. Leiden: Brill.

Backhaus, H.G., (1997). *Dialektik der Wertform. Untersuchungen zur marxschen Ökonomiekritik*. Freiburg: ça ira.

Backhaus, H.G., (2016). *Ricerche sulla critica marxiana dell'economia. Materiali per la ricostruzione della teoria del valore*, R. Bellofiore and T. Redolfi Riva (eds). Milano: Mimesis.

Backhaus, H.G. and Reichelt, H., (1995). Wie ist der Wertbegriff in der Ökonomie zu konzipieren? Zu Michael Heinrich: Die Wissenschaft vom Wert, in Beiträge zur Marx–Engels–Forschung. Neue Folge. *Engels' Druckfassung versus Marx' Manuskripte zum III. Buch des 'Kapital'*, Argument, Hamburg, pp. 60–94.

Behrens, D., and Hafner, K., (1993). *Totalität und Kritik*. In D. Behrens, *Gesellschaft und Erkenntnis: zur materialistischen Erkenntnis und Ökonomiekritik*. Freiburg: ça ira, pp. 89–128

Bellofiore, R., (2014). Lost in Translation: Once Again on the Marx–Hegel Connection. In F. Moseley and T. Smith (eds), *Marx's* Capital *and Hegel's* Logic. *A Reexamination*. Brill: Leiden, pp. 164–188.

Bellofiore, R., (2016). Chrysalis and Butterfly, Ghost and Vampire. In S.R. Farris (ed), S.R. *Returns of Marxism. Marxist Theory in a Time of Crisis*. Chicago, IL: Haymarket Books, pp. 41–62.

Bellofiore, R., (2018a). *Le avventure della alienazione. Dalla teoria monetaria del valore alla teoria macro-monetaria della produzione capitalistica*. Milano: Mimesis.

Bellofiore, R., (2018b). The Adventures of Vergesellschaftung. *Consecution Rerum*, 3 (5): 503–544.

Bellofiore, R., (2019). Forever Young? Marx's *Critique of Political Economy* after 200 Years. *PSL Quarterly Review*, 71 (287): 353–388.

Bellofiore, R. and Coveri, A., (2021). The Transformation Problem. In *The SAGE Handbook of Marxism*. Volume I. London: SAGE, pp. 171–177.

Blunden, A., (2022). *Hegel, Marx and Vygotsky. Essays on Social Philosophy*. Leiden: Brill.

Brentel, H., (1989). *Soziale Form und ökonomisches Objekt: Studien zum Gegenstands-u. Methodenverständnis d. Kritik d. polit. Ökonomie*. Opladen: Westdeutscher Verlag.

Campbell, C., (2017). Marx's Transition to Money with No Intrinsic Value in *Capital*, Chapter 3. *Continental Thought and Theory*, 1 (4): 207–230.

Colletti, L., [1969] (1972). *From Rousseau to Lenin. Studies in Ideology and Society*. London: New Left Books.

Colletti, L., [1969] (1973). *Marxism and Hegel*. London: New Left Books.

Colletti, L., (2012). *Il paradosso del Capitale. Marx e il primo libro in tredici lezioni inedite*. Roma: Fondazione Liberal.

Doz, A., (1996). Le sens du mot 'absolu' chez Hegel. *Revue des Sciences philosophiques et théologiques*, 80 (1): 5–11.

Ehrbar, H.G., (2010). *Annotations to Karl Marx's 'Capital'*, 26 August. https://content.csbs.utah.edu/~ehrbar/akmc.pdf.

Fineschi, R., (2001). *Ripartire da Marx. Processo storico ed economia politica nella teoria del 'capitale'*. Napoli: La città del sole.

Furner, J., (2004). Marx's Critique of Samuel Bailey. *Historical Materialism*, 12 (2): 89–110.

Gehrke, C., (1998). Absolute Value and the Invariable Measure Of Value. In H.D. Kurz and N. Salvadori (eds), *The Elgar Companion to Classical Economics*. Cheltenham, UK and Lyme, NH, USA: Edward Elgar Publishing, Vol. 1. pp. 1–6.

Graziani, A., [1983] (1997). Let's Rehabilitate the Theory of Value. *International Journal of Political Economy*, 27 (2): 21–25.

Hartmann, K., (1970). Die Marxsche Theorie: Eine philosophische Untersuchung zu den Hauptschriften. Berlin: de Gruyter.

Hegel, G.W.F., [1831] (2010). *The Science of Logic*. Transl. and ed. by George Di Giovanni. Cambridge: Cambridge University Press.

Heinrich, M., (1999²). *Die Wissenschaft vom Wert. Die Marxsche Kritik der politischen Ökonomie zwischen wissenschaftlicher Revolution und klassischer Tradition*. Berlin: Westfälisches Dampfboot.

Heinrich, M., (2021). *Wie das Marxsche 'Kapital' lesen? Leseanleitung und Kommentar zum Anfang des 'Kapital' Teil 2*. Stuttgart: Schmetterling Verlag.

Kliman, A.J., (2000). Marx's Concept of Intrinsic Value. *Historical Materialism*, 6 (1): 89–114.

Lippi, M., [1976] (1979). *Value and Naturalism in Marx*. London: New Left Books.

Luxemburg, R., [1900²] (2004). Reform or Revolution. In P. Hudis (ed), *The Rosa Luxemburg Reader*. New York: Monthly Review Press, pp. 128–167.

Martin, C.G., (2016). Wittgenstein on Perspicuous Presentations and Grammatical Self-Knowledge. *Nordic Wittgenstein Review*, 5 (1): 79–108.

Meyer, L., (2005). *Absoluter Wert und allgemeiner Wille. Zur Selbstbegründung dialektischer Gesellschaftstheorie*, transcript Verlag.

Moseley, F., (2016). *Money and Totality. A Macro-Monetary Interpretation of Marx's Logic in* Capital *and the End of the 'Transformation Problem'*. Leiden: Brill.

Murray, P., (2016). *The Mismeasure of Wealth. Essays on Marx and Social Form*. Leiden: Brill.

Napoleoni, C., (1972). *Lezioni sul capitolo sesto inedito*. Torino: Boringhieri.

Napoleoni, C., (1974). Introduzione. In C. Boffito (ed), *Teorie della moneta. Ricardo, Wicksell, Marx*. Torino: Einaudi, pp. 9–17.

Napoleoni, C., (1976). *Valore*. Milano: Isedi.

Napoleoni, C., [1988] (1991). Value and Exploitation. Marx's Economic Theory and Beyond. In G. Caravale (ed), *Marx and Modern Economic Analysis.* Aldershot, UK and Brookfield, VT, USA: Edward Elgar Publishing, p. 222–238.

Nyikos, E., (2010). *Das Kapital als Prozeß.* Frankfurt am Main: Peter Lang.

Pennavaja, C., (1976). Introduzione. In K. Marx, *L'analisi della forma di valore.* Bari: Laterza, pp. v–liv.

Redolfi Riva, T. (2018). Samuel Bailey and David Ricardo in Karl Marx's Dialectic of the Form of Value. *Dialogue and Universalism,* 28 (3): 55–68.

Reichelt, H., [2002] (2007). Marx's Critique of Economic Categories: Reflections on the Problem of Validity in the Dialectical Method of Presentation in *Capital. Historical Materialism,* 15 (4): 3–52.

Reichelt, H., (2005). *Social Reality as Appearance: Some Notes on Marx's Conception of Reality.* In W. Bonefeld and K. Psychopedis (eds), *Human Dignity. Social Autonomy and the Critique of Capitalism.* London: Routledge, pp. 31–67.

Reichelt, H., (2008). *Neue Marx-Lektüre, Zur Kritik sozialwissenschaftlicher Logik.* Hamburg: VSA Verlag.

Roncaglia, A., [1975] (1978). *Sraffa and the Theory of Prices.* London: John Wiley & Sons.

Roncaglia, A., (2009). *Piero Sraffa.* Basingstoke: Palgrave Macmillan.

Rubin, I.I., [1929] (2018). The Dialectical Development of the Categories in Marx's Economic System. In R.B. Day and D. Gaido (eds), *Responses to Marx's* Capital: *From Rudolf Hilferding to Isaak Illich.* Leiden: Brill, pp. 728–817.

Sachs, J., (2004). *Aristotle's Physics: A Guided Study.* New Brunswick, NJ: Rutgers University.

Tran, Hai-Hac, (2003). *Relire Le Capital.* Lausanne: Page deux.

Tairako, T., (2017). Versachlicung and Verdinglichung – Basic Categories of Marx's Theory of Reification and their Logical Construction. *Hitotsubashi Journal of Social Studies,* 48: 1–26.

APPENDIX I: LOST IN TRANSLATION?

Ausdrücken = 'to express' (from the inner to the outer).

Darstellung = 'exhibition', 'display' or 'presentation' (also 'exposition', which may be trickier in English); and accordingly, for *darstellen*, 'to exhibit', 'to display', 'to present' (also 'to expose').[77]

---

[77] In this case something more must be said. *Darstellung* derives etymologically from 'to *put* something *there*'. Here the accent is on the exposition through which the truth of the object of the inquiry emerges, thanks to the connections that that exhibition reveals in its course, which is at the same time an outer expression and transformation of the thing itself. What Albinus (2016, p. 353), writes about Wittgenstein also applies to Marx: he 'did not point to a revocation of something already self-identically present as implicitly suggested by the word "re-presentation", but rather wanted to point to something that emerges from the very construction of joining links.' 'Represent', the usual translation, is inappropriate since it derives from *re-ad-praesenns*, meaning to present again. A better choice, but awkward in English (as it is not in Italian, which partially explains the preference by Fineschi), is 'expose', from *ex-ponere*. The one

Dasein = 'being-there', but also sometimes 'existence'.

Ding, Sache = the former as 'physical or natural thing'; the latter as 'matter, case', and the like.

Einverleiben = 'to embody' (meaning including some as a part).

Enthalten = 'to contain'; and hence 'contained labour' (definitely not 'embodied' labour, as in most translations; the expression embodied labour is appropriate for concrete labour, not abstract labour).

Erscheinung = (necessary) 'phenomenal manifestation' (of the essence), the way the latter cannot but appear; *erscheinen* = 'to appear' or, better, 'to manifest'. Important: 'appear' is never to be used for *scheinen*. There is no essence separated from the form of 'appearance'.

Fetisch-charakter and *Fetischismus* = 'fetish character' and 'fetishismus' (not to be identified).

Gegenständlich and related terms = it refers to 'becoming objective'; the objectivity standing in front of human beings, as something which has its origin in the processual moment of labour as activity. I am in favour of Fineschi's Italian translation of *Gegenständlichkeit* as *oggettualità*, 'objectuality', but I fear this term would be problematic for most English readers, so here I rather use objectivity as objectification).

Gestalt = 'shape', 'figure' (distinguishing it from 'form').

Materiatur = I leave this unusual old term in German; in *Capital I* it expresses the fact that the material representing value in money as a commodity must have some peculiar properties which make it adequate to be a proper expression and form of manifestation of value itself.

Naturwüchsige gesellschaftliche = 'natural-spontaneous but social', in contrast to the 'natural and spontaneous' division of labour in pre-existing communities. It is meant in a negative sense, referring to connections not yet subjected to a conscious human action:

Offenbarung = 'revelation', belonging to a theological vocabulary; accordingly, *offenbaren*, 'to reveal'.

Schein = 'semblance', 'seeming' (may be illusory, opening to 'vulgar' explanations); *scheinen* = to seem.

Übergreifen and related terms = 'overgrasping', but also 'overreaching' and 'overriding', bordering on 'dominant'.

Unterschied = 'distinction'.

Veräusserung and related terms = it is an 'alienation' which is first of all an 'externalization'.

I choose is 'to exhibit', which is very much a synonym of the latter, meaning 'to present (to view)', 'to show', to 'display', and the like.

Verkörperung = 'embodiment'; and hence *verkörpern* = 'to embody' (meaning 'to present in a physical shape'). I do not render them as 'incarnation', 'to incarnate', since Marx uses *Inkarnation* with a specific emphasis.

Verrückte Formen = 'perverted and crazy', 'deranged' forms of appearance.

Vorstellung = 'representation' of imagination; *vorstellen* = 'to represent' (meaning, forming ordinary conceptions and idea, hence also leading to notional anticipations).

Wirklich = 'actual', or 'effective' (better than 'real').

APPENDIX II: LOST IN INTERPRETATION?

What precedes is an exercise about reading Marx's confrontantion with Bailey and Ricardo on 'absolute value', orientated by an interpretation of his economic writings as a monetary value theory *of labour*. In this Appendix I cannot provide a survey of the secondary literature. I will just give a list of some references intersecting my topic, with a few telegraphic comments.

On Marx on Bailey, the debate between James Furner (2004) and Patrick Murray (2016) is vitiated, as almost all Anglo-Saxon commentaries, by not paying attention to the (serious) errors of translation, which are therefore cropping up in their quotes. Andrew Kliman (2000) as well as Martha Campbell (2017) do not distinguish intrinsic and absolute value. Kliman denies the presence of the latter notion in Marx. Campbell is blind to the essentiality of money as a commodity for Marx's value theory. The key role of 'money as a commodity' in *Capital I*, and hence of money as embodied value, in anticipating the existence of value before the exchange, is usually lost in most interpreters.

Tony Smith, at least to my knowledge, does not seem to have room for absolute value in his books and articles, but only for intrinsic value, unproblematically identified with the value dimension. Geert Reuten never discussed absolute and intrinsic value; he considered, though, its immanent/extroversive or inner–outer aspects in a way that is partially different than mine. Tommaso Redolfi Riva (2018) is a very well-researched and careful dissection of Marx on Bailey, but like Murray (2016), fast forwards to the polarity of the form of value, with the inconvenient of obscuring the specificity Marxian meaning of 'absolute value' in *TSV*. Tran (2003), on the contrary, accurately depicts Marx's position that the value 'relation' must be analysed, turning the couple relative–absolute value of *TSV2* into the polarity relative–equivalent form of value in *Capital I*. He overlooks that absolute value in *TSV* is 'cancelled' by being 'maintained' in *Capital I*, and it is important to understand how this *sublation* happens. Isaak Il'ic Rubin was the one who most thoroughly articulated a sensible theoretical presentation on his own, which is the nearest to Marx, of what is at issue in this chapter. But strangely, his appraisal is disappointing when dealing with Marx's engagement with Bailey, especially on absolute value. But in Rubin ([1929] 2018), he gets the point absolutely right when he concludes that '[f]rom being a modest representative of commodities, money has become the *absolute* existence of value'.[78] In his own conceptual development of Marx, Rubin eventually understood 'absolute value' much better than in his review of Marx versus Bailey and Ricardo.

Christian Gehrke (1998) considers Marx's notion of absolute value in the context of an entry opposing that concept to relative value. His reading is immediately Ricardian: a commodity's absolute value is the value of that commodity measured against an invariable standard. About Marx, the absolute value of a commodity would be the amount of socially necessary abstract labour required to produce it. All of Marx's mediations are cancelled, which may lead to different conclusions at lower levels of concretizations. The identification of absolute value with 'embodied' labour in the single commodity as the 'substance' of value is, unfortunately, also in Alessandro Roncaglia (2009), following Marco Lippi ([1976] 1979). A much more open (though somehow hesitant) discussion about Marx on Bailey and Ricardo was in Roncaglia ([1975] 1978) (abridged, partially merged and partially contradicted in the 2009 book).

More accurate and profound interpretations of Marx's position were, in Italy, those by Lucio Colletti and Claudio Napoleoni; and in Germany, those by Hans-Georg Backhaus and Helmut Reichelt.[79] They all share the view that Marx's value theory *is* the theory of absolute value.

Colletti (2012), recollecting his *Lectures on Capital* in Rome of the early 1970s, but already Colletti ([1969] 1973) (in a surprisingly *malgré soi* quite Hegelian last chapter of his *Marxism and Hegel*), connect the separate and abstract existence of abstract labour and absolute value to a process of *hypostatization*. Colletti, however, commits a serious error. He maintains that in the commodity as a sensuously supersensuous 'thing', the use value aspect *of its own* natural body becomes nothing more than a means that the commodity employs to embody its supersensuous aspect *as if in its own body*.

For Napoleoni ([1988] 1991), in his last essay, one can speak in Marx of absolute value in a sense quite different from Ricardo, that is, *as the product of capital itself*, the nature of which is thus highlighted as a historical, and not a natural, form of production. In his Turin University lectures in the early 1970s Napoleoni came very near the interpretation which I have provided. Money is value 'detached' from the *particular* bodies of commodities and entered into the unique *body* that is money, as a circumstance intrinsic to the

---

[78] Rubin ([1929] 2018), p. 786.
[79] The key role of absolute value was already in Klaus Hartmann (1970, p. 271), who however criticizes the notion.

production of value. Napoleoni (1974) was perceptive in associating absolute value with money as a particular and the excluded commodity. Unfortunately, he committed the same blunder as Colletti, arguing that autonomization means that when there is money, *exchange value* has detached itself from the material body of the commodity and is exhibited in an autonomous form by a particular commodity. This is incorrect. Money is *not* 'exchange value' made autonomous. It *is* 'value' – namely, intrinsic value, the *ghost* – made autonomous *and* materialized in a sensible *thing*, in gold as money, which is then *value embodied*. This is, properly speaking, *exchange value*.[80]

Hans-Georg Backhaus is very outspoken in emphasizing the pivotal place of the universal character of value as abstract value, objective value; namely, 'absolute value'. In his introduction to Backhaus (1997), the recognized founder of the 'monetary value theory' perspective highlights that one should beware of refuting *pre-monetary* value as such. It is not true that *absolute* pre-monetary value is unthinkable, he writes. Marx's surplus value *is* a pre-monetary value. The same value 'in general' (that is, what in my interpretation is *intrinsic* value), whose 'general characteristics' contradict its *being-there* within a determinate commodity, is *likewise* a pre-monetary value. Even though this 'pre-monetary' value cannot be realized *as such* in a pre-monetary 'exchange value', and it is rather manifested in a monetary structure of commodity *and* money, in its own pre-monetary character '[it] is the *ens realissimum* in Adorno's sense, it is the motor of dialectical development, it is a principle that is ultimately only realized in the movement of the world market of capital'.[81]

Backhaus's revisitation of 'pre-monetary value' within a monetary value theory of labour is inseparable from his point of view about 'absolute value'. The most insightful discussion is in an essay from the early 1980s, available not in the original German (which has been lost) but in Italian[82] (as well as in Castillano and Danish), that Redolfi Riva and I published a few years ago in Backhaus (2016). The problem is that quite often for Backhaus, like already in Colletti and Napoleoni, immanent and absolute value (and value 'as such') are one and the same, as when he writes that *money* can only be understood as the phenomenal form of *absolute* value. He correctly argues that the existence of value cannot be immediately perceived, and is exhibited in the being-there of money; but this is true for intrinsic value, while absolute value is exactly

---

[80]   If I understand well, a similar confusion has been detected in Napoleoni (1976, p. 55) by Nyikos (2010, p. 109).

[81]   Backhaus (1997, pp. 32–33), my translation.

[82]   'Sulla problematica del rapporto tra "logico" e "storico" nella critica marxiana dell'economia politica' (On the problematics about 'logical' and 'historical' in the Marxian critique of political economy), in Backhaus (2016, pp. 353–414).

the phenomenal form of intrinsic value. Moreover, Backhaus takes for granted (like Marx) that the unity making commodities identical is labour: 'If I can only talk reasonably about "labour-value" when it manifests itself in something sensible, and if I am furthermore able to describe certain states of affairs as sensuously suprasensible, then the suprasensible has to some extent also become "perceivable" as an "existing universal" or an "existing principle"'.[83]

A very similar emphasis on 'absolute value' as part of the formation of the money form is found in Helmut Reichelt's interpretation of Marx's dialectical development of categories as a preliminary to his critique of Marx proposing an alternative approach building on the concept of validity. Examples are Reichelt (2005, [2002] 2007, 2008).

The centrality of 'absolute value' is confirmed in Backhaus and Reichelt (1995), the critical review they wrote together in 1995 about the first edition (1992) of Michael Heinrich's *Die Wissenschaft vom Wert.* According to the two reviewers, Marx's view of value as an ethereal ghost is truly exposed to the risk of landing into a theory of the 'two worlds'. The first world is about *the use value dimension* of the real, the material, and the concrete. The second world is about *the value and monetary dimension* of the ideal, the social, and the abstract. This risk is fully actualized in Heinrich, where the process of abstraction is inevitably conceived in a *nominalist* way. Backhaus and Reichelt object that it is impossible to regard value as a *Real-Universal* along this path, as Marx did. The peculiar 'objectivity' that is at issue – in Marx, not in Heinrich – is a universal which is *at the same time* sensible. In their argument, the movement of thought characterized by them as the *absolute value* (here the authors should write, in my view, 'intrinsic value') presents itself as an interior which is *externalized* as an exchange value (here the authors are talking of 'absolute value', properly speaking). Discarding the terminological confusion, I think that the notion of absolute value is what Backhaus and Reichelt are trying to deliver.

In Heinrich's (1999) second edition, Marx's 'absolute value' in Marx's *TSV* is not really discussed, only Ricardo's according to Marx. Nor does Heinrich enter in any detailed consideration of Marx's critique of Bailey. He just affirms that the exposition of the value form in the first chapter of the first edition is dialectically more precise than in *Contribution,* primarily because of Marx's confrontation with Bailey's critique of Ricardo. Heinrich maintains that the value-objectivity of commodities can only exist in their value relation, acquiring social form in exchange value. In *Wie das Marxsche Kapital lesen?*

---

[83] Backhaus (2016, p. 389), my translation. I agree with Ehrbar (2010) that 'sensible suprasensible' means *sensuous things which are at the same time extrasensory or social.*

Leseanleitung und Kommentar zum Anfang des 'Kapital' Teil 2 Heinrich (2021) writes that for Marx while value was initially only one of the two factors of the commodity, it acquires an autonomous shape (*selbstständige Gestalt*) in money as money.[84] All this is correct, but only if it goes hand-in-hand with the inner–outer movement (the movement of 'expression'), and the understanding that for Marx, the *essential* role of money as a commodity allows the quantitative anticipated existence of value *before* exchange (embodied value as a notional expected magnitude). However, this side of Marx is strongly turned down by Heinrich, and if recognized, it is theoretically rejected.

Backhaus supervised Helmut Brentel's PhD dissertation in Frankfurt, which was delivered in 1984, and then revised and updated to become Brentel (1989). Contrary to Diethard Behrens and Kornelia Hafner, who[85] defined Brentel's as 'an unusual reading, to say the least', I find Chapter 3 of *Soziale Form und ökonomisches Objekt*[86] to be one of the most accurate investigations about Marx's critique of Bailey, to which I cannot do justice here. I limit myself to remind that rightly Brentel – quoting Marx about the *absolute(s) Verhältnis* (the *absolute relation*) – claims that in Marx, the attributions of the absolute and the relative are reversed: what Bailey takes as the metaphysically 'absolute value' of commodities turns out to be a *relative* relation of the commodity output to the labour of *society as a whole*. It is the 'absolute' expression of its 'relative value'. Value is expressed as something relative, *but now in the absolute relation by which it is value*. It is the competitively enforced totality of private labours in their relation to one another. What is 'absolute' is this specific determination of commodities through labour, not the concrete computability of individual values.

Like Colletti and Napoleoni, as well as Rubin, Brentel maintains that the individual commodity does have, *in advance*, an 'immanent' value. Abstract labour depends on circulation, but *not* as a phase distinct from production, only as the totality of the circle production–circulation, where commodities are produced *for* the market. Abstract labour is *latent* but, as such, already exists in immediate production. Indeed, for Brentel, abstract-universal labour is an *anticipatory* concept of the totality of the socialization of labour under universalized capitalist commodity production. The economic form is always a *thingly* and *reified* one because value as a social relation can only be expressed in a *material* (that is, in a gold-matter as something 'volumetric'). This *sensible* character of the economic form is the basis of its generally 'valid' character *as a thought form* about what people must reckon with and

---

[84]   Heinrich (2021), p. 193
[85]   Behrens and Hafner (1993), fn. 259, p. 217.
[86]   Brentel (1989), pp. 103–133.

how they must act in the economic intercourse: and this is an echo both of Backhaus and Reichelt.

Lars Meyer, in his *Absoluter Wert und allgemeiner Wille* (*Absolute Value and General Will*) (Meyer 2005), also moves from a conceptual landscape very near to Backhaus and Reichelt. 'Absolute value' is even inscribed in the title. An enlightening theme chased by this author is that in dialectical social theory the universal is *not* imagined as a 'substance' but as the constant mediation of the *unity* of society (made abstract and autonomous) *through* the singular and the particular; something which very much resembles what Marx was doing in *TSV* and beyond.

Before concluding this summary review of the reception of 'absolute value', I cannot avoid mentioning Arthur (2022), though it is neither an interpretation of Marx, strictly speaking, nor a comment on Bailey. It is, however, useful to look at how the same concept emerges in Arthur's personal line of reasoning. In a perspective where labour is *not* the 'substance' of value, Arthur's absolute value mimics many of Marx's notion characteristics. For Arthur, 'money, as the unique universal equivalent, is necessary to the *actuality* of value', and '[i]n its own activity money makes itself necessary *by taking on the position of "absolute value" against commodities*'.[87] 'Absolute' does not mean 'unconditioned', but that value is presented substantively as *independent* of exchange value.[88] Arthur asserts that '[m]oney is value in *absolute* form because it exists in *seeming* autonomy from the commodity relations originally supposed to be characterised by value. Determined as "absolute", *it simply exhibits itself as what it is.*'[89] In my view, the autonomy of absolute value cannot be reduced simply to a 'semblance', as Arthur's formulation may induce to think: that autonomy springs from those commodity relations themselves. Last but not least, the 'embodiment' of *intrinsic* value (as the ghostly objectivity of latent abstract labour) in money *as a commodity* as absolute value – the point I underlined in my *interpretation* of Marx – is nowhere to be found in Arthur.[90]

---

[87] Arthur (2022), p. 117.

[88] This notion in Arthur indicates a *relative* exchange ratio, differently from my convention in this chapter where it is a sort of *absolute* exchange ratio.

[89] Arthur (2022), p. 118.

[90] I very much agree with Arthur's argument that the 'unity' of commodities in labour is not categorically justified in Marx in the first chapter of *Capital I*, in whatever edition, in an adequate way. Yet, even if I am convinced that the total labour as the social unity behind the world of commodities is not justified in the early chapters (and provided an alternative ground in the Conclusion), I refrain from Arthur's bold move of completely severing the link between value and labour at the opening of Marx's theoretical discourse in *Capital*. As I have argued in the past, the expository structure of the three volumes of *Capital* is such that it begins with *seemingly subjective* ('for us') abstractions. They must be brought about *objectively*, going beyond a merely mental

The interpreter who probably more than anybody else came near to Marx's argument on absolute value, at the same time problematizing it rather than taking it for granted, is Pennavaja (1976) in her Introduction and editorial apparatus to her translation of Marx's analysis about the form of value in the first edition of *Capital*. Pennavaja was, so to speak, at the intersection point of the network connecting the authors I privileged among the interpreters. Pennavaja studied with Lucio Colletti and Claudio Napoleoni in Rome in the late 1960s. In the early 1970s, after attending the Department of Social Sciences at the Goethe Universität in Frankfurt am Main, she obtained a Doctorate in Economic and Social Sciences at the University of Bremen under Helmut Reichelt. In these years, she was in contact with Hans-Georg Backhaus.

Not that her own understanding is without ambiguities, but she came very near to what I see as a correct interpretation. Human labour's objectification as an abstract object is a 'thing of thought' (*ein Gedankending*), an 'imaginary thing' (*Hirngespinst*). Yet, Marx writes, commodities are *things*:

> What they are, they must be *materially*: that is, they must show it in their material relations. A certain amount of human labour-power has been expended. Its value is the purely objective reflection of the labour thus expended in the linen. But this value is not reflected in its own body. It 'reveals itself' [*offenbart sich*], and takes on a *sensible expression* through its relation of value to *another* commodity, the coat. While the linen makes the coat the same with itself as value, and at the same time distinguishes itself from it as a use value, the coat becomes the form of manifestation [*Erscheinungsform*] of the value of the linen in contrast to the body of the coat, that is it becomes the 'form of value' of the cloth in contrast to its natural form.[91]

Not only does Pennavaja understand the thrust of Marx's reasoning, but she also perceives how shaky is the foundation on which Marx's argument is erected. She rightly claims that the category of labour as the substance of absolute value is not sufficiently explained in its logical-historical implications. Instead, it is developed through connotations and other analogical concepts which, although related to the supposed identity between value and (the monetary expression) of labour, do not properly ground it. She adds, convincingly, that Marx gives no reason as to *why* the labour expended to produce a commodity – 'crystallized' or 'coagulated' in it – is assumed to be the creative

---

abstraction and achieving a real abstraction. This is what Marx accomplishes with his account (since Chapter 7 of Volume I) of the constitution of capital thanks to his *method of comparison* and with his conceptualization of the *practical* abstraction of wage labour.

[91]   Pennavaja (1976), p. xxvii.

substance of value.[92] In truth, I have shown that the reason Marx offers is assuming money as a commodity, that is, a product of labour. But, put in this way, Marx's value theory stands or falls with the approach to money as a commodity (as Napoleoni, and Backhaus and Reichelt, more or less recognized). I do not find that alleged 'foundation' for Marx's value theory persuasive.

---

[92] Pennavaja (1976), p. xvi.

6. Money, measurement and quantification

Frank Engster

6.1   MARX'S *CAPITAL* AS CAPITAL-THEORY OF MONEY, VALUE AND THEIR COMMON VALORIZATION

One way to read Marx's *Capital* is to read it as a theory and critique of money.[1] Vol. 1 can be read along the logical-categorial development of its main functions, a development that in the Hegelian sense is a 'retreat to the ground' and an accounting for presuppositions;[2] here, the capitalist ground of money is developed through the attainment of its capital-form and through the valorization of labour and capital. Vol. 2 then explains the reproduction circuits accomplished by money. Finally, Vol. 3 deals with the manifestation of valorization in prices, with money's finance-forms such as credit-money and fictitious capital, and with capitalist crises.

It is crucial to note that throughout the whole development, money's functions are always inseparably combined with value; that is, with the social relation which money: (1) realizes and quantifies *qua* measure; (2) mediates and transfers *qua* means of exchange and circulation; and (3) brings into effect and expands through its (finance) capital-form.

In all three determinations, not only is money combined – or rather, to use a suitable term from quantum physics, entangled – with value, but also the entanglement takes on a form. By developing these forms, Marx shows how money receives its functions and 'properties' through the social

---

[1]   In *Capital*, Marx's concept of money differs radically from all previous conceptions, even from the so-called *Grundrisse*. In the various editions of *Capital*, Vol. 1, he not only sets out the final three versions of his value-form analysis, but he now also distinguishes between value and exchange-value; he replaces 'common labour' with 'abstract labour'; he clearly indicates the double character of labour and of the commodity; and he underlines the particularity of the commodity labour-power, and so on.

[2]   'Rückgang in den Grund' (Hegel 2010, p. 49) and 'Einholen der Voraussetzungen'.

relations which it determines and constitutes, realizes and transfers, valorizes and expands. *Capital* Vol. 1 begins with the value-form analysis which exposits the measure of value (Marx [1867] 1996, pp. 58–93). The exposition then shows that this measure becomes practical in money's function as means of exchange and circulation and takes on the form of simple commodity-circulation: Commodity-Money-Commodity (C-M-C) (Marx [1867] 1996, pp. 58–93), before finally generating the overarching capital-form of money: Money-Commodity-more Money (M-C-M´) (Marx [1867] 1996, pp. 157–186). Through this exposition, *Capital* demonstrates that the value realized in commodities comes from the valorization of labour and capital, and that realized profit comes from unpaid labour-time. These three steps are finally the condition to reason that the form of finance capital M-M´ (Money-more Money) is an abbreviated, yet 'irrational form' (Marx), as it depends on this productive valorization and on the exploitation of labour-power, and yet seems to generate profit without it (Marx 1998, pp. 313–438).

6.2 THE CRITICAL OUTCOME OF THE LOGICAL-CATEGORIAL READING OF *CAPITAL*

It was the decisive insight of the 'logical reading'[3] developed in the 1960s, especially by the so-called New Reading of Marx (NRM),[4] that Marx's analysis of the form *x commodity A = y commodity B* (Marx [1867] 1996, p. 58) at the very beginning of *Capital* should not be interpreted as an exchange, whether in the sense of a historical reconstruction or in that of a logical-systematic genesis.[5] Instead, the analysis logically shows the necessity of money by the failure of a direct, pre-monetary exchange of commodities: the status of a commodity already presupposes money and therefore cannot be derived from

---

[3]   This logical reading of *Capital* in general, and of the value-form analysis in particular, was established in the 1960s in opposition to the existing logical-historical reading, which was even propagated by Engels (Engels [1859] 1971, esp. pp. 475–477; Engels [1894] 1998, pp. 5–23). This dominant reading was first challenged by I.I. Rubin's ([1928] 1972) *Essays on Marx's Theory of Value*, and from the mid-1960s on by R. Rosdolsky, J. Zelený, and the different new – workerist, structuralist, form-analytic – readings of *Capital*.

[4]   Pioneers were Hans-Georg Backhaus and Helmut Reichelt, working groups around the student movement in West Germany, and research groups in East Germany, especially a circle around the Halle-based *Arbeitsblätter zur Marx-Engels-Forschung* (W. Jahn, T. Marxhausen, R. Hecker).

[5]   The necessity of the logical reading of *Capital* was an outcome not only of discussions of how to read *Capital*, but of how to begin a critique of the mode of production if it has to be presented as a totality which reproduces itself.

direct commodity-exchange. The value-form analysis rather has to be read as a critique of all pre-monetary value theories (Backhaus 1980, pp. 99–120) and as a '*monetary* theory of value' (Heinrich 2021).[6]

This decisive insight gets lost, however, and the whole further development of the capitalist mode of production goes in the wrong direction when money is subsequently once again reconstructed as a means of commodity-exchange.[7] To be analysed – regardless of what Marx himself intended to show, but as it is quite obvious in the 'x' and 'y' – is how the quantification of a social relation is possible. This quantitative status is decisive for the whole capitalist mode of production, since it is an economy based not on exchange, but on the realization, mediation and productive valorization and accumulation of quantitative values (and, in cases of crisis, also on their de-valorization and annihilation). In capitalism, it is also due to this quantitative status that labour and the commodity become what Marx calls the 'substance' and 'form of value', respectively, while Marx determines value itself as an undetermined, pure 'social relation'. It is only by sublating this social relation quantitatively that both labour and the commodity determine society in a double sense, namely by their famous 'twofold character' which Marx exposes right at the beginning of *Capital*: the 'dual character of labour embodied in the commodities' (Marx [1867] 1996, p. 51), and hence the dual character of the commodity itself (Marx [1867] 1996, pp. 45ff.). Both labour and the commodity can be infinitely different qualitatively, and they can even be infinitely differentiated and developed; this is not in spite of, but precisely due to the circumstance that it is the relation of all individual labours – and the relation of all commodities – that becomes their identical quality by being determined quantitatively (Marx [1867] 1996, p. 57). Marx's *Capital* further shows that the whole 'capitalist production process is a unity of the labour process and the valorisation process' (Marx [1861–63] 2010, p. 92). Hence, wealth in capitalism has a dual character in that its qualitative dimension is an infinite multiplicity of possible use-values, while its quantitative dimension is an ever-finite, but endlessly self-referential, 'accumulation for accumulation's sake' (Marx [1867] 1996, p. 591).

---

[6]   A proper monetary theory of value, influenced by the logical reading, was elaborated in the works of H.-G. Backhaus and H. Reichelt, É. Balibar, D. Behrens, R. Bellofiore, H. Brentel, S. de Brunhoff, I. Elbe, R. Fineschi, A. Haesler, J. Hoff, U. Krause, J. Milios, F. Moseley, H.-J. Lenger, O. Schlaudt, G. Sgro, H. Strauss, A. Szepanski, and others.

[7]   Historically, there has never been anything like a direct exchange of goods or barter carried out by two individual owners from which money could originate, whether logically or historically. This myth – this Robinsonade with two Robinsons – was first deconstructed in the 1920s by ethnologists and anthropologists such as M. Mauss, B. Laum and W. Gerloff.

To capture this double determination, which is as divisive in the economy as it is thoroughgoing, in one inconspicuous term: the whole capitalist economy is qualitative reproduction as quantitative valorization and accumulation. Therefore, real wealth is neither the capitalist economy's qualitative nor its quantitative dimension, neither material reproduction nor quantitative accumulation. Real wealth is the mode of their mutual production hidden in the inconspicuous term 'as', which nevertheless stands for nothing less than a speculative identity: the transformation of the qualitative into the quantitative dimension, and vice versa.

This transformation is what money as a measure accomplishes. Through this transformation, the measure itself changes its function and becomes the means to realize the speculative identity between the qualitative and the quantitative dimension of the economy. But Marx finally demonstrates that this realization is a moment of money's own 'turnover' as capital, and that it is the latter which becomes the form of the processing of the qualitative reproduction of the capitalist society *as* quantitative magnitudes.

6.3 QUANTIFICATION AS A TECHNIQUE OF MEASUREMENT

It is important to emphasize that in capitalism money constitutes value as a social relation into which 'not an atom of matter enters' (Marx [1867] 1996, p. 57; a similar formulation occurs on p. 48), and that this relation is hence pure in the non-empirical, Kantian sense (Kant [1781] 1998, A 20, p. 156). According to Marx, however, this purity belongs to a purely – and here 'purely' can rather be linked to Hegel's notion of 'pure Being' in his *Science of Logic* (Hegel 2010, pp. 45ff., 59ff.) – 'social being' or a purely 'social relation'. This purely social relation – with labour as its substance and the commodity as its form – is constituted not simply by quantification, but by quantification through measurement. Quantification through measurement is something totally different from the way in which quantification has been conceptualized in the few attempts which have thus far been made to theorize it using Marx's critique of political economy (and different from how money might have quantified social relations before capitalism). What was overlooked in these attempts (and what Marx himself overlooked or underestimated, but also prepared the way for theoretically) is the constitutive status of money: by quantifying through measurement, money paradoxically constitutes the same quality – the purely social relation, 'value' – which it simultaneously actualizes objectively and represents. This paradoxical status has to be emphasized against all essentialist and substantialist conceptions of value and abstract labour, especially in the tradition of classical Marxism which interpreted Marx's *Capital* as a 'labour theory of value',[8] but also against the tradition of Western Marxism and critical theory (for example, Lukács, Sohn-Rethel, Adorno), which, in thematizing exchange, social synthesis, equalization and (real) abstraction, conceptualized the opposite pole, as it were, to labour and production, and thus based their critique rather on the form of social exchange and mediation.

What is enigmatic here – and this is what gives rise to the notorious 'money riddle' – is that it is only through money that the relation between labours and the relation between commodities are constituted and realized in the first place; and yet, through this realization by money, these relations manifest themselves as if they existed independently of money, and as if money were merely a neutral means of their representation. In short, these social relations are realized through money's quantification by measurement as though they exist without money.

This quantification by measurement has nothing to do with a mere passive representation of an independently existing quality or relation; nor has it anything to do with counting, reduction, equation or even with an abstraction, be it an abstraction from the qualitative dimension, from the use-values of commodities, or from concrete labours. The strange entanglement which constitutes that which must seem to be independent also renders spurious the question as to whether money itself has value or only represents it: that is, whether money's value is based on a commodity with value, as is claimed by a metallist interpretation; or whether, on the contrary, value is conventional and ultimately imaginary, as is asserted by nominalists. (And although the ambition in the following is to go with Marx beyond these oppositions in the concept of value and money, this means also going beyond his own ambivalences in this regard.)

All these discussions are redundant as they disregard the primary question, namely that as to how quantification is possible at all; that is, a quantification that appears like an objective self-reflection of the quantified relation. As will be shown, this quantification which appears like a self-reflection falls within the logic and technique of measure, and here money has the same fundamental constitutive status as measurement in natural science and, especially, in quantum physics.[9] However, whereas measurement and quantification in natural science constitute a first nature, money constitutes a second, purely social nature. Furthermore, the entanglement is reversed. Whereas the first

---

[8]   A term which Marx himself never used. Nevertheless, a (left-)Ricardian interpretation was predominant both in the realm of classical Marxism and in that of critiques of the latter.

[9]   Two other analogies to determine the technique of measure would be possible: Hegel's logic of being in his *Science of Logic* (2010), and A. Badiou's use of set theory in *Being and Event* (2005).

nature is, by means of the measured magnitudes, actualized and reflected as an independent, given and unconscious relation opposed to society, money actualizes the same social relations which, through this very actualization, become real and possible as such. It is as if, through money, society enters into a supra-individual, unconscious but practical reflection of its own second, quantitative nature in the first place, hence into: itself.

6.4 HOW A MEASURE AND ITS OBJECT ARE GIVEN: THE VALUE-FORM ANALYSIS AND THE CONSTITUTION OF SOCIAL OBJECTIVITY

Bringing Out the Truth of Finite Being: The Total Unfolding and its Conversion

By developing in a logical way how a measure is 'given', Marx's value-form analysis shows how capitalist society, by turning social into quantitative relations, can exhibit its own relation as in a (self-)reflection.

To show how money can constitute the same social self-relation that it simultaneously exhibits, Marx fully unfolds the simple form of value of an arbitrary commodity A: 'z Com. A = u Com. B or = v Com. C or = w Com. D or = x Com. E or = &c' (Marx [1867] 1996, p. 73). Yet this unfolding leads to a 'bad infinity' (Hegel 2010, pp. 109, 190ff.; there is a similar formulation in Marx [1867] 1996, p. 74f.) of an infinite progress, indicated in the '= &c', without a final, definitive conclusion, as one commodity must always determine and present its own social relation through another, different commodity, and ultimately every commodity has to be determined by its endless relation to all other commodities. No commodity can be finally determined; nowhere can their relation be determined as such and consummated in a final, objective determination: the social relation can find its determination only in its own enduring, endless progress without ever coming to a final determination.

Yet instead of going endlessly further into this bad infinite relativity of an unresolvable relation, the analysis returns back to commodity A and turns the equation around; and with the equation, finitude itself (Marx [1867] 1996, pp. 75–79). This turn, which is akin to a conversion, exposes the truth of the bad infinity: the 'true infinity' (Hegel 2010, pp. 119ff.). In actual fact, it was the total unfolding itself that already brought out its own truth, as it constructs a social relation in the first place, and hence the negative quality or pure being of a relation as such. But to demonstrate this truth, the becoming of this quality is necessarily accompanied by an inversion: it is only insofar as finitude is led through the form of its own determination that the truth can be exhibited in one of its elements, commodity A. This commodity A, which stands for every individual commodity, can end the endless progress by taking on the form unfolded vis-à-vis it, and it can hence be a 'general equivalent' (Marx [1867] 1996, pp. 80ff.) of its own form of determination. Moreover, it is an equivalent for the quality produced by this form, the relation as such, pure being, or – and in fact all of these mean the same – the negative quality, or quality of negativity. Hence, commodity A can be a universal equivalent for this quality by taking on the form not only of the determination of something by something else – of one commodity by another – but of the determination of the relation as such: that is, of the relation constituted as the identical being or negative quality opposed to it by the total unfolding of its own form of determination.

In short, in one commodity A (which stands for every single being), the bad infinity of the endless relation is considered to be speculatively completed and accomplished (Marx [1867] 1996, pp. 75, 80). It is as if, by returning to commodity A, the finitude in this one commodity returns to itself, but as if it were now totally and completely accomplished. Commodity A, having completely passed through the form or logic to determine its own social relation, becomes – in striking analogy to the scenario of crucifixion – converted (Marx [1867] 1996, p. 77) by its own infinity und universality, a universality which comes into being in this relation as the identical quality or pure being as such which is constituted by this form or logic. Converted in this way, commodity A, as the 'universal equivalent' (Marx [1867] 1996, p. 77), exposes all other commodities to the universal form or logic of their determination. And when they are related to their universal equivalent, commodities in turn become representatives of the determination they share through this equivalent, and yet they thereby become commodities in the first place: beings which can sublate their own social (and, as will be shown, capitalist) relation.

Counting a Relation as One; Turning a Negative Being into the Quality of Quality: Quantity as the Truth of Quality

If one commodity can take on the pure relation of all commodities as such, it converts into the one commodity that counts the negative and identical quality of all other commodities as one. Therefore, commodity A becomes an equivalent not only for its own relation, but also for the negative identical quality which is constituted with this relation, and this means that the form to determine-by-relating, to determine something through another thing, becomes reflexive in an immediate and unconscious manner. The quality of determination becomes reflexive by turning a relation as such into a quantitative being. Thus, commodities share their own relation, their own negative being, and not only are they related as one to a common equivalent: thereby they also share this unity or oneness quantitatively. Counting itself as one and turning into quantitative being, this is how finitude, through one of its elements, can become reflexive and determine its own finitude purely as such.

When the common relation of commodities is counted as one by a commodity which stands for the relation as such, this commodity represents an ideal, void and undetermined unit, determined to be determined by the relation which it turns into a quantitative relation, thereby exhibiting its truth in quanta. The 'truth' exhibited *is* this turning of social into quantitative relations, exhibiting the negativity of their (social) being through the positivity of quanta.

The Fixing of an Ideal Unit as the Measure of Value: The Permanent Exclusion of One Commodity from All Others

The form of a universal equivalent can 'be assumed by any commodity' (Marx [1867] 1996, p. 80). But to be in this decisive, universal position (the position of sovereignty, to use a term of political theology), one single commodity has to be permanently 'excluded from the rest' (Marx refers to logical exclusion: Marx [1867] 1996, p. 77; and to practical exclusion: p. 97). It is through this exclusion that both sides, in one stroke, take on a totally new status: the universal equivalent fixes an ideal unit of value, and by this fixing, the excluded commodity becomes the 'money-commodity', while all the other commodities in turn become its object and are set in a quantitative relation as pure values; thereby becoming commodities in the first place (Marx [1867] 1996, pp. 80ff.).

It is only by virtue of its permanent excluded position that the money-commodity fixes an ideal unit. Money itself is nothing, but it is absolutely necessary that something, an arbitrary being, exists in this excluded position and stands in for what is not to be found in all beings: an ideal unit and a measure to exhibit the truth of the relation which becomes the object by being turned into a quantitative being. Nothing, no being, can – and nothing has to – be adequate to this ideal unit, since money becomes adequate to it negatively, as the analysis has shown: if the bad infinity is speculatively posited as accomplished in one commodity, in this commodity the logic of determination becomes reflexive and the commodity can turn into a universal equivalent, and through its permanent exclusion this equivalent fixes an ideal unit that counts the whole relation as one and turns it into a quantitative being.[10] Although money always exists not only as some particular being (gold, paper-money, electronic impulse, crypto-code), but also as an already finite quantum – a 'scarce good' – logically it stands for an undetermined unit of value which

---

[10]   The position of money and its status for the economy which it activates, can be seen to be analogous to the position and status of the figures of sovereignty and religious and political power. Negative theology, especially in the tradition of Heidegger, Benjamin, Schmitt, Foucault, Agamben and so on, also revolves around the included–excluded position of a sovereign who occupies the void, that is, the empty locus of power, especially the power to mark and make differences.

acquires its own quantitative determination and specification through the economy it realizes, mediates and converts, as will be shown in the next sections retracing the development in Marx's *Capital*.

To understand this logic of the measure, it is crucial also to understand the status of the analysis. The value-form analysis concerns neither a historical nor a logical genesis of money. What is analysed is a genesis that never occurred, yet it must seem as if the genesis becomes true by virtue of being always already assumed – and put into effect – by the validity of money. It is only from an already given validity of money that this quantitative relation and its pure validity can be reconstructed, but this reconstruction is necessary only because of money's own 'lost cause': instead of leading to its historical or logical origins, such a reconstruction only leads to the non-derivability of money's validity. Money is a common equivalent for a form that never occurred. The form is always already in the state of having been replaced, since in place of the necessity of determining every commodity by its relation to all other commodities, in money this bad infinity of a total relation is merely posited as accomplished, and as having been 'taken over' by money's validity; therefore, all commodities can enter into their social being by sharing it purely quantitatively right from the outset. In short, the genesis of money becomes true by virtue of its validity, and this validity is pure and timeless, just like the quality that money realizes quantitatively; yet it follows that money has to realize its own genesis together with this quantitative realization.

The task of the analysis, hence, is to reveal the measure as the common excluded third already present in 'x' and 'y', but as its vanished condition; that is also the reason why the analysis describes a non-linear and non-chronological genesis. That which is analysed is the blind spot of quantification: the absent measuring unit that presents social being in an always already quantitative way by means of determined magnitudes.

The whole quandary of the reconstruction of money's genesis can be captured in one term: through its turn into quantitative relations, the social relation presents itself as reflected. That the quantitative finitude of being is always already reflected is the truth which money exhibits in – or, more immediately, with – the values it realizes (and that these reflected magnitudes become reflexive in a self-relation will be the truth of money's own turnover as capital). Quantity is the quality of a relation that can become reflexive as such; that is, as a relation and hence as a negative being or negative quality: the measure is the means for this reflexivity. The reflection carried out by money is as unconscious as it is objective – it occurs as a self-reflection – and it is this self-reflection that, through money, is given to the subject *qua* objectivity in realized values. With money, therefore, what the subject is given is the means to turn the social relations of things into an objectivity that presents itself in its quantitative being in an already reflected way. To enter into this relation, the measure 'merely' has to be used as a means of social mediation.

6.5   MONEY AS A MEANS AND THE NECESSARY FALSE SEMBLANCE: EXCHANGE AND CIRCULATION AS MEASUREMENT

So far, the analysis has only shown in a purely logical-categorial way how, through the exclusion of a money-commodity, an ideal unit becomes fixed and the logic of quantification is given by a measure. However, the realization of the ideal unit which money as a measure stands for has yet to acquire its function as a means of 'exchange' and its function in the 'circulation of commodities', as the ideal unit becomes real through the actualization of commodities as values. Marx describes this actualization immediately after the value-form analysis, in Chapters 2 and 3 (Marx [1867] 1996, pp. 94–103, 103–156). While the value-form analysis has a purely logical-categorial status, the commodity-circulation process describes a practical social mediation; and its exposition is at the same time its critique, as circulation produces a necessary false semblance.

This critique has two facets, just like exchange, circulation and social mediation itself have an ambiguous status between money as a measure of value, and money as the capitalist form of its valorization. The first facet is the previous analysis which shows that an exchange and circulation process of quantitative values presupposes a fixed, common measure and therefore must turn out to be something else: what seems to be merely an exchange of money against a commodity is in fact a form of measurement. And the other facet, which will be developed in the sections following this one, is that the measured and objectified 'object' is not, as it seems, the relation of commodities, but rather the relations which obtain in their production.

What initially regards the presupposed measure: in the exchange process the logical status of an excluded money-commodity becomes practical. Hence, the realization of the ideal unit by the quantification of the relation of the commodities also becomes practical. Whereas, in the analysis, the exclusion of the money-commodity and the fixing of an ideal unit was shown only logically, in the circulation process money enters in practice into the same mediation of commodities from which it falls out (more drastically in the so-called *Grundrisse*; Marx [1857–58] 2010b, pp. 479, 497). With its practical exclusion of the money-commodity, the circulation process is, so to say, an ongoing repetition of the origin of the money-commodity and its position and status.

Or, more accurately, both money and commodities practically enter into mediation and circulation and fall out. But while commodities fall out of circulation to disappear in consumption, money which mediates this process not only determines and presents this mediation in the values realized, but it also divides this mediation in time and space into the acts of buying and selling (Marx [1867] 1996, pp. 116–124), while it holds the realized values identical in time and space in a determinate way by transferring and circulating them (Marx [1867] 1996, p. 122). This is why the ideal unit, fixed by the excluded money-commodity as a measure of value, not only becomes real through all the acts of selling and buying and through all the values realized and trans-ferred (that is, by the processes executed by money as a means): the ideal unit thereby also takes on a form, the form 'of simple circulation', Commodity–Money–Commodity (C–M–C) (Marx [1867] 1996, p. 115). Moreover, by taking on the form of commodity and money, value becomes an 'automatic subjectivity' (Marx [1867] 1996, pp. 164f.), by being simultaneously the objectivity of social being.[11]

This is how, of all things, the ideality of the fixed unit becomes the material-ism, as it were, to realize and present the finitude in its hardest and purest, most objective and immediate mode: as pure quanta. However, money presents this objective reality only in its passing and vanishing. Moreover, this objective, present reality, is a false immediacy and a necessary semblance. Although – unlike the value-form analysis before – money, value and commodities are now situated in a chronological and linear social mediation, what money now presents in these values of commodities is already an actualization of the relations in their production, and through this actualization it gives the possible future a quantitatively determined reality. The values realized define and open up this future, and money *is* this passage between realized past and its possible future. This leads to the other aforementioned facet of Marx's critique of medi-ation as a necessary false semblance.

6.6   THE CAPITAL-FORM OF MONEY M–C–M′. THE SELF-RELATION OF MONEY BY MEANS OF THE SELF-VALORIZATION OF VALUE: CAPITALISM'S SELF-MEASUREMENT

> The whole difficulty arises from the fact that commodities are not exchanged simply
> as *commodities*, but as *products of capitals*[12]

---

[11]   Much more Hegelian is the German version of *Capital*, Vol. 1 (MEW Bd. 23, p. 169), where Marx (1962) also refers to an '*übergreifendes Subjekt*' (overarch-ing subject) and '*Identität mit sich selbst*' (identity with itself). The English version of *Capital*, Vol. 1 has fewer Hegelian terms, and in the French version 'subject' is replaced by 'substance'.

[12]   Marx (1998, p. 174).

Marx's *Capital* demonstrates that the ideal unit for which money as a measure stands not only becomes a means which posits all commodities in a social relation that they quantitatively share: money thereby also posits in a relation the elements of the production of commodities, labour and capital. Money posits all private and isolated concrete labours and all individual capitals – at least in the respective branches of commodity production – in a relation by constructing a totality of all labour-time spent and all individual capitals used, and by this it simultaneously deduces average magnitudes. What therefore seems to be an exchange process is not only a form of measurement; likewise, the measured and objectified 'object' consists not of commodities, but rather of the valorization accomplished by labour-power and capital in their production process. In short, 'to measure' means to set all labours and all capitals in a common – or even global – relation and to deduce simultaneously the average magnitudes necessary for their productive valorization. What Marx therefore develops as 'abstract labour', and calls the 'substance of value', is labour-power valorized by capital and set in a social relation, measured and quantified by money.

But the crucial point has still not been reached yet, since – paradoxically – measuring money and the values it realizes will be reconverted into, and thus return back to, these elements of commodity production which have been actualized by money. As a measure of value and means of its realization, money opens up its own self-relation through capitalist valorization. Marx describes this metamorphosis as the 'capital form': Money–Commodity–Money with a profit, M–C–M', where C stands for labour-power and capitalist means of production (Marx [1867] 1996, pp. 157–186).

Hence, what money in capitalism posits in a quantitative status is not only commodities, but also producers and their means of production, which take on the historically new status as labour-power and capital, and are thus commodified as well. Marx shows this new status at the end of *Capital* Vol. I, in the chapter 'The So-Called Primitive Accumulation' (Marx [1867] 1996, p. 704), and thereby traces an arc to its beginning by showing the historical and logical origins of the valorization process that he had developed throughout *Capital* Vol. I. However, this development has revealed that, through its capitalist form, money must, as in a reproduction of this origin of accumulation, again and again activate the same elements of valorization which are encompassed in overarching fashion by its own capitalist metamorphosis; likewise, the exposition has demonstrated that money internalizes by means of the values realized what its own externalization into these elements has been worth.

Thereby, the social objectivity for which money seems to be the means of mediation dissolves into a process in which money, in order to reproduce its capitalist functions, its pure and universal validity and its own economic value, has to externalize this value into elements which have to be released into the independence of their valorization. During this independent valorization, all the different kinds of labour and individual capital quantitatively share the same common social being to which they contribute, but to which they contribute only in a speculative way, while money becomes their overarching form, being the actualization of their quantitative being and becoming the actual identity of their process. This is why *Capital*, Vol. 1, finally demonstrates that the ideal unit of value becomes real not only through the exclusion of a money-commodity which functions as a measure and becomes the means for the realization and mediation of quanta: to exist, this ideal unit of value must be split by money's overarching capital-form and capital-process into the forms of labour-power and capital.

6.7   THE MEASUREMENT OF PRODUCTIVITY: SPECIFICATION OF MONEY THROUGH THE CONSTRUCTION OF AVERAGE MAGNITUDES OF NECESSARY LABOUR-TIME AND PROFIT

The entanglement between money and value has to be developed in order to generate on the one hand the capital-form of money, and on the other hand the valorization of value by labour and capital, and their entanglement itself has to be developed as a measurement; although Marx himself does not speak of measurement, but rather of 'a complicated social process' (Marx 1998, p. 815) and of the 'transformation' of values into prices (Marx 1998, p. 153). What seems, however, to be a transformation in time and in space, leading to the notorious 'transformation problem', is again not a chronological-linear, not a causal and not an arithmetic calculation, and many of the misunderstandings to which Marx himself gave rise are due to the arithmetic calculations he presents in a manner resembling a left-Ricardian objective labour theory of value. What do occur in chronological time and in space, however, are all the 'decisions' made when money breaks and interrupts a processing relation with a measurement which brings this process to a quantitative determination by prices. That which is 'transformed' by its measurement is the status of the relation, namely from a not-yet-determined social relation (valorization of value) which, through prices, becomes quantitatively determined, fixed and made manifest. Money's essence *is* to make value manifest as price, but also to dissolve these prices – this manifestation of social being – back into social relations (this manifestation of value as price is the reason why it appears as if value were quantitatively traceable or reconstructible; Marx indeed attempted such a quantitative reconstruction in *Capital*). What therefore seems to be money's essence, namely the exchanging of commodities and the realization of values, is rather to be taken as the moment of this decision and determination of our social relation *qua* measurement; a timeless and spaceless interruption which is the necessary passage to determine and to continue society's self-relation, and its endless processing and accumulation by means of finite, determinate and regulative quanta.

Yet nor is this passage a transformation in time and in space as if both were given as per classical Newtonian physics. It is, rather, a transformation of time and space themselves, as money literally brings the same time with itself which it quantitatively realizes, transfers and converts, thereby defining the chronological and the spatial dimension of social relations. By actualizing values, money interrupts a valorization which is functioning as a process and spatially dispersed in the totality of capitalist relations, and by means of this break and interruption a realized past which is actualized by magnitudes becomes separated from – but is also rendered regulative for – its own further, future productive valorization. Not only is measurement by money the separation between the realized past and its future, but money is also the means to convert these magnitudes back into its functioning as a process, becoming the passage between the past and future of valorization. In short, quantification by measurement is a passage for both: a spatialization of time and space, and a temporalization of space and time.

It is therefore impossible to quantitatively reconstruct or calculate values from prices, as individual prices necessarily lead back to this process of the measurement of a relation of labour-power and capitalist means and conditions which is in process and not quantitatively fixed. Economic science, like everyday consciousness, has no concept for this indeterminacy. Yet nor do they have any need of such a concept, since money is the technique which can literally induce value, as a quantitatively indeterminate relation, to become manifest in a quantitatively determinate way in the prices of individual things. Money therefore allows economic science and economic subjects a calculation with prices only, a calculation in which prices lead back to prices and the indeterminacy 'in between' is resolved by the negative essence of money.[13] Nevertheless, only capitalism, which comprises a measurement which functions like a practical reflection and decision, opens up this difference between value and price; a difference which entails nothing less than social mediation

---

[13]   Although Marx presents labour-time and values often as if they are already quantified, he nevertheless emphasizes – especially in Vol. 3 – that the quantitative existence of this social relation is only price, hence monetarily determined value. While mainstream political economy calculates with prices only and regards 'value' as metaphysical, critique has to start with the difference of value and price to reconstruct the social mediation which literally vanishes by means of its own manifestation. Marx's critique is not only located within this distinction, it is also his criterion for distinguishing 'classical' from a 'vulgar-economy' (see Marx [1867] 1996, pp. 14ff., Afterword, and in particular pp. 65 (fn), 169, 538–542, 592–594).

in its totality, or as totality. As money makes value manifest in prices and makes value disappear, the difference also becomes the critical distinction as such, and opens up the problem of a 'transformation' between value and price. It is only in capitalism that money, in its functions and its capitalist movement: (1) individualizes the same labour-powers and capitals that it sets in a common relation; by (2) making their relation manifest in a quantitative, determinate way in individual prices; in (3) a way that all labours and all capitals quantitatively share the same valorization process to which they contribute; while (4) money from past valorization determines and deduces the average socially necessary magnitudes of labour-time and of profit decisive for their future productive valorization (for 'socially necessary labour-time', Marx [1867] 1996, pp. 49f., 55f., 63f., 86, 116f; for 'surplus-value', pp. 177–186, 221–233, 239–243; for the 'average profit', pp. 320ff.). In short, in capitalism the socialization of labour, of capital and of all things is accomplished by this quantification and measuring process. And the ideal value unit, for which the excluded money-commodity stands, is for its part quantitatively specified and, as it were, socialized by the measurement of the results of the valorisation process and the measured magnitudes. Money is always a finite quantum, quantitatively specified by the measurement it enacts through its own metamorphosis as capital, and by the magnitudes it realizes, converts and transfers.

6.8   THE ENTANGLEMENT: THE INTERFERENCE OF MONEY'S FUNCTIONS AND THE SUPERPOSITION OF VALUE

The character of a measurement is captured in the correspondence between the magnitudes money actualizes, transfers and converts on the one hand, and money's own value and quantitative specification on the other hand. Although Marx develops the single functions of money in a linear way, in the capitalist process these functions overlap each other and interfere, and that is because they are entangled with a value which likewise has different conditions or statuses according to these different functions. Marx's development of money and value hence requires more than the dialectical understanding shown so far. We have to grasp that money's functions interfere with each other, and that value, our very own 'social relation', exists in a kind of 'superposition', to conceptualize it with a post-Newtonian quantum physics which Marx could not yet make use of.

First, with regard to money's overlapping functions, its logically first function as a measure only comes into being by the exclusion of one commodity which fixes an ideal unit and becomes the 'money-commodity'. This unit, however, only becomes a measure of value through money's function as a means of the actualization and mediation of value in the form of what seem to be commodity-exchanges. And finally, both the measure of value and the means of its realization always already actualize and extrapolate money's own self-reference as capital in the values of commodities (making exchange-value a necessary false semblance).

It is only in capitalism that money, as a medium of exchange and circulation, measures the results of a valorization into which money itself was converted and from which it returns, closing the circle of its self-reference by arcing across the elements of the independent valorization process: labour-power and the means and conditions of production.

Second, the overlapping of money's function is entangled with a corresponding different status of value. As a measure, money – whichever shape it might take as a money-commodity, and in whatever quantity and value it exists – stands in the last instance for an ideal unit of value that is completely indefinite and at the same time universally valid. As a medium of exchange, money realizes this unity always already through finite, quantitatively determinate values; and thereby the ideal unit always already exists in single quanta, taking on the form of commodity-circulation. But as capital, money has to split and metamorphose the ideal unit for which it stands and which it realizes, by converting these realized values back into the elements of their valorization. To summarize, the ideality and unity of the ideal unit of value becomes real only: (1) by being represented and fixed (money as measure); (2) by being disseminated into the relation of beings and their mediation (money as means); and (3) by being split in the overarching self-relation which is in process in the forms of labour-power and capital (money's capital-form).

This entanglement is why money's own value must correspond to that which, on the side of the economy, it realizes, transfers and converts: money is nothing but a quantum, specified by its own processing in the forms of the economy. However, one big riddle is still open: How can this necessity of a correspondence, this entanglement between measure and measured relations, quantitatively transcend itself and enlarge its own process and its reproduction?

6.9 EXPLOITATION OF TIME BY ITS QUANTIFICATION

The self-measurement of valorization in money's self-relation as capital contains the riddle of how this self-measurement can overcome itself: the quantification of labour and capital and the measurement of their valorization *qua* its results leaves – or, more accurately, yields – a quantitative surplus, marked in the dash in the capital-form M–C–M′. Moreover, the whole entanglement is *a priori* oriented to the increase of both value and money, and this quantitative accumulation not only has to take on qualitative forms in labour-power, its means of production, and in the commodities produced; the latter are all constantly modified, developed and even revolutionized qualitatively by the necessity to go beyond themselves quantitatively (Marx and Engels [1848] 2010, p. 487).

In order to understand the emergence of this surplus, the entanglement of valorization and capital-form has to be once again understood as a self-measurement. Thus far, the accumulation of capital has been an infinite and immeasurable valorization process beyond all measures, precisely because the relations are constantly measured and the measured values not only determine the necessary magnitudes for a productive valorization of labour-power and capital, but also these magnitudes are transferred and converted into them by the measuring unit for which money stands. However, money also literally brings out – or extracts – an excessive dimension. With money, a surplus value is exploited and receives an independent existence in a pure quantum. Only money can extract a surplus value which, according to Marx, is labour-time which goes beyond the labour-time necessary for the reproduction of the commodity labour-power (which the worker receives as a wage) (Marx [1867] 1996, pp. 177–186, 187–316). Only money can realize this difference between the value produced by labour and the value of the commodity labour-power itself by quantitatively realizing this difference and, as it were, extracting it as profit; only money can convert this exploited surplus-time back into the valorization process it came from; and finally – or rather, first of all – it is only in money that it pays off for capitalist society to increase productivity by reducing labour-time and the reproduction costs of the commodity labour-power in order to convert the reduced labour-time and the reduced reproduction costs into surplus labour-time (the two methods for this conversion are described in Marx [1867] 1996, pp. 317–534).

Outside of money, this surplus-time can exist only in a spatial dimension. Like time-relations in general, this excess dimension of time must take on the forms of labour-power, capitalist means and conditions of production, and commodities, and it must fall within their spatial reproduction circuits. Meanwhile, only money can 'translate' these spatial forms and reproduction circuits into time by quantifying them, giving the excess surplus labour-time an independent existence.

6.10   CONCLUSION: THE TRANSLATION OF MEASUREMENT AND QUANTIFICATION INTO AN 'ECONOMY OF TIME'

The next step would be to transfer both the technique of money and the valorization of labour-power and capital, hence both the measuring 'subject' and the measured object or substance, into an 'economy of time', and literally to dissolve their entanglement in time (Marx [1857–58] 2010a, p. 109).[14] Money – with the ideal unit it stands for and with the relations it quantitatively realizes, mediates and converts – calculates or reckons with the identity of time; yet this time must obtain in the forms and in the relations of labour-power and its capitalist means and conditions of (re-)production.

As regards the dimension of valorization, Marx explicitly dissolves the substance of value and its valorization into two temporal relationships. Or rather, he shows that it is the capitalist self-relation of money which dissolves into these two time-relations. The first relation is present and past labour-time, contained in labour-power and accumulated in the value of the capitalist means of production (Marx [1867] 1996, pp. 187ff., esp. 221); Marx develops this relation under the term 'organic composition of capital' (Marx [1867] 1996, pp. 607–703). The second relation is necessary and surplus labour-time. Through this relation, time becomes excessive through the commodification of labour-time and the reproduction circuit of this particular, 'ecstatic' commodity. What is measured and exhibited in average magnitudes of labour-time, but also in profit, is in the last instance the actual productive power of these two time-relations.

The technique of putting into effect and regulating these time-relations falls within a measurement and a quantification that now can be summarized and epitomized as a calculation – or a reckoning – with the identity of time. This calculation is twofold and ambivalent. It is a rational – and even a mathematical – calculation executed with money by all individuals; however, these are always already moments of the supra-individual, speculative calculation which money puts into effect when it posits all the qualitative forms of labour and capital in a social relation which they quantitatively share by means of the construction of the average magnitudes necessary for their own productive valorization and reproduction. Furthermore, money *is* this metamorphosis and this passage between past and future valorization. The individual calculation must therefore – in a second-order operation, as it were – reckon with this supra-individual reckoning which money puts into effect for the capitalist totality and for individuality.

---

14 There have been several attempts to reconstruct such an economy of time, for example by J. Derrida, M. Postone, D. Bensaïd, S. Tombazos, P. Osborne, D. Harvey, W. Bonefeld, M. Tomba, H. Rosa, J. Martineau and H. Harootunian. However, even where the connection between economy and time was sought in money, it was mostly determined in a rather 'exoteric' way, whereas the 'esoteric' connection has, in my view, to be sought in quantification and measurement (see Engster 2014).

To recapitulate this reckoning, the main functions of money must be translated, or transposed, into the technique of measurement through time:

1. As a measure, the excluded money-commodity – with the fixed ideal unit of value – holds time identical or timeless. The negative and identical quality which emerges through quantification by a measure, hence the quality of quantitative relations, seems to be an abstract, homogenous time which exists timelessly by virtue of its quantification.
2. Through this quantification, however, this timeless, self-identical time always already comes into being via the magnitudes of commodities. It thereby exists in a determinate and finite way, and it seems that money, *qua* means of exchange and circulation, realizes and presents this time by quantifying it, and that money holds time as quantitatively identical and stores it by transferring and circulating it.
3. Yet this presence of time is also a semblance, as money realizes in the magnitudes of commodities the productive power of the time-relations which regulate their production; that is, the productive power of living-present and past-dead, but accumulated, labour-time. This quantitative realization turns out to be an actualization of the productive power of the relation of past and present labour-time by average magnitudes; just as if this relation had been measured through time. Although money stands for a negative, pure and universal time, this becomes regulative by means of the average magnitudes which money deduces, determining from past valorization the magnitudes necessary for future productive relations and for future 'organic compositions' of past and present labour-time, and money itself converts these magnitudes back into these relations, becoming the passage of a present between past and future presence.
4. Whereas the capital-form brings into effect a productive relation of past and present labour-time and encompasses it in an overarching manner, as in a time-spanning movement, the finance-forms of capital calculate (with) the future of this relation, and deal with different possibilities which turn into probabilities and entangle the present with its anticipated future.

To summarize, in the quanta actualized, money makes the valorization of labour-power through capital manifest as if the relation between these two were measured through time. Through money's functions and circuits, society as a whole is held to the measure of time, and becomes fractured by time, as in a total self-reflection, and in a reflection of social totality. On the one hand, this time comes to exist in all the measured and quantified social relations which, on the other hand, are constantly realized, transferred and converted by money. The entanglement between measured valorization and measuring money is an entanglement between, on the one hand, a detached and external natural or, better, naturalized time which, at once, becomes socialized by the valorization of labour and capital; and, on the other hand, its measurement through money, making money the interface between naturalized and socialized time. This is how, finally, both measuring money and measured valorization dissolve their entanglement in a temporalization of time. This dissolution of social relations in time is simultaneously the solution of the money riddle: money quantitatively realizes a time which money itself brings with it: money *is* this temporalization of time by quantifying social relations; reckoning with the identity of a time which becomes the identity of society in the circuits of the latter's reproduction.

REFERENCES

Abbreviations:
  MECW = Marx–Engels Collected Works. London: Lawrence & Wishart.
  MEW = Marx–Engels Werke. Berlin: Dietz.

Backhaus, H.-G., (1980). On the Dialectics of the Value-Form. *Thesis Eleven* 1(1), pp. 99–120.
Badiou, A., (2005). *Being and Event.* London: Continuum.
Engels, F., [1859] (1971). Review of A Contribution to the Critique of Political Economy. In: *MECW*, vol. 16. Digital edition. London: Lawrence & Wishart, pp. 465–477.
Engels, F., [1894] (1998). Preface of Vol. III. In: *MECW*, vol. 37. Digital edition. London: Lawrence & Wishart, pp. 5–23.
Engster, F., (2014). *Das Geld als Maß, Mittel und Methode. Das Rechnen mit der Identität der Zeit.* Berlin: Neofelis.
Hegel, G.W.F., (2010). *The Science of Logic.* Cambridge: University Press.
Heinrich, M., (2021). *The Science of Value. Marx's Critique of Political Economy Between Scientific Revolution and Classical Tradition.* Leiden: Brill.
Kant, I., [1781] (1998). *Critique of Pure Reason.* Trans. P. Guyer and A.W. Wood, Cambridge: Cambridge University Press.
Marx, K., [1857–58] (2010a and 2010b). *Grundrisse. Manuscripts 1857–61.* In: *MECW*, vol. 28 and 29. Digital edition. London: Lawrence & Wishart.
Marx, K., [1861–63] (2010). Manuscripts 1861–63. In: *MECW*, vol. 30. Digital edition. London: Lawrence & Wishart.
Marx, K., [1867] (1996). *Capital. Critique of Political Economy Vol. I.* In: *MECW*, vol. 35. Digital edition. London: Lawrence & Wishart.
Marx, K., (1962). *Das Kapital. Kritik der politischen Ökonomie* Bd. I. In: *MEW* Bd. 23. Berlin: Dietz Verlag.
Marx, K., (1998). Capital Vol. III. In: *MECW*, vol. 37. Digital edition. London: Lawrence & Wishart.
Marx, K. and Engels, F., [1848] (2010). Manifesto of the Communist Party. In: *MECW*, vol. 6. Digital edition. London: Lawrence & Wishart. pp. 477–517.
Rubin, I.I., [1928] (1972). *Essays on Marx's Theory of Value.* Detroit: Black & Red.

7.   Automatic subject

Luca Micaloni

7.1   SUBJECTIVITY AS ACTIVITY: FROM THE EARLY WRITINGS TO THE GENERAL FORMULA OF CAPITAL

In the fourth chapter of *Capital* Volume One Marx analyses the transformation of money into capital. While in simple circulation the independent, monetary form of value serves only the purpose of mediating the exchange of commodities and 'vanishes in the final result of the movement', in the M-C-M circulation the form of value is 'constantly changing from one form to the other without thereby becoming lost' (Marx [1890] 1991, p. 141; transl. p. 171). The conservation of money and the expansion of value through the constant alternation of money-form and commodity-form induce Marx to describe value as an 'automatic subject', or as the subject that dominates (or overarches) such a process[1] and is endowed with the ability to add value to itself.[2] In the course of this process, value 'repels itself as surplus-value from itself as original value' (Marx [1890] 1991, p. 141, transl. p. 171, trans. mod.), and thus 'It enters now, so to say, into private relations with itself' (Marx [1890] 1991, p. 142, transl. p. 172). In order to describe capital's recursive self-reference, Marx also resorts to theological jargon: value 'differentiates itself as original value from itself as surplus-value, just as the Father differentiates himself from himself quâ the Son' (Marx [1890] 1991, p. 142, transl. p. 172, trans. mod.).[3] The 'trinitarian' similitude adopted in the general formula introduces a dialectical coexistence between capital's real dynamics and the fetishized character

---

[1]   '*Das übergreifende Subjekt eines solches Processes*'.

[2]   This ability is initially defined as 'occult'. Marx's illustration of the production of surplus-value is meant to unravel its enigmatic character.

[3]   Compare Hegel's account of the transition from 'Force and the Understanding' to 'Self-Consciousness' in the *Phenomenology of Spirit* (Hegel [1807] 1986, p. 135, transl. p. 102): 'I, the selfsame being, repel myself from myself; but what is posited as distinct from me, or as unlike me, is immediately, in being so distinguished, not a distinction for me'.

of its self-relation, which will also play an essential role at later stages of the exposition.

Both notions of 'subject' and 'automaticity' raise some interpretative and theoretical issues, also reflected in the recurring tendency to expunge them from translations.[4] Marx derives his notion of subjectivity from German Idealism, particularly from Hegel, who perhaps more than any other thinker bestowed on the Subject a set of features belonging to the semantic area of 'activity': self-motion, self-relation,[5] negation of otherness, self-negation, 'return' from otherness, circular movement. Without reaching (nor pursuing) systematic coherence, Marx often refers to this cluster of meaning in his use of the concept of 'Subject', including his recurring definitions of capital as Subject in the critique of political economy.

Since his early writings, to be a subject means to be an active and self-moving entity that moves itself through a specific (circular and 'returning') form of movement and by virtue of endogenous power. Marx puts this argument forth already in his critique of Hegel's theory of the state, when he comments on the famous §262 of the *Elements of the Philosophy of Right*. Hegel is criticized for having improperly attributed to the Idea of the state subjective, active features and the capacity to 'posit' family and civil society as moments of its self-development; while – Marx argues – family and civil society are the 'real presuppositions' and the truly active spheres:

> The Idea is subjectivized and the *real* relationship of the family and civil society to the state is conceived as its[6] inner, *imaginary activity*. The family and civil society are the preconditions of the state; they are the true agents; but in speculative phi-

---

[4]   Since the first edition of *Capital*, Marx described capital as 'an automatic Subject that sets itself in motion' (Marx [1867] 1983, p. 109): '*ein automatisches, in sich selbst prozessirendes Subjekt*'. In the second German edition, Marx kept the references to the automatic Subject he had made in the first edition, but added the phrase 'a self-moving substance in process' (Marx [1873] 1987, p. 172): '*eine processirende, sich selbst bewegende Substanz*', which continued to appear up to the fourth German edition (Marx [1890] 1991, p. 142, transl. p. 172): 'an independent substance, endowed with a motion of its own'. The 'processual' feature of the automatic subject is no longer present in the French edition, where the phrasing of the second German edition is replaced by 'automatic substance, endowed with its own life' (Marx [1872–75] 1989, p. 124: '*une substance automatique, douée d'une vie propre*'. As for the English translations, in the Aveling–Moore translation the phrases 'subject of a process' and 'automatic subject' were replaced by 'active factor in a process' and 'automatically active character' (of value) respectively (see Marx [1887] 1990, p. 133) and have been restored in Ben Fowkes's Penguin translation.

[5]   On the applicability of the concept of self-relation to Hegel's philosophy, see Henrich (1982, pp. 142–208).

[6]   In the translation: 'their'.

losophy it is the reverse. When the Idea is subjectivized the real subjects ... are all transformed into unreal, objective moments of the Idea (Marx [1843] 1982, p. 8, transl. p. 62)

In Marx's theory, this notion of Subject as activity cooperates with the Aristotelian concept of *hypokeimenon* in order to put forth a critique of subject/predicate inversions:[7] while in actual reality the subject is the material bearer of properties and the logical subject that holds predicates, in Hegel predicates are made independent and become themselves subjects (Marx [1843] 1982, p. 25, transl. p. 80).

A similar notion of subjectivity (along with other shades and uses of the concept of Subject) recurs then in several loci of Marx's work, from the *Economic and Philosophic Manuscripts* to the *Grundrisse*, particularly in the definition of labour, of its alienation, and of its opposition to objectified labour.[8]

As we have seen in the general formula, Marx's formulations in the critique of political economy indicate quite clearly that being an automatic subject, that is, possessing the ability to move itself in an endless circle[9] without resorting to any external moving cause, is an essential feature of capital.

The conjunction of subjectivity and automaticity might seem paradoxical at a first glance, but the oxymoron dissipates when we consider automaticity as equivalent to self-motion.[10] Far from denoting a conditioned and passive entity moved by external factors, the notion of 'automaton' underlying the general formula of capital entails the subjective prerogative of being principle, cause, beginning and end of one's own movement.

In the following, I show how Marx's characterization of large-scale industry and of interest-bearing capital proves to be coherent with the circular

---

[7]   See Marx ([1843] 1982, p. 12).

[8]   For example, Marx ([1844] 1982a and 1982b, pp. 258 and 384, respectively; transl. p. 343; Marx [1857/58] 1976, p. 196, transl. p. 272). I must omit the philological issues regarding the publication of both the *Economic and Philosophical Manuscripts* and the *Grundrisse*. The translations I indicate were not based on the MEGA edition.

[9]   'Value therefore now becomes value in process, money in process, and, as such, capital. It comes out of circulation, enters into it again, preserves and multiplies itself within its circuit, comes back out of it with expanded bulk, and begins the same round ever afresh' (Marx [1890] 1991, p. 142, transl. p. 173).

[10]   Western thought offers multiple uses of the notion of 'automaton' and of the contiguous, but not overlapping, notion of 'self-motion'. The idea of self-motion plays a crucial role in several debates, both ancient and modern (see Cambiano 1994; Gill and Lennox 1994), regarding: (a) the nature of the soul and its relation with the body (e.g. Plato, *Phaedr.* 245c–245e); (b) physics and cosmology, and the movement of celestial objects in particular (e.g. Aristotle, *Phys.* VIII.5, 257a–258b); and (c) automatic machines (see Bedini 1964; Chapuis and Gélis 1984; Berryman 2003).

self-movement illustrated in the general formula. Lastly, I present a few remarks on the Hegel–Marx connection and I add some arguments in favour of the 'homology thesis'.

7.2 THE SUBJECT OF LARGE-SCALE INDUSTRY: FIXED CAPITAL AS SELF-MOVING AUTOMATON

The subjective structure of self-motion that defines the concept of capital also characterizes the increasing mechanization of production processes, which culminates (at least at the stage of development Marx could observe) in large-scale industry. In the transition from manufacture to large-scale industry we witness capital's growing ability to assume properties formerly ascribed to human subjectivity. Coherently with its nature of automatic subject, capital presents itself as an automatic system of machinery, dead labour that shows subjective, 'living' capacity of self-motion.

In manufacture, each operation still 'retains the character of a handicraft, and is therefore dependent on the strength, skill, quickness, and sureness, of the individual workman in handling his tools. The handicraft continues to be the basis. This narrow technical basis excludes a really scientific analysis of the production process' (Marx [1890] 1991, p. 305, transl. p. 371, trans. mod.).

The analytic subdivision of the labour process leads to the annexation of the workers to a partial operation. Yoked to a limited function, 'the individual himself is divided up, and transformed into the automatic motor [*das automatisches Triebswerk*] of a fractional operation' (Marx [1890] 1991, p. 325, transl. p. 396, trans. mod.). It is worth dwelling a little on the specific meaning of 'automatic' at this stage, as it is significantly different from the one examined in the general formula. For the workers, the automatic character entails absence of control over their own movement and the labour process of which it is part. Deprived of freedom of initiative and of rational control, living labour-power is reduced to motive power of a 'working machine', which carries out the operation in its stead. The automatic character of the movement means the complete spoliation of the essential features of human subjectivity. Not coincidentally, Marx is to some extent in tune with Adam Ferguson, according to whom 'manufactures … prosper most where the mind is least consulted' (Marx [1890] 1991, p. 326, transl. p. 397); and with the even more radical idea formulated by Adam Smith according to which the worker 'has no occasion to exert his understanding' and only acquires dexterity in his partial operation 'at the expense of his intellectual, social, and martial virtues' (Marx [1890] 1991, p. 327, transl. pp. 397–398). As we shall see, the removal of subjectivity from the workers that takes place in manufacture by means of the automatization of their movement, in large-scale industry is reinforced through a more thorough automation of the whole labour process that bestows subjective qualities on fixed capital.

Marx explicitly maintains that in the logical-historical progression from 'cooperation' to 'manufacture' and to 'machinery' as regulative principles of capitalist production, the superior functions of mental reconstruction and conscious command of the labour process are increasingly transferred from the bearers of labour-power to capital:

> The knowledge, the judgement, and the will, which, though in ever so small a degree, are practised by the independent peasant or handicraftsman … are now required only for the workshop as a whole. Intelligence in production expands in one direction, because it vanishes in many others. What is lost by the detail labourers, is concentrated in the capital that employs them. It is a result of the division of labour in manufactures, that the labourer is brought face to face with the intellectual potencies [*geistige Potenzen*] of the material process of production, as the property of another, and as a ruling power. This separation begins in simple co-operation, where the capitalist represents to the single workman, the oneness and the will of the associated labour. It is developed in manufacture which cuts down the labourer into a detail labourer. It is completed in modern industry, which makes science a productive force distinct from labour and presses it into the service of capital. (Marx [1890] 1991, pp. 325–326, transl. pp. 396–397)

The adequation of capital to its definition as 'automatic subject' is gradually accomplished as machine-based production gains centrality. More thoroughly than cooperation and manufacture, large-scale industry production approximates capital to the full historical coincidence with its general formula. While in manufacture 'the workman becomes adapted to the process', but 'the process was previously made suitable to the workman', in production with machinery 'this subjective principle of the division of labour no longer exists' (Marx [1890] 1991, p. 341, transl. p. 415), and the instruments of labour, instead of labour-power, are the starting point of the analysis of the process of production.[11]

Intolerant of the anthropic limitations to the expansion of relative surplus-value, capital overcomes them through technological development:

> Here, the process as a whole is examined objectively, in itself, that is to say, without regard to the question of its execution by human hands, it is analysed into its constituent phases; and the problem, how to execute each detail process, and bind them all into a whole, is solved by the aid of machines, chemistry, &c. (Marx [1890] 1991, p. 341, transl. p. 415)

---

11   See Marx ([1890] 1991, p. 333, transl. p. 405).

In the paragraph on the English factory legislation, this crucial allusion to technology becomes more explicit:

> The principle which it pursued, of resolving each process into its constituent movements, without any regard to their possible execution by the hand of man, created the new modern science of technology. The varied, apparently unconnected, and petrified forms of the industrial processes now resolved themselves into so many conscious and systematic applications of natural science to the attainment of given useful effects. Technology also discovered the few main fundamental forms of motion, which, despite the diversity of the instruments used, are necessarily taken by every productive action of the human body. (Marx [1890] 1991, p. 438, transl. p. 532)

At the core of the capitalistic extraction of surplus-value lies *die ganz moderne Wissenschaft der Technologie*, which hinges on the application of natural science and on the ergonomic knowledge of the human body.[12] This tendency to the 'objectification' of the production process and of the workers employed in it, to the demystification of the 'mysteries' of handicraft, takes place along with the dislocation, the marginalization, the ever-growing expulsion of labour-power from production. The industrial worker can be replaced, both as motive force and as keeper of indispensable knowledge, which have now been concentrated in capital through the separation of the 'intellectual potentialities' from the worker, and through the radicalization and the 'carrying out of the automatic principle' (Marx [1890] 1991, p. 342, transl. p. 416).

The motor mechanism has become 'a self-acting prime mover' (Marx [1890] 1991, p. 342, transl. p. 416), and the entire labour process is now carried out by 'an organized system of machines, to which motion is communicated by the transmitting mechanism from a central automaton' (Marx [1890] 1991, pp. 342–343, transl. p. 416). Despite apologetic descriptions of machinery that present the 'combined collective worker' as 'the dominant subject [*übergreifendes Subjekt*], and the mechanical automaton as the object' (Marx [1890]

---

[12] While the references to Charles Babbage and Andrew Ure are preserved in *Capital*, references to the German coté of *Technologie* that Marx read at least since 1851 (see Marx [1851/56] 1982) featured in the *1861–63 Manuscript* but were for the most part removed from the first edition of Volume One. A further significant element, from both a philological and a theoretical point of view, is the progressive systematic substitution of many occurrences of the adjective 'technological' (*technologisch*), widely used in the first German edition of Volume One, with 'technical' (*technisch*) in the successive German editions. On this issue, see Müller (1992), Tribe (2016), Frison (1992, 1993a, 1993b). Bellofiore (2018) makes interesting remarks regarding the peculiar kind of socialization linked to technology and its structural function in capitalist economy, as well as its systematic, pivotal position within the architecture of *Capital*. On the text alterations in the second edition of Volume One, see Jungnickel (1987).

1991, p. 377, transl. p. 458), in the new organization of the labour process 'the automaton itself is the subject' (Marx [1890] 1991, p. 377, transl. p. 458).

The adequation of capital to its concept, that is, to the subjective and automatic (and 'overarching') character established by the general formula, involves once again the coexistence of actual functioning and fetish-like pretension, which cannot be reduced one to the other. Though it strives to be an automatic subject, capital cannot wholly reduce the alterity of nature and of labour-power to a product of its own absolute positing, and needs instead to internalize and subsume external factors of production through a constant, asymptotic effort. One might be thus tempted to ground the (actual or latent) possibility of struggle and conflict in this inescapable constraint that imposes on capital the constant renewal of subsumption of nature and labour-power (as well as the extraction of labour and value from the latter). On the other hand, both the high degree of technical domination of nature, and capital's exertion of social power over the working class (up to the determination of the psycho-physical, cognitive and libidinal constitution of it), may lead to subsumption being conceived of as an irreversible result.[13] In fact, Marx's text is ambivalent enough to support the fluctuation of Marxist theory between these two kinds of reading: on the one hand, the interpretation of automaticity as the ultimately unattainable aim of capital; on the other, the full integration of otherness and of potentially insubordinate elements.

Be that as it may, for the scope of this chapter it is sufficient to say that the multiple references to the semantic field of automaticity and self-motion, as well as the connection between automaticity and subjectivity, indicate the extent to which the automation of the labour process in large-scale industry represents for Marx an implementation of the general formula of capital as 'automatic subject'.

7.3 INTEREST-BEARING CAPITAL AS AUTOMATIC FETISH AND REAL BEGINNING

In the fifth part of Volume Three[14] ('The Division of Profit into Interest and Profit of Enterprise'), Marx introduces – particularly in chapters 21 and 24 –

---

[13]   See Arthur (2002), Bellofiore (2013). A different perspective can be found in Finelli (2014).

[14]   Volume Three is the result of a posthumous edition conducted by Engels on the basis of Marx's manuscript. Engels' interventions affect the subdivision into chapters, the repositioning and reworking of text portions and the theoretical determination of ambiguous phrases and passages. On these problems, see Jungnickel 1991; Vollgraf and Jungnickel 1994; Vollgraf 1995; Vygodsky 1995; Heinrich 1996. On Volume Three in general, see Campbell and Reuten 2002. As regards the chapters analyzed

the category of 'interest-bearing capital'. In this shape (M-M'), money exhibits the ability to derive its expansion from itself alone, that is, to pursue and to obtain self-valorization exclusively through self-relation.

This 'meaningless abbreviation' (Marx [1894] 2004, p. 381, transl. p. 515) of the whole process and of the general formula of capital seems to be homologous with an idealistic subjectivity yearning to disregard every external reality and to relate only to itself in a pure and unperturbed self-reference. The loss of meaning is a consequence of the fact that a purely abstract form has not only subsumed the concrete entities and subjects that grant its subsistence, but has also removed the entire series of mediations it presupposes and has – seemingly – managed to become a fully autonomous and automatic Subject.

The form of interest-bearing capital appears logically autonomous from the series of transitions of which it is the result. Moreover, it conceals its nature of product of social relations, and condenses it in a simple, 'thingly' givenness: 'The *thing* (money, commodity, value) is now already capital simply as a thing; the result of the overall reproduction process[15] appears[16] as a property devolving on a thing in itself'[17] (Marx [1894] 2004, p. 381, transl. p. 516). All that appears in this shape is a given quantity of money which begets more money, free from contamination by empirical processes of production.

However, the self-valorization of interest-bearing capital is a real property, not a mere semblance. Money here is a commodity that is alienated (in this case, loaned out) because of its capacity to act later as functioning capital, that is, to valorize itself in production and to realize itself in circulation. Borrowed capital is a peculiar commodity that is 'alienated only on condition that it is, first, returned to its starting-point after a definite period of time, and second,

---

in this section (XXI and XXIV), the partition of the matter substantially follows the Manuscript (chapters XXI-XXIV follow chapters I-IV of section V of the manuscript). Also, the text edited by Engels is fairly accurate when compared with the manuscript; however, at least for the quotations, I indicate in the endnotes where the edited text differs from it.

[15]   In the manuscript: 'of production and circulation'. On the interchangeability, in Engels's editorial work, of this hendiadys and of the terms 'production' and 'reproduction', see Vollgraf and Jungnickel (1994).

[16]   '*Erscheint*'. Added by Engels. Marx often distinguishes phenomenic 'appearance', the (partially reliable) mode of manifestation of an essence and its necessary correlate, from 'semblance', a superficial, illusory and deceptive projection of an underlying reality. Such a distinction is drawn from the Hegelian one between 'appearance' (*Erscheinung*) and 'shine' or 'illusory being' (*Schein*), but does not overlap it.

[17]   '*Eine, einem Ding von sich selbst zukommende Eigenschaft*': interpolation by Engels. In the manuscript (Marx [1863–67] 1992, p. 462): '*eine dem Ding inhärente Eigenschaft*'.

is returned as realized capital, so that it has realized its use-value of producing surplus-value' (Marx [1894] 2004, p. 335, transl. p. 465).

Both the initial act and the final return of money to the lending capitalist are 'legal transactions which take place before and after the real movement of capital and have nothing to do with it as such' (Marx [1894] 2004, p. 339, transl. p. 469).

It is important to notice that the expansion of capital by means of a legal transaction which is indifferent to the real process of production and realization is not a mere sleight of capital carried out by a fetishized abstract form that removes and mystifies the actual process of valorization. The fetish-character coexists, within the same figure, with actual properties that are not reducible to the condensation and concealment of the social relations of production, and of the process of production and circulation. The disappearance of the mediations that allow capital's relation with itself is both the way in which interest-bearing capital mystifies its genesis, and a part of the way in which interest-bearing capital subsists and acts as self-expanding money.

The coexistence of these two descriptions characterizes chapters 21 and 24 of Volume Three. On the one hand, Marx restates that 'in interest-bearing capital, the capital relationship reaches its most superficial and fetishized form' (Marx [1894] 2004, p. 380, transl. p. 515). On the other hand, the reification of the social relationship and the seemingly immediate self-valorization are not the only ontological functions that pertain to this form. The same figure is also 'the original starting point of capital' (Marx [1894] 2004, p. 381, transl. p. 515), that is, the real starting point of the entire economic dynamics: no longer the starting point seen as the beginning of the systematic exposition (commodity), but capital, by now capable of providing an ontological foundation to the whole process and, moreover, capital that, being lent out as capital, becomes itself 'a thing for sale' [*verkaufbares Ding*] (Marx [1894] 2004, p. 382, transl. p. 517), and thus reconnects with the 'mediated immediacy' of the initial category of Volume One. Two different social and economic functions are thus reunited in the same shape: the highest mystification of the real process,[18] and the real ontological starting point, that which is more fundamental and not simply most readily knowable by ordinary consciousness.

On the one hand, the exposition has spread out the whole complexity of capitalist production and reproduction, which culminates in 'capital in its finished form [*das fertige Kapital*], the unity of the production and circulation processes, and hence capital yielding a definite surplus-value in a specific period of time' (Marx [1894] 2004, p. 381, transl. pp. 515–516). However,

---

[18]   '[T]he power of producing surplus-value in geometric progression by way of an inherent secret quality, as a pure automaton' (Marx [1894] 2004, p. 388, transl. p. 523).

on the other hand, by virtue of the same shape, the highest mystification of the whole process also takes place. This direct valorization is both true and false: the reliable expression of reality, and the mystification of it; endowed with ontological consistence and systemic necessity. In order to define the mystification of capital, Marx once again invokes the notion of automaticity: 'in interest-bearing capital, therefore, this automatic fetish is elaborated[19] into its pure form, self-valorizing value, money breeding money, and in this form it no longer bears any marks of its constitution [*Entstehung*]' (Marx [1894] 2004, p. 381, transl. mod. p. 516).

The 'finished form' of the automatic fetish has removed the process mediating its genesis, but the process itself and its moments enjoy neither ontological consistence nor logical justification outside the generative power of the 'real starting point' which coexists with the fetish in the same shape. This shape represents, as we have seen, 'the capital mystification in its most flagrant form' (Marx [1894] 2004, p. 382, transl. p. 516), but also the real logical and ontological basis of the entire actual movement, that is, 'the simple form [*die einfache Gestalt*] of capital, in which it is presupposed [*vorausgesetzt*][20] to its own reproduction process' (Marx [1894] 2004, p. 382, transl. mod. p. 516): that is, it activates, as financing (the real starting point), its reproduction process. The real beginning and the fetishized form are joined but do not coincide, and represent distinct aspects of the same category.

7.4 WHICH HOMOLOGY? RE-DISCUSSING THE HEGEL–MARX RELATION

The vast array of positions regarding the relation between Marx's critique of political economy and Hegel's logic can be reduced to two main sets: on the one hand, 'methodological' interpretations that investigate the influence of the Hegelian mode of exposition of categories on the Marxian one;[21] on the other hand, 'ontological' interpretations, which maintain that the use of Hegelian categories and structures hinges on the isomorphism between those (idealistic) categories and socio-economic reality.[22] Methodological readings, despite their insistence on the development of the 'thing itself', remain most often below

---

[19]   '*Herausgearbeitet*'. In the manuscript: '*Vollendet*'.
[20]   The translation 'taken as logically anterior' annuls all of the ontological value of the presupposition.
[21]   See Noske (1976), Jahn and Noske (1980), Škedrow (1989), Fineschi (2008).
[22]   See Arthur (2002), Moseley and Smith (2014). See also Backhaus (1997). Backhaus's perspective, as well as that of other authors, does not fall univocally into one side of the methodological/ontological couple, which is not meant to work as a rigid distinction.

the genuinely ontological commitment that a Hegelian exposition requires in order to be justified and not be merely arbitrary. Ontological readings, instead, conceive of the 'homology' between economic reality and Hegelian logic focusing on the domination of 'pure forms', a putative historical embodiment of philosophical idealism; in so doing, they not only offer a one-sided account of the 'idealistic' nature of value and capital, but also fail to recognize the actual ground of the systematic-dialectical framework of *Capital*.[23]

The thesis of a Marxian use of Hegelian metaphysics in order to grasp the metaphysic structure of capitalist society was introduced by Colletti (1973), though within an interpretative framework according to which Marx's 'problematic' – and accordingly, to a certain extent, his method – were to be understood as one and the same, from the early writings to the critique of political economy: a critique of subject–predicate inversions, of the subjectification of abstract forms and of their domination over the concrete, legitimate subjects (Colletti 1991, p. 47).[24] Marx's relation to Hegel was thus no longer conceived of as a materialistic appropriation of the dialectic (at last put back on its feet), but as a materialist critique of Hegel's inversions (including the dialectic) which nevertheless were the keystone of the analysis of the capitalist mode of production. This idea, along with some results of the *Neue Marx-Lektüre*,[25] flows into the more recent 'value-form approach', and in the systematic-dialectic account of the critique of political economy it is again

---

[23]   See Arthur (2002, p. 82): 'Just as Hegel's logic follows the self-movement of thought ... so the dialectic of exchange sets up a *form-determined system*. Here the formal structures are indeed "self-acting" ... the forms are in effect of such abstract purity as to constitute a real incarnation of the ideas of Hegel's logic'. Compare Colletti (1973, pp. 280–282):

> This society based on capital and commodities is therefore the metaphysics, the fetishism, the 'mystical world' – even more so than Hegel's Logic itself ... This overturning, this quid pro quo, this *Umkehrung*, which, according to Marx, rules Hegel's Logic, rules also, long before the Logic, the objective mechanisms of this society.

See also Reichelt (1970, p. 80): 'Hegel's Idealism ... is the bourgeois civil society as ideology'. The critique of the 'deranged forms' (*verrückte Formen*) is a relevant motif in Backhaus (1997). Arthur (2003a) has summarized the results of his approach. See the criticism by Smith (2003) and Arthur's reply (Arthur 2003b). A further development of the discussion is in *Historical Materialism*, 13(2). For a critical examination of the homology thesis, see also Bellofiore (2018).

[24]   'His discussion of subject–predicate inversion in Hegel's logic, his analysis of estrangement and alienation, and (finally) his critique of the fetishism of commodities and capital can all be seen as the progressive unfolding, as the ever-deepening grasp of a single problematic.'

[25]   See Reichelt (1970), Backhaus (1997).

combined with a dialectical reconstruction of the exposition of economic categories.

In what follows I will maintain, first, that Marx's *Capital* meets the requirements of Hegel's 'philosophical science', as regards its difference from empirical sciences.[26] Second, that this systematic collocation lies on an ontological foundation, which is the proper terrain upon which the discussion regarding the similarities between Hegel's logic and Marx's *Capital* should be grafted. Third, that the 'Hegelian' traits of modern economy should be redefined, in order to outline a non-extrinsic relation between logic and ontology within *Capital*.

Hegel claims that experimental or empirical sciences (*Erfahrungswissenschaften*) 'have found for their own purposes their own peculiar method, such as it is, of defining and classifying their material' (Hegel [1831] 1986, p. 48, transl. p. 53).[27] What empirical sciences aim at 'are laws, general propositions, a theory, i.e. the thoughts of what there is [of what is given, *des Vorhandens*]' (Hegel [1830] 1986, § 7). In the 'scientific manner' of empirical science 'the Universal ... is on the one hand left indeterminate for itself and is not intrinsically connected to the particular [*das Besondere*]. Instead, both are external and contingent in relation to each other, as are likewise the combined particularities vis-à-vis each other in their reciprocal relationship' (Hegel [1830] 1986, § 9).

According to Hegel, political economy (*Staats-Ökonomie*) is an eminent example of an empirical 'intellectual' science – that is, that relies on connections established by understanding, or 'intellect' (*Verstand*) – in which the universal and the particular are related in an extrinsic fashion. It is important to notice that such a methodological configuration of political economy is not due to a theoretical limit, but rather to the nature of its ontological domain, which for Hegel is characterized by an analogous extrinsic composition of universality and particularity and by the reciprocal externality of the particulars: 'its development affords the interesting spectacle (as in Smith, Say and Ricardo) of thought working upon the endless mass of details which confront it at the outset and extracting therefrom the simple principles of the thing, the understanding [*Verstand*] effective in the thing and directing it' (Hegel [1821] 1986, § 189).

---

[26]   This does not mean, of course, that the Marxian critique of political economy is devoid of any claim to empirical validity.

[27]   One might of course object that such a laconic formulation does not do justice to the richness of experimental methodology, which does not (or not solely) consist in 'defining and classifying'; and that Hegel's view is too narrow, not only in the light of the more recent philosophy of science, but also in regard to the epistemology of his time.

The Intellect is able to grasp the economic 'Thing' (*Sache*) adequately, only insofar as the Thing is informed and regulated by 'intellectual' ontological principles. The only mediation between particularity and universality – between the peculiar needs of individual agents on the one hand, and their reciprocal dependence on the other – of which the System of needs is capable, is the intellectual form of rationality (*Verständigkeit*) (Hegel [1821] 1986, § 187). The 'System of needs' replicates a salient feature of 'civil society', in which the individuals' efforts to fulfil their egoistic aims gave birth to 'a system of complete interdependence' (*ein System allseitiger Abhängigkeit*), regarded as 'external state', as a 'state of Necessity and of Intellect' (*Not- und Verstandes-Staat*) (Hegel [1821] 1986, § 183).

For Hegel, methodological differences rest on ontological reasons: the Intellect governs the Thing, and therefore the Thing can be grasped by 'intellectual' knowledge. In the *Encyclopedia*, Hegel suggests that:

> as satisfactory as this [empirical] knowledge may initially be in its sphere, there is, in the first place, yet another domain of objects that are not contained therein, namely freedom, spirit, and God ... they are not found in that sphere, because in terms of their content these objects immediately present themselves as infinite. (Hegel [1830] 1986, § 8)

Infinite objects require a different kind of knowledge. The previous illustration of Marx's characterization of capital as 'automatic Subject' should allow us to go beyond the formulaic opposition between metaphysical idealism and materialism, and to understand that Marx's real detachment from Hegel ultimately hinges on the identification of capital as infinite object (or rather, infinite Subject). The Hegel–Marx methodological connection in *Capital* is of both continuity and discontinuity. On the one hand, Marx builds his critique of political economy according to Hegel's model of a philosophical science; on the other hand, he extends this model to an objectual domain that Hegel entrusts to a corresponding empirical science, legitimate in its field. If Marx concurs with Hegel on the evaluation of classical political economy as extraction of simple principles from the manifoldness of empirical facts,[28] he supersedes Hegel's viewpoint through the critique of political economy, having shed light on the infinity of its object. Thus, methodological continuity entails Marx's implicit 'systematic' disagreement, which in its turn is rooted

---

[28]   Marx sees in Adam Smith's work a methodological contradiction between the attempt 'to penetrate the intimate physiology of bourgeois society' and the need 'to find a nomenclature and corresponding concepts of intellect (*Verstandesbegriffe*) for these phenomena' (Marx [1861–63] 1978, p. 817). Such a claim seems to be utterly in line with Hegel's description of political economy as 'intellectual' science.

in an ontological difformity: for Hegel (and for classical political economy), no economic entity is capable of true infinity; while for Marx, capital is a truly infinite entity[29] that is able to derive from itself an organic and circular totality, and hence is a suitable subject-matter for a 'science with Hegelian characteristics'. Methodological continuity is therefore based on an ontological break, that is, on a different theoretical acquisition of the social content of civil society. In order to treat political economy as a philosophical science in the Hegelian sense, Marx needs to dismiss the Hegelian view of political economy and of the economic sphere, and to recognize the existence of a Subject that is isomorphic with the infinite dynamics of the Concept.[30] Capital is 'Hegelian' not only because it fetishizes and reifies the process of its valorization, and strives to interiorize, through formal and real subsumption, all external and possibly conflictual elements, but also because – precisely in its most fetishized form – capital is the real starting point of the entire economic dynamic, already 'present' from the beginning of the exposition. Drawing on this Hegelian concept of a result of a series of mediations that is also the beginning of the series, and that after the deduction condensates itself and releases itself into reality, Marx sets the ground for its macro-monetary theory of production and of the *Kreislauf* (or circuit) of capital (see Bellofiore 2002, 2004).

REFERENCES

Aristotle (1984). *Physics.* In *The Complete Works of Aristotle. Revised Oxford Translation. Vol. 1*, edited by Johnathan Barnes. Princeton, NJ: Princeton University Press.

---

[29] It is of course possible to perceive a resemblance between this connotation of capital and Hegel's 'bad infinite'. Being a determinate quantity of money, capital constantly relapses from its putative universality into a quantitative limit, which it strives to overcome by increasing its magnitude. Its movement can thus be defined as '*maßlos*' (Marx [1890] 1991, p. 139): literally, 'measureless'. However, capital's effort to become a true infinite also displays an autotelic structure. The bad infinity of the linear infinite progress coexists with the circular infinite movement that defines the concept of capital. In the light of this remark, the quotation from Galiani (Marx [1890] 1991, p. 141, transl. p. 171), '*questo infinito che le cose non hanno in progresso, hanno in giro*', that is, 'when moving in a circle, things possess the infiniteness which they lack when advancing in a straight line', acquires greater significance. Arthur (2002, p. 140) has rightly pointed out that both the bad or spurious infinity and the true infinity are relevant to an adequate description of Marx's concept of capital, in which the linear and cumulative logic of infinite progress and the circular self-motion are combined. The linear and the circular motion are synthesized in the image of the 'spiral' (Marx [1857/58] 1976, p. 189, transl. p. 266).

[30] On the relevance of the distinction between Intellect and Reason in Marx's critique of political economy, see Reichelt (1970, p. 93).

Arthur, C.J., (2002). *The New Dialectic and Marx's Capital*. Leiden and Boston: Brill.
Arthur, C.J., (2003a). The Hegel–Marx Connection. *Historical Materialism*. 11 (1). pp. 179–183.
Arthur, C.J., (2003b). Once More on the Homology Thesis. A Response to Smith's Reply. *Historical Materialism*. 11 (1). pp. 195–198.
Backhaus, H.G., (1997). *Dialektik der Wertform*. Freiburg im Breisgau: Ça ira.
Bedini, S., (1964). The Role of Automata in the History of Technology. *Technology and Culture*. 5. pp. 24–42.
Bellofiore, R., (2002). Transformation and the Monetary Circuit. Marx as a Monetary Theorist of Production. In M. Campbell and G. Reuten (eds), *The Culmination of Capital. Essays on Volume III of Marx's* Capital, Basingstoke: Palgrave. pp. 102–127.
Bellofiore, R., (2004). Marx and the Macro-economic Foundation of Microeconomics. In R. Bellofiore and N. Taylor (eds), *The Constitution of Capital: Essays on Volume One of Marx's* Capital. Basingstoke: Palgrave. pp. 170–210.
Bellofiore, R., (2013). Il capitale come feticcio automatico e come soggetto, e la sua costituzione: sulla (dis)continuità Hegel–Marx. *Consecutio Temporum*. 5. pp. 43–78.
Bellofiore, R., (2018). The Adventures of Vergesellschaftung. *Consecutio rerum*. 5. pp. 503–540.
Berryman, S., (2003). Ancient Automata and Mechanical Explanation. *Phronesis*. 48. pp. 344–369.
Cambiano, G., (1994). Automaton. *Studi storici*. 35 (3). pp. 613–633.
Campbell, M. and Reuten, G., (2002). *The Culmination of Capital. Essays on Volume III of Marx's* Capital. Basingstoke: Palgrave.
Chapuis, A. and Gélis, E., (1984). *Le Monde Des Automates: Etude Historique et Technique*. Géneve: Éditions Slatkine.
Colletti, L., (1973). *Marxism and Hegel*. London: New Left Books.
Colletti, L., (1991). Introduction. In K. Marx, *Early Writings*. London: Penguin Books. pp. 7–56.
Finelli, R., (2014). *Un parricidio compiuto. Il confronto finale di Marx con Hegel*. Milano: Jaca Book.
Fineschi, R., (2008). *Un nuovo Marx. Filologia e interpretazione dopo la nuova edizione storico-critica (MEGA2)*, Roma: Carocci.
Frison, G., (1992). Smith, Marx and Beckmann: Division of Labour, Technology and Innovation. In H.P. Müller and U.Troitzsch (eds), *Technologie zwischen Fortschritt und Tradition*. Frankfurt am Main: Peter Lang. pp. 17–40.
Frison, G., (1993a). Linnaeus, Beckmann, Marx and the Foundation of Technology. Between Natural and Social Sciences: A Hypothesis of an Ideal Type – First Part: Linnaeus and Beckmann, Cameralism, Oeconomia and Technologie. *History and Technology*. 10 (3). pp. 139–160.
Frison, G., (1993b). Second and Third Part: Beckmann and Marx. Technologie and Classical Political Economy. *History and Technology*. 10 (3). pp. 161–173.
Gill, M.L. and Lennox, J., (1994). *Self-Motion from Aristotle to Newton*. Princeton, NJ: Princeton University Press.
Hegel, G.F.W., [1807] (1986). *Phänomenologie des Geistes*. Frankfurt am Main: Suhrkamp. Transl. by A.V. Miller (1977). *Phenomenology of Spirit*. Oxford: Oxford University Press.
Hegel, G.F.W., [1821] (1986). *Grundlinien der Philosophie des Rechts*. Frankfurt am Main: Suhrkamp. Transl. by T.M. Knox, revised by S. Houlgate (2008). *Outlines of the Philosophy of Right*. Oxford: Oxford University Press.

Hegel, G.F.W., [1830] (1986). *Enzyklopädie der philosophischen Wissenschaften im Grundrisse. Erster Teil Die Wissenschaft der Logik.* Frankfurt am Main: Suhrkamp. Transl. by K. Brinkman and D. Dahlstrom (2010). *Encyclopedia of the Philosophical Sciences in Basic Outline. Part I: Science of Logic.* Cambridge: Cambridge University Press.

Hegel, G.F.W., [1831] (1986). *Wissenschaft der Logik. Erster Teil. Die Objektive Logik. Erstes Buch.* Frankfurt am Main: Suhrkamp. Transl. by A.V. Miller (1969). *Science of Logic.* London: Allen & Unwin. pp. 25–388.

Henrich, D., (1982). *Selbstverhältnisse. Gedanken und Auslegungen zu den Grundlagen den klassischen deutschen Philosophie.* Stuttgart: Reclam.

Jahn, W. and Noske, D., (1980). Ist das Aufsteigen vom Abstrakten zum Konkreten die wissenschaftlich richtige Methode? *Arbeitsblätter zur Marx-Engels-Forschung.* 11. pp. 38–47.

Jungnickel, J., (1987). Zu den Textänderungen von der 1. zur 2. deutschen Auflage des ersten Bandes des 'Kapitals'. *Beiträge zur Marx-Engels-Forschung.* 23. pp. 18–27.

Jungnickel, J. (1991). Bemerkungen zu den von Engels vorgenommenen Veränderungen am Marxschen Manuskript zum dritten Band des 'Kapitals. In *Beiträge zur Marx-Engels-Forschung Neue Folge: Studien zum Werk von Marx und Engels.* Hamburg: Argument. pp. 130–138.

Marx, K., [1843] (1982). *Zur Kritik der Hegeischen Rechtsphilosophie.* In *Werke, Artikel, Entwürfe. März 1843 bis August 1844. MEGA* Abteilung I, Band 2. Berlin: Dietz Verlag. pp. 3–137.

Marx, K., [1844] (1982a). *Ökonomisch-philosophische Manuskripte (Erste Wiedergabe).* In *Werke, Artikel, Entwürfe. März 1843 bis August 1844. MEGA* Abteilung I, Band 2. Berlin: Dietz Verlag. pp. 187–322. Transl. by G. Benton, (1991). *Economic and Philosophical Manuscripts (1844).* In K. Marx, *Early Writings.* London: Penguin Books. pp. 279–400.

Marx, K., [1844] (1982b). *Ökonomisch-philosophische Manuskripte (Zweite Wiedergabe).* In *Werke, Artikel, Entwürfe. März 1843 bis August 1844. MEGA* Abteilung I, Band 2. Berlin: Dietz Verlag. pp. 323–438.

Marx, K., [1851/56] (1982). *Die technologisch-historischen Exzerpte.* Frankfurt and Berlin: Ullstein.

Marx, K., [1857/58] (1976). *Ökonomische Manuskripte. 1857/58. Teil 1.* In: *MEGA* Abteilung II, Band 1. Berlin: Dietz Verlag. Transl. by Martin Nicolaus (1973). *Grundrisse. Foundations of the Critique of Political Economy* (Rough Draft). London: Penguin Books.

Marx, K., [1861–63] (1978). *Zur Kritik der Politischen Ökonomie (Manuskript 1861–1863).* Teil 3. In: *MEGA* Abteilung II, Band 3. Berlin: Dietz Verlag.

Marx, K., [1863–67] (1992). *Ökonomische Manuskripte 1863–1867.* In: *MEGA* Abteilung II, Band 4, Teil 2. Berlin: Dietz Verlag.

Marx, K., [1867] (1983). *Das Kapital. Kritik der politischen Ökonomie. Erster Band. Hamburg 1867.* In: *MEGA* Abteilung II, Band 5. Berlin: Dietz Verlag.

Marx, K., [1872–75] (1989). *Le Capital. Paris 1872–75.* In: *MEGA* Abteilung II, Band 7. Berlin: Dietz Verlag.

Marx, K., [1873] (1987). *Das Kapital. Kritik der politischen Ökonomie. Erster Band. Hamburg 1872.* In: *MEGA* Abteilung II, Band 6. Berlin: Dietz Verlag.

Marx, K., [1887] (1990). *Capital. A Critical Analysis of Capitalist Production. London 1887.* In: *MEGA* Abteilung II, Band 9. Berlin: Dietz Verlag.

Marx, K., [1890] (1991). *Das Kapital. Kritik der politischen Ökonomie. Erster Band, Hamburg 1890.* In: *MEGA* Abteilung II, Band 10. Berlin: Dietz Verlag. Transl. by

S. Moore and E. Aveling (1906). *Capital. A Critique of Political Economy. Volume One*. New York: Modern Library.

Marx, K., [1894] (2004). *Das Kapital. Kritik der Politischen Ökonomie. Dritter Band. Hamburg 1894*. In: *MEGA* Abteilung II, Band 15. Berlin: Akademie Verlag. Transl. by D. Frenbach (1981). *Capital. A Critique of Political Economy. Volume Three*. London: Penguin Books.

Moseley, F. and Smith, T. (eds), (2014). *Marx's Capital and Hegel's Logic: A Re-examination*. Leiden and Boston: Brill.

Müller, H.P., (1992). *Karl Marx über Maschinerie, Kapital und industrielle Revolution. Studien zur Sozialwissenschaft*. Wiesbaden: Springer.

Noske, D., (1976). Über Weg und Ziel dialektischer Unterschungen der Marxschen politischen Ökonomie. *Arbeitsblätter zur Marx-Engels-Forschung*. 2. pp. 79–91.

Plato (1997). *Phaedrus* in *Plato. Complete Works*, edited by John M. Cooper. Indianapolis, IN: Hackett Publishing Company.

Reichelt, H., (1970). *Zur logischen Struktur des Kapitalbegriffs bei Karl Marx*. Frankfurt am Main: Europäische Verlagsanstalt.

Škedrow, V.P., (1989). Die Unterschung der Dialektik der Warenform des Arbeitsprodukts in der 1. und 2. Auflage des ersten Bandes 'Kapitals' von Karl Marx. *Beiträge zur Marx-Engels-Forschung*. 27. pp. 187–191.

Smith, T., (2003). On the Homology-thesis. *Historical Materialism*. 11 (1). pp. 184–194.

Tribe, K., (2016). De l'atelier au procès de travail : Marx, les machines et la technologie. In F. Jarrige, ed. *Dompter Prométhée. Technologies et socialismes à l'âge romantique (1820–1870)*. Besançon: Presses Universitaires de Franche-Comté. pp. 229–250.

Vollgraf, E., (1995). *Engels' Druckfassung versus Marx' Manuskripte zum III. Buch des 'Kapital'*. Hamburg: Argument.

Vollgraf, E. and Jungnickel, J., (1994). Marx in Marx's Worten? Zu Engels' Edition des Hauptmanuskripts zum dritten Buch des 'Kapitals'. *MEGA-Studien*. 1 (2). pp. 3–55.

Vygodsky, V., (1995). Was hat Engels in den Jahren 1885 und 1894 eigentlich veröffentlicht? *MEGA-Studien*. 2 (1). pp. 117–120.

8. Reproduction

Roberto Fineschi

In this chapter, I consider Marx's concept of reproduction. On the one hand, it is articulated according to the 'specific logic of the specific object': the typical capitalist form of reproduction is accumulation; on the other hand, it appears as a historically determined form of the general concept of human reproduction. We have two sides of the same coin: a combination of trans-historical continuity of human development, and its specific discontinuous forms.

8.1 REPRODUCTION IN MARX'S THEORY OF CAPITAL

In the structure of Marx's theory of capital, reproduction is a key concept, on which the soundness of its entire logic relies. It is not by chance that this part underwent several changes as his project started to assume a more defined form, second only to value-form in this regard. Reproduction is strictly connected to capital accumulation, which is the historically specific form under which reproduction takes place in the capitalistic mode of production. Differently from value-form, which in spite of many variants has always been at the beginning of theory of capital, reproduction was articulated in several passages and sections throughout the three books and their several manuscripts, and its position changed in the different versions of the theory; it can be considered as a litmus paper for establishing the progress in the articulation of Marx's theory of capital as a whole.

It is also strictly connected with Marx's dialectical method: a theory has to reproduce as its own results those elements that at the beginning were presuppositions, not posited by the theory itself. This is the realization of 'posited-presuppositions', only thanks to which capital can properly become a process, move from itself to become itself. This procedure through which a theory comes back to its foundations, founding itself, is a key point of the dialectical method, but at the same time it focuses on the 'limits' of this same method. Marx argues that the capitalistic mode of production, both logically and historically, has a starting point which is not posited by itself; therefore, Marx can claim that an *a priori* universal deduction of the entire history is not possible; the intrinsic, historically determined logical dialectics that characterizes each mode of production cannot, as such, be abstractly projected over other ones: each mode of production has its own logic. This phenomenally appears in historical dynamics which have to be logically theorized (way of exposition) on the basis of a reconstruction that begins from their factual appearance (way of research).

If, on the one hand, this creates discontinuities which avoid the criticisms of historical teleology, on the other hand it could potentially determine theoretical aporias: a conceptual model would be lacking of its starting points, if they depend on the results of another exogenous mode of production that obeys to different rules. The above-mentioned positing of presuppositions represents the solution to this issue. Reproduction is then a structural, but also methodo-logical, key point; this explains why it underwent so relevant changes.

In regard to the place that reproduction/accumulation has in the structure of the theory, a first change was in its position and articulation through the different levels of abstractions. This question connects with the *vexata quaestio* of the passage from *Grundrisse* to *Capital*.[1] My starting point is the result of decades of philological investigations connected to the publication of the second *Marx–Engels-Gesamtausgabe*;[2] according to these, Marx began a more consistent development of his theory of *Capital* only starting with the *Grundrisse*. In a plan he sketched in that period,[3] he wrote about three levels of abstraction: Universality, Particularity and Singularity, which recalls the

---

[1]   For an outline of this question see Fineschi (2009a).

[2]   On the MEGA[2], see Bellofiore and Fineschi (2009). See Tuchscheerer (1968), Vygodskij (1967), Jahn and Nietzold (1978).

[3]   See Marx ([1857–58] 1976–81, p. 199. Eng. Transl. Marx [1857–58] 1986, p. 205):

> Capital. I. Generality: (1) (a) Evolution of capital from money. (b) Capital and labour (mediating itself by alien labour). (c) The elements of capital, distin-guished according to their relationship to labour (product, raw material, instru-ment of labour). (2) Particularisation of capital: (a) Circulating capital, fixed capital. Turnover of capital. (3) Singularity of capital: Capital and profit. Capital and interest. Capital as value, distinct from itself as interest and profit.
> II. Particularity: (1) Accumulation of capitals. (2) Competition of capitals. (3) Concentration of capitals (quantitative difference of capital as at the same time qualitative, as measure of its volume and effect).
> III. Singularity: (1) Capital as credit. (2) Capital as share-capital. (3) Capital as money-market.

A similar structure is also in a letter to Engels of 2 April 1858 (Marx and Engels 1973, p. 312ff.; Eng. transl. Marx and Engels 1986, p. 298):

> 1. Capital falls into four sections. a) Capital en général. (This is the substance of the first installment.) b) Competition, or the interaction of many capitals. c) Credit, where capital, as against individual capitals, is shown to be a universal element. d) Share-capital as the most perfected form (turning into communism) together with all its contradictions.

Hegelian theory of judgement and syllogism.[4] This was initially just a schematic frame that was useful for Marx to give a first arrangement to the economic content; therefore, it would be mistaken considering this mere outline as Hegelian, inasmuch as an application of an external given logic to a separate content is exactly the opposite of Hegel's method, and dialectics in general. But Marx did not stop at this mere formalism: he moved forward, and changed important passages of his theory – the position and role of reproduction in particular – exactly to improve its dialectical soundness.[5] This made his theory properly dialectic because of the development of the logic of the thing itself (*Auslegung der Sache selbst*), not for a mere use of words.[6]

What is meant by Universality, Particularity and Singularity? Universal capital – or 'capital in general' – was conceived as one and all at the same time, and developed until it reached the category of profit; at that point, it doubles in itself – 'begetting its son' – and generating multiple particular capitals; this is the passage to competition and particularity. Particularity inquires into the dynamics of 'many' capitals: in each particular capital, the universal laws developed before act as such. In singularity, finally, one particular capital works as universal – that is represents as individual the most abstract and universal form of valorization: money begetting money – in relationship with other particular capitals functioning in the different branches. This is the content of the section on credit and fictitious capital.

What is the position of reproduction in this outline? Marx initially placed accumulation/reproduction in Particularity, after capital has posited profit, after its first 'turn' and return to the starting point; even after the theory of capital circulation. Marx seems here to believe that the position of presuppositions might be possible without considering the reproduction conditions of capital. But this is actually not possible: if not just production, but also reproduction conditions are considered, capital will not become a process, since it would perpetually need external starting points. Marx had actually considered accumulation in the *Grundrisse*, but just the 'primitive' one, which dealt with the position of the general presuppositions of capital through a process external to capital itself; this could not be enough. This is why he gradually started to distinguish between primitive and actual capitalistic accumulation, and at first occasionally then more consistently, added elements of a proper capitalistic

---

[4]   See Hegel (1995/96, § 163). English translations of both Marx's and Hegel's works are not very precise on this point.

[5]   I dealt extensively with the relationship between Marx and Hegel in Fineschi (2006b).

[6]   Dialectics was then not reduced, but improved. This comment refers to the debate on the 'reduction of dialectics': see Reichelt (1973), Backhaus (1997), Göhler (1980), and others. For a summary of part of this debate see Fineschi (2009b).

accumulation in the right place: before the capital–profit relationship (the final step of capital in general). In the *Manuscripts of 1863–65* (Marx [1863–68] 1988–2012), when for the first time he adopted the three-book structure, Marx finally outlined accumulation into two steps: reproduction of a single capital in the future 7th section of vol. 1, and that of many capitals (not yet in competition) in the future 3rd section of vol. 2 (sections mentioned according to Engels's editions). Both moments are required by capital in order to posit its presuppositions, to reach profit as final step of the treatment of capital in general. Marx came to this conclusion while writing the *Manuscripts of 1861–63* (Marx [1861–63] 1976–82) and consequently adopted this new structure in the final three-book plan.[7]

In the different editions of vol. 1, especially the French one, he further specified a few elements that made the whole more consistent. The first edition of 1867 (Marx [1867] 1983) was immediately considered inadequate under several regards; starting with the second German edition, Marx modified the text, in particular the first three chapters. More variants could be found in the French one, in particular in the 7th section on accumulation. These variants are the reason why Marx wrote that the French edition also had its own value in regard to the German one, although the translation was simply unacceptable. As a matter of fact, Marx never considered this edition as the last one: if we look at his manuscripts left for future editions or even translations, we see how he always referred to the second German edition as to be updated with determined, specific passages from the French one;[8] passages that mostly come from the section on accumulation. The most relevant changes are the following:

1. the introduction of the concept of organic composition;
2. the distinction between concentration and centralization of capitals;
3. the structure of the section, based on the finalized distinction between primitive and proper capitalistic accumulation.

Organic composition consists of two moments: on the one hand, the value composition of capital, the ratio of capital investment in constant or variable capital, that is, the value of means of production and labour-power; on the other hand, the technical composition, that is, the corresponding material parts: the mass of means of production and workers employed. The complex interaction of these two moments is crucial for the determination of the rate

---

[7]   Marx ([1861–63] 1976–82, p. 1134; Eng.: Marx 1989, p. 143). For a more accurate investigation into this development, see Fineschi (2013).

[8]   On the development of Marx's theory in the various editions of vol. 1, see: Hecker et al. (1989), Lietz (1987a, 1987b) and Fineschi (2006a).

of surplus value (and profit), and total social reproduction as a material reproduction process in value-form. This was not in the second German edition and appears only with the French one (Marx [1872–75] 1989, p. 534); it was added by Engels to the third German edition and kept in the fourth one (Marx [1883] 1989, p. 574). Here Marx confirms that he is dealing just with the ideal average: (1) not including the many capitals yet; and (2) not including their free interaction in competition. The former is considered in the 3rd section of vol. 2 (within capital in general), and the latter in the 3rd section of vol. 3 (within particularity/competition).

The other relevant change in the French edition is the distinction between concentration and centralization. The second term is introduced here and refers to the competitive inclusion, or voluntary unification, of different capitals. This of course accelerates the accumulation dynamics if compared with the slower pace of the concentration process (simple accumulation). Some have commented that this seems to anticipate the future analysis of competition, where this process will actually take place; I disagree, because here we have just the abstract possible conditions, not the reality of that process; therefore, claiming that competition is already taking place would be mistaken. It is a different level of abstraction; actually not even the abstract ratio between these capitals (total social reproduction), which would still be before competition is considered yet (Marx [1872–75] 1989, p. 546; Marx [1883] 1989, p. 588).

The third issue is a structural change. Now primitive accumulation is distinguished from the actual capitalist one, and exposed in a separate section, the 8th one. Since Engels did not take this change into account, although it was outlined in the manuscripts left by Marx for future editions, German readers (and all those that read translations from the fourth German edition) have missed this crucial passage. Here Marx explicitly distinguishes and separates the factual 'history' of the exogenous presuppositions of the capitalist mode of production in a specific moment and in a specific part of the world, and the intrinsic logic of its accumulation process, which does not have to correspond to a factual historical chronology (Marx [1872–75] 1989, p. 631ff.; Marx [1883] 1989, p. 667). This makes also evident that the concept of primitive accumulation as such is not part of the proper theory of capital accumulation. Marx shows also how the theoretical reconstruction has a mediated relationship to historical contingencies. The distinction between logical and logic-historical methodology is here finally accomplished.

This point is often mistaken in the interpretations: some think that the use of 'explicit' violence in the current forms of accumulation would represent a presence of primitive accumulation still within the proper capitalistic one. Instead, primitive accumulation shows how: (1) money is accumulated; and (2) labour-power and means of production are separated in a non-capitalist way, and without capitalist goals in the undertaking (that is, without maximizing profit in the capitalist sense). This is not the case with the current use of violence, because now the goals and money employed to use violence have been capitalist since the beginning. The current dynamic has to be explained at a more concrete level of abstraction, which includes not just capital accumulation, but also states and their interaction. Unfortunately, Marx did not reach that concreteness.

Lack of space does not allow me to follow the more complex articulation of social reproduction in the schemata, and even later when the abstraction clause of capital in general (supply = demand) is dropped in competition. At this more concrete abstraction level, the theory becomes more complex, and includes the issue of commodity realization, which affects the category of value (market values). The same complexity emerges in the sketched theory of cycle, or even in the relationship between real and fictitious accumulation in the final section on credit and fictitious capital. The apparent autonomy and the correlation between these two different accumulations as part of a unified reproduction process was formulated for the first time in the final part of *Manuscript of 1863/65*,[9] by exposing the lowest level of abstraction of the general theory of capital, as he had already planned in the draft of *Manuscripts of 1857/58* and letters. In the entire traditional debate started by Rosdolsky, no one has ever considered that there is a further level of abstraction next to capital in general and competition: credit and fictitious capital (or singularity as it was also called by Marx).[10] This peculiar misunderstanding was in part due to the poor edition of this part of the manuscript by Engels: in fact, credit and fictitious capital is not presented for what it is, that is, the general title of the last section of capital theory, but as a chapter among others.[11]

8.2   REPRODUCTION IN BROADER SENSE

As we saw in the previous section, in the capitalist mode of production social reproduction as a whole takes place in the historical-specific form of capital accumulation. This is a determined phase of the development of human history, and therefore has a form-specific structure. Marx has analysed it extensively, but could not finish his work; he got to the point of sketching the relationship

[9]   See Marx ([1863–65] 1988–2012), vol. 4.2. It is the main manuscipt used by Engels to edit *Capital* vol. 3.
[10]   See Rosdolsky ([1968] 1977), Vygodskij (1967), Reichelt (1973) and especially Müller (1978), Schwarz (1978). See also Heinrich (1989), Arthur (2002) and Moseley (2009). For a summary of this debate, see Fineschi (2009a). I showed that for the first time in Fineschi (2001; see also 2013).
[11]   Compare Marx ([1863–68] 1988–2012), vol. 4.2, and Marx ([1894] 1991, p. 525ff).

between real and fictitious accumulation. However, a more general element emerges here: the relationship between specific historical forms of reproduction, and the fact that human beings, whatever the form, always need to reproduce themselves. The issue is how we can include as coherent parts of one theory the general reproduction of humans, which is trans-historical, with the fact that it always occurs in historically specific systems: the issue of the dialectic of historical continuity/discontinuity.

Marx's theory of historical process focuses on two moments. On the one hand, a 'general' dimension: how what happens trans-historically can be said to be 'human'; on the other hand, their history is not a simple sequence of identical phases, but there are leaps that characterize each period as something specific. The whole of this process, at every stage, can, in its continuity, specifically change and develop. These passages are not just different, but constitutive: the same definition of what is human changes accordingly. It is a dynamic of phases that, in their particularity, make the whole move, and get redetermined at every stage.[12] Reproduction through the labour process is the knot that permits the articulation of this complex framework in its different levels.[13]

Natural-social reproduction takes place through labour process: it is, first, what keeps together continuity and discontinuity with nature.[14] Since humans do not live in emptiness or come from nothing, they are themselves to be conceived as constitutive parts of natural evolution; they are that peculiar animal that is able to work: their own activity is one moment of a whole that includes a final goal that they posit, and interaction with means and objects; the result is a product, since they are able to give external, permanent existence to their subjective action (Marx [1890] 1991, p. 162ff.; Eng. transl. Marx 1976, p. 284ff.). Their reproduction through work is what makes them natural/human, and this determines a continuity/discontinuity with nature in general.

However, this does not mean that what they are 'socially' is determined just through this first moment; their identity as humans is not completely given just thanks to this first continuity/discontinuity with nature. What humans are is the result of their reproduction throughout history, and this implies that the same concept of human being, or labour process in general, is historical. What the words 'human', 'society', and so on mean is redefined in every phase of natural-historical reproduction in a specific determined form. Therefore, Marx's theory cannot be an anthropology, if by this we mean

---

[12]   Marx refers to the dialectic of trans-historical elements and their historical specificity in several passages: see Marx ([1890] 1991, pp. 44, 167, 506, 508; Eng: Marx 1976, pp. 133, 287, 711, 713).

[13]   Marx ([1890] 1991, ch. 5; Eng. transl. Marx 1976, ch. 7).

[14]   Marx ([1890] 1991, p. 162; Eng. transl. Marx 1976, p. 283).

that 'human beings' is an essence that is given since the beginning and just alienated (and not co-defined) by its historical determinations.[15] This growth and co-determination is what Marx and Engels mean when they say that they know just one science, the science of history. What every period has in common is that humans will produce and reproduce themselves, and always in a somehow associated form; however, the form of this reproduction will always be specific, and historically determined.[16] If all societies are forms of human reproduction, they are different, first, in the way the elements of the labour process combine (Marx [1885] 2008, p. 38; Eng. transl. Marx [1885] 1978, p. 120): the different bearers of its moments stand one in front of another apparently as 'persons' – individuals that are formally free and equal, each one legitimate owner of the labour-power, the worker, and means of production, the capitalist – but actually as classes defined by their function in the capitalist production process. Their union takes place through a contract, an exchange of equivalents, because all is reduced to commodity, inclusive of labour-power (Marx [1890] 1991, p. 152ff.; Eng. transl. Marx 1976, p. 270 f.). Then, more laws further specify reproduction in capitalist form (exploitation, absolute and relative surplus value and specific way of working under capital, subsumption, accumulation, and many others), but here there is not enough space for a detailed analysis of this (Marx [1890] 1991, chs 10ff.; Eng. transl. Marx 1976, chs 12ff.).

The distinction between labour in general and specific forms in which it takes place parallels that of reproduction in abstract terms and its historical forms. Labour process and the general concept of reproduction are then the 'naked' forms of effective historical processes, a material content that as such has never existed in history, because it has always been instantiated in historical-specific forms of its development, and formulated in general only through abstraction from their concrete reality. 'Material content' always has a 'social form'; it does not exist outside of that form or get deformed by that: form is the way of actualization of content. Content develops through its forms and, at some point, enters in contradiction with its old form/content configuration; it was its own, but later becomes inadequate to its further development. Historical continuity/discontinuity is articulated through the dialectic of content and form, universal and particular, and of their distinct/interconnected levels of abstraction. Reproduction is a key moment of that.

---

[15]   More remarks on this in Fineschi (2020).
[16]   I have developed this theme in Fineschi (2001). It takes up points made first by Mazzone (1980, 1987) in his classic studies.

8.3 CONCLUSIONS

At the end of this investigation, I can conclude that in reproduction we can, on the one side, distinguish its capitalist-specific way as a peculiar form of a determined stage of human development; and on the other, thanks to abstraction, focus on the existence of the general necessity of that reproduction. We have seen how the historical-specific forms are not just merely different from the general level, but they change and configure it: each peculiar historical form is a moment of a constitutive process. Therefore, the same concepts of human being or human labour in general are specific products of it.

REFERENCES

Abbreviations:
MECW = Marx–Engels Collected Works. London: Lawrence & Wishart.
MEW = Marx–Engels Werke. Berlin: Dietz.
MEGA = Marx–Engels-Gesamtausgabe. Berlin: Dietz.

Arthur, C., (2002). Capital in General and Marx's *Capital*. In: M. Campbell, G. Reuten, eds, *The Culmination of Capital*. Basingstoke: Palgrave, pp. 42–64.
Backhaus, H.G., (1997). *Dialektik der Wertform*. Freiburg: ça ira.
Bellofiore, R., Fineschi, R., eds, (2009). *Re-reading Marx. New Perspectives after the Critical Edition*. Basingstoke: Palgrave Macmillan UK.
Fineschi, R., (2001). *Ripartire da Marx. Processo storico ed economia politica nella teoria del 'capitale'*. Napoli: La città del sole.
Fineschi, R., (2006a). Nochmals zum Verhältnis Wertform – Geldform – Austauschprozess. In: *Neue Aspekte von Marx' Kapitalismus-Kritik*. Berlin: Argument, pp. 115–133.
Fineschi, R., (2006b). *Marx e Hegel. Contributi a una rilettura*. Roma: Carocci.
Fineschi, R., (2009a). 'Capital in General' and 'Competition', in the Making of Capital: The German Debate. *Science and Society*. 1, 54–76.
Fineschi, R., (2009b). Dialectic of the Commodity and Its Exposition: The German Debate in the 1970s – A Personal Survey. In: Bellofiore, R. Fineschi, *Re-reading Marx. New Perspectives after the Critical Edition*. Basingstoke: Palgrave Macmillan UK, pp. 50–70.
Fineschi, R., (2013). The Four Levels of Abstraction of Marx's Concept of 'Capital'. In: R. Bellofiore, G. Starosta, P. Thomas, eds, *In Marx's Laboratory. Critical Interpretations of the 'Grundrisse'*. Boston, Leiden, Tokyo: Brill, pp. 71–98.
Fineschi, R., (2020). Real Abstraction: Philological Issues. In: A. Oliva, A. Oliva, I. Novara, eds, *Marx and Contemporary Critical Theory. The Philosophy of Real Abstraction*. Basingstoke: Palgrave Macmillan, pp. 61–78.
Göhler, G., (1980). *Die Reduktion der Dialektik durch Marx: Strukturveränderungen der dialektischen Entwicklung in der Kritik der politischen Ökonomie*. Stuttgart.
Hecker, R., Jungnickel, J., Vollgraf, C.E., (1989). Zur Entwicklungsgeschichte des ersten Bandes des 'Kapitals' (1867 bis 1890). *Beiträge zur Marx-Engels-Forschung*. 27, 16–32.

Hegel, G.F.W., (1995/96). *Enzykopädie der philosophischen Wissenschaftten*. Frankfurt am Main: Suhrkamp.

Heinrich, M., (1989). Capital in General and the Structure of Marx's *Capital*. New Insights from Marx's 'Economic Manuscript of 1861–63'. *Capital and Class*. 38, 63–79.

Jahn, W., Nietzold, R., (1978). Probleme der Entwicklung der Marxschen politischen Ökonomie im Zeitraum von 1850 bis 1863. *MarxEngels-Jahrbuch*. 1, 145–174.

Lietz, B., (1987a). Zur Entwicklung der Werttheorie in den 'Ergänzungen und Veränderungen zum ersten Band des "Kapitals" (Dezember 1871–Januar 1872)'. *Beiträge zur Marx-Engels-Forschung*. 23, 26–33.

Lietz, B., (1987b). Ein Ausgangsmaterial für die 2. deutsche Auflage und die autorisierte französische Ausgabe des ersten Bandes des 'Kapitals'. *Beiträge zur MarxEngels-Forschung*. 24, 76–84.

Marx, K., [1857–58] (1976–81). *Ökonomische Manuskripte 1857/58*, Teil I-II. In: *MEGA*, Abteilung II, Band 1. Berlin: Dietz.

Marx, K., [1857–58] (1986). Economic Works 1857–1858. In: *MECW*, vol. 28, transl. by Ernst Wangermann. London: Lawrence & Wishart.

Marx, K., [1861–63] (1976–82). *Zur Kritik der politischen Ökonomie (Manuskripte 1861–1863)*. In: *MEGA*, Abteilung II, Band 3. Berlin: Dietz.

Marx, K., [1863–68] (1988–2012). *Ökonomische Manuskripte 1863–1868*. In: *MEGA*, Abteilung II, Band 4.1–3. Berlin: Dietz.

Marx, K., [1867] (1983). *Das Kapital. Kritik der politischen Ökonomie. Erster Band. Hamburg 1867*. In: *MEGA*, Abteilung II, Band 5. Berlin: Dietz.

Marx, K., [1872–75] (1989). *Le Capital, Paris 1872–75*. In: *MEGA*, Abteilung II, Band 7. Berlin: Dietz.

Marx, K., [1883] (1989). *Das Kapital. Kritik der politischen Ökonomie. Erster Band. Hamburg 1883*. In: *MEGA*, Abteilung II, Band 8. Berlin: Dietz.

Marx, K., [1885] (1978). *Capital, Volume II*, transl. by David Fernbach. Harmondsworth: Penguin.

Marx, K., [1885] (2008). *Das Kapital. Kritik der politischen Ökonomie. Zweiter Band. Herausgegeben von Friedrich Engels. Hamburg 1885*. In: *MEGA*, Abteilung II, Band 13. Berlin: Dietz.

Marx, K., [1890] (1991). *Das Kapital. Kritik der politischen Ökonomie. Erster Band. Hamburg 1890*. In: *MEGA*, Abteilung II, Band 10. Berlin: Dietz.

Marx, K., [1894] (1991). *Capital. A Critique of Political Economy*, Volume III, transl. by David Fernbach. London: Penguin.

Marx, K., (1976). *Capital: A Critique of Political Economy*, Vol. 1, transl. by Ben Fowkes. London: Penguin.

Marx, K., (1989). *Economic Manuscript of 1861–3*. In: *MECW*, vol. 32. London: Lawrence & Wishart.

Marx, K., Engels, F. (1973). *Briefe. Januar 1856 bis Dezember 1859*. In: *MEW*, Band 29. Berlin: Dietz.

Marx, K., Engels, F. (1986). Letters. January 1856–December 1859. In: *MECW*, vol. 40. London: Lawrence & Wishart.

Mazzone, A., (1980). *Questioni di teoria dell'ideologia*. Messina: La libbra.

Mazzone, A., (1987). La temporalità specifica del modo di produzione capitalistico. (Ovvero: 'la missione storica del capitale'). In: *Marx e i suoi critici*. Urbino: QuattroVenti, pp. 224–260.

Moseley, F., (2009). The Development of Marx's Theory of the Distribution of SurplusValue in the Manuscript of 1861–63: In: Bellofiore, Fineschi eds, *Re-reading*

Marx. New Perspectives after the Critical Edition. Basingstoke: Palgrave Macmillan UK, pp. 128–147.

Müller, M., (1978). *Auf dem Wege zum 'Kapital'. Zur Entwicklung des Kapitalbegriffs von Marx in den Jahren 1857–1863.* Berlin DDR: das europäische Buch.

Reichelt, H., (1973). *Zur logischen Struktur des Kapitalbegriffs bei Karl Marx.* 4., durchges. Auflage. Frankfurt am Main: Europäische Verlagsanstalt.

Rosdolsky, R., [1968] (1977). *The Making of Marx's 'Capital'.* London: Pluto Press.

Schwarz, W., (1978). *Vom 'Rohentwurf' zum 'Kapital'. Die Strukturgeschichte des Marxschen Hauptwerkes.* West Berlin: das europä ische Buch.

Tuchscheerer, W., (1968). *Bevor 'Das Kapital' entstand.* Berlin: Akademie Verlag.

Vygodskij, V., (1967). *Geschichte einer grossen Entdeckung.* Berlin: Die Wirschaft.

9.   Primitive accumulation

Sebastiano Taccola

9.1   PRIMITIVE ACCUMULATION AS A STARTING POINT

The chapter on primitive accumulation begins with an extraordinary example of Marx's typical anti-bourgeois irony (a literary style that often appears in *Capital* and that probably much owes to Shakespeare, Goethe and, mostly, Heine):[1]

> This primitive accumulation [*Ursprüngliche Akkumulation*] plays in Political Economy about the same part as original sin in theology. Adam bit the apple, and thereupon sin fell on the human race. Its origin is supposed to be explained when it is told as an anecdote of the past. In times long gone-by there were two sorts of people; one, the diligent, intelligent, and, above all, frugal elite; the other, lazy rascals, spending their substance, and more, in riotous living. The legend of theological original sin tells us certainly how man came to be condemned to eat his bread in the sweat of his brow; but the history of economic original sin reveals to us that there are people to whom this is by no means essential. Never mind! Thus it came to pass that the former sort accumulated wealth, and the latter sort had at last nothing to sell except their own skins. (Marx [1867] 1906, pp. 784–785)

Thus, primitive accumulation is the historical background of the constitution of the bourgeois social relations. Marx wants to unmask the apologetic and idyllic vision proposed by political economy, which makes of the bourgeoisie a class of virtuous men and of the proletarians (or, more generally, of the poor people) a class of lazy squanderers. Through the category of 'primitive accumulation' , Marx wants to unmask that the ways that lead to the capitalistic mode of production are based on methods that 'are anything but idyllic' (Marx [1867] 1906, p. 785). Therefore, there is a primitive accumulation that precedes the accumulation *sans phrase* and distinguishes itself from it insofar

---

[1]   For an analysis of the influence that literature had on the formation of Marx's theoretical and political thought, see: Prawer (1976).

as it is 'an accumulation not the result of the capitalist mode of production, but its starting point' (Marx [1867] 1906, p. 784).

Posing the bourgeois categories at the beginning of history, the classical political economy naturalizes the capitalistic social relations and, thus, makes them eternal; but according to Marx, money, means of production and of subsistence cannot always be considered *sub specie capitalistica*: they need to be transformed into capital. The necessary presupposition of such a transformation is the accomplishment of the process of separation between the worker and his conditions of labour; historically speaking, this is the process that lead to the genesis of the modern free worker, who has nothing to sell but his labour-power (that is, James Steuart's 'free hands'). In this perspective, Marx presents a more specific definition of primitive accumulation:

> The process, therefore, that clears the way for the capitalist system, can be none other than the process which takes away from the laborer the possession of his means of production; a process that transforms, on the one hand, the social means of subsistence and of production into capital, on the other, the immediate producers into wage-laborers. The so-called primitive accumulation, therefore, is nothing else than the historical process of divorcing the producer from the means of production. It appears as primitive, because it forms the pre-historic stage of capital and of the mode of production corresponding with it. (Marx [1867] 1906, p. 786)

Here Marx highlights the historical side of primitive accumulation as a history of the expropriation of the workers' conditions of production and of the constitution of those historically determined social relations that enable capitalist accumulation through the exploitation of the labour power. The result is that in the capitalistic society, the worker is no more immediately dependent on personal power-relationships (as happened in the pre-capitalist forms of relations of production, such as ancient slavery or feudal serfdom), but is enslaved by capital in a more mediated and mystified way.

9.2   BRITISH PRIMITIVE ACCUMULATION: A HISTORICAL CASE

Marx finds the illustrative case of primitive accumulation in modern England. He outlines the plural strategies that brought to the dissolution of feudal relations and to the creation of the *ex-lege* proletariat in some central passages of the chapters concerning primitive accumulation. It is possible to sum up these strategies in a few points:

1. The redefinition of the property rights over the lands: a process that, through the expropriation of the ecclesiastic and public property and of the

yeoman's lands, and the privatization of communal property through the Enclosure Acts, led to the birth of modern private property.

2. The redefinition of the property rights over the means of production through the phenomenon of the clearing of the estates (that is, peasants forced to leave their lands, and their means of production as well).

3. A brutal legislation to discipline the expropriated so that they were forced to accept low wages and to conform to the coercive market laws.

4. The violent creation of a home market that, going hand in hand with brutal colonialism, and using means such as public debt and protectionism, posed the presuppositions for the capitalist dynamics to evolve on a global, systematic and perpetual scale.[2]

5. The transformation of the money-capital accumulated as loan capital and commercial capital into industrial capital through the dissolution of the feudal bonds and the appropriation of the means of production by the rising bourgeoisie.[3]

In all of these passages, Marx highlights that 'force' (*Gewalt*)[4] is an essential means for the realization of such strategies. In the Marxian presentation, force

---

[2]   Marx dedicates chapter 33 ('The Modern Theory of Colonization') to an analysis of the colonialism. It is worth noting that, for Marx, the examination of modern phenomena such as colonialism cannot exist without a synchronic and systematic critical theory of capitalistic society; that is, without having first understood the structural conditions according to which 'capital is not a thing, but a social relation between persons, established by the instrumentality of things' (Marx [1867] 1906, p. 839).

[3]   It is worth noting that Dobb's *Studies in the Development of Capitalism* is probably one of the first works that explicitly follows the strategies of primitive accumulation outlined by Marx in order to give a historical account of the growth of proletariat between the sixteenth and eighteenth centuries. See: Dobb (1946, pp. 221–254).

[4]   The huge semantic spectrum evoked by the German term *Gewalt* can hardly be translated in English. It means at the same time force, violence, power. This leads many interpreters to state that the word *Gewalt* has an immanent ambiguity. In this perspective, for example, Balibar has written:

> In German (the language in which Marx, Engels and the first Marxists wrote), the word *Gewalt* has a more extensive meaning than its 'equivalents' in other European languages: *violence* or *violenza* and *pouvoir, potere, power* ... Seen in this way, 'from the outside', the term *Gewalt* thus contains an intrinsic ambiguity: it refers, at the same time, to the negation of law or justice and to their realisation or the assumption of responsibility for them by an institution (generally the state). (Balibar 2009, p. 101)

Tomba, analysing this passage by Balibar (and proposing an interpretation that is shared in this chapter) has stated:

> Dividing *Gewalt* into 'power' and 'violence', one must not think of two sides of violence, the institutional and the anti-institutional, because much apparently extralegal violence ends up written into the institutional record. Furthermore, a great deal of state violence, which is denounced as illegitimate, is of rather vital

becomes a crucial category to read the whole history of Modern Europe in a critical way, and to sketch a sort of counter-history of the genesis of the present social relations:

> The different momenta of primitive accumulation distribute themselves now, more or less in chronological order, particularly over Spain, Portugal, Holland, France, and England. In England at the end of the 17th century, they arrive at a systematical combination, embracing the colonies, the national debt, the modern mode of taxation, and the protectionist system. These methods depend in part on brute force, e.g., the colonial system. But, they all employ the power of the State, the concentrated and organised force of society, to hasten, hot-house fashion, the process of transformation of the feudal mode of production into the capitalist mode, and to shorten the transition. Force is the midwife of every old society pregnant with a new one. It is itself an economic power. (Marx [1867] 1906, pp. 823–824)

An economic power that, with the force of the whip and of the law, realizes 'that artificial product of modern society', which consists, on the one hand, in the foundation of a new anthropological standard, namely the owner-individual,[5] and on the other hand, in the birth of 'the "eternal laws of Nature" of the capitalist mode of production' (Marx [1867] 1906, p. 833).

9.3   THE SYSTEMIC CHARACTER OF PRIMITIVE ACCUMULATION

These are the methods of primitive accumulation as a lever of the capitalistic social relations and the process of dissolution of the feudal society.[6] In this

---

    importance for maintaining the state machinery. In this ambivalence is hidden the violent character of law, that violence that funds the state and preserves it. (Tomba 2009, p. 127)

[5]   In these pages Marx writes that 'in the nineteenth century, the very memory of the connection between the agricultural labourer and communal property had, of course, vanished' (Marx [1867] 1906, p. 800).

[6]   Here I cannot deal with the questions concerning the historical trajectories of the transition from feudalism to capitalism; questions that gave rise to a debate known as 'the transition debate' or 'the Dobb–Sweezy debate' (since it followed the publication of the *Studies on the Development of Capitalism* by Maurice Dobb and the critical review dedicated to it by Paul Sweezy). For a complete collection of the articles composing the debate, see Aston and Philpin (1987). Anyway, it is important to underline that in this debate, primitive accumulation played a marginal role, since the scholars who took part in it (in addition to Dobb and Sweezy, also H.K. Takahashi, R. Hilton, C. Hill, H. Lefebvre, G. Procacci, J. Merrington, E. Hobsbawm) focused especially on some chapters from *Capital Volume III* (namely, chapter 20 'Historical Facts about Merchant's Capital', chapter 36 'Pre-Capitalist Relationships', chapter 47 'The Genesis of Capitalist Ground-Rent'). For a reconstruction of the whole debate: Hilton (1978). Similar issues had been at the centre of a later debate, known as 'the Brenner

horizon, it is possible to identify the founding processes of the capitalist mode of production in a diachronic perspective, which can help to shed light on the historical differences existing between the capitalist and the pre-capitalist modes of production, and thus to lay the basis for the elaboration of a pre-history of the bourgeois society.

The antediluvian character of primitive accumulation is undeniable, but at the same time it is not the only one. If we consider only the antediluvian side of primitive accumulation, we remove its processual nature, reducing it to a historical phenomenon which occured once in history. And, moreover, we would run the risk of falling back into those old interpretations that attributed to Marx a vision of history identifiable with a simple and mechanical succession of modes of production founded, *in primis*, on the abstract concept of progress.

Rather, primitive accumulation is a crucial moment of the capitalist system that synchronically realizes itself within the dynamic that characterizes the whole capitalist reproduction. In fact, as Marx also states in the *Grundrisse*, capital, to achieve its perpetual reproduction, needs at the same time the reproduction of those conditions that opens to it new spatial-temporal margins of accumulation. Once the fundamental separation between the worker and the means of production is presupposed, 'the production process can only produce it anew, reproduce it, and reproduce it on an expanded scale' (Marx [1857/58] 1993, p. 462). That is why the tendency to create a world market is immanent to capital.

Nowadays, many Marxist scholars, following a thesis originally proposed by Rosa Luxemburg,[7] think that it is necessary to highlight the perpetual character of primitive accumulation in order to understand phenomena such as imperialism, underdevelopment, geo-politics, the reproductive and conflicting

---

debate' (opened by the article 'Agrarian Class Structure and Economic Development in Pre-Industrial Europe' by the Marxist historian Robert Brenner). But if the Dobb–Sweezy debate was an intra-Marxist debate, the Brenner debate also involved non-Marxist scholars, and evoked a much more complex range of themes concerning the European long-term economic development. For a complete collection of the articles composing the debate, see: Aston and Philpin (1987). For a more recent and theoretically brilliant overview from a Marxist perspective on issues concerning the origin of capitalism see: Meiksins Wood (2002).

[7]   The following passage from *The Accumulation of Capital* is paradigmatic:

Accumulation, with its spasmodic expansion, can no more wait for, and be content with, a natural internal disintegration of non-capitalist formations and their transition to commodity economy, than it can wait for, and be content with, the natural increase of the working population. Force is the only solution open to capital; the accumulation of capital, seen as an historical process, employs force as a permanent weapon, not only as its genesis, but further on down to the present day. (Luxemburg [1913] 2003, p. 351)

temporalities of the capitalist society, and so on. Among them, it is worth mentioning at least David Harvey, who, to erase the pre-historic character of primitive accumulation, coined the notion of 'accumulation by dispossession' in order to propose a critical inquiry into some recent phenomena such as gentrification, privatization of commons, commodification and privatization of public assets, and so on.[8] Acknowledging the crucial role that these processes have in the reproduction and the expansion of the capitalistic social relations on a global scale, Harvey also highlighted the political potentiality that could be opened by articulating in a productive way the socio-political conflicts given on only apparently independent or residual grounds.

In these processes, characteristic and still current expressions of the primitive accumulation, the economic and the political, are deeply interrelated in a dialectical way.[9] For Marx the *Gewalt* is an 'extra-economic force' (Marx [1867] 1906, p. 809) and an 'economic power' (Marx [1867] 1906, p. 824) at the same time. Their relation cannot be reduced to a linear and deterministic one: in the totality of the capitalistic society, the political cannot exist without the economic, and *vice versa*. A totality – 'concentration of many determinations, hence unity of the diverse' (Marx [1857/58] 1993, p. 101) – identifiable with those reproductive processes of a historically determined mode of production, whose immanent tendency is to spread on a global scale according to plural spatial-temporal coordinates. Keeping in mind these plural spaces and times is important to understand why in capitalism a non-contemporaneity (for example, according to Samir Amin, the underdevelopment) co-exists with

---

[8] Accumulation by dispossession is a topic that is present in many of Harvey's works. See, for example: Harvey (2003, pp. 137–182), Harvey (2006), Harvey (2010, pp. 289–313), Harvey (2014, pp. 53–61).

[9] In this sense, two passages in which Marx talks about public debt and protectionism as two political-economic strategies intelligible within the theoretical framework of the primitive accumulation appear very interesting (mostly nowadays):

> The public debt becomes one of the most powerful levers of primitive accumulation. As with the stroke of an enchanter's wand, it endows barren money with the power of breeding and thus turns it into capital, without the necessity of its exposing itself to the troubles and risks inseparable from its employment in industry or even in usury ... the national debt has given rise to joint-stock companies, to dealings in negotiable effects of all kinds, and to agiotage, in a word to stock-exchange gambling and the modern bankocracy. (Marx [1867] 1906, p. 827)

> The system of protection was an artificial means of manufacturing manufacturers, of expropriating independent labourers, of capitalising the national means of production and subsistence, of forcibly abbreviating the transition from the medieval to the modern mode of production. (Marx [1867] 1906, p. 830)

a contemporaneity identifiable with the most developed countries;[10] capital aims at synchronizing these plural (and conflicting) temporalities thanks to the (economic and extra-economic) force of the state. Thus, in the synchronic moment we can include the tendency of the capitalistic process to posit its own presuppositions, that is, to form-determine the other, what it finds beyond its limits, *sub specie capitalistica*.

As many authors have already shown, capitalistic temporalities are essentially conflicting. Counter-temporalities (often posed by capital itself in its evolutionary spiral-like movement)[11] immediately contrast the temporality of capital and its process of accumulation, hence producing a tension between different strata of time.[12] In this horizon, the bourgeois society no longer appears as a static object of analysis, but as an organism whose physiology is intelligible from the point of view of the antagonisms, conflicts and contradictions that take place in it.[13] In this perspective, primitive accumulation reveals itself as a category that is able to unveil these conflicting temporalities that play their roles on an ever-increasing global scale. The extraction of surplus value in different geographical areas of the world is a good exemplification of this process: the investment of capital in the technological sector (with the following extraction of relative surplus value) in Western countries has become possible only though the simultaneous forced extraction of absolute surplus value that took places in other countries, such as China or India (where the working day has reached the peak of 12 or more hours). Such a phenomenon occurs in the frame of the world market, that is, a system about which Marx

---

[10]   Relations between the formations of the 'developed' or advanced world (the center), and those of the 'underdeveloped' world (the periphery) are affected by transfers of value, and these constitute the essence of the problem of accumulation on a world scale. Whenever the capitalist mode of production enters into relations with precapitalist modes of production, and subjects these to itself, transfers of value take place from the precapitalist to the capitalist formations, as a result of the mechanisms of *primitive accumulation*. These mechanisms do not belong only to the prehistory of capitalism; they are contemporary as well. It is these forms of primitive accumulation, modified but persistent, to the advantage of the center, that form the domain of the theory of accumulation on a world scale. (Amin 1974, p. 3)

[11]   I take the image of the 'spiral-like movement' of capital from Harvey (2017).

[12]   See: Tomba (2012). Here Tomba, following other authors (such as Bensaïd 2002), considers the conflict between different temporalities as a pivotal element in the construction of a Marxian theory of political praxis.

[13]   This self-contradictory nature of capital is an essential feature of the capitalistic physiology, and a concept that, from a theoretical standpoint, sheds light on the specific differences existing between the pre-capitalist and capitalist modes of production. Self-moving and self-sublating contradiction constitutes a fundamental form-determination of capital (Marx [1857/58] 1993, pp. 704–706; Calabi 1975).

began to think in the years of his first attempt to write *Capital*, as the following passage from a letter he wrote to Engels on 8 October 1858 witnesses:

> The proper task of bourgeois society is the creation of the world market, at least in outline, and of the production based on that market. Since the world is round, the colonisation of California and Australia and the opening up of China and Japan would seem to have completed this process. (Marx [1858] 2010a, p. 347).[14]

Plural spaces mean plural temporalities as well. Plural temporalities that, from the point of view of capital, need to be synchronized with the temporalities of an ever-increasing production and realization of surplus value that take place on the world market.

Maybe, the reflections of the late Marx must be contextualized within this wide conceptual constellation: from the *Ethnological Notebooks* to the *Preface* to the 1882 Russian edition of the *Communist Manifesto*, going through the *Letter to Vera Zasulič* and its drafts.[15] In these works, beyond some important reflections on the conditions of possibility of a communist revolution, we can find some interesting considerations about the limit of the Eurocentric historical-philosophical *Weltanschauung* and a deep critique of its theoretical framework based on a linear, teleological and deterministic idea of progress. In this regard, it is worth quoting a passage from a letter Marx wrote to the Russian newspaper *Otechestvennye Zapiski* in November 1877. Here, in a few lines, Marx criticizes those interpreters who want to see in the pages dedicated

---

[14]   The question of the developing creation of a world market was at the centre of Marx and Engels's interests since the beginning of the 1850s. See the letter Engels wrote to Marx on 24 August 1852: 'California and Australia are two cases which were not foreseen in the *Manifesto*: creation of large new markets out of nothing. They will have to be included' (Engels [1852] 2010, p. 165). See also this passage from the article Marx published in the *New York Daily Tribune* on 14 June 1853:
> Notwithstanding California and Australia, notwithstanding the immense and unprecedented emigration, there must ever, without any particular accident, in due time arrive a moment when the extension of the markets is unable to keep pace with the extension of British manufacturers, and this disproportion must bring about a new crisis with the same certainty as it has done in the past. But, if one of the great markets suddenly becomes contracted, the arrival of the crisis is necessarily accelerated thereby. (Marx [1853] 2010, pp. 95–96)

[15]   For a presentation of the late Marx's writings about Russia (1882 *Preface* to the Russian edition *The Communist Manifesto*, the *Letter to Vera Zasulic* and the *Letter to the Editorial Board of Otechestvennye Zapiski*), see: Shanin (1983). For a deeper and historically wider examination of the Marxian writings about non-capitalist societies, see: Anderson (2010).

to primitive accumulation a 'philosophy of history' aimed at foreseeing the future of every country according to prearranged evolutionary patterns.

> The chapter of *Capital* on primitive accumulation claims no more than to trace the path by which, in Western Europe, the capitalist economic order emerged from the womb of the feudal economic order. It therefore presents the historical movement which, by divorcing the producers from their means of production, converted the former into wage-labourers (proletarians in the modern sense of the world) and the owners of the latter into capitalists. (Marx [1877] 1983, p. 135)

9.4   PRIMITIVE ACCUMULATION AND THE LOGICAL REPRODUCTION OF CAPITAL

The systemic and structural role played by primitive accumulation represents a pivotal articulation in the explanation of some economic, social and political phenomena typical of capitalism. But if we try to stay within the more restricted borders of the critique of political economy, it will be necessary to take an additional step and go deeper. If the project of the critique of political economy is to be understood, as Marx writes to Lassalle, as a '*Critique of Economic Categories* or, IF YOU LIKE, a critical exposé of the system of the bourgeois economy', as 'at once an exposé and, by the same token, a critique of the system' (Marx [1858] 2010b, p. 270), then it should be clear that our interpretation of primitive accumulation is not accomplished, since this category has not yet been explained on the basis of the inner genesis of the categories of the whole system.

To put it a different way: the object of *Capital* is not capitalism as a historical and particular phenomenon, but capital as a determined abstraction; the critique of capital consists in an exposition that is logically guided by 'the correct observation and deduction' (Marx [1857/58] 1993, p. 460) of the laws constituting social relations, which show themselves in a fetishized way, on the one side, in political economy, on the other, in society. Therefore, the critique of political economy, with its articulation between the method of inquiry (*Forschungsweise*) and the method of presentation (*Darstellungsweise*),[16] needs to be interpreted as a system (with its own structural laws), whose synchronic validity relates to a diachronically constituted matter. Such a scientific

---

16   Of course the method of presentation must differ in form from that of inquiry. The latter has to appropriate the material in detail, to analyse its different forms of development, to trace out their inner connexion. Only after this work is done, can the actual movement be adequately described. If this is done successfully, if the life of the subject-matter is ideally reflected as in a mirror, then it may appear as if we had before us a mere a priori construction. (Marx [1867] 1906, pp. 24–25).

model is not a static one; on the contrary, as the Italian Marxist philosopher Cesare Luporini has also highlighted, the formal-genetic construction of *Capital* would not be possible without the integration of historical-genetic data in specific moments of the exposition.[17]

Primitive accumulation, as a systematic category of the critique of political economy, has a hybrid nature: it is located between the historical-genetic and the formal-genetic moments.[18] In the first case, it shows the presuppositions of the historical genesis of capitalistic relations; in the latter, it defines that 'it is in fact this divorce between the conditions of labour on the one hand and the producers on the other that forms the concept [*Begriff*] of capital' (Marx [1894] 1991, p. 354). From this latter perspective, primitive accumulation is, then, the category that sets the conditions for the reproduction of the concept of capital itself. In this sense, we can maybe explain the reason for its position at the end of that circular exposition that characterizes *Capital Volume I*, that is, primitive accumulation is the necessary condition for commodity and money to assume their capitalistic form.

Those scholars who, like David Harvey for example, consider primitive accumulation not only for its systematic character within the capitalistic accumulation, but also as a strategy consciously employed by the ruling class, run the risk of ignoring its essential role in the reproduction of the capitalistic fetish. They describe capitalist reality, but they do not inquire about its conceptual constitution. In so doing, they lose the theoretical constitution of capital as a determined abstraction.

The fetish character of commodities finds its first presupposition in the separation between the capitalist (as a 'personification' of capital), on the one side, and the worker selling his labour-power, on the other. 'The whole mystery of commodities, all the magic and necromancy that surrounds the products of

---

[17] See: Luporini (1975).

[18] In this sense, we could say that in these pages Marx gives us a hint of the tension existing between morphology and chronology in the realm of historiographical reconstruction. In the horizon of the critique of political economy, the historical dimension cannot be represented as a sequence of events; instead, it is a montage that requires the mediation of the formal determination of the categories implied by the systematic reproduction of the dominant mode of production. Hence, it is only after having identified the logic specific to the capitalist mode of production that we can talk about its specific temporalities and, finally, land in the domain of historiography. The conceptual reproduction of the capitalist society is the condition for the morphological analysis of its structural dynamics and its historical becoming and presuppositions. In this theoretical framework, we can see the anti-historicist nature of the Marxian critique: history is not something we can presuppose, but something we have to explain in its specific forms of constitution and becoming. This is the point where the critique of political economy can make its contribution to the foundation of a critical historiography.

labour' (Marx [1867] 1906, p. 87) is built over this particular social relation. This 'bewitched, distorted and upside-down world haunted by *Monsieur le Capital* and *Madame la Terre*, who are at the same time social characters and mere things' (Marx [1894] 1991, p. 969), is founded on a perpetual separation process, which is achieved through primitive accumulation. Its importance is tangible even in the political domain, since the reproduction on an 'expanded scale' (Marx [1857/58] 1993, p. 462) of the separation between the subjective and objective conditions of production represents an element of tension that animates class struggle. Proceeding in this direction, Marx has managed to radically demystify the nature of the bourgeois social relations, to show the actual division that makes them effectual.

Capital needs to perpetually reproduce its own presuppositions, it needs to keep the workers away from the possession of the conditions of production, it needs to renovate its 'eternal laws of nature', whose genesis is then removed in the result (assumed as an isolated fact) of a social relation that assumes the form of a relation between things. That is why, as Werner Bonefeld has written, primitive accumulation is 'the presupposition of capital and the result of its reproduction. In short primitive accumulation is the social constitution of capitalist social relations'.[19]

This is an essential feature to distinguish political economy from its critique: the critique of political economy – as Horkheimer states – 'does not labor in the service of an existing reality but only gives voice to the mystery of that reality',[20] and makes a contribution for its removal with an unscrupulous praxis aimed at the transformation of the social totality. It is a critique, which is able to tear up the fetishistic veil that masks the exploitation upon which capitalist reproduction is founded. Marx's critical apparatus can guide us in this comeback from the result to the genesis. In such 'anamnesis of the genesis',[21] primitive accumulation, as we have seen, can play a crucial role. It sheds a light on the ever-renewing constitution of the capitalist social relations. The destiny, then, of this perpetual reproduction of the presuppositions of capital – a reproduction that always comes back to weigh on the proletarians' back as the toil of Sisyphus – will be decided on the ground of class struggle.

---

[19] Bonefeld (2001, p. 2). Bonefeld has given a synchronic interpretation of the primitive accumulation starting from the different perspectives. See: Bonefeld (1988, 2011).

[20] Horkheimer ([1937] 2002, p. 217).

[21] Adorno (1965, p. 223). For an interpretation of Adorno's 'anamnesis of the genesis' and of its relation to the Marxian critique of political economy, see: Redolfi Riva (2013), Bellofiore and Redolfi Riva (2015).

REFERENCES

Abbreviation:
MECW = Marx–Engels Collected Works, London: Lawrence & Wishart.

Adorno, T.W., (1965). Notizen von einem Gespräch zwischen Th. W. Adorno und A. Sohn-Rethel am 16. 4. 1965. In: A. Sohn-Rethel, *Geistige und körperliche Arbeit. Zur Epistemologie der abendländischen Geschichte*. Wenheim: VCH, pp. 221–226.

Amin, S., (1974). *Accumulation on a World Scale. A Critique of the Theory of Underdevelopment*. New York and London: Monthly Review Press.

Anderson, K.B., (2010). *Marx at the Margins*. Chicago, IL: Chicago University Press.

Aston, T.H. and Philpin, C.H.E., eds, (1987). *The Brenner Debate. Agrarian Class Structure and Economic Development in Pre-Industrial Europe*. Cambridge: Cambridge University Press.

Balibar, É., (2009). Reflections on *Gewalt. Historical Materialism* 17(1), pp. 99–125.

Bellofiore, R., and Redolfi Riva, T., (2015). The Neue Marx-Lektüre. Putting the Critique of Political Economy Back into the Critique of Society. *Radical Philosophy* 189, pp. 24–36.

Bensaïd, D., (2002). *Marx For Our Times. Adventures and Misadventures of a Critique*. London and New York: Verso.

Bonefeld, W., (1988). Class Struggle and the Permanence of Primitive Accumulation. *Common Sense* 6(1), pp. 54–65.

Bonefeld, W., (2001). The Permanence of Primitive Accumulation: Commodity Fetishism and Social Constitution. *The Commoner* 2, https://thecommoner.org/wp-content/uploads/2019/10/The-Permanence-of-Primitive-Accumulation-Bonefeld.pdf (accessed 1 June 2021).

Bonefeld, W., (2011). Primitive Accumulation and Capitalist Accumulation: Notes on Social Constitution and Expropriation. *Science and Society* 75(3), pp. 379–394.

Calabi, M.L., (1975). Su 'barriera' e 'limite' nel concetto del capitale. *Critica Marxista* 14(2–3), pp. 55–69.

Dobb, M., (1946). *Studies in the Development of Capitalism*. London: Routledge.

Engels, F., [1852] (2010). Letter to Marx, 24 August 1852. In: *MECW*, vol. 39. Digital edition. London: Lawrence & Wishart, pp. 164–165.

Harvey, D., (2003). *The New Imperialism*. Oxford: Oxford University Press.

Harvey, D., (2006). *Spaces of Global Capitalism. Towards a Theory of Uneven Geographical Development*. London and New York: Verso.

Harvey, D., (2010). *A Companion to Marx's 'Capital'*. London and New York: Verso.

Harvey, D., (2014). *Seventeen Contradictions and the End of Capitalism*. London: Profile Books.

Harvey, D., (2017). *Marx, Capital and the Madness of Economic Reason*. London: Profile Books.

Hilton, R.H., ed., (1978). *The Transition from Feudalism to Capitalism*. London: Verso.

Horkheimer, M., [1937] (2002). Traditional and Critical Theory. In: M. Horkheimer, *Critical Theory: Selected Essays*. New York: Continuum, pp. 188–243.

Luporini, C., (1975). Reality and Historicity: Economy and Dialectics in Marxism. *Economy and Society* 4(2), pp. 206–231; 4(3), pp. 283–308.

Luxemburg, R., ([1913] 2003). *The Accumulation of Capital*. Routledge: London.

Marx, K., [1853] (2010). Revolution in China and Europe. In: *MECW*, vol. 12. Digital edition. London: Lawrence & Wishart, pp. 93–100.

Marx, K., [1857/58] (1993). *Grundrisse. Foundations of the Critique of Political Economy*, 2nd edn. Harmondsworth: Penguin.

Marx, K., [1858] (2010a). Letter to Engels, 8 October 1858. In: *MECW*, vol. 40. Digital edition. London: Lawrence & Wishart, pp. 345–357.

Marx, K., [1858] (2010b). Letter to Ferdinand Lassalle, 22 February 1858. In: *MECW*, vol. 40. Digital edition. London: Lawrence & Wishart, pp. 268–271.

Marx, K., [1867] (1906). *Capital. A Critique of Political Economy. Volume One*. New York: Modern Library.

Marx, K., [1877] (1983). A Letter to the Editorial Board of *Otechestvennye Zapiski*. In: T. Shanin, ed., *Late Marx and the Russian Road. Late Marx and the 'Peripheries of Capitalism'*. New York: Monthly Review Press, pp. 134–37.

Marx, K., [1894] (1991). *Capital. A Critique of Political Economy. Volume Three*, 8th edn. Harmondsworth: Penguin.

Meiksins Wood, E., (2002). *The Origin of Capitalism. A Longer View*. London and New York: Verso.

Prawer, S.S., (1976). *Karl Marx and the World Literature*. London and New York: Oxford University Press.

Redolfi Riva, T., (2013). Teoria critica della società? Critica dell'economia politica. Adorno, Backhaus, Marx. *Consecutio Temporum* 3(5), http://www.consecutio .org/2013/10/teoria-critica-della-societa-critica-delleconomia-politica-in-adorno -backhaus-marx/ (accessed 1 June 2021).

Shanin, T., ed., (1983). *Late Marx and the Russian Road. Late Marx and the 'Peripheries of Capitalism'*. New York: Monthly Review Press.

Tomba, M., (2009). Another Kind of *Gewalt*: Beyond Law. Re-reading Walter Benjamin. *Historical Materialism* 17(1), pp. 126–144.

Tomba, M., (2012). *Marx's Temporalities*. Leiden: Brill.

10. Domination

Chris O'Kane

10.1 INTRODUCTION

Marx's voluminous writings contain historical, theoretical and conjunctural accounts of domination. They span his corpus from his earliest to his last writings, from his best-known works to numerous less well-known manuscripts, notes and letters. One can then say, without exaggeration, that domination is a core issue in Marx's work.

Coupled with Marx's stature as a thinker, this means that the secondary literature on Marx's theory of domination is massive. In this secondary literature, Marx's conception of domination is often primarily treated as a theory of class domination, a theory of alienation, or a theory of reification.

In the theory of class domination, domination is construed trans-historically. The classes that own the means of production dominate the labouring classes, forcing them to produce wealth that enriches the ruling classes and deprives the labouring classes. In capitalism, this type of class domination consists in the domination of the proletariat by the capitalist class (see Engels [1878] 1975; Lenin [1914] 1974).

In domination as alienation, domination is also conceived trans-historically. Like the theory of class domination, alienation as domination is premised on the classes that own the means of production appropriating the proceeds of labour from the labouring classes. Yet following the early Marx's writings, alienation as domination conceives of this process on the basis of a notion of human nature as collective production for need. Consequently, rather than exclusively focusing on class oppression and deprivation, alienation as domination holds that the working classes are dominated by the world they have collectively created, which has estranged them (and even the ruling classes) from their own nature. In capitalism, domination as alienation consists of the alienated world of commodities and the market, which are created by and dominate the proletariat and capitalist class because the capitalist class owns the means of production (see Lefebvre 2009; Olman 1978; Mészáros 2006; Sayers 2011).

The interpretation of domination as reification resembles that of alienation. Yet it focuses specifically on capitalism and bases the theory of reification on Marx's critique of political economy. Like alienation as domination, the working class creates the reified second nature of the capitalist economy, which capitalists and proletarians perceive as a first nature, leading them to act in accordance with what they perceive to be the natural laws of the economy (see Lukács [1923] 1972; Markus 1982).

The lesser well-known approach of value-form theory argues that Marx possessed two theories of domination. Pre-capitalist societies were characterized by 'personal domination'. In feudalism, for instance, authority was vested in the person of the lord. Serfs were obligated to produce and distribute a surplus to the lord on the basis of this personal authority. Hence the lord's domination of the serfs was personal domination. Capitalism, in contrast, is distinguished by a historically specific form of 'impersonal domination'. The historically specific social form of the capitalist mode of production is manifest in the supraindividual forms of value that dominate capitalists and proletarians and mediate class antagonism. Individual capitalists thus dominate proletarians on the basis of the impersonal power of the money they possess, not the hereditary right of lords (see Heinrich 2012).

There is certainly evidence for the theory of class domination in Marx's political writings (particularly *The Communist Manifesto* and *The 18th Brumaire*). The theory of alienation as domination is also a central theme of Marx's early work on political economy (particularly the *1844 Manuscripts*). Finally, domination as reification and the value-theoretic idea of impersonal domination are present in the critique of political economy.

In what follows, I take a different approach to understanding Marx's conception of domination than the aforementioned approaches. In contrast to the theory of class of domination, I do not conceive of Marx's theory of domination as a trans-historical account of class oppression, nor do I hold that such a theory completed English political economy. In opposition to alienation as domination and alienation as reification, I do not conceptualize Marx's idea of domination as premised on human nature, nor do I show how this idea drew on Hegel. Finally, in distinction to value-form theory, I do not provide a detailed reconstruction of the critique of political economy that shows how Marx's theory of the value-form draws on Hegel and distinguishes itself from English political economy.

I focus instead on indicating how Marx's early and later writings on political economy can be seen to amount to a critical social theory of domination. I do so by drawing on and developing the insights of a number of critical theorists' interpretations of Marx.[1] These thinkers' conceptions of Marx's idea of domination are often associated with the interpretations of domination as reification or 'impersonal domination'. It is certainly true that these thinkers, particularly Horkheimer and Adorno, use the term 'reification'. The impersonal domination of the forms of value is also central to their interpretations of Marx's theory of domination. Yet as the other terms these thinkers use such as 'social objectivity' and 'social domination' indicate, reification and impersonal domination are used as part of an interpretation of Marx's theory of domination as a critical theory of social domination. In this critical theory interpretation, domination is inherent to the 'social reality' of bourgeois society due to the organization of bourgeois society.

I build on this interpretation of Marx's theory of domination from two theoretical vantage points intended to illuminate such a critical theory of domination. The first vantage point entails 'detourning' Lenin's famous depiction of Marx as 'the genius who continued and consummated the three main ideological currents of the nineteenth century ... classical German philosophy, classical English political economy, and French socialism combined with French revolutionary doctrines in general' (Lenin [1914] 1974, p. 50). As I previously suggested, this interpretation has certainly provided important purchase for understanding the development of Marx's thought, including the theories of class domination and alienation and reification as domination. In what follows, I aim to show that focusing on Marx's critique of these 'currents' can also illuminate and develop the interpretation of Marx's theory of domination as a critical social theory of domination. I do so within the confines of this chapter by focusing on Marx's critique of Smith, Hegel and Proudhon's theories of the historical realization of freedom in contemporary society.

The second vantage point entails adapting Alfred Schmidt's approach to interpreting the development of Marx's work. Following Schmidt (1968), I interpret Marx's early critique of Smith, Hegel, Proudhon and bourgeois society from the perspective of Marx's later critique of political economy. Adapting Schmidt, I also conceive of Marx's critical social theory of domination as possessing a:

> double meaning ... first as a critique of real, political economic conditions as they necessarily arise from capitalist forms of production and circulation, and secondly,

---

[1] This approach draws on the insights of the strand of value-form theory associated with Frankfurt School critical theory (see esp. Reichelt 2001; Backhaus 1992; Postone 1993; Reichelt 2005). Yet I also develop the insights of earlier thinkers from the Frankfurt School, notably Max Horkheimer, Theodor W. Adorno and Alfred Schmidt. Finally, I also extend the insights of Simon Clarke (1991), Werner Bonefeld (2013) and William Clare Roberts (2018).

as a criticism of [Smith, Hegel and Proudhon's] political economy as the science [*Wissenschaft*] of the whole vital process ... within which the theoretical under-standing ... bourgeois society had of itself found its most adequate conception.

I do so by taking up Schmidt's point that 'by sticking closely to the theoretical premises of bourgeois economy' Marx 'reveals the contradictions between these premises and social reality (as thought) and thereby the objective contra-dictions within social reality itself' (Schmidt 1968, p. 95).

From these two vantage points I argue that the 'double meaning' of Marx's critical social theory of domination can be interpreted as criticizing Smith's, Hegel's and Proudhon's theories of social freedom in modern society by demonstrating how the moral and institutional aspects of bourgeois society which these figures argued realize freedom are instead premised on the historically specific organization of a society that consists in domination. Consequently, these thinkers' conceptions of social freedom only propose to perpetuate social domination. Social freedom is only possible through the emancipatory abolition of bourgeois society and the creation of a communist society. This is why Marx's theory of domination can be conceived as a critical social theory of domination.

Section 10.2 provides a short outline of Smith, Hegel and Proudhon's theories of social freedom. Section 10.3 focuses on Marx's early critiques of Hegel, Smith, Proudhon and bourgeois society. Section 10.4 provides an interpretation of the critique of political economy as a critical theory of social domination and develops Marx's critiques of Hegel, Smith and Proudhon by demonstrating how the historically specific organization of bourgeois society is founded on violent expropriation and is realized in the interrelated social dynamic of impersonal domination and class antagonism. Section 10.5 draws together my discussion of the late and early Marx's theory of domination and his critiques of Smith, Hegel and Proudhon's ideas of social freedom in order to substantiate my characterization of Marx's theory of domination as a critical social theory of domination. I conclude by summarizing my interpretation of Marx's theory of domination, discussing Marx's idea of social freedom, and pointing towards their importance today.

10.2   SMITH, HEGEL AND PROUDHON'S THEORIES OF SOCIAL FREEDOM

English political economy, German idealism and French socialism claimed to apprehend the normative principles of social development inherent to modern society. Thinkers in these schools of thought further argued that if institutions and individuals within modern society followed these normative principles, freedom, well-being and affluence would be attained. The confines of this chapter prevent a nuanced discussion of these schools of thought and of the ambiguities and differing interpretations of their foremost thinkers. I focus instead on interpreting Smith, Hegel and Proudhon's theories of social freedom as emblematic of bourgeois society's understanding of itself as a free society that culminates historical development, in order to anticipate Marx's critiques of these thinkers.

Smith

In *Theory of Moral Sentiments, Lectures on Jurisprudence* and *Wealth of Nations* (Smith [1759] 1984; [1763] 1982; [1776] 1982), Adam Smith developed a systematic theory of moral philosophy, jurisprudence and political economy intended to apprehend the normative principles inherent to the development of modern society that could achieve freedom and well-being for all members of society. Smith conceived of these normative principles on the basis of the human propensity to benevolently truck and barter, creating a division of labour based on human needs that had become more complex over time. According to Smith, this process of historical development had occurred in progressive historical stages and led to the emergence of the institutions of money (which facilitated exchange on markets with a sophisticated division of labour) and the modern state.

In Smith's time the division of labour had developed into 'commercial society'. In 'commercial society' three classes contributed to the production of historically unparalleled wealth. According to Smith, each class would receive compensation in the distribution of wealth via the allocative mechanism of the invisible hand of the market, which in turn would facilitate the further development of the division of labour. However, greedy and immoral capitalists often tried to appropriate too much wealth for themselves. Inept politicians also promoted mercantile economic policies. These immoral acts and ill-conceived policies led to inequality and prevented the further development of the division of labour. For Smith, the state should stand above the particular interests of these immoral and greedy capitalists, uphold laws that protect property and the market, and provide necessary moral education that teaches individuals to benevolently truck and barter, thus facilitating the progressive development of the division of labour and the realization of freedom, wealth and well-being for all.

Hegel

Hegel's philosophical system paralleled Smith's, but pointed to a different normative principle of social development. Like Smith, Hegel argued that a dynamic principle of modern society could realize freedom and human well-being. Like Smith, Hegel also developed a theory of social freedom and human well-being that combined moral philosophy and political economy that was premised on this dynamic principle. Yet, unlike Smith, Hegel did not ground this normative principle in the natural human activity of trucking and bartering, nor contend that the invisible hand of the market and the laissez-faire state were necessary to achieve freedom and prosperity. Instead, the dynamic historical principle that Hegel identified was the development of human consciousness as the progressive realization of *Geist*. Although Hegel's overarching theory held that such a process ultimately amounted to the coming to self-consciousness of nature, the development of society as a second nature whose institutions realized freedom was integral to this process. In *Philosophy of Right* (Hegel [1821] 1991), Hegel thus argued that modern society was typified by the spheres of the state, civil society and the family. Each of these spheres possessed norms that should be actualized in the harmonious order of modern society. A constitutional monarchic state should play the superordinate role, realizing these norms in laws. For Hegel, the attainment of freedom and human well-being thus consisted in identifying and acting in accordance with these modern norms and laws.

Proudhon

Pierre-Joseph Proudhon was the first radical socialist to develop an immanent critique of English political economy, German idealism, and French socialism.[2] In *The System of Economic Contradictions: Or, The Philosophy of Poverty* (Proudhon [1846] 1888), Proudhon drew on Smith and Hegel to develop a schematic dialectic that purportedly apprehended the normative principles of the progressive historical development of freedom and human flourishing that were present in modern society. Like Smith and Hegel, Proudhon argued that human nature and freedom could only be achieved through the social institutions of modern society. Yet Proudhon's radical immanent critique of Smith and Hegel argued that human nature and freedom could only be achieved in an equal society. This was because the institutions that undergirded Smith and Hegel's philosophy – property and law – were unequally distributed and unfairly enforced in modern society. According to Proudhon, labour created all wealth. Yet the distribution of wealth was unequal, due to monopolies, the commodity character of money, and elite-run banks. In Proudhon's analysis, these institutions were all creatures of the state and violated the just principles of equal exchange, leading to poverty and misery. Proudhon proposed to

---

[2]   As Mattick (2018) states, Lenin's aforementioned characterization of Marx's thought is a more accurate characterization of Proudhon.

remedy inequality and create a just society by equally distributing property, abolishing the commodity character of money, and creating people's banks. Proudhon also held that the moral legal institution of the contract would be necessary to promote and preserve the equality enacted by these reforms. Together these reforms would bring into being the just principles of exchange in a free society. Hence, according to Proudhon, production within the modern division of labour premised on equal, just and free exchange would lead to freedom on the basis of the realization of the mutualist morality of human nature.

10.3 MARX'S EARLY CRITIQUES OF HEGEL, SMITH, PROUDHON AND BOURGEOIS SOCIETY

Marx's theoretical writings in the 1840s moved from a critique of Hegel's *Philosophy of Right*, to his initial critiques of Smith and Proudhon. Following Alfred Schmidt's approach of reading the ideas developed by the young Marx from the perspective of the ideas developed by the older Marx, I will not focus on how Marx's early theories of class struggle or alienation persist in the critique of political economy. Nor will I focus on the status of his theory of value in the 1844 and 1867 manuscripts. Rather, I will show that it was during the 1840s that Marx originated his critique of Hegel, Smith, Proudhon and bourgeois society that he would develop and refine in his critique of political economy. I will also demonstrate that these earlier critiques of Marx's anticipated the double-character of his critique of political economy as a critical social theory of domination. For it was during the 1840s that Marx first argued – in contrast to Hegel, Smith and Proudhon – that historical development had not led to the prospect of attaining freedom in modern society. For the institutions, norms and social relations of modern society were not the bases for social freedom as Hegel, Smith and even Proudhon's theories held. Rather, they were tantamount to the social domination of bourgeois society. Consequently, rather than grasping the principles of social freedom, Hegel, Smith and Proudhon's theories propounded social domination. Only the emancipatory abolition of bourgeois society and the overcoming of estrangement in a communist society would realize freedom.

In his writings on Hegel's *Philosophy of Right*, Marx argued that rather than realizing freedom in the spheres, norms and constitutional state of modern society, bourgeois society is characterized by separation and unfreedom. Individuals in civil society are separated from private property and from each other. Civil society is separated from the state. Rather than serving the general interest and embodying freedom, 'the political constitution is … the constitution of private property'. Hence, according to Marx, Hegel's concept of freedom in the modern Prussian constitutional state captures the unfreedom of 'estrangement within unity' (Marx [1843] 1975, p. 98).

Marx's manuscripts on Smith from several months later critiqued Smith's theory of freedom. Rather than the division of labour being premised on human nature, Marx holds that 'political economy presupposes [the] property owner' and 'defines the estranged form of social intercourse as the essential and original form corresponding to man's nature' (Marx [1844] 1975a, p. 217). Contra Smith's notion of benevolence, 'The social connection or social relationship between the two property owners is therefore that of reciprocity in alienation.' Therefore, rather than a division of labour based on production for need, 'The division of labour is the economic expression of the social character of labour within estrangement' (Marx [1844] 1975b, p. 317). Finally, rather than the expansion of the division of labour leading to social harmony and affluence, the division of labour in bourgeois society amounts to misery. Hence, 'in a declining state of society – increasing misery of the worker; in an advancing state – misery with complications; and in a fully developed state of society – static misery' (Marx [1844] 1975b, p. 239). Therefore:

> Since ... according to Smith, a society is not happy, of which the greater part suffers – yet even the wealthiest state of society leads to this suffering of the majority – and since the economic system (and in general a society based on private interest) leads to this wealthiest condition, it follows that the goal of the economic system is the unhappiness of society. (Marx [1844] 1975b, p. 239)

In *The Poverty of Philosophy* and elsewhere, Marx was critical of Proudhon's emancipatory theory. He argued that Proudhon's moral ethos of mutualism was grounded on a trans-historical theory of human nature that failed to grasp historical specificity. Consequently, like classical political economy and Hegel:

> Mr Proudhon, chiefly because he doesn't know history, fails to see that, in developing his productive faculties, i.e. in living, man develops certain inter-relations, and that the nature of these relations necessarily changes with the modification and the growth of the said productive faculties. He fails to see that *economic categories* are but *abstractions* of those real relations, that they are truths only in so far as those relations continue to exist. Thus he falls into the error of bourgeois economists who regard those economic categories as eternal laws and not as historical laws which are laws only for a given historical development, a specific development of the productive forces. (Marx [1846] 1982, p. 100)

Like Smith and Hegel, Proudhon thus failed to grasp how the division of labour characteristic of bourgeois society creates a dynamic of unfreedom that compels production and consumption:

> The producer, the moment he produces in a society founded on the division of labour and on exchange (and that is Mr Proudhon's hypothesis), is forced to sell. Mr Proudhon makes the producer master of the means of production; but he will agree with us that his means of production do not depend on free will. Moreover, many of these means of production are products which he gets from the outside, and in modern production he is not even free to produce the amount he wants. The actual degree of development of the productive forces compels him to produce on such or such a scale. The consumer is no freer than the producer. His estimation depends on his means and his needs. Both of these are determined by his social position, which itself depends on the whole social organization ... But the difference in their estimations is explained by the difference in the positions which they occupy in society, and which themselves are the product of social organization. (Marx [1847] 1975, pp. 118–119)

Consequently, in Marx's view, Proudhon's proposal to remedy distribution could not overcome this social organization of unfreedom. Hence, in Marx's view, 'Mr Proudhon does not provide a false critique of political economy because his philosophy is absurd – he produces an absurd philosophy because he has not understood present social conditions in their engrènement' (Marx [1846] 1982, p. 95), trying to pass off as a '"revolutionary theory of the future" what Ricardo expounded scientifically as the theory of present-day society, of bourgeois society' (Marx [1847] 1975, p. 121).

In sum, in these early writings Marx argued that the institutions and intersubjective norms of modern society that Hegel, Smith and Proudhon argued had and should realize freedom, were premised on estrangement and realized in the domination, antagonism and misery of bourgeois society. Adhering to their theories would propound domination, not realize freedom. According to Marx, emancipation could only be attained by the proletariat's abolition of bourgeois society and of itself as a class. While these criticisms of bourgeois society and Marx's notions of communism were premised on his idea of human nature, his later work on the critique of political economy, to which I now turn, would develop these insights outside of the anthropological standpoint of estrangement and within one of the critiques of the historically specific constitution and reproduction of the political economy of bourgeois society.

10.4 MARX'S CRITICAL THEORY OF SOCIAL DOMINATION

Marx famously described the critique of political economy in a letter to Lassalle as 'a critical *exposé* of the system of bourgeois economy. It is at once an *exposé* and, by the same token, a critique of the system' (Marx [1858] 1983, p. 270). Since the critique of political economy is riddled with ambiguities and was not completed by Marx, many authors have offered interpretations of this passage in conjunction with their reconstruction of the critique of political economy. In this chapter, on Marx's critical social theory of domination, adapting Schmidt, I use this passage to argue that the critique of political economy set out to expose how the historically specific organization of bourgeois society was realized in the constitution and ensuing dynamic of reproduction of unfreedom and misery, rather than Hegel's, Smith's and Proudhon's notions of freedom and well-being. Consequently, freedom and human flourishing could not be attained by the further development of the institutions and social relations of modern society, only their emancipatory negation. In order to show this, I first focus on Marx's delineation of the historical specificity of the capitalist social form of production, then his critical *exposé* of its dominating and class antagonistic dynamic, before turning to the state. I do so by drawing on the relevant passages in the *Grundrisse*, *Capital Volume I* and the incomplete manuscripts that were published as part of *Capital Volume III*.

The *Grundrisse*

I begin by turning to Marx's discussion of the historical specificity of capitalist domination in the *Grundrisse*. In these passages Marx is at pains to grasp modern society in a markedly different way than Smith and Proudhon. First, by criticizing accounts of the 'prehistorical' development of market society as eminently historical. Then, by arguing, contra Smith, that the organization of modern society, via market dependence, has not superseded domination but led to the emergence of a new type of domination. Whereas the organization of previous societies had consisted in 'personal dependence', 'personal imprisonment' and 'personal domination', the organization of bourgeois society consists in 'all around dependence' and 'thing-like objective dependency [*sachlicher Abhängigkeit*]'.

According to Marx, this historically specific type of social domination arose because bourgeois society is premised on 'the dissolution of all production and activities into exchange value' and 'the dissolution of all fixed personal (historical) relations of dependence in production' (Marx [1857/58] 1973, p. 156). Consequently, the 'objective bond' of 'bourgeois society', which 'rests on exchange value', seems to be natural and premised on the freedom of exchange. However, 'they seem [*scheinen*] thus only for someone who abstracts ... from the conditions of existence within which these individuals enter into contact (and these conditions, in turn, are independent of individuals and, although created by society, manifest [*erscheinen*] as if they were natural conditions not controllable by individuals)' (Marx [1857/58] 1973, p. 164).

By not abstracting from these historically specific conditions, Marx reveals that since 'this reciprocal dependence is expressed in the constant necessity for exchange and for exchange-value as the all-sided mediation', the capitalist division of labour is not premised on production for need. Rather:

> the social character of activity, as well as the social form of the product, and the share of individuals in production manifest [*erschein*] as something alien and objective, confronting the individuals, not as their relation to one another, but as their subordination to relations which subsists independently of them and which arise out of collisions between mutually indifferent individuals. (Marx [1857/58] 1973, p. 157)

Consequently, 'individuals are now ruled by abstractions' which are nothing 'more than the theoretical expression of those material relations which dominate [*herrschaft*] themselves' (Marx [1857/58] 1973, p. 164). Marx would unpack how these historically specific forms of domination pertain to their constitution, the class antagonism and capital accumulation, in the argument of *Capital Volume I*.

Capital

Part VIII on 'so-called primitive accumulation' in *Capital Volume I* provides a historical account of the process of the dissolution and creation of the historically specific social form of the capitalist mode of production alluded to in the *Grundrisse*. According to Marx, rather than Smith's account of entrepreneurs accumulating wealth due to their frugal spending habits, this state-facilitated process consisted in 'conquest, enslavement, robbery, murder, briefly force' (Marx [1867] 1906, p. 785). Such a history of expropriation was 'written in the annals of mankind in letters of blood and fire' and 'forms the pre-historic stage of capital and of the mode of production corresponding with it' (Marx [1867] 1906, p. 786). This is because the transformation of money and commodities into capital:

> can only take place under certain circumstances that ... that two very different kinds of commodity-possessors must come face to face and into contact, on the one hand, the owners of money, means of production, means of subsistence, who are eager to increase the sum of values they possess, by buying other people's labour-power; on the other hand, free labourers, the sellers of their own labour-power, and therefore the sellers of labour. (Marx [1867] 1906, p. 785)

The 'capital-relation' thus 'pre-supposes the complete separation of the labourers from all property in the means by which they can realize their labour'. Moreover, 'As soon as capitalist production is once on its own legs, it not only maintains this separation, but reproduces it on a continually extending scale' (Marx [1867] 1906, pp. 785–786).

The preceding Parts in *Volume I* on the commodity, money, capital, production and accumulation elaborate how the constitution of this historically specific social form is realized in the forms of value, the circuit of capital, the organization of production, and the ensuing dynamic of capital accumulation. This social dynamic consists in the 'objective thing-like dependency' (*sachlicher Abhängigkeit*) typified by the internally related impersonal class antagonistic domination of value, and is realized in the reproduction of separation on a 'continually extending scale' (Marx [1867] 1906, p. 786).

Commodities are goods produced for sale that possess use value and value. Concrete labour entails the particular activities that give particular commodities specific use value. Abstract labour is the historically specific substance of value. The value of a commodity is determined by socially necessary labour time. Exchange value is the form of appearance of value. Buying and selling commodities on markets necessitates money, which is the form and measure of value. However, in contrast to Smith, money is not a neutral entity that simply makes exchange more efficient. Rather, since money is the necessary appearance of value and the sole means of exchange, it possesses a 'social power' that is magnified by its central role in the endless process of capital accumulation (M-C-M'). Since the capitalist social form 'reifies persons and personifies things', the 'endless process' of capital accumulation is an 'automatic subject'. Capitalists and workers are 'bearers of social relations' compelled to act in this manner by this process characteristic of a society in which 'their own social action takes the form of the action of objects, which rule the producers instead of being ruled by them' (Marx [1867] 1906, p. 86).

Capitalists, as 'personifications of economic categories', are thus compelled by these forms of value to compete to acquire money in the form of profit. Since workers are free from the means to sustain themselves and free to sell their labour power, they are compelled to compete with other proletarians to sell their labour power for money in order to survive. Since profit is incumbent upon selling commodities while maximizing surplus value, in accordance with socially necessary labour time, capitalists compete to increase working hours, lower wages and increase productivity. Increased productivity leads to the revolutionizing of production.

As this trajectory indicates, in contrast to Smith, the development of the division of labour within the factory does not lead to increased wages, freedom and livelihood. Nor in contrast to Proudhon is cooperation within the production process a mutualist enterprise that is badly distributed by the corrupt institutional mechanisms. Rather, the capitalist is a 'despot'. Factory production is organized to maximize productivity by deskilling and intensifying work and introducing machinery that makes workers redundant.

This dynamic is replicated across the whole social division of labour in the crisis-ridden dynamic of capitalist accumulation and reproduction. The development of the division of labour does not then lead to the proliferation of small businesses, nor increased livelihood, but to the centralization of ownership in large firms and the multiplication of the proletariat. At best, proletarians are increasingly deskilled, supervised and compelled to ramp up productivity. Other proletarians are pushed out of work in dying sectors of the economy, and pulled into work in growing sectors of the economy. The rest are permanently unemployed.

For those who are lucky to remain employed, work becomes 'the martyrdom of the producer; the instrument of labour becomes the means of enslaving, exploiting, and impoverishing the labourer' and 'the social combination and organisation of labour-processes is turned into an organised mode of crushing out the workman's individual vitality, freedom, and independence' (Marx [1867] 1906, p. 555). Those who become unemployed are members of the surplus population who live as paupers and depress the market for wage labour, increasing the rate of exploitation. Hence, whether employed or unemployed, the working population experiences 'chronic misery' (Marx [1867] 1906, p. 471).

Consequently, rather than realizing freedom and well-being, the general law of capital accumulation is tantamount to unfreedom and misery. Not only is the accumulation of capital an 'increase of the proletariat' (Marx [1867] 1906, p. 673), but also the reproduction of separation on a 'continually extending scale' (Marx [1867] 1906, p. 786). Moreover, as Marx himself neatly states, 'all means for the development of production undergo an inversion so that they become means of domination and exploitation of the producer'. The '[a]ccumulation of wealth at one pole is, therefore, at the same time accumulation of misery, agony of toil slavery, ignorance, brutality, mental degradation, at the opposite pole, i.e., on the side of the class that produces its own product in the form of capital' (Marx [1867] 1906, p. 709). Yet ultimately, as befits a theory of social domination and objective 'thing-like dependency' (*sachlicher Abhängigkeit*), 'As, in religion, man is governed by the products of his own brain, so in capitalistic production, he is governed by the products of his own hand' (Marx [1867] 1906, p. 681).

The State

Marx himself at one point planned to devote a volume of the critique of political economy to the state. Yet many have rightly pointed to the absence of a systematic theory of the state in *Capital*. Others have drawn on Marx's discussion of the state to develop a theory (see O'Kane 2014). Clearly there is, then, a lacuna on the state in the critique of political economy. Yet the scattered discussion which Marx provides of the state in *Volume I* is still enough to establish the contours of a critique of the state on the basis of the state's role in the accumulation and reproduction of the capitalist social form. These aspects of Marx's critique of the state can also be seen as indicating that the state is neither a means of actualizing freedom in modern society (as in Hegel), nor is it responsible for preventing it (as in Proudhon), nor in reinforcing the freedom provided by the division of labour (as in Smith).

For, as Marx noted in *Volume III*, the state mirrors the categories of bourgeois political economy insofar as it is an autonomous social form constituted by the historically specific social relations that mediate and compel these relations. As we have seen, the state did so in primitive accumulation by facilitating the constitution of the capitalist social form. In the rest of *Capital*, Marx shows how the normative and minimal role that Smith ascribes to the state facilitates accumulation, and in so doing domination, antagonism and the reproduction of the capitalist social form. Moreover, as Marx's discussion of contract and law indicates, contra Proudhon, the state's enforcement of neutral laws in the idealized conditions of fairness enforce and preserve the class antagonistic capitalist social form. Finally, in what might be read as a damning inversion of *Philosophy of Right*, as the 'organized force of society', the night watchman state supplements 'the silent compulsion of economic relation', by stepping in during moments of crisis to revive accumulation and reproduction in order to guarantee the worker's dependence on capital. Rather than the obstacle to or realization of freedom in modern society, the state perpetuates domination in bourgeois society.

The critique of political economy thus develops Marx's earlier critiques of Smith, Hegel, Proudhon and his critique of bourgeois society. As was shown above, Marx's earlier work critiqued these thinkers' notion of social freedom for being premised on a society characterized by separation, estrangement and unfreedom. Hence, rather than advocating the actualization of freedom, these theories advocated the further realization of social domination. Rather than proceeding from the standpoint of estranged human essence, Marx's later work developed these insights, in the 'double meaning' of the critique of political economy. On one level, the critique of political economy developed Marx's earlier critiques of property, separation, the division of labour and the state into Marx's critical *exposé* of the bourgeois system. This aspect of the critique of political economy demonstrated that the historically specific organization of bourgeois society was based on the separation of producers from the means of reproduction. It then proceeded to show how the organization of such a society was realized in the social forms of value and the state mutually mediating indifferent class antagonistic social relations in a social dynamic of accumulation and reproduction, which results in 'separation on an extended scale'. Accordingly, bourgeois society is not premised on human nature, nor do the institutions of bourgeois society actualize freedom. Rather, bourgeois society is premised on separation and realizes 'all around', 'objective', 'thing-like dependency' (*sachlicher Abhängigkeit*) resulting in unfreedom and misery.

Hence, on the second level, Marx's critique of political economy demonstrates the faulty premises of bourgeois society's self-understanding of itself as marking the culmination of historical development and the attainment of freedom. Smith, Hegel and Proudhon's theories are representative of such a self-understanding. Yet the institutions, norms and interpersonal relations which they hold can and should serve as the bases of social freedom are in fact the bases of unfreedom, indifference, antagonism and misery. In contrast to Smith, the division of labour and the state do not facilitate 'benevolent' 'trucking', 'bartering' and freedom in accordance with human nature. Nor do they even grant prosperity. Rather, the invisible hand is a 'Moloch' that compels indifferent bartering and antagonistic trucking by personifications of economic categories, culminating in 'all-around dependency' and social misery. Moreover, since the state is integral to primitive accumulation and the reproduction of capital, it does not realize the freedom that Hegel envisioned. The state is a 'public force organized for social enslavement' (Marx [1871] 1974, p. 207). Finally, contra Proudhon, the unfreedom and inequality of modern society does not stem from the state's maldistribution of property, nor monopolies, nor the commodity character of money, and cannot be remedied by contracts or currency schemes that ensure just distribution. Rather, 'equal right is still constantly encumbered by a bourgeois limitation ... right by its nature can exist only as the application of an equal standard; but unequal individuals ... it is therefore a right of inequality in its content, like every right' (Marx [1875] 1989, p. 86).

In sum, by taking up the theoretical premises of Smith's, Hegel's and Proudhon's theories, Marx reveals the contradictions between their normative conceptions of social freedom and the social reality of domination. From this it follows that the social unfreedom of bourgeois society cannot be changed by convincing people to act in accordance with modern norms, or to embrace these modern institutions. Nor can these institutions be remedied to ensure fair distribution on the basis of fair contracts and just monetary schemes. Adhering to these theories would only perpetuate the inherent unfreedom and misery of bourgeois society. Therefore, by developing his earlier criticisms of the state, market and the division of labour, Marx's critique of political economy is a critical theory of the historically specific constitution and reproduction of bourgeois society. Such a society is premised on separation. It is realized in the social domination of the division of labour and the state, indifference and class antagonism, and the ensuing dynamic of accumulation and reproduction that is realized in expanded separation and misery. This is how Marx's theory of domination can be seen as a critical social theory.

10.5   CONCLUSION

Much has been written about Marx's conception of domination. Those in the classical Marxist tradition emphasize class domination. Marxist humanists focus on alienation and reification. Value-form theory examines the impersonal domination of the value-form. There are certainly many bases for these conceptions in Marx's writings. Yet this chapter has focused on building on the critical theory interpretation of Marx, conceptualizing Marx's theory of domination as a critical social theory. In order to do so, this chapter has inverted Lenin's famous saying, focusing on how Marx's theory of domination can be seen as a critique of Smith's English political economy, Hegel's German idealism and Proudhoun's French socialism. Moreover, following Alfred Schmidt, I have read Marx's early work from the perspective of his later work. This has led me to focus on Marx's early critique of Hegel, Smith and Proudhon and bourgeois society from the perspective of his critique of political economy. On this basis, developing Alfred Schmidt's interpretation of the critique of political economy, I have argued that Marx's theory of social domination can be seen as a double-faceted critical theory of society: one that is critical of the self-conception of bourgeois society by exposing its historically specific social reality. Hence while Hegel, Smith and Proudhon embody bourgeois science's self-understanding, elucidating theories of how the norms and institutions of modern society can and should realize freedom and well-being, Marx argues that bourgeois society consists in domination and leads to misery. In so doing, such an account of domination has drawn on and broadened the interpretation of social domination developed by critical theory, highlighting that rather than merely a theory of impersonal domination, it is a critical social theory of domination.

More importantly this interpretation of Marx's conception of domination illuminates Marx's notion of emancipation. For Marx, contra the currents of social democracy and progressivism that are influenced by Hegel, Smith and Proudhon, emancipation does not consist in the institutions of the market and the state realizing the normative potential of the social relations of bourgeois society. Rather, such a society, even at its best, is realized in domination, antagonism and misery. Accordingly, emancipation is made possible only by the abolition of such a society.

For Marx, an emancipated society would no longer be grounded on the separation of producers from the means of production, nor of a class antagonism, nor would they be realized in the social forms of labour, the market, or the state. Social relations would be grounded on the common ownership of the means of production. Therefore, in contrast to Smith and Proudhon, the capitalist division of labour and distribution would be abolished. Moreover, in contrast to

Hegel, the bourgeois state would wither away. In addition, contra Smith's idea of human nature, the working day would be minimized and individuals would have free time to pursue their own interests. Finally, contra Proudhon's notion of justice, distribution would proceed on the basis of 'from each according to their ability, to each according to their need'. Such a communist society would realize social freedom, human flourishing, autonomy and heterogeneity.

REFERENCES

Abbreviation:
MECW = Marx–Engels Collected Works, London: Lawrence & Wishart.

Backhaus, H.G., (1992). Between Philosophy and Science: Marxian Social Economy as Critical Theory. In W. Bonefeld, Richard Gunn and Kosmos Psychopedis (eds), *Open Marxism Volume 1*. London: Pluto, pp. 54–92.
Bonefeld, W., (2013). *Critical Theory and The Critique of Political Economy*. London: Bloomsbury.
Clarke, S., (1991). *Marx, Marginalism and Modern Sociology*, 2nd edn. London: Palgrave Macmillan.
Engels, F., [1878] (1975). Anti-Dühring. In: *MECW*, Vol. 25. London: Lawrence & Wishart, pp. 1–312.
Hegel, G.W.F., [1821] (1991). *Elements of The Philosophy of Right*. New York: Cambridge University Press.
Heinrich, M., (2012). *An Introduction to the Three Volumes of Karl Marx's* Capital. New York: Monthly Review Press.
Lefebvre, H., (2009). *Dialectical Materialism*. Minneapolis, MN: University of Minnesota Press.
Lenin, V.I., [1914] (1974). Karl Marx. In idem, *Collected Works*, Vol. 21. Moscow: Progress Publishers, pp. 43–91.
Lukács, G., [1923] (1972). *History and Class Consciousness*. Boston, MA: MIT Press.
Markus, G., (1982). Alienation and Reification in Marx and Lukács. *Thesis Eleven* 5(1), pp. 139–161.
Marx, K., [1843] (1975). A Contribution to the Critique of Hegel's Philosophy of Law. In: *MECW*, Vol. 3. London: Lawrence & Wishart, pp. 3–129.
Marx, K., [1844] (1975a). Comments on James Mill *Élémens d'économie politique*. In: *MECW*, Vol. 3. London: Lawrence & Wishart, pp. 211–228.
Marx, K., [1844] (1975b). Economic and Philosophic Manuscripts of 1844. In: *MECW*, Vol. 3. London: Lawrence & Wishart, pp. 229–346.
Marx, K., [1846] (1982). Letter to Annenkov, 28 December 1846. In: *MECW*, Vol. 38. London: Lawrence & Wishart, pp. 95–106.
Marx, K., [1847] (1975). The Poverty of Philosophy. Answer to the *Philosophy of Poverty* by M. Proudhon. In: *MECW*, Volume 6. London: Lawrence & Wishart, pp. 105–212.
Marx, K., [1857/58] (1973). *The Grundrisse*. London: Penguin.
Marx, K., [1858] (1983). Letter to Ferdinand Lassalle, 22 February 1858. In: *MECW*, Vol. 40. London: Lawrence & Wishart, pp. 268–271.
Marx, K., [1867] (1906). *Capital: A Critique of Political Economy, Volume 1*. New York: Modern Library.

Marx, K., [1871] (1974). *The Civil War in France*. Peking: Foreign Language Press.
Marx, K., [1875] (1989). Critique of the Gotha Programme. In: *MECW*, Vol. 24. London: Lawrence & Wishart, pp. 75–99.
Mattick, P., (2018). *Theory as Critique*. Leiden: Brill.
Mészáros, I., (2006). *Marx's Theory of Alienation*, 5th edn. London: Merlin Press.
O'Kane, C., (2014). State Violence State Control: Marxist State Theory and the Critique of Political Economy. *Viewpoint*, 3. https://viewpointmag.com/2014/10/29/state-violence-state-control-marxist-state-theory-and-the-critique-of-political-economy/.
Olman, B., (1978). *Alienation: Marx's Concept of Man in a Capitalist Society*, 2nd edn. New York: Cambridge University Press.
Postone, M., (1993). *Time, Labor and Social Domination*. New York: Cambridge University Press.
Proudhon, P.J., [1846] (1888). *System of Economic Contradictions: Or, The Philosophy of Poverty*. Readers Against DRM.
Reichelt, H., (2001). *Zur logischen Struktur des Kapitalbegriffs bei Karl Marx*. Freiburg: ça ira.
Reichelt, H., (2005). Social Reality as Appearance: Some Notes on Marx's Conception of Reality. In W. Bonefeld and K. Psychopedis eds, *Human Dignity, Social Autonomy and The Critique of Capitalism*. London: Routledge, pp. 31–67.
Roberts, W.C., (2018). *Marx's Inferno: The Political Theory of Capital*. New York: Princeton University Press.
Sayers, S., (2011). *Marx and Alienation: Essays on Hegelian Themes*. London: Palgrave Macmillan.
Schmidt, A., (1968). On The Concept of Knowledge in The Criticism of Political Economy. In G. Mann et al. (eds), *Karl Marx 1818/1968*. Bad Godesberg: Inter Nationes, pp. 92–102.
Smith, A., [1759] 1984. *The Theory of Moral Sentiments*. Indianapolis, IN: Liberty Fund.
Smith, A., [1763] 1982. *Lectures on Jurisprudence*. Indianapolis, IN: Liberty Fund.
Smith, A., [1776] 1982. *An Inquiry into the Nature and Causes of The Wealth of Nations*. Indianapolis, IN: Liberty Fund.

11. Real abstraction

Gianluca Pozzoni

11.1 INTRODUCTION

Karl Marx never used the term 'real abstraction' in his published or unpublished work. Nonetheless, he used similar expressions to characterize the conversion of labour activity into exchangeable goods within capitalist production. In his *A Contribution to the Critique of Political Economy* (1859), Marx argued that to determine the exchange value of a commodity, all labour that is necessary to its production must be quantifiable. Different kinds of labour – for example, the labour of a shoemaker, miner, spinner, painter, and so on – must be reduced to mere quantitative expenditure of muscles, nerves, brain, and so on; only in this way can the exchange value of produced commodities be measurable by the average labour which, in a commodity-producing society, the average person can perform. This reduction of labour activity to labour time, Marx wrote, 'appears to be an abstraction, but it is an abstraction which is made every day in the social process of production' (Marx [1859] 1987, p. 272). As a consequence, the resolution of all commodities into labour time 'is no greater an abstraction, and is no less real, than the resolution of all organic bodies into air' (Marx [1859] 1987, p. 272).

Not too dissimilarly, in his 1857 *Introduction* to the *Outlines of a Critique of Political Economy* (*Grundrisse*) Marx spoke of labour as an 'abstraction' that is nonetheless 'true in practice' within capitalist society. In criticizing the way classical economists casually used the abstract category of 'labour' to designate productive human activity in all society, Marx observed that this concept only corresponds to a concrete social entity within specifically capitalist societies. The concept of 'labour' as such designates productive activity regardless of both the individuals carrying it out and the particular kinds of labour being performed. However, Marx noted, it is only under capitalism that labour has ceased in practice 'to be tied with the individuals in any particularity'. In a capitalist form of society, 'individuals easily pass from one kind of labour to another, the particular kind of labour being accidental to them and therefore indifferent'. Therefore, it is only in bourgeois-capitalist society that:

> the abstract category 'labour', 'labour as such', labour *sans phrase*, the point of departure of modern [political] economy, is first seen to be true in practice. The simplest abstraction which plays the key role in modern [political] economy, and which expresses an ancient relation existing in all forms of society, appears to be true in practice in this abstract form only as a category of the most modern society. (Marx [1857] 1986, p. 41)

The idea of abstraction thus appears to play a crucial role in Marx's distinctive approach to the critique of political economy. His use of the concept in reference to economic categories can be traced back to as early as his 1840s criticism of Proudhon's ideas, which culminated in his anti-Proudhonian pamphlet *The Poverty of Philosophy* (Marx [1847] 1976). Although Marx's economic work from that period can be seen in many important respects as a mere critical application of classical political economy to the issues at the centre of the political debate (see, e.g. Heinrich 2017), at that time he had nonetheless developed an early critique of the ahistorical use of economic categories on the part of bourgeois economists; which he would expand into a fully fledged critique of political economy beginning in the 1950s.

Thus, in a famous 1846 letter to his correspondent Pavel Vasilyevich Annenkov, which anticipates much of the content of his forthcoming anti-Proudhonian book, Marx chastises both bourgeois political economy and Proudhon's interpretation of economic development on accounts of their failure to see that economic categories are abstractions. For Marx, Proudhon:

> falls into the error of bourgeois economists who regard those economic categories as eternal laws and not as historical laws which are laws only for a given historical development, a specific development of the productive forces. Thus, instead of regarding politico-economic categories as abstractions of actual social relations that are transitory and historical, Mr Proudhon, by a mystical inversion, sees in the real relations only the embodiment of those abstractions. Those abstractions are themselves formulas which have been slumbering in the bosom of God the Father since the beginning of the world. (Marx [1846] 1982, p. 100)

This passage testifies to the pivotal role that the idea of abstraction played in the development of Marx's critique of political economy from an early stage (O'Kane 2020). However, the import of Marx's early reference to the method of abstraction for critical purposes should not be taken too far. At this stage, Marx's usage of the concept of 'abstraction' plays out primarily, if not exclusively, at the level of methodology. Here, the conceptual value of abstraction lies chiefly in its capacity to expose the intellectual fallacies of speculative philosophy and classical political economy alike. For Marx, both approaches fall prey to idealism insofar as their constituent categories are assumed rather than abstracted from concrete historical processes and relations. As a consequence, economic categories are deemed applicable indistinctly to all forms of society rather than to the sole forms of society from which they are abstracted.

The political implications of Marx's methodological critique of political economy should not go unnoticed. His critique of the universalization of economic categories also entails a critique of ideology: for Marx, assuming the abstractions of bourgeois society as eternally valid categories is tantamount to presenting the tenets of bourgeois society as also valid eternally. The naturalization of economic categories makes the capitalist mode of production appear eternal, while the method of abstraction implicitly unearths its transiency. The method of abstraction thus paves the way, at least in principle, for the political overcoming of capitalism. Nonetheless, it is only as Marx's methodological critique evolves into a comprehensive scientific approach to political economy that the idea of abstraction reveals its conceptual potential.

11.2   ABSTRACTION AND *CAPITAL*

After his expulsion from France in 1845, Marx spent a few years between Brussels and Cologne before he finally found refuge from political persecution in London in the summer of 1849. There, he was able to devote himself to a more constant study of political economy by availing himself of the British Museum Library. Having intensified his studies, by April 1851 he was hoping to be able to license a systematic work of political economy for publication soon afterwards (Marx [1851] 1982, p. 325). Although the first volume of *Capital* would not see the light of day for another 16 years, Marx began to actually write his planned book with the aforementioned 1857 *Introduction* to the *Grundrisse*.

In Marx's economic manuscripts from this period, the critique of bourgeois economists has matured into a rational and scientific approach to the study of the capitalist mode of production. As Engels wrote in an instant review of *A Contribution to the Critique of Political Economy* (1859):

> the purpose of Marx's work cannot simply be a desultory criticism of separate propositions of political economy or a discussion of some economic issue or other in isolation. On the contrary, it is from the beginning designed to give a systematic résumé of the whole complex of political economy and a coherent elaboration of the laws governing bourgeois production and bourgeois exchange. (Engels [1859] 1980, p. 472)

On this basis, the abstractions implicitly assumed by bourgeois economists correspond to abstractions in the reality of bourgeois production and exchange.

This is what has become known in the subsequent Marxist vernacular as 'real abstraction'.

Let us return briefly to Marx's economic manuscripts from the late 1850s. *A Contribution to the Critique of Political Economy* (1859) opens, like *Capital*, with the famous observation that the wealth of bourgeois society presents itself as 'an immense accumulation of commodities', and proceeds to explaining the distinction between the 'use value' and the 'exchange value' of those commodities. As we have already seen, this is where abstraction enters the equation. As exchange values of different magnitudes, Marx argues, different amounts of commodities such as 1 ounce of gold, half a ton of iron, 3 bushels of wheat and 5 yards of silk 'represent [*darstellen*] larger or smaller portions, larger or smaller amounts of simple, uniform, abstract general labour, which is the substance of exchange value' (Marx [1859] 1987, p. 271).

As mentioned at the beginning, this abstraction is located by Marx in the social process of production: the abstraction of the labour time contained in a commodity is 'the labour time *necessary* for its production, namely the labour time required, under the generally prevailing conditions of production, to produce another unit of the same commodity'. For this reason, abstract labour is also referred to as 'average labour' and as 'social labour' (Marx [1859] 1987, pp. 272–273). The 'reality' of this abstraction is analysed at length in the first volume of *Capital*; the only one that Marx published in his lifetime. Labour, writes Marx in the first chapter, assumes a social form 'from the moment that men in any way work for each other' (Marx [1867] 1906, p. 82). The commodity form acquires an exchange value alongside a use value on accounts of 'the peculiar social character of the labour that produces them' (Marx [1867] 1906, p. 83). Let us see how.

In bourgeois society, producers are private individuals who work independently of each other and only come into social contact when they exchange the products of their labour. Commodities are the social product of the dressmaking, tailoring, shoemaking, sewing, hat-making, and so on, of private individuals. At the same time, private individuals do not produce commodities in isolation by their own means, but only as parts of an integrated system of production: in a commodity-producing system, individuals must sell their labour-power to the owners of the means of production in order to be able to work and produce commodities. This is where abstract labour emerges: through the exchange of labour-power for money, private labour enters the commodity-producing process and therefore becomes social labour. Labour-power is exchangeable because it is a commodity too; that is, it has an exchange value. The amount of its exchange value, like that of the exchange values of all commodities, is determined by the labour time that is socially necessary to produce it under the conditions prevailing at the time.

In its turn, the socially necessary labour time is determined through what Marx calls the 'subsumption of labour under capital'. As said before, workers produce commodities collectively, not on their own account. This requires that individuals be placed under the direct control of a capitalist. Such subordination of the labour process to capital, or subsumption of labour under capital, characterizes capitalist production vis-à-vis other modes of production such as, for example, handicraft agriculture in independent peasant economies. Through subsumption, capitalists become the directors, or managers, of the labour process. In this way, the labour process becomes the instrument for the creation of value in capitalist production: by acting as supervisors and directors of the labour process, capitalists determine the amount of labour time that is socially necessary for the production of commodities. Not only can they raise the quantity of production, but they can also multiply and diversify the spheres of production and their sub-spheres through co-operation, division of labour, the use of machinery, and in general through the transformation of production by the use of technology. Through subsumption, labour becomes socialized and value-producing, and the exchange value of commodities becomes the deciding factor of capitalist production.

The reality of the value abstraction thus resides, ultimately, in the social relations of capitalist production, that is, in the social position of the agents of capitalist production in relation to each other. The relationship between capital as the buyer, and the worker as the seller of labour-power, creates the conditions for the domination of workers by capital; the sale and purchase of labour-power creates the conditions for the emergence of the value of commodities. Indeed, this relationship is vital to the very existence of the capitalist mode of production. The subsumption of labour under capital is essential to the creation of surplus value, which in turn is essential to the reproduction and perpetuation of capitalist production: only insofar as they dominate the labour process can capitalists ensure that enough value is produced not only for the production and reproduction of labour-power, but also for capital accumulation and for their own private consumption. Subsumption is thus necessary to extort the maximum value from labour so that, when the commodities produced are exchanged, their production proves profitable.

11.3   REAL ABSTRACTION AND THE CRITIQUE OF SOCIETY

The term 'real abstraction' in reference to the analysis of this process, has been popularized by German Marxist Alfred Sohn-Rethel. In his *Intellectual and Manual Labour* (first published in German in 1970, English translation 1978 cited here), Sohn-Rethel set out to present a 'critique of the traditional theories of science and cognition' based on Marx's commodity analysis and complementing Marx's own critique of political economy (Sohn-Rethel 1978, p. xi). In particular, Sohn-Rethel argues that the principles of thought basic to science and cognition emerge with the growth of commodity production as a consequence of the structuring of society into a coherent network of relations, which Sohn-Rethel calls the 'social synthesis'. For Sohn-Rethel, the social synthesis in a commodity-producing society is made possible by the function of money as a 'general equivalent', to use Marx's expression, and it is from the formal characteristics of money that the categories of thought are formed: the abstractions of thought arise socially from the abstraction of exchange.

As a general equivalent, money determines the proportion in which commodities are exchanged. Therefore, it is money that makes labour exchangeable and turns it into a commodity, making it 'abstract labour' (Sohn-Rethel 1978, p. 20). This abstraction, Sohn-Rethel comments, 'must be viewed as a *real abstraction* resulting from spatio-temporal activity'. Insofar as it implies the negation of the quality and physical reality of use and use value, Sohn-Rethel argues, the exchange of commodities is an abstraction, but it is an abstraction that 'in no way lacks physical reality itself':

> Exchange involves the movement of the commodities in time and space from owner to owner and constitutes events of no less physical reality than the activities of use which it rules out … It is in its capacity of a real event in time and space that the abstraction applies to exchange, it is in its precise meaning a real abstraction and the 'use' from which the abstraction is made encompasses the entire range of sense reality. (Sohn-Rethel 1978, pp. 27–28)

Now, for Sohn-Rethel all cognition emerges when real abstraction assumes conceptual form. What characterizes intellectual activity, Sohn-Rethel argues, is the use of non-empirical, 'pure' concepts. However, this type of activity does not exist unless it is separated from manual labour. Intellectual activity is the product of the social system of the division of labour: only in commodity-producing societies does a class system emerge in which the educated class can perform exclusively intellectual labour. Intellectual labour thus depends on the social synthesis of commodity-producing society down to its very form: intellectual activity is a reflection of the social synthesis within a society based on the exchange of commodities, and the 'abstractions' of the intellect are a reflection of the real abstraction of commodity exchange. In the second part of *Intellectual and Manual Labour*, Sohn-Rethel identifies the origins of Western forms of reasoning, including science and its technological applications, in the introduction of coinage. According to Sohn-Rethel, the minting of coins in Greek antiquity led to the institution of a monetary economy of which commodity exchange is characteristic, and in which real abstraction becomes dominant. This is the presumed origin of a conceptual mode of thinking based on abstractions, as can be seen in the purely deductive philosophy of the Milesian school or in that of great thinkers such as Pythagoras, Heraclitus and Parmenides.

Importantly, Sohn-Rethel does not aim at merely contributing a materialist approach to the history of human cognition. His argument about the correspondence of thought abstraction and real abstraction extends to the very form of Western conceptual categories, which are, in Sohn-Rethel's own words, 'historical by origin and social by nature' (Sohn-Rethel 1978, p. 7). Such a 'critique of the traditional theories of science and cognition' is directed primarily at Kantian and neo-Kantian transcendental idealism, and more specifically to the idea that the categories of thought are timeless features of the human intellect.

But two particular aspects of Sohn-Rethel's critique should be noted for present purposes. First, as the above quotation shows, Sohn-Rethel locates real abstraction in the exchange of commodities, not in their production. In his understanding, real abstraction is a feature of all monetary-mercantile societies, including, but not limited to, capitalist-bourgeois society. This allows him to situate the emergence of real abstraction in seventh-century BC Ionia rather than in the formation of modern capitalism. Second, Sohn-Rethel's approach has strong political undertones. The development of a critical theory of knowledge, writes Sohn-Rethel, was not among Marx's own primary concerns. But in a highly technological society, accounting for the genesis of the division of intellectual and manual labour 'should ... help us in perceiving the preconditions of its historical disappearance and hence of socialism as the road to a classless society' (Sohn-Rethel 1978, p. 7). The unification of intellectual and manual labour is inherent to the disappearance of the class system; the critical scrutiny of intellectual labour, understood as a separate activity within the 'social synthesis', is a precondition of the socialist transformation of society.

These aspects of Sohn-Rethel's interpretation of real abstraction draw his 'critique of the traditional theories of science and cognition' closer to a 'critique of society' in the sense of Theodor W. Adorno's later philosophy. This affinity is not accidental. *Intellectual and Manual Labour* was first published in 1970, one year after Adorno's death. In fact, it was at Adorno's funeral that Sohn-Rethel met Siegfried Unseld, Adorno's publisher with Suhrkamp, who contracted him for the publication of his book. By that time, however, *Intellectual and Manual Labour* had already been decades in the making. In 1951, Lawrence & Wishart had turned down a long manuscript on *Intellectual and Manual Labour* on the grounds that it was too unorthodox. But Sohn-Rethel self-reportedly began investigating the problem of knowledge from a materialist standpoint as early as during World War I (Sohn-Rethel 1978, pp. xi–xiv). Interestingly, his early written work on the subject dates back to 1936 in the form of a letter to Adorno (Sohn-Rethel 1971; see Lange 2022); from that moment on, as their correspondence shows, the two continued to discuss the themes of Sohn-Rethel's work until Adorno's death (Adorno and Sohn-Rethel 1991).

In *Negative Dialectics* (1966), Adorno speaks approvingly of Sohn-Rethel's interpretation of real abstraction: 'Alfred Sohn-Rethel', he writes, 'was the first to point out that hidden in this principle, in the general and necessary activity of the mind, lies work of an inalienably social nature' (Adorno 1973, p. 177). Indeed, Adorno's overall endeavour in *Negative Dialectics* can be character-ized as 'a far-reaching critique of society as real abstraction' (Bonefeld 2020, p. 155): in it, the abstraction of exchange is presented as a social force capable of exerting no less than a 'universal domination of mankind' which 'a priori keeps the subjects from being subjects and degrades subjectivity itself to a mere object' (Adorno 1973, p. 178).

Very much like Sohn-Rethel, Adorno sees real abstraction as translating into an all-encompassing system of social domination that extends far beyond the production and exchange of commodities. In his 1969 Introduction to the volume collecting the contributions to the famous dispute about positivism in German sociology (*Positivismusstreit*), Adorno eloquently writes:

> The abstraction of exchange value is a priori allied with the domination of the general [*des Allgemeinen*] over the particular, of society over its captive mem-bership. It is not at all a socially neutral phenomenon as the logistics [*Logizität*] of reduction, of uniformity of work time pretend. The domination of men over men is realized through the reduction of men to agents and bearers of commodity exchange. The concrete form of the total system requires everyone to respect the law of exchange if he does not wish to be destroyed, irrespective of whether profit is his subjective motivation or not. (Adorno 1976, p. 14)

As Adorno makes clear in his lectures collected in *Introduction to Sociology*, in capitalist society the exchange of commodities is the relationship through which socialization comes about on the basis of the antagonistic interests of the individuals engaging in exchange. The abstraction that materializes in exchange thus appears as the principle that binds together society as a 'totality' (Adorno 2000). Hence, the critique of abstraction doubles as a comprehensive critique of the abstract totality of (capitalist) society.

11.4   REAL ABSTRACTION AND THE CRITIQUE OF POLITICAL ECONOMY

For all their originality, Sohn-Rethel's and Adorno's critical theories of society are not unrelated to Marx's own critique of political economy. By exchanging labour products, Marx argues, individuals exchange values as amounts of homogeneous human labour ('abstract labour'). However, Marx adds, 'we are not aware of this, nevertheless we do it' (Marx [1867] 1906, p. 85). This social fact conceals what Marx calls the 'secret' of the fetish character of commodities: insofar as they are produced as exchangeable commodities, the products of labour embody and reflect social relations between human beings, and therefore manifest themselves as fetishes, as autonomous figures endowed with a life of their own.

Most importantly, the exchange of commodities is made possible by money as the general equivalent of all their exchange values. However, as Marx ([1867] 1906, p. 98) put it, only 'a social act' can set apart a particular type of commodity and turn it into the universal equivalent. Society thus appears to be endowed with an independent agency of its own. But despite Marx's deliberate choice of quasi-theological wording, there is nothing supernatural in this fact; the independent agency of the social process is but the manifestation of the form of value. In presenting the 'general formula' of capital, Marx describes it as a circular movement which 'a commodity is bought with money, and then money is bought with a commodity' (Marx [1867] 1906, p. 164). Yet, Marx drily comments, this exchange would be 'purposeless' and 'absurd' if a commodity were exchanged for the same amount of money; it would be 'merely a roundabout way of exchanging money for money, the same for the same' (Marx [1867] 1906, p. 167). What is really being exchanged in this movement is value for more value, of which money and commodity are but different 'modes of existence'. This makes value an 'automatic subject', or the 'dominant subject' of a comprehensive process through which it creates surplus value and therefore 'expands spontaneously' (Marx [1867] 1906, p. 172).

Marx's own economic reasoning thus leads to extensive implications. In light of this, it comes as little surprise that 'real abstraction' as a key category in the critical theory of society has been readopted in later contributions to the critique of political economy, and that some of its proponents have been directly influenced by the work of Adorno. Helmut Reichelt's engagement with real abstraction, for instance, can be interpreted as part of an attempt at reconstructing Marx's theory within the framework of what has become known as the *Neue Marx-Lektüre* ('new reading of Marx'), an approach initiated in the 1960s by some of Adorno's former students, including Reichelt himself (Reichelt 2008; see also Lange 2022). One of the main thrusts of this 'new reading', and the one that most strongly bears the imprint of Adorno's critical theory, is an interpretation of Marx's critique of political economy as a critique of the mystifying categories of bourgeois economists that are nonetheless rooted in the mystified constitution of capitalist society itself (Bonefeld 2014; Bellofiore and Redolfi Riva 2015).

Within this framework, Reichelt (1973, 2007) also sought to bridge the gap between the critique of political economy and Adorno's critical theory of society. Possibly because of his outspoken aversion to economic theory, Reichelt argues, Adorno did not elaborate on how the exchange principle develops into the autonomization of society as a 'totality', nor did he analyse the central concepts of his critical theory, including 'real abstraction'; or, as Adorno called it, 'objective abstraction' (*objektive Abstraktion*) (Adorno 1976, p. 13, see also Adorno 2018). For Reichelt, the concept of 'validity' is required to bridge this gap and make sense of abstraction as a process that is carried out in exchange through the monetary form of value without the individuals performing the exchange being conscious of it.

Reichelt argues that the concept of 'validity' as used by Marx is different from 'recognition' in that it does not presuppose a conscious agent as its subject, whence its importance in understanding abstraction and the role that money plays in it. As a general equivalent, money expresses the exchangeability of all commodities. Yet the character of 'general equivalent' denotes the form of money, not its sensory objectivity: the general equivalent cannot be directly perceived as such; that is, as money-form, or as the monetary form of value. Therefore, the money-form can ensure the 'acceptance' (*Akzeptanz*) of value without the individuals who exchange commodities being conscious of it. This, for Reichelt, is the true nature of real abstraction. Through it, the exchange principle can become autonomous from the individuals who actually exchange commodities, thereby developing into an overarching social totality that dominates them.

Not too dissimilarly from Reichelt's intention, Moishe Postone also engaged in what he described as a 'reinterpretation of Marx's critical theory' in his seminal *Time, Labor, and Social Domination* (Postone 1993). Like Reichelt, Postone attempts to remedy what he sees as certain faults of critical theory as canonized by Adorno and other members of the Frankfurt School. In particular, he sees the characteristic political pessimism of the Frankfurt School as fuelled by a combination of misapprehensions of Marx's critical theory and theoretical inconsistencies, such as pertain, for example, to Adorno's theory of society as a vaguely defined 'totality'. To this, Postone opposes a reconstruction of critical theory that assumes the centrality of 'abstract labour' at its core. Postone's reconstruction moves from Marx's own characterization of the capitalist mode of production as one in which people do not consume what they produce but produce and exchange commodities in order to acquire other commodities. This, for Postone, makes capitalism a 'form of social interdependence' that relates commodity, value and abstract labour.

Importantly, Postone identifies the source of such interdependence in abstract labour itself:

> In a society characterized by the universality of the commodity form ... an individual does not acquire goods produced by others through the medium of overt social relations. Instead, labor itself – either directly or as expressed in its products

– replaces those relations by serving as an 'objective' means by which the products of others are acquired. (Postone 1993, p. 150)

Thus, abstract labour is 'a self-grounding social mediation' that 'constitutes a determinate sort of social whole – a totality' (Postone 1993, p. 151). The social domination of individuals by production is tantamount to their domination by social – or 'abstract' – labour. It is from this standpoint that Postone criticizes Sohn-Rethel's concept of real abstraction for being 'not a labor abstraction but an exchange abstraction'. According to Postone, the creation of the 'alienated social structures' characteristic of the capitalist form of social interdependence has its origin in the labour abstraction, not in the exchange abstraction (Postone 1993, p. 178).

11.5   NEW DEVELOPMENTS

Postone's reconstruction of critical theory does not exclusively engage with the Frankfurt School of critical theory. His understanding of 'abstract labour' explicitly draws also on the work of Italian Marxist Lucio Colletti, whose independent reading of Marx in the 1960s and 1970s already insisted on the identification of 'abstract labour' with '*alienated* labour, labour separated or estranged with respect to man himself' (Colletti 1972, p. 84). Thus, the recasting of the critique of society as a critique of political economy via the critique of real abstraction is not exclusive to the *Neue Marx-Lektüre*.

Chris Arthur's critical theory, for instance, converges with the reading proposed both by Colletti and by the *Neue Marx-Lektüre* (Micaloni and Arthur 2018, p. 482), yet it borrows most directly from Hegel's *Logic*. For Arthur, Marx did not simply '*coquet*' with Hegel's peculiar mode of thinking; as a self-professed 'pupil of that mighty thinker' (Marx [1867] 1906, p. 25), Marx adopted both the categories of Hegel's logic and Hegel's view of them as 'pure categories independent of any contingent empirical instantiation' (Arthur 2004, p. 80). According to Arthur, this idealist ontology is the necessary complement to Marx's critique of political economy. Only by taking the idealizations of thought as efficacious on their own account can one make sense of the social efficaciousness of the labour abstraction, and therefore consistently interpret it as a real abstraction.

Ironically, similar Hegelian considerations can be found in Lucio Colletti's (1973) radically anti-Hegelian reading of Marx. In fact, Colletti's realization that Marx's approach was irreducibly Hegelian at its core would later lead him to the rejection of Marxism as a speculative and anti-scientific philosophy (Colletti 1975). More recently, however, other authors have insisted positively on this 'Hegelian' reading of real abstraction for the sake of reconstructing Marx's critique of political economy. Roberto Finelli, for instance, agrees with

Arthur's idealist reading of abstraction, and even presents *Capital* as rooted in a 'spiritualist' ontology (Finelli 2007, p. 64): according to Finelli, abstraction cannot be perceived in its concrete determination, but only as part of an ideal totality. However, Finelli criticizes Arthur for locating abstraction in the sphere of monetary exchange; according to him, the abstraction of labour in postmodern society is performed by capital not in the form of money, but in the form of an impersonal machine that dominates the 'mental-informational' component of labour (Finelli 2007, p. 67).

Michael Heinrich (2017) also views the labour abstraction as a real abstraction made in commodity exchange through a process of 'a posteriori socialization' (*nachträgliche Vergesellschaftung*) of private labours. Riccardo Bellofiore emphasizes instead the role of the banking system in financing the initial purchase of labour-power on the part of capitalist firms and therefore in 'ante-validating' labour-power; however, like Colletti and Arthur, Bellofiore insists on a 'Hegelian' reading of capital as the subject of the process of real abstraction (Bellofiore 2018). Although Heinrich does not subscribe to a strictly Hegelian reading of Marx's concept of abstraction, his perspective converges with Bellofiore's in placing his reconstruction of Marx's critique of political economy within a broader monetary framework. Their conclusions differ in that Heinrich sees the monetary socialization of labour – or, its abstraction – as something that happens *a posteriori* in exchange rather than *a priori* through informational domination (as per Finelli) or throughout the completion of a 'macro-monetary' process (as per Bellofiore; according to Bellofiore, the sale of commodities in the sphere of circulation is the final monetary step that completes the validation process which begins with finance to production).

11.6   CONCLUSION

What is most important to note about the critique of real abstraction after Marx is that it shows how the concept of 'real abstraction' can serve to recast Marx's critique of political economy as an open research programme rather than as a closed system. Before concluding, however, let us briefly pause again on the relationship between the critique of political economy and the critical theory of society. The role of real abstraction in unravelling this connection has been recently thematized by Alberto Toscano. In an article that revisited the Marxist debate on abstraction, Toscano (2008) highlighted its relevance for investigating the relationship between abstract thought and the concrete reality of contemporary capitalism. This argument has proved particularly influential in spurring more work on the subject.

Building on Toscano, Jason W. Moore (2015) has argued that the labour abstraction transcends into the creation of a further abstraction, namely that of 'abstract social nature', along with its 'natural' counterpart. According to Moore, the resulting Nature/Society dichotomy is the original dualism that consolidated early capitalism as it arose from the original separation of the peasant from the land. Moore also stresses the political importance of this abstraction insofar as it leads to viewing capitalism as a flexible totality that co-produces nature rather than confronting it. Accordingly, Moore argues, the limits to capital are not given 'externally' by an abstract 'nature'; instead, they can only emerge 'internally' – that is, historically – from human relations.

The critique of real abstraction has been expanded independently in other directions, too. Maya Gonzalez and Jeanne Neton of the Endnotes collective, for instance, explicitly frame gender in the terms of real abstraction (Gonzalez and Neton 2013). Moving from a Marxist feminist perspective, they see gender as a category reflecting patriarchal domination, but only in that it is a historically specific feature of capitalism: on this view, the abstraction of gender is the outcome of the material separation between different spheres – production and reproduction, paid and unpaid labour, public sector and private sphere, sex and gender – which are in various ways functional to the commodification of labour-power and which take on materiality as a consequence of this.

The creative application of real abstraction to domains other than the critique of political economy is hardly peculiar to the most recent developments of critical theory. In the 1970s, Henri Lefebvre already broadened Marx's notion of real abstraction – or as he calls it, 'concrete abstraction' (*abstraction concrète*) – to include the production of space as the site in which social relations materialize and acquire social power (Lefebvre 1991). But the list of modern contributions to the critique of real abstraction can also be extended to those authors who critically applied the idea of abstraction in ways that are less directly related to the above lineage of thinking (see, e.g., Althusser 1969; Jameson 1981; Žižek 1989; Laclau 2000, to name but the most renowned), as well as to a variety of recent interventions in the current debate (such as, e.g., Virno 2004; Bonefeld 2014; Lotz 2014; Bhandar and Toscano 2015; Toscano 2017; Moreno 2019; Sorentino 2019).

On the one hand, the fact that the concept of real abstraction regularly rekindles intellectual debate attests to the great power that Marx's key concepts continue to exert in the present. On the other hand, this can be seen as a natural outcome of linking the critique of political economy to the critique of capitalist society at large. But more substantive conclusions could also be drawn. As mentioned, the fact that the critique of real abstraction appears to be an indefinitely open-ended intellectual project reflects the fact that Marx's own critique of political economy is an unfinished work. In turn, this is the direct consequence of the ever-changing nature of capitalism as a system of production and societal organization. A red thread running through the contributions overviewed in this chapter is the attempt to update Marx's analysis to the societal changes that occurred since the time of his writing.

However, the fact that the nature of capitalism cannot be grasped once and for all may also be due to conceptual, alongside historical, reasons. If capitalist reality can only be framed as an abstract totality, as the critique of real abstraction seems to assume, then by its very nature it cannot be apprehended through any determinate analysis. As Georg Lukács put it, 'No path leads from the individual to the totality; there is at best a road leading to aspects of particular areas, mere fragments for the most part, "facts" bare of any context, or to abstract, special laws. The totality of an object can only be posited if the positing subject is itself a totality' (Lukács 1971, p. 28). What it means for a subject to be a totality, Lukács argues, is to preserve the unity of theory and action. If capitalism is a totality, then theory, on its own, can only lead to intellectual impotence before it; on the contrary, only the unity of theory and action can 'actively penetrate the reality of society and transform it in its entirety' (Lukács 1971, p. 39).

REFERENCES

Adorno, T.W., (1973). *Negative Dialectics*. New York: Seabury Press.
Adorno, T.W., (1976). Introduction. In: T.W. Adorno, H. Albert, R. Dahrendorf, J. Habermas, H. Pilot, and K.R. Popper, *The Positivist Dispute in German Sociology*. London: Heinemann Educational Books, pp. 1–67.
Adorno, T.W., (2000). *Introduction to Sociology*. Cambridge, UK: Polity Press / Blackwell Publishers.
Adorno, T.W., (2018). Theodor W. Adorno on 'Marx and the Basic Concepts of Sociological Theory'. *Historical Materialism* 26(1), pp. 154–164.
Adorno, T.W. and Sohn-Rethel, A., (1991). *Briefwechsel 1936–1969*. Munich: edition text + kritik.
Althusser, L., (1969). *For Marx*. London: Penguin.
Arthur, C.J., (2004). *The New Dialectic and Marx's* Capital. Leiden and Boston: Brill.
Bellofiore, R., (2018). The Adventures of 'Vergesellschaftung'. *Consecutio Rerum* 3(5), pp. 503–540.
Bellofiore, R. and Redolfi Riva, T., (2015). The 'Neue Marx-Lektüre'. Putting the Critique of Political Economy back into the Critique of Society: A Sympathetic Assessment and Critique of the Beginnings of. *Radical Philosophy* 189, pp. 24–36.
Bhandar, B. and Toscano, A., (2015). Race, Real Estate and Real Abstraction. *Radical Philosophy* 194, pp. 8–17.
Bonefeld, W., (2014). *Critical Theory and the Critique of Political Economy: On Subversion and Negative Reason*. New York and London: Bloomsbury.
Bonefeld, W., (2020). On Capital as Real Abstraction. In: A. Oliva, Á. Oliva and I. Novara, eds, *Marx and Contemporary Critical Theory: The Philosophy of Real Abstraction*. Cham: Palgrave Macmillan, pp. 153–170.
Colletti, L., (1972). Bernstein and the Marxism of the Second International. In: *From Rousseau to Lenin: Studies in Ideology and Society*. London: NLB, pp. 45–108.
Colletti, L., (1973). *Marxism and Hegel*. London: NLB.

Colletti, L., (1975). Marxism and the Dialectic. *New Left Review* 93, pp. 3–30.

Engels, F., [1859] (1980). Karl Marx, *A Contribution to the Critique of Political Economy*. In: K. Marx and F. Engels, *Collected Works*, vol. 16: *Marx and Engels 1858–1860*. New York: International Publishers, pp. 465–477.

Finelli, R., (2007). Abstraction versus Contradiction. Observations on Chris Arthur's 'The New Dialectic and Marx's "Capital."' *Historical Materialism* 15(2), pp. 61–74.

Gonzalez, M. and Neton, J., (2013). The Logic of Gender: On the Separation of Spheres and the Process of Abjection. *Endnotes* 3, pp. 56–91.

Heinrich, M., (2017). *Die Wissenschaft vom Wert. Die Marxsche Kritik der politischen Ökonomie zwischen wissenschaftlicher Revolution und klassischer Tradition*, 7th expanded edn. Münster: Westfälisches Dampfboot.

Jameson, F., (1981). *The Political Unconscious: Narrative a Socially Symbolic Act.* Ithaca, NY: Cornell University Press.

Laclau, E., (2000). Identity and Hegemony: The Role of Universality in the Constitution of Political Logics. In: J. Butler, E. Laclau, and S. Žižek, *Contingency, Hegemony, Universality: Contemporary Dialogues on the Left*. London and New York: Verso, pp. 44–89.

Lange, E.L., (2022). Real Abstraction. In: B. Skeggs, S.R. Farris, A. Toscano and S. Bromberg (eds), *The SAGE Handbook of Marxism*, vol. I. London: SAGE, pp. 593–608.

Lefebvre, H., (1991). *The Production of Space*. Oxford and Cambridge, MA: Blackwell.

Lotz, C., (2014). *The Capitalist Schema: Time, Money, and the Culture of Abstraction.* London: Lexington Books.

Lukács, G. (1971). *History and Class Consciousness: Studies in Marxist Dialectics.* Cambridge, MA: MIT Press.

Marx, K., [1846] (1982). Letter to Pavel Vasilyevich Annenkov, 28 December 1846. In: K. Marx and F. Engels, *Collected Works*, vol. 38: *Marx and Engels 1844–1851*. New York: International Publishers, pp. 95–106.

Marx, K., [1847] (1976). *The Poverty of Philosophy*. In: K. Marx and F. Engels, *Collected Works*, vol. 6: *Marx and Engels 1845–1848*. New York: International Publishers, pp. 105–212.

Marx, K., [1851] (1982). Letter to Frederick Engels, 2 April 1851. In: K. Marx and F. Engels, *Collected Works*, vol. 38: *Marx and Engels 1844–1851*. New York: International Publishers, pp. 325–326.

Marx, K., [1857] (1986). *Introduction*. In: K. Marx and F. Engels, *Collected Works*, vol. 28: *Marx 1857–1861*. New York: International Publishers, pp. 17–48.

Marx, K., [1859] (1987). *A Contribution to the Critique of Political Economy*. In: K. Marx and F. Engels, *Collected Works*, vol. 29: *Marx 1857–1861*. New York: International Publishers, pp. 257–388.

Marx, K., [1867] (1906). *Capital: A Critique of Political Economy*, Volume One. New York: Modern Library.

Micaloni, L. and Arthur, C.J., (2018). The Logic of Capital: Interview with Chris Arthur. *Consecutio Rerum* 3(5), pp. 476–484.

Moore, J.W., (2015). *Capitalism in the Web of Life: Ecology and the Accumulation of Capital*. London and New York: Verso.

Moreno, G., ed. (2019). *In the Mind but Not From There: Real Abstraction and Contemporary Art*. London and New York: Verso.

O'Kane, C. (2020). The Critique of Real Abstraction: From the Critical Theory of Society to the Critique of Political Economy and Back Again. In: A. Oliva, Á. Oliva, and I. Novara, eds, *Marx and Contemporary Critical Theory: The Philosophy of Real Abstraction*. Cham: Palgrave Macmillan, pp. 265–287.

Postone, M., (1993). *Time, Labor, and Social Domination: A Reinterpretation of Marx's Critical Theory*. Cambridge: Cambridge University Press.

Reichelt, H., (1973). *Zur logischen Struktur des Kapitalbegriffs bei Karl Marx*. Frankfurt a.M.: Europäische Verlagsanstalt.

Reichelt, H., (2007). Marx's Critique of Economic Categories: Reflections on the Problem of Validity in the Dialectical Method of Presentation in 'Capital'. *Historical Materialism* 15(4), pp. 3–52.

Reichelt, H., (2008). *Neue Marx-Lektüre: zur Kritik sozialwissenschaftlicher Logik*. Hamburg: VSA.

Sohn-Rethel, A., (1971). Statt einer Einleitung: Exposé zur Theorie der funktionalen Vergesellschaftung. Ein Brief an Theodor W. Adorno (1936). In: *Warenform und Denkform. Aufsätze*. Frankfurt and Vienna: Europäische Verlagsanstalt / Europa Verlag, pp. 7–27.

Sohn-Rethel, A., (1978). *Intellectual and Manual Labour: A Critique of Epistemology*. London and Basingstoke: Macmillan.

Sorentino, S.-M., (2019). Natural Slavery, Real Abstraction, and the Virtuality of Anti-Blackness. *Theory and Event* 22(3), pp. 630–673.

Toscano, A., (2008). The Open Secret of Real Abstraction. *Rethinking Marxism* 20(2), pp. 273–287.

Toscano, A., (2017). *Fanaticism. On the Uses of an Idea*, new expanded edn. London and New York: Verso.

Virno, P., (2004). *A Grammar of the Multitude*. New York: Semiotext(e).

Žižek, S., (1989). *The Sublime Object of Ideology*. London and New York: Verso.

12. Social reproduction

Kirstin Munro

12.1 INTRODUCTION

Over the past five decades, Marxist-feminist theorizing has been hampered by confusions over the multiple meanings of 'reproduction' (Barrett [1980] 2014, pp. 19–29). Overcoming the haziness with which these concepts are too often treated is especially urgent given the current popularity of social reproduction theory, a recent offshoot of Marxist-feminism. The potential for misunderstanding is exacerbated by the existence of an additional use of the term 'social reproduction' outside of Marxist scholarship: in a Bourdieu-influenced subfield in education scholarship. I argue that precision in the application of political economic categories related to reproduction is not merely desirable for precision's sake: these categories lose their critical explanatory power when applied carelessly.

The reproduction of capitalist society as a whole – that is, social reproduction – cannot be examined without an understanding of the contribution of the reproduction of labour-power and the reproduction of capital to social reproduction. Indeed, the concepts of labour-power and the reproduction of capital from Marx's critique of political economy are meaningless if divorced from their explicit roles in the perpetuation of capitalist society as a whole, and from their recursive relationship to each other in the reproduction of capitalist social relations of production. In this chapter I define these concepts, drawing on Marx and Marxist-feminism, use these definitions to demonstrate the relationships between these concepts, and show how these concepts have been misapplied in some strains of recent Marxist-feminist research. Finally, I discuss the consequences of the incorrect application of these concepts.

12.2 THE INTERGENERATIONAL TRANSMISSION OF STATUS AND CULTURE

Prior to the recent popularity of the new Marxist-feminist inspired offshoot (Bhattacharya 2017; Ferguson 1999, 2019), the term 'social reproduction theory' was primarily used to describe a particular strand of research in the field of education influenced by Bourdieu (1973) and Bourdieu and Passeron (1977). These writings focus on how cultural reproduction – the intergenerational transmission of status, identity and culture via institutions such as formal education – contributes to the reproduction of society as a whole via 'symbolic relationships between classes' and the 'distribution of cultural capital' among these classes (Bourdieu 1973, pp. 71–72), 'classes' here being something more akin to Weberian social classes[1] rather than Marxist classes. And while words such as 'reproduction' and 'capital' may have Marxist connotations,[2] these theories of cultural reproduction are more accurately linked to Durkheim and his notion of 'the conservation of a culture inherited from the past' from his writings on education: that is, 'the transmission from generation to generation of accumulated information' (Bourdieu 1973, p. 72). While Bourdieu is critical of the role of educational institutions in the socialization of students into social classes, Durkheim is a 'defender of the bourgeois social order' and sees this process as a good thing (Allen and O'Boyle 2017, p. 145). Furthermore, Bourdieu specifically draws a distinction between his own theory and that of Durkheim, as Durkheim does not emphasize the link between cultural reproduction and social reproduction – that is, the reproduction of society as a whole – while Bourdieu is concerned with how societies reproduce themselves via culture (Desan 2013).

As absorbed into the field of education research, however, the focus has become the dominating effect of education and how it leads to cultural reproduction and the accumulation of cultural capital by individuals who can cash it in. So while these theorists in education follow Bourdieu in critiquing this process of cultural transmission of identity and status, it is in some ways a more strictly Durkheimian application, dropping the 'social' in 'social reproduction theory'[3] by de-emphasizing the role of these acculturation processes in the reproduction of capitalist society as a whole. Rather, the emphasis is on an unfair initial distribution of 'cultural capital' which is intensified by educational institutions, leading to the persistence of inequality and advantaged and disadvantaged Weberian socio-economic classes or dominant and subordinate 'cultures' (stratified by race and gender). Later developments in social reproduction theory in education build on Giroux's (1983) critique of the 'reproduction thesis' in education as being excessively Marxist, economistic and

---

[1]   Some authors in this field move away from any concept of class entirely, preferring instead to discuss dominant and subordinate cultures.

[2]   Some scholars who use social reproduction theory as developed in the field of education claim that it draws on Marxist roots (see e.g. Collins 2009; Giroux 1983).

[3]   Sometimes the 'social' is literally dropped, for example by Fergus (2016), who discusses 'reproduction theory' in the context of the transmission of teachers' beliefs and racial prejudices.

deterministic. None of this, however, can tell us anything about how 'societies ... perpetuate themselves' (Collins 2009, p. 34).

This brief discussion of the term 'social reproduction theory' as used in the field of education has been included here because the existence of two distinct social reproduction theories – one Marxist-feminist and one Durkheimian – has the potential to cause confusion, as words can mean more than one thing. This usage of social reproduction in the field of education research to mean the intergenerational transmission of status and culture will be set aside for the remainder of the chapter, as it is unrelated to Marx or Marxist usages,[4] and the phrase 'social reproduction theory' going forward will refer to the recent Marxist-feminist offshoot.

12.3   BIOLOGICAL REPRODUCTION

In the context of radical feminism or a dual systems approach to Marxist-feminism,[5] biological reproduction and the capacity to give birth are central to understandings of women's oppression in a transhistorical notion of 'patriarchy'. However, Mark Cousins writes that:

> The argument that a theory of reproduction must include childbirth is based simply upon a pun. It is one thing to list what every child knows is necessary for the continuation of an economy: it is quite another to give any one of them a discursive priority in relation to the problem of reproduction. (Cousins 1978, p. 66)

Thus, the use of the term 'reproduction' by Marxist-feminists is fraught with danger, as 'it tends to conflate ... the biological reproduction of the species with the historically specific question of ... the reproduction of ... labour power and in maintaining the relations of dominance and subordinacy of capitalist production' (Barrett [1980] 2014, p. 27). At its worst, this conflation results in biologically determinist theories of women's oppression in capitalist society and the gender division of labour (Arruzza 2016).

---

[4]   One possible additional source of confusion is the elements of Marxist-feminist social reproduction theorist Sears's (2017) work, which in part concerns socialization and the transmission of heteronormativity and gay identity, and Susan Ferguson's work on childhood and education, both of which draw on this other version of social reproduction theory from the field of education.

[5]   Dual systems or socialist feminist approaches are those that combine aspects of radical feminism and Marxism to theorize gender-based oppression as the result of two systems: patriarchy and capitalism. See Young (1981) for a seminal critique of dual systems approaches, and Vogel (1981) in the same book for a critical history of the 'socialist feminist synthesis'.

When Marx writes that 'the seller of labour-power must perpetuate himself, "in the way that every living individual perpetuates himself, by procreation"', he is not referring to just any biological procreation but rather to the replenishment of the 'race of peculiar commodity-owners' in order to 'perpetuate its appearance in the market' (Marx [1867] 1906, p. 191).

12.4   THE REPRODUCTION OF LABOUR-POWER

Labour-power is 'the aggregate of those mental and physical capabilities existing in a human being, which he exercises whenever he produces a use-value of any description' (Marx [1867] 1906, p. 186).[6] Labour-power only becomes a commodity when it is offered for sale on the market. The commodity labour-power is sold by the bearer of labour-power – the free labourer – because he has nothing else to sell as the result of the historical process of forcible expropriation. The existence of the capitalist necessitates the existence of the seller of labour-power, and the imperative of accumulation necessitates that labour-power remains constantly available on the market. While he viewed the reproduction of labour-power as a key component of the reproduction of capitalist society, Marx 'never provided a thoroughgoing exposition of just what it entailed' (Vogel [1983] 2013, p. 188). Thus, precisely how labour-power, this peculiar commodity, is replenished with fresh labour-power both day-to-day and intergenerationally has been a focus of Marxist-feminist scholarship for over 50 years, as have debates over the specific relationship of these activities to the production of surplus value.

The classical theory of wage determination states that the 'natural price of labour is that price which is necessary to enable the labourers, one with another, to subsist and to perpetuate their race' (Ricardo [1817] 1951, p. 93), or for Marx, that 'the value of labour-power is the value of the means of subsistence necessary for the maintenance of the labourer' (Marx [1867] 1906, p. 190). Ricardo writes that the wage is dependent on but not exactly equal to the money price of the commodities the waged worker and their household need to survive; and Marx argues that, at its minimum level of subsistence, the value of the commodity labour-power is 'determined by the value of the commodities, without the daily supply of which the labourer cannot renew his vital energy' (Marx [1867] 1906, p. 192). However, in making the simplifying jump from the means of subsistence generically to the value of commodities specifically, both Ricardo and Marx bypass the fact that commodities must be

---

[6]   In order to successfully produce use-values, the capacity to produce use-values that exists in a human being – actualized as labour – must be combined with means of production that likewise must possess the capacity to produce use-values.

transformed in order to serve as final use-values; that is, before they are consumed (Vogel [1983] 2013, p. 159). Though this production process frequently takes place in family-households, this need not be the case (Vogel [1983] 2013, p. 189). The quantity of unwaged work spent by the working-class in this production of use-values is dynamic as both a substitute for and complement to commodities purchased with money from waged labour, and thus also impacts upon the range of the ultimate and minimum levels of the value of labour-power in terms of commodities.

The wage is not exactly equal to the full amount of labour time necessary for the reproduction of labour-power day-to-day or intergenerationally because of the unwaged time involved in transforming commodities into use-values and raising children (Quick 2018; Vogel [1983] 2013), what Lise Vogel ([1983] 2013, p. 158) calls the 'domestic component of necessary labour'. State programmes such as public education, healthcare, and other welfare state benefits also contribute to the non-equivalence of the worker's wage and the worker's subsistence level (Conference of Socialist Economists 1977, p. 4). Just as the wage is not static, so the quantity of unwaged labour and the quantity of welfare state benefits involved in the subsistence of the working class are not static. Understanding the cultural norms that prescribe working class 'needs', the specific proportions of inputs, the social assignment of tasks, and the arrangement of people in space is an empirical question for historians; the reproduction of labour-power has been carried out in a variety of ways during the history of capitalism (Vogel [1983] 2013, p. 154). The imperative of accumulation means that capital must 'tend to socialise (that is turn into a collective activity) the general conditions of capitalist accumulation' (Cockburn 1977, p. 63). While the focus is frequently on women, households and household production, and their role in the reproduction of labour-power, labour-power can be replenished via other means – such as proletarianization – and in other sites, such as schools, 'labour-camps, barracks, orphanages, hospitals, prisons, and other such institutions' (Vogel [1983] 2013, p. 159).

One thing that is not clear is whether the unwaged work that goes into this transformation of commodities into final use-values by the working class and the reproduction of labour-power, when unwaged, more generally represents a subsidy to the capitalist class that allows for the realization of higher profits. Some authors, for example Vogel ([1983] 2013, p. 162), suggest that there is no subsidy involved, and in fact that reductions in domestic labour may increase surplus value. Others, such as Dalla Costa and James (1975), suggest that unwaged work does represent a subsidy to the capitalist class. If Vogel's analysis is correct, then from the perspective of the capitalist class, unproductive work involved in reproducing labour-power 'is simultaneously indispensable and an obstacle to accumulation' (Vogel [1983] 2013, p. 163).

Following Brenner and Laslett (1991) and Brenner (2000), the recent Marxist-feminist offshoot social reproduction theory initially redefined social reproduction as the reproduction of labour-power (Bhattacharya 2017, pp. 6–7), without a specific examination of how the reproduction of labour-power relates to capitalist society as a whole. Social reproduction theory (SRT) borrows from Dalla Costa and James (1975) the idea that women who perform tasks on an unwaged basis related to the reproduction of labour-power are members of the working class and thus capable of participating in class struggle. From Lise Vogel ([1983] 2013), social reproduction theory borrows the notion that labour-power is reproduced not only in the family-household on an unwaged basis by mothers and wives, but also on a waged basis by unproductive workers. In borrowing these aspects of 20th-century Marxist-feminist scholarship, social reproduction theory argues for the working-class position and revolutionary capacity of people outside the 'productive' economy: those engaged in either waged or unwaged work related to the reproduction of labour-power, if not surplus value directly. While it is gestured towards in places, this social reproduction theory does not specifically examine how the reproduction of labour-power relates to the crisis-ridden reproduction of capitalist society. What is offered instead is a foreshortened account in which exploitation and domination are extrinsic to the organization of production and reproduction, and the activities involved therein. For this reason, social reproduction theory is not a theory of capitalist society, but rather can be best described as a revolutionary strategy aimed at correctly identifying the working class on the assumption that the correct definition can help to bring about communism.

More recently, social reproduction theorists such as Alan Sears (2016, 2017), Susan Ferguson (2019) and Tithi Bhattacharya have moved away from redefining social reproduction as the reproduction of labour-power, and have begun to use the term 'life-making'. The vague term 'life-making' straddles the line between biological reproduction and the reproduction of labour-power. Ferguson argues that capitalism proceeds by 'reorganizing and devaluing all of people's life-making activities, most of which have been the tasks assigned to women' (Ferguson 2019, p. 2). Social reproduction itself is defined by Bhattacharya as 'life-making activities' (Jaffe 2020). Others in this niche define social reproduction as 'the domain of life-making' (Thompson 2020, p. 278), 'the under-remunerated effort of producing use-values essential to "life-making"' (Rao et al. 2021, p. 2), and 'the renewal and maintenance of life and of the institutions and work necessary therein' (Arruzza 2016, p. 10). Social reproduction is said to give 'a name to the activities that constitute life making … in capitalist society' (Miranda and Lane-McKinley 2017). The shift by social reproduction theorists from redefining social reproduction to meaning the reproduction of labour-power, to redefining social reproduction, to meaning 'life-making', generically represents a further evolution in the stripping away of the explanatory political economic power in these Marxist categories, as it divorces them from their explicit relationship to capitalist society as a whole. 'It substitutes for an economic category, a sycophantic phrase – voilà tout' (Marx [1867] 1906, p. 654).

While social reproduction theorists may speak about 'life-making' in order to paint these 'life-making activities' (and the people who perform them) in a virtuous light, the life that is made is a worker who must compete with other workers for the opportunity to sell her labour-power, spending the majority of her life maximizing surplus value. Seen in this way, the task of reproductive workers is the reproduction of not just any life, but that of this race of peculiar commodity-owners, the sellers of labour-power. Thus, the reproduction of labour-power in capitalist society is not virtuous 'life-making', but rather one aspect of a larger process that perpetuates the capitalist organization of society. After all, 'the reproduction of labour-power … [is] a factor in the reproduction of capital itself. Accumulation of capital is therefore increase of the proletariat' (Marx [1867] 1906, p. 673, trans. mod.).

12.5 ACCUMULATION AND THE REPRODUCTION OF CAPITAL

Another aspect of a larger process that perpetuates the capitalist organization of society is accumulation. Labour-power cannot be sold on the market without Mr Moneybags on the other end to buy it: individual capitalists are compelled to continually buy labour-power in order to continually produce commodities for sale on the market, or else face ruin. Surplus value is realized if these commodities are successfully sold for more than the cost to produce them, and the resulting money must be immediately and constantly returned into circulation in order to purchase additional labour-power and means of production to begin the cycle again for reproduction on an increasing scale. '[B]y the side of the newly-formed capital, the original capital continues to reproduce itself, and to produce surplus-value, and that this is also true of all accumulated capital, and the additional capital engendered by it' (Marx [1867] 1906, p. 637). In this way, 'the consumption of labour-power is at one and the same time the production of commodities and of surplus-value', assuming, of course, that those commodities are sold.

This process is portrayed by traditional Marxists[7] as a 'theft' of surplus by 'greedy' capitalists (Postone 1993; Clarke 1995), but this is not the case:

> It is the market that imposes its capitalist character on each individual capital ... The action of the individual capitalist is not an expression of his individual will, but of the social character of capital, and its social character is only imposed on the individual capital through its insertion into the sphere of exchange, as the individual capitalist seeks to valorise his capital. (Clarke 1995, p. 4)

The individual capitalist, like the individual worker, is compelled to act in particular ways by the market and the imperatives of accumulation: 'the effect of the social mechanism, of which he is but one of the wheels' (Marx [1867] 1906, p. 649). And besides, workers are being paid the market price of the commodity labour-power that they are compelled to sell to capitalists (Heinrich 2012).

In traditional Marxist theories, class struggle involves workers attempting to recapture a portion of the value created through their labour for their own use and enjoyment, while the capitalist class uses the state as an instrument to allow the continued 'theft' of the surplus (Postone 1993). According to these theories, the short-term amelioration of this theft can be achieved through the redistribution of both monetary wealth and political power from capital to workers. This redistribution appears to be conceived of as a stepping stone towards the ultimate end of workers – now broadly defined to also include those engaged in the work of reproducing labour-power – seizing power and centrally planning an equitable form of distribution while leaving the existing production processes intact. However, 'the more or less favourable circumstances in which the wage-working class supports and multiplies itself, in no way alter the fundamental character of capitalist production' (Marx [1867] 1906, pp. 672–673), and improvements in well-being can only be secured within capitalism to the extent that these improvements do not interfere with accumulation. Furthermore, '[T]he class struggle over production is not a matter of the subjective motivation of the capitalist, but is imposed on every capitalist by the pressure of competition, which is the expression of the tendency for capitalism to develop the forces of production without regard to the limits of the market' (Clarke 1995, p. 4).

An expanded definition of the working class to include people whose waged and unwaged work contributes to the reproduction of labour-power has helped to shed light on previously under-studied activities that are not productive of surplus value. However, in examining capitalism from the standpoint of waged and unwaged labour – with 'good' workers and 'bad' capitalists – traditional

---

[7]   For an overview of the critique of traditional Marxism, see O'Kane (2018).

Marxists concerned with the reproduction of labour-power have largely refrained from examining how this labour relates to accumulation, and as a consequence how the reproduction of labour-power relates to the whole of capitalist society.

12.6 REPRODUCTION OF CAPITALIST SOCIETY AS A WHOLE

Recently, social reproduction theory has attempted to redefine 'social reproduction' to mean the reproduction of labour-power alone, and these theorists use the phrase 'societal reproduction' to refer to the reproduction of capitalist society. Contra social reproduction theory, there is no social reproduction without 'societal reproduction', as all production and reproduction in capitalist society are indelibly shaped by accumulation. In correct Marxist usage, 'social reproduction' refers to the reproduction of society as a whole, rather than one element of that society, and when Marxist-feminists such as Lise Vogel, Martha Gimenez, and others, refer to 'social reproduction' this is the sense in which they use the term. Furthermore, one must identify precisely what sort of society is being produced, as both Vogel ([1983] 2013) and Gimenez (2018) do when they specify capitalist social reproduction.

The capitalist class and the working class are inextricably linked to one another via their own processes of production and reproduction, discussed above, with these processes shaped by the imperative of endless accumulation and together implicated in the reproduction of capitalist society as a whole: 'a historically specific form of the social production process in general' (Marx [1894] 1981, p. 957). The imperative of accumulation arose out of the historical process of primitive accumulation that divided people and production into these classes. It is this imperative of accumulation as a law of the whole – rather than one class or another – that ultimately prescribes and constrains the possible actions taken by people, firms and institutions. Following the convention in classical political economy starting with Quesnay, ending with Marx's critique of political economy – in which the capitalist economy is conceived of as a system with interconnected parts – I will briefly present a simple model of capitalist society adapted from Munro (2019) in which individual members of the working class and capitalist class each must reproduce themselves to perpetuate their own existence, and in doing so contribute to the reproduction of capitalist society as a whole.[8]

---

[8] In this version, the role of the state is largely absent. See Munro (2019, 2021a, 2021b) for discussions of the role of the state in this process.

Capitalist society is defined here as not just a capitalist division of labour within the so-called 'formal economy', but divisions of labour that compel and constrain the activities of people within society as a whole. These divisions of labour are a consequence of the specific organization of society's productive capacities in capitalism, in which the imperatives of capitalist accumulation ultimately shape institutions and dictate the activities of people. Within the larger social division of labour in capitalist society, there are further divisions of labour within each sector that comprises it. Working-class households must purchase commodities using money from waged work, and combine these commodities with their unwaged labour in order to survive, and are thus reliant on capitalist firms for both these wages and the commodities purchased with these wages. Capitalist firms must purchase labour-power, must drive down costs to earn profits from the sale of commodities, and must constantly reinvest these profits to avoid being put out of business by other capitalist firms. Both working-class households and capitalist firms are compelled by the larger structure to act in particular ways to ensure their own survival, and in doing so perpetuate the existence of the whole. The way each class goes about reproducing itself involves mutual reliance on the other class, perpetuating their existences. At the same time as the classes are reliant on one another, each class has interests that are at odds with the others, resulting in conflict. Furthermore, there are tensions within each class, as capitalist firms must compete with other capitalist firms for their survival, and workers compete with other workers for theirs.

The individual capitalist firm must compete with other firms, both for the supply of workers and in the market selling commodities. The firm does this by driving down costs and by reinvesting profits to perpetuate its own existence. Firms must hire workers to produce commodities, and firms pay wages to the workers that are equal to the value of the commodity labour-power. Because the value of the commodity labour-power is less than the value of the commodities produced by these workers during the working day, the firm realizes surplus value in the form of profit when the commodities are sold. The market price of labour-power is equal to the money price of the commodities used as inputs into the transformation of these commodities into the use-values necessary and customary for survival, though this money price may be higher or lower depending on the portion of the household's subsistence provided by inputs from the state and unwaged work of household members. Firms contribute to accumulation by purchasing commodities from other firms as inputs into their production processes. The firm contributes to social reproduction by remitting payments to the state in the form of taxes. The firm also contributes to social reproduction by paying wages and providing other benefits to workers, who use the money from this wage to buy commodities needed for inputs into the household production process to reproduce labour-power.

The individual working-class household in capitalism contributes to accumulation and is thus implicated in social reproduction in four main ways. First, household members who are compelled to sell part of their time for wages contribute to accumulation because their wage is less than the value produced thanks to the consumption of their living labour-power over the course of the working day. Second, the household is the primary site in which the next generation of workers is raised, providing the future source of labour-power. Third, the household purchases commodities as inputs into its household production process, and in doing so surplus value is realized in the form of profit. Fourth, household members may have additional unwaged work shifted onto them by the firms from whom they purchase goods and services without a corresponding decrease in the purchase price of those goods or from the state in the form of volunteer work (Glazer 1984, 1993). The household also contributes to social reproduction by remitting payments to the state in the form of taxes, providing labour to the state in the form of military service, and other employment in the state sector, by and reproducing the population.

The capitalist process of production is:

> a historically specific form of the social production process in general. This last is both a production process of the material conditions of existence for human life, and a process, proceeding in specific economic and historical relations of production, that produces and reproduces these relations of production themselves, and with them the bearers of this process, their material conditions of existence, and their mutual relationships, i.e. the specific economic form of their society. For the totality of these relationships which the bearers of this production have towards nature and one another, the relationships in which they produce, is precisely society, viewed according to its economic structure. Like all its forerunners, the capitalist production process proceeds under specific material conditions, which are however also the bearers of specific social relations which the individuals enter into in the process of reproducing their life. Those conditions, like these social relations, are on the one hand the presuppositions of the capitalist production process, on the other its results and creations; they are both produced by it and reproduced by it. (Marx [1894] 1981, p. 957)

Accumulation and the reproduction of capital cannot be divorced from the reproduction of labour-power, and the reproduction of labour-power cannot be divorced from the reproduction of capitalist society, nor from the social misery inherent to it.[9]

---

[9]   It establishes an accumulation of misery, corresponding with accumulation of capital. Accumulation of wealth at one pole is, therefore, at the same time accumulation of misery, agony of toil slavery, ignorance, brutality, mental degradation, at the opposite pole, i.e., on the side of the class that produces its own product in the form of capital. (Marx [1867] 1906, p. 709)

12.7   CONCLUSION

In correct Marxist usage, social reproduction refers to the reproduction of capitalist society as a whole, a process shaped by the imperative of endless accumulation. While Marx was clear that the reproduction of labour-power played a crucial role in this process, Marxist-feminists have made important theoretical and empirical contributions to our understanding of precisely how this process is carried out. Along the way, the multiple meanings of reproduction – the reproduction of labour-power, the reproduction of capital, and biological reproduction – have caused confusion, as has the existence of a non-Marxist 'social reproduction theory' in the field of education that concerns the intergeneration transmission of culture and status.

I have outlined above a simplified model showing how the reproduction of capitalist society depends on the capitalist continually reproducing himself as a capitalist, and the worker continually reproducing themself as a worker; compelled to do so both 'physically and socially' (Clarke 1995, pp. 19–20) as they are each at once produced by the capitalist production process and reproduced by it. The Marxist-feminist offshoot social reproduction theory has attempted to redefine social reproduction to mean the reproduction of labour-power alone; and more recently to redefine social reproduction to mean 'life-making'. However, these redefinitions set back our theoretical understanding of capitalist society and the essential role that the reproduction of labour-power plays in accumulation and capitalist social reproduction, and how these supposedly virtuous 'activities of life-making' in fact perpetuate the antagonism and social misery inherent to capitalism.

REFERENCES

Allen, K. and O'Boyle, B., (2017). *Durkheim: A Critical Introduction.* London: Pluto Books.

Arruzza, C., (2016). Functionalist, determinist, reductionist: social reproduction feminism and its critics. *Science and Society* 80(1), pp. 9–30.

Barrett, M., [1980] (2014). *Women's Oppression Today: The Marxist/Feminist Encounter.* London: Verso.

Bhattacharya, T., (2017). Introduction. In T. Bhattacharya, ed., *Social Reproduction Theory: Remapping Class, Recentering Oppression.* London: Pluto Press, pp. 1–20.

Bourdieu, P., (1973). Cultural production and social reproduction. In R. Brown, ed., *Knowledge, Education and Social Change.* London: Taylor & Francis, pp. 71–84.

Bourdieu, P., and Passeron, J-C., (1977). *Reproduction in Education, Society, and Culture.* London: Sage Publications.

Brenner, J., (2000). *Women and the Politics of Class.* New York: Monthly Review Press.

Brenner, J. and Laslett, B., (1991). Gender, social reproduction, and women's self-organization: considering the U.S. welfare state. *Gender and Society* 5(3), pp. 311–333.

Clarke, S., (1995). Marx and the Market. https://homepages.warwick.ac.uk/~syrbe/pubs/LAMARKW.pdf.

Cockburn, C., (1977). *The Local State: Management of Cities and People.* London: Pluto Press.

Collins, J., (2009). Social reproduction in classrooms and schools. *Annual Review of Anthropology* 38, pp. 33–48.

Conference of Socialist Economists, (1977). *On the Political Economy of Women.* CSE Pamphlet no. 2, London: Stage 1.

Cousins, M., (1978). Material arguments and feminism. *m/f* 2, pp. 62–70.

Dalla Costa, M. and James, S., (1975). *The Power of Women and the Subversion of the Community.* Bristol: Falling Wall Press.

Desan, M.H., (2013). Bourdieu, Marx, and Capital: a critique of the extension model. *Sociological Theory* 31(4), pp. 318–342.

Fergus, E., (2016). Social reproduction ideologies: teacher beliefs about race and culture. In D.J. Connor, B.A. Ferri and S.A. Annamma, eds, *DisCrit: Disability Studies and Critical Race Theory in Education.* New York: Teachers College Press, pp. 117–127.

Ferguson, S., (1999). Building on the strengths of the socialist feminist tradition. *Critical Sociology* 25(1), pp. 1–15.

Ferguson, S., (2019). *Women and Work: Feminism, Labour, and Social Reproduction.* London: Pluto Press.

Gimenez, M., (2018). *Marx, Women, and Capitalist Social Reproduction.* Chicago, IL: Haymarket Books.

Giroux, H., (1983). Theories of reproduction and resistance in the new sociology of education: a critical analysis. *Harvard Educational Review* 53(3), pp. 257–293.

Glazer, N.Y., (1984). Servants to capital: unpaid domestic labour and paid work. *Review of Radical Political Economics* 16(1), pp. 61–87.

Glazer, N.Y., (1993). *Women's Paid and Unpaid Labour: The Work Transfer in Health Care and Retailing.* Philadelphia, PA: Temple University Press.

Heinrich, M., (2012). *An Introduction to the Three Volumes of Karl Marx's* Capital. New York: Monthly Review Press.

Jaffe, S., (2020). Social reproduction and the pandemic, with Tithi Bhattacharya. *Dissent Magazine* 2 April. Accessed 6 February 2021. https://www.dissentmagazine.org/online_articles/social-reproduction-and-the-pandemic-with-tithi-bhattacharya.

Marx, K., [1867] (1906). *Capital: A Critique of Political Economy.* New York: Modern Library.

Marx, K., [1894] (1981). *Capital: Volume III.* Trans. David Fernbach. London: Penguin Books.

Miranda, M. and Lane-McKinley, K., (2017). Artwashing, or, between social practice and social reproduction. *A Blade of Grass,* 1 February. Accessed 6 February 2021. https://abladeofgrass.org/fertile-ground/artwashing-social-practice-social-reproduction/.

Munro, K., (2019). 'Social reproduction theory', social reproduction, and household production. *Science and Society* 83(4), pp. 451–468.

Munro, K., (2021a). The welfare state and the bourgeois family-household. *Science and Society* 85(2), pp. 199–206.

Munro, K., (2021b). Unproductive workers and state repression. *Review of Radical Political Economics* 53(4), pp. 623–630.

O'Kane, C., (2018). Moishe Postone's new reading of Marx: the critique of political economy as a critical theory of the historically specific social form of labour. *Consecutio Rerum* 3(5), pp. 485–501.

Postone, M., (1993). *Time, Labour, and Social Domination.* Cambridge: Cambridge University Press.

Quick, P., (2018). Labour power: a 'peculiar' commodity. *Science and Society* 82(3), pp. 386–412.

Rao, S., Ramnarain, S., Naidu, S., Uppal, A. and Mukherjee, A., (2021). Work and social reproduction in rural India: lessons from time-use data. University of Massachusetts Amherst Political Economy Research Institute Working Paper #535.

Ricardo, D., [1817] (1951). *On the Principles of Political Economy and Taxation.* Indianapolis, IN: Liberty Fund.

Sears, A., (2016). Situating sexuality in social reproduction. *Historical Materialism* 24(2), pp. 138–163.

Sears, A., (2017). Body politics: the social reproduction of sexualities. In T. Bhattacharya, ed., *Social Reproduction Theory: Remapping Class, Recentering Oppression.* London: Pluto Press, pp. 171–191.

Thompson, M., (2020). Sounding the arcane: contemporary music, gender and reproduction. *Contemporary Music Review* 39(2), pp. 273–292.

Vogel, L., (1981). Marxism and feminism: unhappy marriage, trial separation or something else? In L. Sargent, ed., *Women and Revolution: A Discussion of the Unhappy Marriage of Marxism and Feminism.* Montréal: Black Rose Books, pp. 195–217.

Vogel, L.., [1983] (2013). *Marxism and the Oppression of Women: Toward a Unitary Theory.* Leiden: Koninklijke Brill.

Young, I., (1981). Beyond the unhappy marriage: a critique of the dual systems theory. In L. Sargent, ed., *Women and Revolution: A Discussion of the Unhappy Marriage of Marxism and Feminism.* Montréal: Black Rose Books, pp. 43–69.

13. Material interchange

Vittorio Morfino[1]

13.1 INTRODUCTION

In the brief space of this chapter, I propose an analysis of Marx's reference to Lucretius and Darwin in *Capital* volume one. These are very quick references, one to Lucretius and two to Darwin. The references are not only quick, but marginal, relegated to footnotes. Of course, if we wished to extend the framework to examine the occurrences of the proper names or concepts of the two authors within Marx's entire theoretical production, we would find much more material to analyse. Marx dedicated a notebook to Lucretius[2] in his youth, and makes a handful of references to him throughout his published works, journal articles and unedited manuscripts.[3] Regarding Darwin, Marx had an important exchange with Engels in addition to a number of other references.[4] However, I do not take this path. Instead, I attempt to respond to a question whose rhetorical form we owe to Alain Badiou: of what are these authors, in *Capital*, the name? In other words, to which theoretical strategy, if there is one, do Marx's notes correspond?

13.2 THE NOTE ON LUCRETIUS IN CHAPTER 7

Marx cites Lucretius in a note added to chapter 7 of the 1872 second edition of *Capital* on 'The Rate of Surplus-Value'. We can briefly note the context in which the great Latin poet is evoked. We are in the first section, 'The Degree of Exploitation of Labour-Power', which culminates with the formulation of the rate of surplus-value in the following terms:

---

[1]   Translated by Dave Mesing.
[2]   Marx ([1838–39] 1976, pp. 9–141). Notebooks 4 and 5 are dedicated to *De rerum natura*. See ibid., pp. 74–117.
[3]   If the bibliography concerning the relation between Marx and Epicurus is relatively long, the same cannot be said about Marx and Lucretius. For Marxian references to Lucretius, see Morfino (2012).
[4]   See Morfino (2009) as well as the essential Lecourt (1983).

s (surplus-value)/v (variable capital) = surplus labour/necessary labour

Marx specifies that the two formulas express the same relation in different forms: the former in the form of objectivized labour, and the latter in the form of living, fluid labour.

Naturally, in order to avoid falling into an error which Marx notes in section three is typified by Senior, it is necessary to pose constant capital equal to zero: surplus-value is in fact the consequence of the change in value to variable capital, but this change is obscured in the formula:

(c [constant capital] + v [variable capital]) + s [surplus-value]

> At first sight it appears a strange proceeding, to equate the constant capital to zero. Yet it is what we do every day. If, for example, we wish to calculate the amount of England's profits from the cotton industry, we first of all deduct the sums paid for cotton to the United States, India, Egypt and other countries; in other words, the value of the capital that merely reappears in the value of the product, is put = 0. Of course the ratio of surplus-value not only to that portion of the capital from which it immediately springs, and whose change of value [*Wertveründrung*] it represents, but also -to the sum total of the capital advanced is economically of very great importance ... In order to enable one portion of a capital to expand its value by being converted [*Umsatz*] into labour-power, it is necessary that another portion be converted [*verwandelt warden*] into means of production. In order that variable capital may perform its function, constant capital must be advanced in proper proportion, a proportion given by the special technical conditions of each labour-process. The circumstance, however, that retorts and other vessels, are necessary to a chemical process, does not compel the chemist to notice them in the result of his analysis. If we look at the creation and the alteration of value [*Wertverschöpfung und Wertveändrung*] for themselves, i.e. in their pure form, then the means of production, this physical shape taken on by constant capital, provides only the material in which fluid, value-creating labour-power has to be incorporated. Neither the nature, nor the value of this material is of any importance. The only requisite is that there be a sufficient supply to absorb the labour expended in the process of production. That supply once given, the material may rise or fall in value, or even be, as land and the sea, without any value in itself; but this will have no influence on the creation of value or on the variation in the quantity of value [*Der Prozeß der Werthschöpfung und Werthverändrung*]. (Marx [1867] 1906, pp. 238–239, trans. mod.)

At the end of this passage, for the second edition published in 1872, Marx adds the following note:

> What Lucretius says is self-evident; 'nil posse creari de nihilo,' out of nothing, nothing can be created. Creation of value is transposition [*Umsatz*] of labour-power into labour. Labour-power itself is, above all else, the material of nature [*Naturstoff*] transposed [*umgesetzer*] into a human organism [*menchlichen Organismus*]. (Marx [1872] 1987, p. 239, trans. mod.)

I should first point out that although it appears at the end of the paragraph, the note serves to elucidate just one expression: 'the creation of value'. Marx wants to dissolve any ambiguity in the use of this expression, and for this reason cites Lucretius. He quotes a verse whose model is found in Epicurus's Letter to Herodotus, but at the same time, it is a broader reference to a group of verses that immediately follow the praise of Epicurus who was first to challenge with his philosophy the religion which oppresses 'human life … [with] serious weight' (Lucretius 1975, pp. 7–9). At the heart of Epicurean philosophy there are 'the first-beginnings of things, / from which nature makes all things [*omnis natura crees*], / and increases and nourishes them, / and into which the same nature again reduces them when dissolved' (Lucretius 1975, p. 7). With this, the darkness of religion (which Lucretius exemplifies through the sacrifice of Iphigenia) can be driven away:

> This terror of mind therefore and this gloom,
> must be dispelled, not by the sun's rays or the bright shafts of day,
> but by the aspect and law of nature.
> The first principle of our study we will derive from this,
> that no thing is ever by divine power produced from nothing [*nullam rem e nilo gigni divinitus umquam*].
> For assuredly a dread holds all mortals thus in bond,
> because they behold many things happening in heaven and earth
> whose causes they can by no means see,
> and they think them to be done by divine power.
> For which reasons, when we shall perceive that nothing can be created from nothing [*nil posse creari de nilo*],
> then we shall at once more correctly understand
> from that principle what we are seeking, both the course from which each thing can be made,
> and the manner in which everything is done without the working of gods.
> For if things came out of nothing [*si de nilo fierent*], all kinds of things could be produced
> from all things, nothing would want a seed. (Lucretius 1975, pp. 15–17)

Lucretius's principle, unlike the Epicurean model, is forcefully played as anti-religious. It is the fundamental principle of reason, whose force is capable of dispersing the darkness of ignorance from which religion arises. This principle is based on the fact that everything in nature has its own determinate origin, its own rhythm, its regularities; the specificity of seeds from which

determinate beings arise, the determinate times in which the birth and growth
of these beings are possible:

> But if [things] came from nothing [*si de nilo fierent*], suddenly they would arise
> at uncertain intervals and at unsuitable times of the year;
> naturally, for there would be no first-beginnings to be restrained
> from generative union by the unfavorable season.
> Nor furthermore would time be needed for the growth of things,
> for seeds to collect, if they could grow from nothing [*si e nilo crescere possent*]
> …
> A fixed material is assigned for making things,
> From which what can arise is fixed …
> Therefore we must confess that nothing can come from nothing [*nil igitur fieri de
> nilo*],
> since all things must have seed, from which each being created
> may be brought forth into the soft breezes of air. (Lucretius 1975, pp. 17–19)

Lucretius's argument works to demonstrate the existence of primordial elements from whose combination all natural beings are generated, a certain,
determinate combination in which the boundary between possible and impossible lies.

In Marx, the citation of Lucretius plays the role of a powerful rationalist and
materialist watchword, a watchword recalled a little less than a century earlier
in the inaugural move of the *Pantheismusstreit*, within the famous debate
between Lessing and Jacobi, which Jacobi summarized in his *Concerning
the Doctrine of Spinoza, in Letters to Herr Moses Mendelssohn*. Here is the
decisive passage:

> I have come to talk to you about my hen kai pan. Yesterday you were frightened. I
> [Jacobi]: You surprised me, and I may indeed have blushed and gone pale, for I felt
> bewilderment in me. Fright it was not. To be sure, there is nothing that I would have
> suspected less, than to find a Spinozist or a pantheist in you. And you blurted it out
> to me so suddenly. In the main I had come to get help from you against Spinoza.
> Lessing: Oh, so you do know him? I [Jacobi]: I think I know him as only very few
> can ever have known him. Lessing: Then there is no help for you. Become his friend
> all the way instead. There is no other philosophy than the philosophy of Spinoza. I
> [Jacobi]: That might be true. For the determinist, if he wants to be consistent, must
> become a fatalist: the rest then follows by itself. Lessing: I see that we understand
> one another. I am all the more anxious to hear what you hold to be the spirit of
> Spinozism; I mean the spirit that inspired Spinoza himself. I [Jacobi]: It is certainly
> none other than the ancient *a nihilo nihil fit*. (Jacobi [1885] 1994, p. 187)

Lessing identifies the principle *a nihilo nihil fit* with the *Geist des Spinozismus* (Spirit of Spinozism), a principle which comes from far away and is ancient, against all religious prejudice, the materialist principle of causality.[5]

The expression 'creation of value' thus does not mean creation from nothing, but rather *Umsatz*, transformation, passage, conversion of labour-power into labour. But, Marx adds, labour-power itself is 'above all else, the material of nature (*Naturstoff*) transposed (*umgesetzer*) into a human organism'. Here Marx seems to allude to a Lucretian ontological horizon in which what there

---

[5] In the Postscript to the second edition of *Capital* Marx cites the polemic in a passage that is famous for other reasons:

> The mystifying side of Hegelian dialectic I criticised nearly thirty years ago, at a time when it was still the fashion. But just as I was working at the first volume of 'Das Kapital,' it was the good pleasure of the peevish, arrogant, mediocre *Epigonoi* who now talk large in cultured Germany, to treat Hegel in same way as the brave Moses Mendelsohn in Lessing's time treated Spinoza, i.e., as a 'dead dog.' I therefore openly avowed myself the pupil of that mighty thinker, and even here and there, in the chapter on the theory of value, coquetted with the modes of expression peculiar to him. The mystification which dialectic suffers in Hegel's hands, by no means prevents him from being the first to present its general form of working in a comprehensive and conscious manner. With him it is standing on its head. It must be turned right side up again, if you would discover the rational kernel within the mystical shell. (Marx [1867] 1906, p. 25)

Marx is clearly citing from memory, as actually it was not Mendelsson who called Spinoza a 'dead dog', but rather Lessing. It is found in Jacobi's account in *Concerning the Doctrine of Spinoza, in Letters to Herr Moses Mendelsohn*: 'I won't leave you be; you must clarify this parallelism … Yet people always speak of Spinoza as if he were a dead dog still' (Jacobi [1885] 1994, p. 193).

> And what this Lange has to say about the Hegelian method and my application of the same is simply childish. First, he understands nothing [*rien*] about Hegel's method and, therefore, second, still less about my critical manner of applying it. In one respect he reminds me of Moses Mendelssohn. That prototype of a windbag once wrote to Lessing asking how he could possibly take 'that dead dog Spinoza' *au sérieux*! In the same way, Mr Lange expresses surprise that Engels, I, etc., take au sérieux the dead dog Hegel, after Büchner, Lange, Dr. Düring, Fechner, etc., had long agreed that they – poor dear – had long since buried him. Lange is naïve enough to say that I 'move with rare freedom' in empirical matter. He has not the slightest idea that this 'free movement in matter' is nothing but a paraphrase for the method of dealing with matter – that is, the dialectical method. (Marx [1870] 2010, p. 528)

> It is a characteristic of nations with an 'historical' development, in the sense given to this term by the Historical School of Law, that they always forget their own history. Thus although during this half century the issue of the relation between commodity-prices and the quantity of currency has agitated Parliament continuously and has caused thousands of pamphlets, large and small, to be published in England, Steuart remained even more of 'a dead dog' than Spinoza appeared to Moses Mendelssohn in Lessing's time. (Marx [1859] 2010, p. 398)

is, all that exists, exists in a permanent conversion, a permanent composition/decomposition, an ontological horizon to which the famous expression '*Stoffwechsel*' refers, which for that reason I would propose to translate in a Lucretian way as 'material interchange':

> So far therefore as labour is a creator of use-value, is *useful labour*, it is a condition of human existence which is independent all forms of society; it is an eternal natural necessity which mediates [*vermitteln*] the material interchange [*Stoffwechsel*] between man and Nature, and therefore human life itself. (Marx [1867] 1906, p. 50, trans. mod.)

Now, this material interchange between man and nature, this material that is converted into an organism on the one hand, and labour-power converted into objectified labour on the other, excludes any creation *ex nihilo*. It is with this framework in the background that both the production of value and the production of surplus-value must be thought:

> It is every bit as important, for a correct understanding of surplus-value, to conceive it as a mere congelation [*Gerinnung*] of surplus labour-time, as nothing but materialised surplus-labour, as it is, for a proper comprehension of value, to conceive it as a mere congelation [*Gerinnung*] of so many hours of labour, as nothing but materialised labour. (Marx [1867] 1906, p. 241)

In other words, what must be established through the principle *ex nihilo nihil fit* is precisely the link between the time of surplus-value and the creation of surplus-value:

> During the second period of the labour-process, that in which his labour is no longer necessary labour, the workman, it is true, labours, expends labour-power; but his labour, being no longer necessary labour, he creates no value for himself. He creates surplus-value which, for the capitalist, has all the charms of a creation out of nothing [*Schöpfung aus Nichts*]. (Marx [1867] 1906, p. 240)

13.3   THE NOTES ON DARWIN

Marx cites Darwin in two notes to chapter 12 and chapter 13. The first note is found in the second section of chapter 12 ('The Specialized Worker and His Tools') on 'The Division of Labour and Manufacture'. Marx highlights the twofold origin of manufacturing: on the one hand, it is a combination of different trades reduced to a one-sidedness 'to such an extent that they are reduced to merely supplementary and partial operations in the production of one particular commodity'; on the other hand, manufacturing arises from a disintegration of one particular trade in its particular operations, making them independent 'to the point where each becomes the exclusive function of a particular worker' (Marx [1867] 1906, p. 457):

> On the one hand, therefore, manufacture either introduces division of labour into a process of production, or further develops that division; on the other hand, it unites together handicrafts that were formerly separate. But whatever may have been its particular starting-point, its final form is invariably the same a productive mechanism whose parts are human beings [*ein Produktionsmechanismus dessen Organe Menschen sind*]. (Marx [1867] 1906, p. 371)

The 'combined overall worker' that is, in Marx's own words, the 'living mechanism of manufacture [*lebendige Mechanismus*]', consists of one-sided partial workers that transform their own body into the 'instrument' of the sole operation that they must perform. In this sense, Marx says, on the one hand 'manufacture ... produces the skill of the detail labourer worker' (Marx [1867] 1906, p. 372), and on the other hand the perfecting of his instruments. Marx concludes with the following long passage, wherein he cites Darwin:

> Tools [*Werkzeuge*] of the same kind, such as knives, drills, gimlets. hammers, &c., may be employed in different processes; and the same tool may serve various purposes in a single process. But so soon as the different operations of a labour-process are disconnected the one from the other, and each fractional operation acquires in the hands of the detail labourer a suitable and peculiar form, alterations become necessary in the implements that previously served more than one purpose. The direction taken by this change of form [*die Richtung ihrer Formwechsel*] is determined by the difficulties experienced in consequence of the unchanged form [*die unveränderte Form*] of the implement. Manufacture is characterised by the differentiation of the instruments of labour a differentiation whereby implements of a given sort acquire fixed shapes, adapted to each particular application, and by the specialisation of those instruments, giving to each special implement its full play only in the hands of a specific detail labourer. In Birmingham alone 500 varieties of hammers are produced, and not only is each adapted to one particular process, but several varieties often serve exclusively for the different operations in one and the same process. The manufacturing period simplifies, improves, and multiplies the implements of labour, by adapting them to the exclusively special functions of each detail labourer. (Marx [1867] 1906, pp. 374–375, trans. mod.)

At the end of this passage, we find the reference to Darwin:

> Darwin in his epoch-making work on the origin of species, remarks, with reference to the natural organs of plants and animals: 'So long as one and the same organ has different kinds of work to perform, a ground for its changeability may possibly be found in this, that natural selection preserves or suppresses each small variation of form less carefully than if that organ were destined for one special purpose alone. Thus, knives that are adapted to cut all sorts of things, may, on the whole, be of one shape; but an implement destined to be used exclusively in one way must have a different shape for every different use.' (Marx [1867] 1906, p. 375)

In this note, Marx finds in Darwin a parallelism between natural organ and technical instrument, which alludes to another parallelism between selection in the natural and socio-historical fields. The citation of this parallelism concludes a long game of postponements, substitutions, and combinations of organicist and mechanist metaphors, including manufacturing as a production mechanism whose organs are humans, as a living mechanism which transforms the worker's body into an instrument, and finally the instrument of the worker as organ.

Marx takes up this last point in the opening section ('The Development of Machinery') of chapter 13, 'Machinery and Large-Scale Industry'. Here again the reference to Darwin lies in a footnote. The context is the distinction between manufacture and large-scale industry: in the former the revolution in the mode of production has its starting point in labour-power, while in the latter the starting point is the means of labour, which is transformed from instrument into machine. 'We are only concerned here', Marx specifies, 'with striking and general characteristics; for epochs in the history of society are no more separated from each other by hard and fast lines of demarcation [*abstrakt strenge Grenzlinien*] than are geological [Erdgeschichte] epochs' (Marx [1867] 1906, p. 405). Darwin enters the scene in a discussion on John Wyatt's spinning machine:

Before his time, spinning machines, although very imperfect ones, had already been used, and Italy was probably the country of their first appearance. A critical history of technology [*eine kritische Geschichte der Technologie*] would show how little any of the inventions of the 18th century are the work of a single individual. Hitherto there is no such book. Darwin has interested us in the history of Nature's Technology [*Geschichte der natürlichen Technologie*], i.e., in the formation of the organs of plants and animals, which organs serve as instruments of production for sustaining life [*auf die Bildung der Pflanzen- und Tierorgane als Produktionsinstrumente für das Leben der Pflanzen und Tiere*]. Does not the history of the productive organs of man, of organs that are the material basis of all social organisation, deserve equal attention [*die Bildungsgeschichte der produktiven Organe des Gesellschaftsmenschen der materiellen Basis jeder besondren Gesellschaftorganisation*]? And would not such a history be easier to compile, since, as Vico says, human history differs from natural history in this, that we have made the former, but not the latter? Technology discloses man's active dealing with Nature [*die Technologie enthüllt das aktive Verhalten des Menschen zur Natur*], the process of production by which he sustains his life, and thereby also lays bare the mode of formation of his social relations, and of the mental conceptions that flow from them [*seiner gesellschaftlichen Lebensverhältnisse und in der ihnen entquellenden geistigen Vorstellungen*]. Every history of religion, even, that fails to take account of this material basis, is uncritical. It is, in reality, much easier to discover by analysis the earthly core [*irdischen Kern*] of the misty creations of religion [*religiösen Nebelbildungen*], than, conversely, it is, to develop from the actual relations of life the corresponding celestialised forms [*ihre verhimmelten Formen*] of those relations. The latter method is the only materialistic, and therefore the only scientific one. The weak points in the abstract materialism of natural science [*des abstrakt naturwissenschtlichen Materialismus*], a materialism that excludes history and its process, are at once evident from the abstract and ideological conceptions [*abstrakten und ideologischen Vorstellungen*] of its spokesmen, whenever they venture beyond the bounds of their own speciality. (Marx [1867] 1906, pp. 493–494)

Again the game of postponements and substitutions between mechanism and organicism, with Darwin's work as the model of a critical history of technology insofar as he is the author of a 'natural history of technology', and with organs as instruments and instruments and machines as organs.

13.4   CONCLUSIONS

What is the meaning of these brief footnotes, these drops of intelligence within the ocean of *Capital*? Of what are Lucretius and Darwin the name? The question can be answered here on a scale from certain to conjectural.

It is certain that Lucretius and Darwin represent in Marx a radical form of anti-finalism, an affirmation of a principle of causality finally free from the age-old mortgage of the principle of reason and the empty rhetoric of its fundamental question. A clear philosophical stance for reason and science. Both Lucretius and Darwin represent a total immersion of the human in the natural, a radical rejection of every form of anthropocentrism, every causality through freedom, every radical separation of the sciences of nature and the sciences of history.[6] That Lucretius was then inhabited by the spectre of Spinoza in Marx's citation is merely conjecture; the importance of the *Spinoza-Debatte*

---

6   In this sense, the following reflections of Alfred Schmidt are quite interesting:
   It has become customary, since the work of Dilthey and the neo-Kantians and South-West Germany, to assign to the historical and the natural sciences modes of investigation which are different in principle. While Dilthey distinguished between the method of causal 'explanation' [*Erklären*] peculiar to the natural sciences, and the method of intuitive 'understanding' [*Verstehen*] peculiar to the historical, human sciences, Windelband and Rickert cut reality still more radically into two entirely distinct parts. Nature was conceived in Kantian fashion as the existence of things subject to laws. The 'nomothetic' character of the natural sciences corresponded to this conception. History was said to consist of a profusion of value-oriented, basically unconnected 'individual' data, only accessible to a descriptive 'ideographic' method. It thus became something beyond all rational analysis. Marx admitted no division between nature and society, and hence no fundamental methodological distinction between the natural sciences and historical science ... Scientific thought cannot recognize any area sui generis absolutely inaccessible to explanation in accordance with uniform laws. The methodological dualism of Dilthey, Windelband and Rickert, despite all the efforts of these authors to deal with history, rests on abstractions foreign to history. (Schmidt [1962] 1971, pp. 48–49)

for German philosophy in the late eighteenth century and the major philosophical culture of Marx renders it not so improbable. But if this were the case, we would see a third champion of anti-finalism as well as a rejection of any anthropocentrism. The human in nature is not an *imperium in imperio*. Naturally, the suggestion should not be taken in the reductionistic sense of the historical to the natural, but rather in the sense of a materialism in which the levels of complexity and historicity are at the same time interconnected and irreducible (as Marx expressly says in the note identifying 'the weaknesses of the abstract materialism of natural science' within 'the abstract and ideological conceptions expressed by its spokesmen whenever they venture beyond the bounds of their own speciality').

And this brings us to the final conjecture. As is well known, the fundamental epistemological thesis announced by Althusser in 'From *Capital* to Marx's Philosophy' sees Marx in his masterpiece grappling with a theoretical problem which he was not able to put in explicit terms: the problem of the efficacy of a structure on its elements, the problem of a structural causality. This is a problem which, according to Althusser, Marx undertakes in order to resolve it 'practically in the absence of its concept, with extraordinary ingenuity, but without completely avoiding a relapse into earlier schemata which were necessarily inadequate to pose and solve this problem' (Althusser [1965] 2015, p. 343). These inadequate schemes are the two systems of concepts that modern philosophy has produced in order to think causality: the Cartesian mechanistic model and the Leibnizian expressive model.

It could therefore be hypothesized that the proper names of Lucretius (with Spinoza behind him) and Darwin, as well as the concepts evoked by means of them – the concept of *Umsatz*, the parallel between animal organ and instrument, the reciprocal reference to natural sciences and historical-social sciences – appear at the same time as a symptom of a difficulty and as a theoretical project, an attempt to think a mechanism that does not give up totality and an organicism that is not entangled in the mesh of a new, powerful teleological model, that of Hegelian internal finality. That this risk was not only effective, but also difficult to avoid, is clear from this 16 January 1861 letter by Marx to Lassalle on Darwin's masterpiece:

> Darwin's book is very important and serves me as a basis in natural science for the class struggle in history. One has to put up with the crude English method of development, of course. Despite all deficiencies, not only is the death-blow dealt here for the first time to 'teleology' in the natural sciences but their rational meaning is empirically explained. (Marx [1861] 1985, pp. 246–247)

REFERENCES

Abbreviations:
MECW = Marx–Engels Collected Works. London: Lawrence & Wishart.
MEGA = Marx–Engels–Gesamtausgabe. Berlin: Dietz.

Althusser, L., [1965] (2015). The Object of *Capital*. In L. Althusser, É. Balibar, R. Establet, J. Rancière and P. Macherey, *Reading* Capital*: The Complete Edition.* London: Verso, pp. 215–356.

Jacobi, F.H., [1885] (1994). Concerning the Doctrine of Spinoza in Letters to Herr Moses Mendelssohn. In G. di Giovanni, ed., *The Main Philosophical Writings and the Novel Allwill.* Montreal: McGill-Queen's University Press, pp. 173–252.

Lecourt, D., (1983). *Marx au crible de Darwin.* In Y. Conry, ed., *De Darwin au darwinisme.* Paris: Vrin, pp. 227–249.

Lucretius (1975). *De rerum natura.* Cambridge, MA: Harvard University Press.

Marx, K., [1838–39] (1976). *Hefte zur epikureischen Philosophie.* In: *MEGA*, Abteilung 4, Band 1. Berlin: Dietz Verlag, pp. 9–141.

Marx, K., [1859] (2010). A Contribution to the Critique of Political Economy. In: *MECW*, Vol. 29. London: Lawrence & Wishart, pp. 257–417.

Marx, K., [1861] (1985). Letter to Ferdinand Lassalle, 16 January 1861. In: *MECW*, Vol 41. London: Lawrence & Wishart, pp. 245–247.

Marx, K., [1867] (1906). *Capital. A Critique of Political Economy.* Volume One. New York: The Modern Library.

Marx, K., [1870] (2010). Letter to Ludwig Kugelmann, 27 June 1870. In: *MECW*, Vol. 43. London: Lawrence & Wishart, pp. 527–528.

Marx, K., [1872] (1987). *Das Kapital*, 1872, *MEGA*, Abteilung II, Band 6. Berlin: Dietz Verlag.

Morfino, V., (2009). Sulla legge dell'evoluzione tra Marx e Darwin. *Il calendario del popolo* 65(741), pp. 19–22.

Morfino, V., (2012). L'interpretazione marxiana di Lucrezio. *Rivista di storia della filosofia* 67, pp. 277–291.

Schmidt, A., [1962] (1971), *The Concept of Nature in Marx.* London: New Left Books.

14. Ethnological notebooks

Emanuela Conversano

Almost 50 years after Lawrence Krader edited *The Ethnological Notebooks of Karl Marx* (Marx [1880–82] 1972), we can definitely state that the research about Marx and the Marxisms has certainly benefited, opening up to topics better suited to a globalized world, in which the critique of the capitalist mode of production cannot be separated from the struggles 'at the margins' of the capitalistic world,[1] whether those struggles be understood as the claims of subaltern groups, such as women or ethnic minorities, or of Western peoples outside the geographical borders of the capitalistic centre. Additionally, Krader's edition has encouraged many non-Marxist scholars to explore the reasons for and the goals of Marx's unfinished investigation on non-capitalist societies and the conditions of their historical development; and also to consider it as a new chance for political theory and praxis. A chance that would have been missed, if Marx's late investigation in the fields of ancient and colonial history, anthropology and ethnology were just reduced to an attempt 'to present the results of Morgan's researches' comparing 'barbarism and civilization', 'in connection with the conclusions of [the] materialistic conception of history', as Engels puts it in his 1884 Preface to the first edition of *The Origin of the Family, Private Property and the State* (Engels [1884] 2010). Marx's companion is referring to the investigation on the history of the family and the systems of consanguinity undertaken in the 1870s by one of the fathers of Victorian anthropology, Lewis Henry Morgan, whose essay *Ancient Society* (1877) Marx had read, noted down and commented a few years after its publication. Engels summarizes alleged 'Morganian' conclusions of Marx's notes in terms of a theory that basically splits history in two, precisely presenting a prehistory as its point of departure, during which the ties of blood and kin (*Geschlechtsbande*) had been dominating the social order, to be then replaced by the 'written history' of productivity of labour, which 'develops more and more, and within it, private property and exchange, differences in

---

[1]   I am referring to the title of Kevin B. Anderson's book (Anderson 2016) that is now a landmark in the discussion of the topics mentioned in the book's subtitle, that is, nationalism, ethnicity and non-Western societies, which could be erroneously taken as minor issues in Marx's thought.

wealth, the possibility of utilizing the labour power of others, and thereby, the basis of class antagonisms'. The transition from the old to the new society should be explained according to the materialist conception that Engels holds to have been discovered by Marx and to share with him 'within certain limits'. In the same Preface of his essay, which he defines as a 'fulfilment of a behest', Engels recognizes as 'determining factor in history, in the final instance, the production and reproduction of the immediate life' in its twofold character: on the one hand, 'the production of the means of subsistence ... on the other, the production of human beings themselves'. Although the development of both aspects contributes to determining the social organization of a certain histor-ical period, the more the productivity of labour grows within the sex-based society, the less the blood ties count as the decisive trigger of history, and history properly begins as a class struggle (Engels [1884] 2010, pp. 131–132). Furthermore, Morgan does not merely reconstruct the origin of what he calls 'civilization', but he also assumes that the law of progress applies to the future as it has to the past. Hence, he foreshadows a third phase, that is a 'higher plane of society' that will be the *'revival, in a higher form, of the liberty, equality and fraternity of the ancient gentes'* (Morgan 1877, p. 562; also quoted in Engels [1884] 2010, p. 276. Engels's italics). In Engels's opinion, Morgan's words about the 'future transformation of the society' might have been used by Marx himself (Engels [1891] 2010, p. 213), to close the picture of the dialectic development that would lead from the prehistory of capital to communist society. Those are indeed Marx's written words, insofar as he recorded the passage of Morgan's *Ancient Society* in his notebooks (Marx [1880–82] 1972, p. 139), and he even envisaged the same outcome in the famous drafts of the letter to the Russian revolutionary Vera Zasulich, with which Marx wanted to answer her question about the destiny of the Russian commune (*obščina*) in the early 1880s (Marx [1881] 1985, p. 220).[2]

But what exactly is the meaning of those words for Marx himself? On the one hand, in the first draft of the letter, he explicitly refers to 'the American writer' (Marx [1881] 1983, p. 107), who undoubtedly deserves credit for his acknowledgement that 'a mere property career is not the final destiny of mankind' (Morgan 1877, p. 561; quoted in Marx [1880–82] 1972, p. 139 and Engels [1884] 2010, p. 276). On the other hand, in another paragraph of the drafts, Marx complains about the inadequacy of the historiography on the ancient communities, which is limited to 'very rough sketches' (Marx [1881] 1983, p. 107, note (c)).[3] Certainly, he has also in mind the historical attempts

---

[2]   See in particular the first draft.
[3]   See the original: '*L'histoire de la decadence des communautés primitives ... est encore à faire. Jusqu'ici on n'a fourni que de maigres ébauches*' (Marx [1881] 1985, p. 229).

of other representatives of the bourgeois historical sciences. In fact, the most
trivial reason for distinguishing the positions of Marx and Engels is that the
former had not been focusing only on Morgan's research in the last years of
his life, unlike Engels in his book on the *Origin of the Family*, but on a wide
variety of themes and texts, often reading them almost hot off the press. It
is worth naming first of all the notes on *Obščinnoe zemlevladenie, pričiny,
chod i posledstvija ego razloženija* [*The Communal Possession of Land.
Causes, Course and Consequences of its Decline*], a work of 1879 by Maxim
Kovalevskij ([1879)] 1977), a Russian sociologist and promulgator of the positivistic historical-comparative method in Russia, that Marx read in the same
year, and where the title of Morgan's book is mentioned (See Harstick, p. 222).
Marx's notebook on Kovalevskji is partially accessible to English-speaking
readers thanks to Lawrence Krader, who translated it as an appendix of his
essay on the Asiatic mode of production (Krader 1975)[4] a few years after
collecting the other ethnological notebooks on the so-called Victorian or evo-
lutionist anthropologists (often involved in the British government either in the
mother country or in the colonies), that is: the book of Sir John Budd Phear,
The Aryan Village in India and Ceylon (1880); *Lectures on the Early History
of Institutions* (1875) by Sir Henry Sumner Maine; *The Origin of Civilisation
and the Primitive Condition of Man* (1870) by Sir John Lubbock. But many
other notebooks are still unpublished.[5]

I am quite persuaded that Marx's remark in the letter's draft is at least a clue
to discuss Engels's interpretation of a complete appropriation of Morgan's discoveries by the late Marx. Since I maintain that the above-mentioned inquiries
are neither a mere fulfilment of the 1840s historical materialism as sketched
in the *Origin*, nor a sudden anthropological turn in the name of Morgan, I also
assume the importance of going beyond those 'certain limits', within which the

---

[4]   A German edition of the notebooks was published by Hans-Peter Harstick in
1977.
[5]   See, among the others, the notes on L. Lange, Römische Alterthümer (1856) collected in the same notebook including Kovalevskji's work (B156), and analysed by H.
Brown (2012); or the notes from J.W.B. Money, 'Java, or How to Manage a Colony'
(1861), in the same notebook of the so-called ethnological ones. These Marxian notes
will presumably be part of the digital volumes of the *Mega Abteilung* IV, vol. 24, 27,
28, 29, but some translations have already been published in recent years based on the
Krader and Harstick editions: see also the partial French translation in a volume collecting many essays on the late Marx (Lindner 2019) and the Italian translation of the
Krader edition by A. Bracaletti, M. Cingoli, G. Sgrò and F. Vidoni (Marx and Engels
2020), which substitutes and corrects the partial and somewhat deceptive translation by
P. Foraboschi (2009). All the original papers by Marx and Engels have been digitalized
by the Amsterdam-based International Institute of Social History: https://search.iisg
.amsterdam/Record/ARCH00860.

positions of Engels, Marx and Morgan can converge, in order to understand what the actual 'legacy' (*Vermächtnis*) of late Marx's so-called ethnological studies as a whole can be in the contemporary world.

Trying to distinguish Engels's effort to put together Marx's late inquiry on the non-Western World from Marx's notes *per se* does not mean to make the former the scapegoat for all the following misleading interpretations of Marx's theory of society and history. Rather, it means to create the conditions to consider all the topics involved in the latter's point of view, to comprehend the spirit of his intellectual and practical activity, and to recognize its potentials both in the current theoretical activity and in today's political claims and struggles. It is a way to grasp the very meaning of Marxian 'anthropological' interest, broader than and different from a simple historical reconstruction in terms of a passage from barbarism to civilization; but, on the contrary, consistent with some key concepts of the contemporary humanities – for instance, the triad of race, class and gender – which appear to reduce the gap between fields such as gender studies and feminisms, postcolonial and subaltern studies on the one hand, and Marxism on the other.[6] Thus, late Marx's research raises the question of whether we can call ourselves Marxists today if even Marx himself claimed he was not. Or at least this is what Engels relates after Marx's death, in a letter in which he tries to differentiate their 'historical materialism' from the 'clichés' using the expression 'to run up a jerry-built system out of their own relatively inadequate historical knowledge' (Engels [1890] 2010a, pp. 7–8).[7]

But since we know that Marx instead never employed that expression, it is worth asking what is Marx's Marxism, and what use the late Marx made of the historical knowledge, if we learn from his 1850s foundation of political economy that the goal of his system was neither 'to write the real history of the production relations' nor to consider the capitalist relations to be 'eternal and natural' (Marx [1857–58] 2010, pp. 388–389).

Marx's historical analysis is part of his method of inquiry (*Forschungsweise*), that 'has to appropriate the material in detail, to analyze its different forms of development, to trace out their inner connection', as he explained in the 1873 *Afterword to the Second German Edition* of *Capital*, volume one (Marx [1867–90] 2010, p. 19).[8]

---

[6]   However, it should not be forgotten that there have also been attempts to detect elements of a theory of intersectionality in Engels's interpretation. See for example the reappraisal of the *Origin* made by Lisa Vogel in connection with the new wave of feminism (Vogel 1996).

[7]   Marx's assessment should have been addressed to the French Marxists. Besides Engels's letter of 5 August 1890 to Conrad Schmidt, see also Engels ([1890] 2010b, p. 70).

[8]   See the German text in Marx ([1872] 1987, p. 709).

Marx's ethnological notebooks give us access to Marx's laboratory, where he is far from formulating a complete theory of 'non-capitalist' systems, but he is dealing with modes of production in which different relationships have been ruling in comparison to those between capital and wage labour in Western Europe (at least before the capital domination penetrated those modes of economic production and social reproduction through either a solely economic or real, systematic colonization, as Marx immediately noticed while articulating his theory of capital itself[9]). At the same time, Marx is also involved in a lower level of abstraction compared to the exposition (*Darstellung*) of the critique of political economy focusing on the logic of the capitalist system. There, Marx is not looking to ancient societies to find categories in the past that can immediately be applied to the future, but he is still reasoning about how specific categories, historically arisen from given circumstances, mutually relate in the modern bourgeois society, and how those specific relations of production contradict each other to such an extent that they lead to their dissolution.[10]

As Moishe Postone points out, the form of presentation of Marx's mature critical theory could not contradict the 'historically-determined character of the analysis', proceeding from a supposedly 'trans-historically valid' starting point.[11] Rather, the starting point 'had to express the historical specificity of its object, and consequently, of the theory itself' (Postone 2019, p. 184).[12] Therefore, Stefano Breda is right to emphasize the 'limits' of Marxian materialist dialectics, which deals with 'the peculiar development of a peculiar object', that is, the capitalist mode of production, not in an empirical but in an analytical way. Nonetheless, apart from its theoretical exposition, it makes use of historical-empirical presuppositions to establish the mutual implications between the categories within the peculiar capitalist relationships (Breda 2018). Breda's definition of the Marxian dialectics in terms of an immanent critique of the empirical immediacy – insofar as it denies how the relationships manifest themselves objectively in the experience by 'showing another content

---

[9] See the last chapters of the first volume of *Capital* related to the 'so-called primitive accumulation' and the 'theory of colonization'.

[10] See Marx ([1857–58] 2010, pp. 44, 389, passim).

[11] See Marx's critique of the general point of view of a 'historico-philosophical theory whose supreme virtue consists in being supra-historical', in his 1877 letter to the Editor of the *Otechestvennye Zapiski* (Marx [1877] 1983, p. 136).

[12] My translation.

placed empirically as its condition of existence' (Breda 2018, p. 140)[13] – contributes to explain as Marx defines it in the 1873 *Afterword* to *Capital*:

> In its rational form it is a scandal and abomination to bourgeoisdom and its doctrinaire professors, because it includes in its comprehension and affirmative recognition of the existing state of things, at the same time also, the recognition of the negation of that state, of its inevitable breaking up; because it regards every historically developed social form as in fluid movement, and therefore takes into account its transient nature not less than its momentary existence; because it lets nothing impose upon it, and is in its essence critical and revolutionary. (Marx [1867–90] 2010, p. 20)

In my opinion, the so-called *Forms which Precede Capitalist Production* are a clear example of this attitude, since this text has not to be understood as a historiographic *excursus* that aims to 'put them all on the same plane' (Marx [1881] 1983, p. 107). The picture resulting from the section of the 1857–58 *Grundrisse* dedicated to non-capitalist forms of production may to some extent fit with the scheme depicted in the introduction to Engels's *Origin*, since Marx describes 'kinship tribes' as historically preceding 'locality tribes' (Marx [1857–58] 2010, pp. 405–406), and corresponding to a limited 'development of the productive forces' that brings in itself to the dissolution of the community-based social form that had become too 'narrow for the unfolding of the progressive human pack' (Marx [1857–58] 2010, p. 420). The 'preservation', which is the object of all the pre-capitalist communities, necessarily entails the 'destruction' of the communities themselves, since:

> [i]n the act of reproduction itself are changed not only the objective conditions – e.g. village becomes city, the wilderness becomes cultivated clearings, etc. – but also the producers, who transform themselves in that they evolve new qualities from within themselves, develop through production new powers and new ideas, new modes of intercourse, new needs, and new speech. (Marx [1857–58] 2010, p. 418)

Marx's scheme of the transition from one socioeconomic form to another does not aim at dividing history into chronological periods or historico-philosophical stages.[14] It is instead coherent with the method of the critique of political

---

13 My translation.
14 See Gianni Sofri in his book on the Asiatic mode of production (Sofri 1969), p. 41; but also, another milestone in the Marxian literature, the almost contemporary essay by Alfred Schmidt ([1962] 1971) on Marx's concept of nature. In the Appendix 'On the Relation between History and Nature in Dialectical Materialism', he underlines the non-evolutionist character of Marxian account of historical development and the qualitative rupture represented by the emergence of bourgeois society as a result of objective conditions 'created by the participants in history' (p. 178). This inter-

economy that, in order to present the laws of the bourgeois economy as a 'mere historical form of production' (Marx [1857–58] 2010, pp. 388–389), runs up in the 'process preceding the formation of the capitalist relationship'.[15] Nonetheless, the fact that in 'broad outline, the Asiatic, ancient, feudal and modern bourgeois modes of production may be designated as epochs marking progress in the economic development of society' (Marx [1859] 2010, p. 263)[16] does not mean either that what happened in the past of the capitalistic forma-tion should necessarily apply to the future, or that it has been so everywhere and in every circumstance.

None of these key points is acquired by Marx after discovering Morgan's research, since not only in the 1875 French edition of *Capital* does he explic-itly delimit the validity of the process that leads towards capitalist production to the countries of Western Europe, as broadly acknowledged by the most of the scholars,[17] but already in a fragment from the early 1850s he had dis-tinguished two possible ways of the 'real history': the decline of the feudal system, slavery and serfdom as in the West, and the decay of the communal property as in the Orient and among the Slav people.[18] Nor is it legitimate to claim that Marx gives Morgan credit for having conceived, independently of himself, of historical development in a multilinear way.

To some extent, for both Marx and Morgan the comprehension of the pre-capitalist societies acts as a sort of litmus test to grasp the dynamics of the capitalist society and its future outcomes. Furthermore, Morgan has the merit of acknowledging the historical character of the bourgeois institutions of family, property and state, in particular through the analysis of the tribal

---

pretation rightly denies that Marx's theory reads history 'in accordance with uniform interpretative Idea' (p. 177), also by separating the positions of Marx and Engels, as Schmidt makes clear through the whole essay (see, in particular, his critique of Engels's *Dialectics of Nature*).

[15]   See the editorial note 133 recording the title of the pages 1–15 of the Notebook V in Marx ([1857–58] 2010, p. 559).

[16]   See the original text of the 1859 'Preface to A Contribution to the Critique of Political Economy': '*In großen Umrissen können asiatische, antike, feudale und modern bürgerliche Produktionsweisen als progressive Epochen der ökonomischen Gesellschaftsformation bezeichnet werden*' (Marx [1859] 1980, p. 101).

[17]   '*Elle [l'expropriation des cultivateurs] ne s'est encore accomplie d'une manière radicale qu'en Angleterre: ce pays jouera donc nécessairement le premier rôle dans notre esquisse. Mais tous les autres pays de l'Europe occidentale parcourent le même mouvement, bien que selon le milieu il change de couleur locale, ou se resserre dans un cercle plus étroit, ou présente un caractère moins fortement prononcé, ou suive un ordre de succession différent*' (Marx [1872–75] 1989, p. 634). For an acknowl-edgement of the importance of this passage, see, among others, Anderson (1983) and Pradella (2011).

[18]   See the fragment (*Bastiat und Carey*), in Marx ([1857–58] 2010, p. 13).

organization of the native American *gens* of the Iroquois in comparison with the ancient Greek and Roman *gentes*. However, we know that for Marx it is not enough to trace a historical account to prevent this account from being transhistorical. Therefore, what we need to understand is how the historical development of those institutions as outlined by Morgan relates to the logic outlined by the Marxian historical and materialist dialectics, and not to a supposed historical materialism.

The precondition of Marxian dialectic understanding of reality is the critique of the essentialism, and naturalization of a historically specific social production, that is the famous critique of the 'Robinsonades' of classical economists – to use the language of the *Grundrisse* – or of the 'judicial blindness' of what we call 'humanities', to which Marx refers in a letter to Engels in 1868.[19] Marx's criticism turns to a series of different but symmetrical errors by 'those who have an interest in remaining blind'.[20] Such an interest aims to justify the capitalist mode of production, to represent it as natural and eternal, and as the model for all societies. The ideological nature and the practical consequences of these theoretical weaknesses have been unmasked throughout Marxian ethnological research. Through his omissions, comments and glosses, throughout his notebooks on the Victorian anthropologists, Marx seems to carry out what I have elsewhere defined as his implicit 'critique of anthropology' in analogy with the 'critique of political economy', which Marx carried out as the foundation of his theory of capital.[21]

His notebooks are composed in a mix of languages: English above all, since Marx transcribes long passages from his Anglo-American sources, and in German, since he shortens some passages or adds some comments. By comparing Marx's excerpts with the original sources, it is not always easy to understand Marx's judgement on what he reads, although it appears that the longer the uncommented-upon excerpts, the greater Marx's agreement. By contrast,

---

[19] See Marx's letter to Engels on 25 March 1868: 'Human history is like palaeontology. Owing to a CERTAIN JUDICIAL BLINDNESS even the best intelligences absolutely fail to see the things which lie in front of their noses. Later, when the moment has arrived, we are surprised to find traces everywhere of what we failed to see. The first reaction against the French Revolution and the period of Enlightenment bound up with it was naturally to see everything as mediaeval and romantic, even people like Grimm are not free from this. The second reaction is to look beyond the Middle Ages into the primitive age of each nation, and that corresponds to the socialist tendency, although these learned men have no idea that the two have any connection. They are therefore surprised to find what is newest in what is oldest and EVEN EGALITARIANS TO A DEGREE which would have made Proudhon shudder' (Marx [1868] 2010, p. 557).

[20] So wrote Marx in the second draft of the letter to Vera Zasulich (Marx [1881] 1985, p. 232).

[21] Let me refer to a previous article of mine on this subject: Conversano (2018).

the disagreement with the 'civilized asses [that] cannot free themselves of their own conventionalities' (Marx [1880–82] 1972, p. 340)[22] is much clearer.

To this extent, Engels is not totally wrong in recognizing the privileged position of Morgan's research in Marx's attitude towards anthropology, because the Morganian history of the family – according to which the modern monogamian family is not the natural family formation but the result of a long historical development which leads from classless and stateless communities based on kin relationships to state societies whose antagonisms are embodied in miniature by the family[23] – is the immediate base through which Marx can criticize the ideological naturalization of the monogamian family and the modern society in the works of Maine, Phear and Lubbock.

All of them 'failed with the gens' (Engels [1884] 2010, p. 206) because the 'coloured glasses' (Marx [1880–82] 1972, p. 324)[24] with which they read the antiquity prevent them from recognizing it as the unit of organization of kinship descending from a common ancestor, which ruled the lineage and therefore the property relationships. In this regard, Marx comments that Lubbock 'knows nothing of the base, i.e. the gens' (Marx [1880–82] 1972, p. 340);[25] that the 'blockheaded Englishman' Maine misunderstands the pre-colonial Indian institutions because he holds the patriarchal family as the original cell (Marx [1880–82] 1972, p. 290); that the 'asinus' Phear lets 'everything be founded by private families' (Marx [1880–82] 1972, p. 283),[26] even the property relationships observed within the colonial communities in India.

The 'coloured glasses' worn by those scholars whom Marx designates under the name of '*klassische Schülergelehrsamkeit*' ('classical school erudition', Marx [1880–82] 1972, p. 200), which obstructs a full comprehension of other economies and social systems, are the glasses of the bourgeois ideology, which has to put its socioeconomic organization as the natural form of society instead of recognizing it as a historical, social relation of production, because of its interest in justifying the capitalist domination.

At first glance, it is hard to imagine that Marx would have attached any of those philistine attributes to Morgan, although a preliminary argument to be made to temper Engels's enthusiasm is that Marx had already made consider-

---

[22]   Here Marx comments: '*diese civilisirten Esel können ihre eignen conventionalities nicht los werden*'.

[23]   '*D. moderne Familie enthält im Keim nicht nur servitus (Sklaverei) sondern auch Leibeigenscft, da sie von vorn herein Beziehg auf Dienste für Ackerbau. Sie enthält in Miniatur alle d. Antagonismen in sich, die sich später breit entwickeln in d. Gesellscft u.ihrem Staat*' (Marx [1880–82] 1972, p. 120).

[24]   '*Der Esel sagt selbst mit welchen gefärbten Brillen er sieht*'.

[25]   '*Lubb. weiss also nichts v. d. Basis - der gens | die innerhalb d. tribe existirt*'.

[26]   '*Der asinus lässt auch alles dch private families gründen*'.

able advancement in his knowledge of the gens – which in the *Grundrisse* was still confused – by reading, before Morgan, at least the works of Kovalevskji and probably also the work on ancient Rome by Lange.[27] Nonetheless, if we consider, for instance, the following passage from the notebook on Morgan, we cannot but think that Marx was positively impressed:

> Mit Bezug auf d.[28] present monogamian family: *it must advance as society advances, and change as society changes*, even as it has done in the past. It is the creature of the social system ... must be supposable that it is capable of still further improvement *until the equality of the sexes is attained*. Should the monogamian family in the distant future fail to answer the requirements of society, assuming the continuous progress of civilization, it is impossible to predict the nature of its successor. (Marx [1880–82] 1972, p. 124)

In addition to the appreciation, which we can only share, of Morgan's reference to gender equality, Marx might have positively interpreted the assumption about the impossibility of prophesying the character of the next stage of the social development in anti-deterministic terms, if we consider the emphasis he was giving in the same years to the non-teleological meaning of his 'historical sketch of the genesis of capitalism in Western Europe', which should not be transformed in:

> an historico-philosophic theory of the general course fatally imposed on all people, whatever the historic circumstances in which it finds itself, in order that it may ultimately arrive at the form of economy which will ensure, together with the greatest expansion of the productive powers of social labour, the most complete development of man. (Marx [1877] 1983, p. 136)[29]

However, elsewhere in his essay, Morgan refers to a general 'plan of a Supreme Intelligence' that would carry humanity from barbarism to civiliza-

---

[27] For a valuable assessment of Lange's unpublished excerpts see Brown (2012) and her essay in Lindner (2019, esp. pp. 117–124). Heather Brown predates Marx's notes on Lange over those on Morgan (Brown 2012, p. 199), although from the notes themselves and the epistolary it is not easy to provide a precise datation to these extracts.

[28] 'With regard to'.

[29] It is the answer that Marx gives to the editor of the Russian journal *Otechestvennye Zapiski* in 1877. He writes the letter in French, discussing the meaning of the famous chapter on the 'so-called primitive accumulation' in the first book of *Capital*. Marx comes back to this point in the drafts of the letter to Vera Zasulich of 1881. The 'man' of the English translation is more properly the 'private producer', since Marx uses the French expression '*producteur individuel*' (Marx [1877] 1985, p. 116).

tion, and Marx repeatedly omits any mention of such finalism.[30] What seems clear to me, reading between the lines of Marx's notes, by matching them with its sources, is that he is not simply passively acquiring a new scientific point of view, but he is interpreting the empirical data which the ethnologists have usefully collected in the field, evaluating them in the light of his own scientific method, and carrying out his own critique. In the case of Morgan, due to his credit in the eyes of Marx, nonetheless, it is a sort of 'in-negative' critique, that can already be glimpsed from the way Marx rearranges the sequence of chapters in *Ancient Society*, by recording the chapter about the rise of the government in history after that on the family and the property, which instead follow in Morgan's account. Marx's adjustments certainly reflect his critique of the idealistic aspects of Morgan's work; a critique that is testified by Marx leaving out systematically the expression 'idea of' which Morgan places before the concepts of family, property and government, when he explains that the modern civilization is the outcome of the development of those ideas during the human history from barbarism forward, according to 'general human intelligence'. It appears that, in the eyes of Marx, Morgan merely juxtaposes the material progress of the means of subsistence, corresponding to the passage from a kinship-based to a property- and state-based society, with a design ideally superimposed to all peoples, which is the end and the goal that all peoples in history are set to achieve sooner or later.

On the contrary, Marx emphasizes the active, primary role of the family relationships as a driving force inside the society, and thus that of being an essential part of the social relations, and not a mere 'reflex of its culture'.[31] However, Marx is not simply 'placing back on its feet' what stands on its head in Morgan's account, confining himself to accepting the materialistic side of Morgan's account. In other words, Marx is not merely turning the cause and effect relationship between the elements involved in the society upside-down, and assigning to the family relationships the priority over culture in giving rise to the supposed 'civilization'.

In order to explain what I mean, let me quote another passage of Marx's notebook on Morgan, in which the former is dealing with the latter's account

---

[30] Compare, for instance, Morgan (1877, pp. 562–563), with Marx ([1880–82] 1972, p. 139).

[31] Marx notes down a passage of Morgan's books referring to the advancement of the family and society as follows: 'Mit Bezug auf d. present *monogamian family: it must advance as society advances, and change as society changes,* even as it has done in the past. It is the creature of the social system ... must be supposable that it is capable of still further improvement *until the equality of the sexes is attained.*' Instead of Marx's ellipsis, Morgan wrote: 'It is the creature of the social system, and will reflect its culture'. See Marx ([1880–82] 1972, p. 124) and Morgan (1877, p. 499).

of the relation between the development of the forms of family in history and the systems of consanguinity (that is, regarding how the kinship bonds are conceived across the epochs), from a sort of communism in the family relations during the primitive condition of mankind to the monogamian family in the modern Western society. The forms of the family develop more rapidly than the consanguinity relationships, and determine the change of the latter, which ultimately seem the fossil record of a previous stage of mankind. While excerpting a passage from Morgan's book on this point, he glosses as follows:

> D. family active principle, steht nie still,[32] passes von a lower form into a higher one. Systems of consanguinity sind dagegen passiv[33]; recording the progress made by the family at long intervals apart, and only changing radically when the family has radically changed (Ebenso verhält es sich mit politischen, religiösen, juristischen, philosophischen Systemen überhaupt).[34] (Marx [1880–82] 1972, p. 112)

It is clear that, in those lines, Marx founds something similar to the notorious 'structure–superstructure' correlation. Nevertheless, since the two terms as such are a *hapax* in Marx's production, they should be considered in the light of the whole of Marx's theory, or even only in connection with the previous quotations from the *Grundrisse* and with regard to the development of sex relations in history. Along with this paragraph, they cannot be interpreted in a unidirectional and deterministic way, but they rather allude to the role that specific relationships assume in a given society, once the family relations have become a historical presupposition inside the social system and interact with the development of the relations of production.

In order to think about historical development, it is thus necessary to take into account all the aspects contributing to social change, thus both social production and reproduction. These aspects are not essential, universal and natural, but are social relationships in a given social context, which have a precise function in the economic structure.

In the *Grundrisse*, Marx also wrote:

> In every form of society there is a particular [branch of] production which determines the position and importance of all the others, and the relations obtaining in this branch accordingly determine those in all other branches. It is the general light tingeing all other colours and modifying them in their specific quality; it is a special ether determining the specific gravity of everything found in it. (Marx [1857–58] 2010, p. 43)

---

[32] 'never stands still'.
[33] 'are passive in contrast'.
[34] 'The same happens with political, religious, legal and philosophical systems in general'.

But, as Moishe Postone rightly clarifies in another paragraph of the essay that I have already quoted above:

> the social relations that form the basis of capitalist society are very different from the explicit and qualitatively determined social relations, such as kinship relations or relations of direct personal domination that characterize non-capitalist societies. Although the latter type of social relations continues to exist in capitalism, what ultimately structures that society is a new underlying level of social relations constituted by labour. (Postone 2019, p. 186)[35]

When comparing the non-capitalist society with capitalist society, Marx has no intention of retracing the line of the human evolution, either as Morgan does by paralleling the Iroquois gens with the ancient ones, or as Engels does by schematizing the transition from the primitive communities to the capitalist society. In this sense, we could say that even Morgan's judgement should be defined as 'blind' from Marx's point of view, because the Victorian anthropologist takes modern American society as the model for his historical framework. On the contrary, Marx detects the irreducible specificity of modern capitalist society in comparison to a whole range of past and present non-capitalist forms, on the one hand; on the other hand, going deeper into the analysis of single cases of non-capitalist societies both in the past and at the borders of the capitalist world, he encounters the existence of different modernities starting from the comparison between the peculiar characters of the communities contemporary with capitalism, in contrast not only to capitalism itself but also to the ancient communities.

In the section of Maine's excerpts on Ireland, in fact, we can read: '*At this point, property in its modern form has been established*; but the Joint Family has not wholly ceased to influence successions. (Keineswegs ist ddch "property in its modern form" established; see *Russian communes* f. i.)' (Marx [1880–82] 1972, p. 308). Marx's comment that 'in no way' is the modern property established, at least in the way described by the coloured eyes of bourgeois Maine, seems to be not only a 'vertical projection' of the present capitalist relationships to the Irish Middle Ages, but also a 'horizontal projection' of the classical form of the capitalist society worldwide.[36] In my opinion, the remark is a clear reference to the fact that there is no unique model of society; and that in such supposed modernity there are different 'historical milieux',[37] in which the production and reproduction of material life

---

[35]   My translation.

[36]   The classification of these two types of perspective errors as an object of Marx's criticism in the ethnological notebooks is due to Arndt (2011, p. 99).

[37]   See the reply to the editor of the Russian journal *Otecestvenniye Zapisky* in 1877 and the drafts of the letters to Vera Zasulich where Marx broadly uses this expression.

are conveyed by different relations than the capitalist ones. The survival of the *obščina* at the time must appear to Marx to be living proof of his interpretation: although embodying 'a superior form of the archaic type of property' (Marx [1881] 1985, p. 232),[38] the communes in Russia were still alive, but facing the penetration of capitalism and the possibility to build an alternative to it without suffering the birth-pangs.

The triadic progress depicted by Morgan, thus, cannot be understood as the same dialectical movement outlined in *Capital*, which would lead to the 'negation of the negation' (Marx [1867–90] 2010, p. 751) of capitalist relations: first because this movement is limited to the analysis, that is to the logic of capital's development and it does not concern universal history; and second, since the progress of the capitalistic laws can be practically questioned by the actual encounter of other historical environments contemporary to capital, as Marx makes explicit in the drafts of his letter to Zasulich. In the first one, Marx states:

> While the commune is being bled and tortured, its lands sterilised and impoverished, the literary flunkeys of the 'new pillars of society' ironically refer to the evils heaped on the commune as if they were symptoms of spontaneous, indisputable decay, arguing that it is dying a natural death and that it would be an act of kindness to shorten its agony. At this level, it is a question no longer of a problem to be solved, but simply of an enemy to be beaten. Thus, it is no longer a theoretical problem (it is a question to be solved, it is quite simply an enemy to be beaten). To save the Russian commune, there must be a Russian Revolution. (Marx [1881] 1983, p. 116)

Such statements in the context of Marx's confrontation with the extra-European societies and revolutionary movements (the Russian in particular) have led Karl Heinz Roth to argue that, in Marx's late analysis, the critique of political economy lags behind the revolutionary theory (Roth 2021).[39] Rather, I would say that it is the critique of political economy itself, as a critique of society that has to be reassessed in the light of structural changes in society, insofar as the objects of the critique are at the same time the subjects of the critique itself.[40] In order to still call ourselves 'Marxists', then, we should understand

---

[38] Elsewhere in the draft Marx also states that the word 'archaic' should not alarm (Marx [1881] 1985, p. 220; tr. Eng. Marx [1881] 1983, p. 107).

[39] See in particular paragraph 8 (pp. 169ss) of Roth's very detailed and interesting contribution.

[40] See the famous statement in the 1873 Afterword to *Capital I*, where Marx suggests that it is the development of contradictions within the modern economic and social relations itself that is the foundation of the critique of political economy:

> Since 1848 capitalist production has developed rapidly in Germany, and at the present time it is in the full bloom of speculation and swindling. But fate is still unpropitious to our professional economists. At the time when they were able

the 'specific gravity' we are immersed in, and build a new dialectics that can be revolutionary today.

REFERENCES

Abbreviations:
MECW = Marx–Engels Collected Works. London: Lawrence & Wishart.
MEW = Marx Engels Werke. Berlin: Dietz.
MEGA = Marx–Engels–Gesamtausgabe. Berlin: Dietz.

Anderson, K.B., (1983). The 'Unknown' Marx's *Capital*, Volume I: The French Edition of 1872–75, 100 Years Later. *Review of Radical Political Economics* 15 (4), pp. 71–80.
Anderson, K.B., (2016). *Marx at the Margins: On Nationalism, Ethnicity, and Non-Western Societies*, 2nd expanded edn. Chicago, IL: University of Chicago Press.
Arndt, A., (2011). *Karl Marx: Versuch über den Zusammenhang seiner Theorie*. De Gruyter: Berlin.
Breda, S., (2018). La dialettica marxiana come critica immanente dell'empiria. In: Bellofiore, R., Fabiani, C.M. (eds), *Marx inattuale. Consecutio Rerum* 3 (5), pp. 129–50.
Brown, H., (2012). *Marx on Gender and the Family: A Critical Study*. Historical Materialism Books series, 39. Leiden: Brill.
Conversano, E., (2018). Zur Kritik der Anthropologie. Marx, Theorie des Kapitals und seine ethnologischen Studien. *Marx-Engels Jahrbuch*. Volume 2017. Issue 1. pp. 9–40.
Engels, F., [1884] (2010). *The Origin of the Family, Private Property and the State*. In: *MECW*, vol. 26. Digital edition. London: Lawrence & Wishart, pp. 129–276.

---

to deal with Political Economy in a straightforward fashion, modern economic conditions did not actually exist in Germany. And as soon as these conditions did come into existence, they did so under circumstances that no longer allowed of their being really and impartially investigated within the bounds of the bourgeois horizon. In so far as Political Economy remains within that horizon, in so far, that is, as the capitalist regime is looked upon as the absolutely final form of social production, instead of as a passing historical phase of its evolution, Political Economy can remain a science only so long as the class struggle is latent or manifests itself only in isolated and sporadic phenomena. (Marx [1867–90] 2010, p. 14)

It is also worth quoting Schmidt again, who, in order to explain in anti-unilinearist and anti-evolutionist terms Marx's famous statement on the anatomy of man being the key of the anatomy of the ape in the 1859 Preface to *A Contribution to the Critique of Political Economy*, comments: 'In itself, the historically higher stage is grounded in the lower; but the qualitative distinction between the lower form and the higher form which has proceeded from it can only be comprehended when the higher form is fully developed and has already become the object of an immanent critique' (Schmidt [1962] 1971, p. 177).

Engels, F., [1890] (2010a). Letter to Conrad Schmidt, 5 August 1890. In: *MECW*, vol. 49, Digital edition. London: Lawrence & Wishart, pp. 6–9.

Engels, F., [1890] (2010b). *Reply to the Editors of the* Sächsische Arbeiter-Zeitung. In: *MECW*, vol. 27, Digital edition. London: Lawrence & Wishart, pp. 69–71.

Engels, F., [1891] (2010). *To the Early History of the Family (Bachofen, McLennan, Morgan) [Preface to the fourth edition of* The origin of the family, private property and the state]. In: *MECW*, vol. 27. Digital edition. London: Lawrence & Wishart, pp. 203–214.

Foraboschi, P., (ed) (2009). *Karl Marx: Quaderni antropologici. Appunti da L. H. Morgan e da H. S. Maine*. Milano: Unicopli.

Harstick, H.-P., (1977). *Karl Marx über Formen vorkapitalistischer Produktion. Vergleichende Studien zur Geschichte des Grundeigentums 1879–80 Aus dem handschriften Nachlaß*. Frankfurt and New York: Campus Verlag.

Kovalevskij, M.M., [1879)] (1977). *Obščinnoe zemlevladenie, pričiny, chod i posledstvija ego razloženija*. Frankfurt/M. and New York: Campus-Verlag.

Krader, L., (1975). *The Asiatic Mode of Production: Sources, Development and Critique in the Writings of Karl Marx*. Assen: Van Gorcum.

Lindner, K., (ed) (2019). *Le dernier Marx.* Toulouse: L'Asymétrie.

Marx K., [1857–58] (2010). *Economic Manuscripts of 1857–58*. In: *MECW*, vol. 28. Digital edition. London: Lawrence & Wishart.

Marx, K., [1859] (1980). Zur Kritik der politischen Ökonomie. Erstes Heft. Vorwort. In: *MEGA* Abteilung II, Band 2. Berlin: Dietz Verlag, pp. 99–104.

Marx, K., [1859] (2010). *A Contribution to the Critique of Political Economy*. Part One. In: *MECW*, vol. 29. Digital edition. London: Lawrence & Wishart, pp. 257–417.

Marx, K., [1867–90] (2010). *Capital. Volume I.* In: *MECW*, vol. 35. Digital edition. London: Lawrence & Wishart.

Marx, K., [1868] (2010). Letter to Friedrich Engels, 25 March 1868. In: *MECW*, vol. 42, Digital edition. London: Lawrence & Wishart. pp. 557–559.

Marx, K., [1872] (1987). *Das Kapital. Kritik der politischen Ökonomie. Erster Band. Hamburg 1872*. In: *MEGA* Abteilung II, Band 6. Berlin: Dietz Verlag.

Marx, K., [1872–75] (1989). *Le Capital. Paris 1872–1875*. In: *MEGA* Abteilung II, Band 7. Berlin: Dietz Verlag.

Marx, K., [1877] (1983). A Letter to the Editorial Board of *Otechestvennye Zapiski*. In: Shanin, T. (ed) (1983), *Late Marx and the Russian Road*. New York: Monthly Review Press, pp. 134–137.

Marx, K., [1877] (1985). À la rédaction de l' «Отечественныя Записки». In: *MEGA* Abteilung I, Band 25. Berlin: Dietz Verlag, pp. 112–117.

Marx, K., [1880–82] (1972). *The Ethnological Notebooks of Karl Marx*, edited by L. Krader. Assen: Van Gorcum.

Marx, K., [1881] (1983). Draft of a Reply (February/March 1881). In: Shanin, T. (ed) (1983), *Late Marx and the Russian Road*. New York: Monthly Review Press, pp. 97–126.

Marx, K., [1881] (1985). Lettre à Vera Ivanova Zassoulitch (Premier projet, deuxième projet, troisième projet, quatrième projet et lettre à Vera Ivanova Zassoulitch). In: *MEGA* Abteilung I, Band 25. Berlin: Dietz Verlag, pp. 217–241.

Marx, K., and Engels, F., (2020). *Opere Complete*. Vol. XXVI. Napoli: La città del sole.

Morgan, L.H., (1877). *Ancient Society, or Researches in the lines of Human Progress from Savagery through Barbarism to Civilisation*, 2nd edn. Chicago, IL: C.H. Kerr.

Postone, M., (2019). Capitale e temporalità. In: Musto, M. (ed), *Marx revival. Concetti essenziali e nuove letture*. Roma: Donzelli, pp. 177–198.

Pradella, L., (2011). Kolonialfrage und vorkapitalistische Gesellschaften: Zusätze und Änderungen in der französischen Ausgabe des ersten Bandes des Kapital. *Marx-Engels Jahrbuch*. Volume 2010. pp. 82–100.

Roth, K.H., (2021). Marx und die revolutionären Umbrüche seiner Zeit: Vom eurozentrischen Determinismus zu einer global offenen Perspektive. In: Sablowski, T., Dellheim, J., Demirović, A., Pühl, K., Solty, I. (eds), *Auf den Schultern von Karl Marx*. Münster: Westfälisches Dampfboot, pp. 141–178.

Schmidt, A., [1962] (1971). *The Concept of Nature in Marx*. London: NLB.

Sofri, G., (1969). *Il modo di produzione asiatico. Storia di una controversia marxista*. Torino: Einaudi.

Vogel, L., (1996). Engels's Origin: Legacy, Burden and Vision. In: Arthur, C.J. (ed), *Engels Today*. London: Macmillan, pp. 129–151.

Index

value, intrinsic 67–68, 70, 75, 84,
    88, 91–92, 100, 102–103, 105
value, real 70
value, relative 69–70, 76, 77, 81,
    101, 104
vampire 87, 92
vicious circle 82
victorian anthropology 228, 230, 235,
    240
Vidoni, Ferdinando 230
Virchow, Rudolf 56–57, 60–61
Virno, Paolo 199
Vogel, Lise 205–208, 211, 231
Vollgraf, Carl–Erich 134–135
von Helmholtz, Hermann 50
von Kölliker, Albert 56
vulgar political economy 84, 99, 121
Vydodskij, Vitalij 134, 146, 150,

wage 6, 71, 93, 124, 158, 180, 206, 208,
    210, 212–213

wage labour 5, 9, 24, 41–42, 53, 55,
    58–59, 106, 181, 207, 232,
    157, 164, 232
wage struggles 34
    see also class struggles
waged work 207–208, 210, 212
Wagner, Adolph 55, 57
Weltanschauung 165
Windelband, Wilhelm 225
Wittgenstein, Ludwig 7, 93, 98
Wolf, Dieter 22
Wolf, Frieder Otto 19–20, 24, 32, 36,
    40–41, 45
Wolff, Richard 36
World market 53, 102, 160, 162–163
Wyatt, John 224

Zasulič, Vera 163, 229, 235, 237, 240,
    241
Zeleny, Jindrich 109
Žižek, Slavoj 199

Φάντασμα 85